Teacher's Edition
DAYBOOK
OF CRITICAL READING AND WRITING

THE AUTHORS
* Fran Claggett
* Louann Reid
* Ruth Vinz

Great Source Education Group

A division of Houghton Mifflin Company

Wilmington, Massachusetts

THE AUTHORS

✻ **Fran Claggett,** an educational consultant, writer, and teacher at Sonoma State University, taught high school and college English for more than thirty years. Her books include *Drawing Your Own Conclusions: Graphic Strategies for Reading, Writing, and Thinking* (1992) with Joan Brown, *A Measure of Success* (1996), and *Teaching Writing: Art, Craft, and Genre* (2005) with Joan Brown, Nancy Patterson, and Louann Reid.

✻ **Louann Reid** taught junior and senior high school English for nineteen years and currently teaches courses for future English teachers at Colorado State University. She has edited *English Journal* and is the author or editor of several books and articles, including *Learning the Landscape* and *Recasting the Text* (1996) with Fran Claggett and Ruth Vinz. She is a frequent consultant and workshop presenter nationally and internationally.

✻ **Ruth Vinz,** currently a professor of English education and Morse Chair in Teacher Education at Teachers College, Columbia University, taught in secondary schools for twenty-three years. She is author of numerous books and articles that focus on teaching and learning in the English classroom. Dr. Vinz is a frequent presenter at conferences as well as a consultant and co-teacher in schools throughout the country.

The authors gratefully acknowledge the assistance of the following teachers in developing the student and teacher material for the *Daybook of Critical Reading and Writing*: Tiffany Hunt, Cammie Kim Lin, Katherine McMullen, and Lance Ozier.

DEVELOPMENT: Bonnie Brook Communications (teacher's edition)
Michael Priestley (assessment)
EDITORIAL: Sue Paro, Bev Jessen
DESIGN AND PRODUCTION: AARTPACK, Inc.

Copyright © 2007 by Great Source Education Group, a division of Houghton Mifflin Company. All rights reserved.

Permission is hereby granted to teachers to reprint or photocopy in classroom quantities, for use by one teacher and his or her students only, the pages in this work that carry the appropriate copyright notice, provided each copy made shows the copyright notice. Such copies may not be sold and further distribution is expressly prohibited. Except as authorized above, prior written permission must be obtained from Great Source Education Group to reproduce or transmit this work or portions thereof in any other form or by any other electronic or mechanical means, including any information storage or retrieval system, unless expressly permitted by federal copyright law. Address inquiries to Great Source Education Group, 181 Ballardvale Street, Wilmington, Massachusetts 01887

Great Source® is a registered trademark of Houghton Mifflin Company.

Printed in the United States of America

International Standard Book Number 13: 978-0-669-53486-3

International Standard Book Number 10: 0-669-53486-2

1 2 3 4 5 6 7 8 9 10 – POO – 11 10 09 08 07 06

CONTENTS

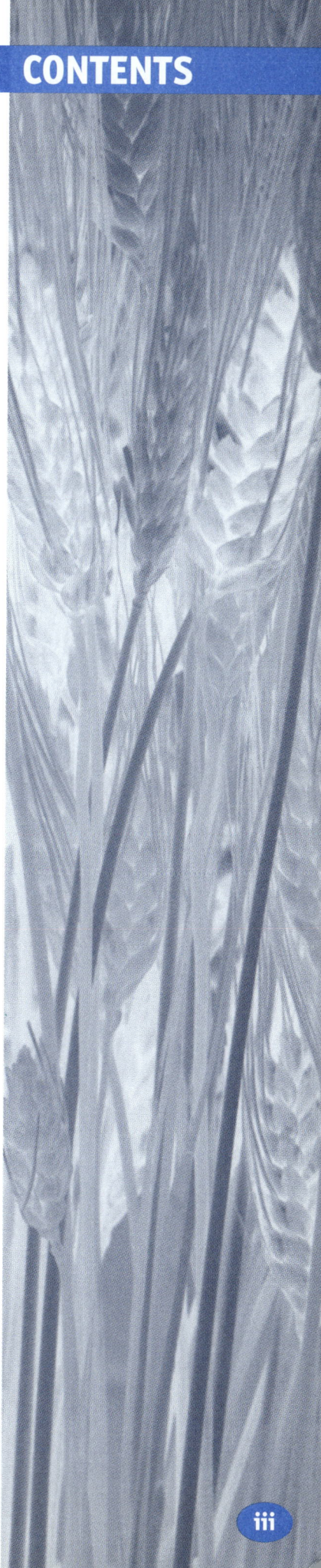

DAYBOOK OVERVIEW
How to Use the *Daybook* vii
A Look Inside a Lesson viii
Frequently Asked Questions x
Writing, Vocabulary, Visual Literacy, and Assessment xi
Five Essential Strategies of Critical Reading and Writing xiii
10 Ways Research Supports the *Daybook* 1

UNIT 1 BUILDING YOUR REPERTOIRE
Critical Strategies for Reading and Writing
LESSON
1. Interacting with the Text 10
2. Making Connections 13
3. Exploring Multiple Perspectives 16
4. Focusing on Language and Craft 19
5. Studying an Author 22

UNIT 2 INTERACTING WITH THE TEXT
Strategic Reading
LESSON
6. Making Predictions 26
7. Questioning the Text 29
8. Summarizing 32
9. Visualizing 34
10. Reflecting 37

UNIT 3 MAKING CONNECTIONS
Story Elements
LESSON
11. Setting 40
12. Point of View 42
13. Characters 45
14. Plot 48
15. Theme 51

UNIT 4 EXPLORING MULTIPLE PERSPECTIVES
Perspectives on a Person
LESSON
16. A Biography 54
17. An Interview 58
18. A Personal Account 62
19. A Poetic Portrait 65
20. A Brief Encounter 67

UNIT 5 FOCUSING ON LANGUAGE AND CRAFT
Personal Narrative and Poetry
LESSON
21. People Are Poems 70
22. Epistle Poems 75
23. Langston Hughes 77
24. Finding Ideas 80
25. Connecting Through Poetry 82

iii

UNIT 6 STUDYING AN AUTHOR
Yoshiko Uchida

LESSON
- 26 A Writer's Heritage 86
- 27 A Writer's Identity 90
- 28 A Writer's Language 93
- 29 A Writer's Themes 96
- 30 A Writer's Intent 99

UNIT 7 ASSESSING YOUR GROWING REPERTOIRE

LESSON
- 31 Interacting and Connecting with a Story 102
- 32 Using Reading and Writing Strategies 106
- 33 Studying an Author 109
- 34 Getting Ready to Write 112
- 35 Revising and Evaluating Your Work 116

UNIT 8 EXPANDING YOUR REPERTOIRE
Reading for Meaning

LESSON
- 36 Interacting with the Text 118
- 37 Making Connections 121
- 38 Exploring Multiple Perspectives 124
- 39 Focusing on Language and Craft 129
- 40 Studying an Author 131

UNIT 9 INTERACTING WITH THE TEXT
Reading Visual Texts

LESSON
- 41 Making Inferences 134
- 42 Characteristics of a Genre 137
- 43 Style and Design 140
- 44 Dialogue, Narration, and Sound 143
- 45 Adapting a Text 145

UNIT 10 MAKING CONNECTIONS
Monitoring Your Connections

LESSON
- 46 Connecting to the Facts 148
- 47 Connecting to the People 151
- 48 Connecting to Fictional Accounts 154
- 49 Connecting Through Photographs 158
- 50 Connecting to Inform Future Actions 160

UNIT 11 EXPLORING MULTIPLE PERSPECTIVES
The Art of Persuasion

LESSON
- 51 Problem and Solutions 164
- 52 Convincing Details 167
- 53 Examining the Alternatives 169
- 54 Making Connections to Our Lives 172
- 55 Persuading Others 175

UNIT 12 FOCUSING ON LANGUAGE AND CRAFT
Reading, Writing, and Symbols

LESSON		
56	Reading, in Other Words	178
57	Writing as Writing	182
58	Writing Goes Extraterrestrial	184
59	From Image to Symbol	186
60	Writing a Poem	190

UNIT 13 STUDYING AN AUTHOR
Will Hobbs

LESSON		
61	Stories from Other Stories	194
62	Real-Life Stories	197
63	Stories in Different Genres	200
64	Characters in Stories	204
65	Revising Stories	207

UNIT 14 ASSESSING YOUR STRENGTHS

LESSON		
66	Interacting and Connecting with a Story	210
67	Studying an Author's Craft	213
68	Focusing on Language and Craft	215
69	Getting Ready to Write	218
70	Revising and Reflecting	221

Becoming an Active Reader, Glossary, Credits 223

RESOURCES 227
Writing Prompts 228
Unit 1 Review 229
Unit 2 Character Sketch 230
Unit 3 Personal Narrative 231
Unit 4 Character Sketch 232
Unit 5 Persuasive Letter 233
Unit 6 Response to Literature 234
Unit 8 Story Continuation 235
Unit 9 Persuasive Letter 236
Unit 10 Expository Essay 237
Unit 11 Expository Essay 238
Unit 12 Descriptive Essay 239
Unit 13 Response to Literature 240
Assessments 241
Pretest 247
Reading Strategy Assessments 253
Posttest 264
Reproducible Graphic Organizers 270
Index 273

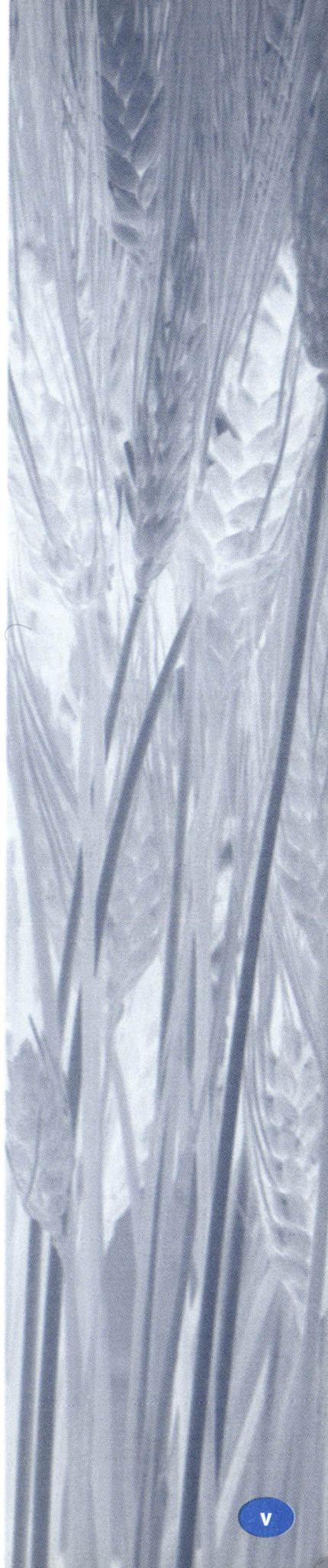

DAYBOOK OVERVIEW

What, exactly, is a *Daybook*, and how can it help my students? Teachers often ask these questions upon their initial encounter with the *Daybook of Critical Reading and Writing*. The answers are simple and compelling:

The *Daybook*
The *Daybook* is a keepable, journal-like book that promotes daily reading and writing experiences. The integrated, interactive pages of the *Daybook* provide students with multiple opportunities to read a variety of literature and other texts, to respond to what they read, and to experiment with their own writing. The *Daybook* honors the relationship between the reader and text, conveying the message that good readers take risks, relate their reading and writing to what they know and want to know, and take ownership of the learning process.

The Literature
Many of the selections complement those commonly found in anthologies or present authors and novels known to be popular with teachers and students. The selections also support curricular content and themes for grades 6-8, reflect the diversity of our world, include a blend of traditional and contemporary authors, and present a wide variety of fiction and nonfiction. Excerpts were chosen carefully to feel "complete" and yet to inspire students to seek out and read the larger works.

The Lessons
Each *Daybook* lesson focuses on a specific strategy or strategies for critical reading and writing, providing students with the tools they need to become more proficient, confident readers and writers. The lessons include instruction on how to respond actively to many kinds of writing, as well as opportunities to practice the strategies, information about writer's craft and genre elements, and support for writing activities.

The Framework
The *Daybook* units are structured around the **Five Essential Strategies of Critical Reading and Writing:**

1. Interacting with the Text
2. Making Connections
3. Exploring Multiple Perspectives
4. Focusing on Language and Craft
5. Studying an Author

These research-based, practical strategies are introduced and summarized in the first unit, "Building Your Repertoire." Subsequent units explore each of the Five Essential Strategies in greater depth. Two assessment units also engage students in an examination of their progress as they move through the book.

HOW TO USE THE DAYBOOK

No two classrooms are alike. That's why the *Daybook* was designed to accommodate a wide range of classrooms and instructional scenarios. The *Daybook's* flexibility and versatility offer something for every teacher.

Supplement an Anthology or Core Novel List
The contemporary selections and multicultural authors provide a needed balance with the more traditional canon in older anthologies. Likewise, for teachers using a list of core novels, the *Daybook* offers a way to add daily writing and reading instruction.

Provide Direct Instruction
The lessons in the *Daybook* are ideal for helping all students develop strong literacy skills. You can use these lessons to

* teach **critical reading skills,** such as predicting, making inferences, and finding the main idea;

* teach **literary elements,** such as plot, setting, characters, and theme;

* teach **writer's craft** and literary devices, such as metaphor, imagery, and dialogue;

* teach **writing traits,** such as organization, word choice and conventions;

* prepare students for **state tests** and teach **standards and benchmarks,** such as writing for a variety of purposes and audiences.

Blend Elements
The *Daybook* allows teachers to provide truly integrated instruction by blending

* direct instruction in how to read and respond to literature critically;

* regular and explicit practice in marking up and annotating texts;

* "writing to learn" activities for each day or week;

* great selections from contemporary and multicultural literature.

> **WHEN TO USE THE *DAYBOOK***
>
> Each 30-to-40 minute lesson can be used
>
> * as the **core instruction** for a literature or language arts class;
>
> * **before other reading or writing instruction**—to introduce a topic, genre, or author or to teach a particular skill or strategy;
>
> * **after other reading or writing instruction**—to provide additional works by a particular author or to provide practice for students needing skill reinforcement.
>
> Teachers who use the *Daybook* only for homework have not reported much success. The *Daybook* is designed to support interaction among teacher and students; students work collaboratively to reflect, question texts, get feedback on writing, and construct knowledge. These opportunities are lost when students use the *Daybook* in isolation.

DAYBOOK OVERVIEW

A LOOK INSIDE A LESSON

STUDENT EDITION

Lesson title • **Lesson focus** • **Literature excerpt** • **Initial response activity**

LESSON 8 SUMMARIZING

Readers show that they understand the main ideas and supporting details when they **summarize** what they read. Finding the main ideas and restating them in your own words is a strategy for you to use when you want to remember key points or ideas.

Sojourner Truth, an African American woman, spoke at a women's rights convention in 1851. Read her speech once to get an idea about the general subject.

✻ When you look at the title and know where and when she gave this speech, what do you predict will be her main point?

"Ain't I a Woman?" by Sojourner Truth

Response Notes

Well, children, where there is so much racket there must be something out of kilter. I think that 'twixt the Negroes of the South and the women at the North, all talking about rights, the white men will be in a fix pretty soon. But what's all this here talking about? That man over there says that women need to be helped into carriages, and lifted over ditches, and to have the best place everywhere. Nobody ever helps me into carriages, or over mud-puddles, or gives me any best place! And ain't I a woman? Look at me! Look at my arm! I have plowed and planted, and gathered into barns, and no man could head me! And ain't I a woman? I could work as much and eat as much as a man—when I could get it—and bear the lash as well! And ain't I a woman? I have borne thirteen children, and seen them most all sold off to slavery, and when I cried out with my mother's grief, none but Jesus heard! And ain't I a woman?

Then they talk about this thing in the head; what's this they call it? ["Intellect," someone in the audience whispers.] That's it, honey. What's that got to do with women's rights or Negro's rights? If my cup won't hold but a pint, and yours holds a quart, wouldn't you be mean not to let me have my little halfmeasure full? Then that little man in black there, he says women can't have as much rights as men, 'cause Christ wasn't a woman! Where did your Christ come from? Where did your Christ come from? From god and a woman! Man had nothing to do with him.

If the first woman God ever made was strong enough to turn the world upside down all alone, these women together ought to be able to turn it back, and get it right side up again! And now they is asking to do it, the men better let them. Obliged to you for hearing me, and now old Sojourner ain't got nothing more to say. ✧

32 LESSON 8

✻ After your first reading, what do you think is the main idea of Sojourner Truth's speech?

✻ Now reread the speech so that you can summarize it. As you read, write the main ideas in the **Response Notes** and circle the details in the speech that support what you have written.

✻ Using your annotations, write a summary of Truth's speech. As a challenge, limit your summary to three sentences that contain all of the important points.

Writing a summary of a selection helps you identify and remember the key points.

SUMMARIZING 33

Space for students' comments, questions, and annotations • **Practice and application of lesson focus** • **Lesson focus summary statement**

viii DAYBOOK OVERVIEW

TEACHER'S EDITION

Prereading activity to build background and/or activate prior knowledge

Preteaching of difficult or significant selection vocabulary

Suggestion for differentiated instruction for students who need language support

Quickly find out whether students have grasped the main focus of the lesson

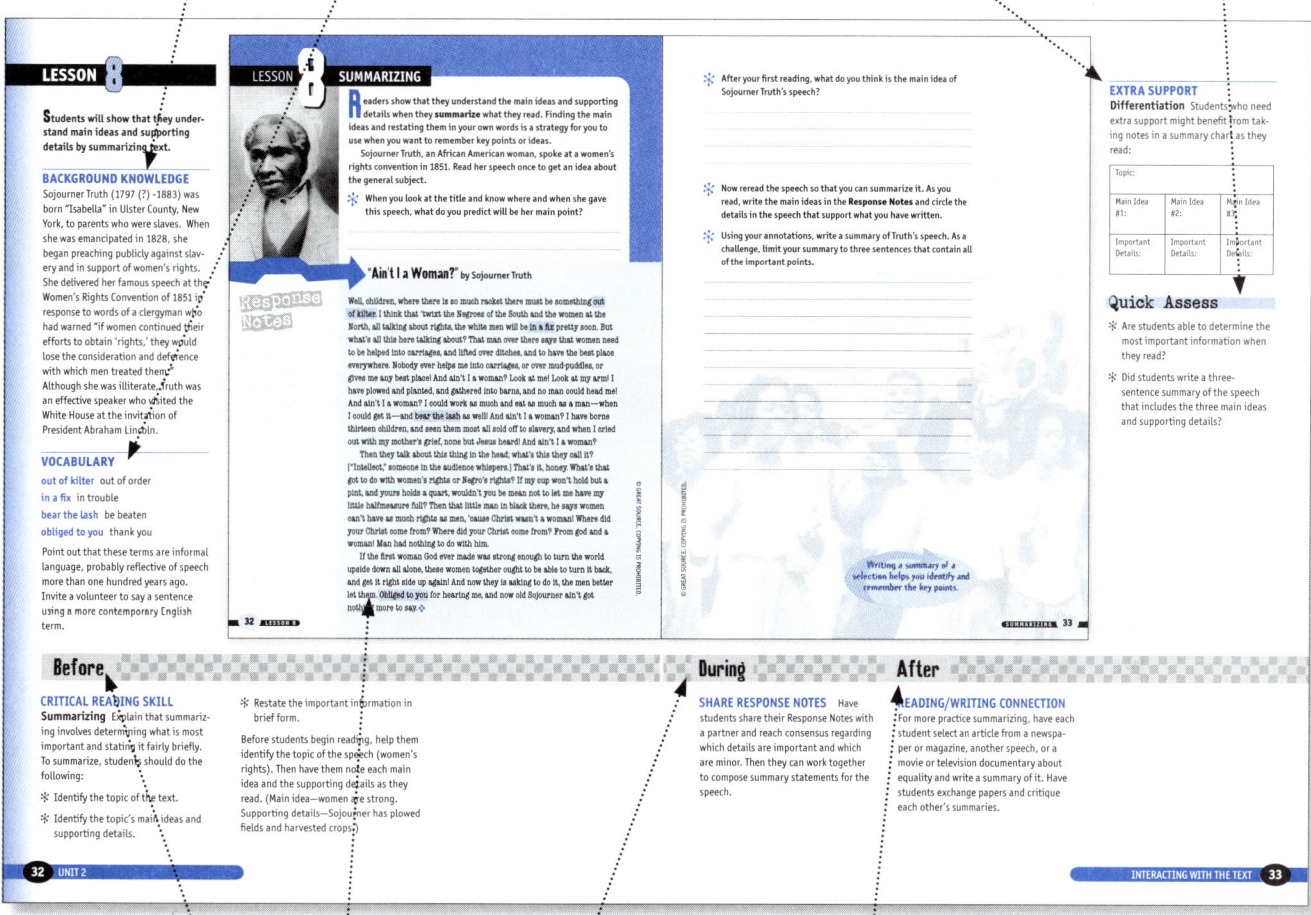

Support for introducing Critical Reading Skill and lesson focus

Support for guiding students through reading the selection and completing response activities

Extension/enrichment activities for further application of the skill or strategy

Reduced facsimiles of student pages eliminate the need for a separate book and include highlighted vocabulary

DAYBOOK OVERVIEW ix

FREQUENTLY ASKED QUESTIONS

Who is the audience for the Daybook?

The *Daybook* can help all students. The length of selections and the scaffolding built into the lessons support students at all levels, while additional suggestions in the Teacher's Edition offer support for differentiated instruction, collaborative learning, and enrichment.

Are students supposed to write in the book?

Absolutely. The immediacy of responding in the *Daybook* is an integral feature of this program. Interacting with text is one of the Five Essential Strategies of Critical Reading and Writing; only by physically marking the text do students become active readers. Writing in the book provides a natural kinesthetic aid to memory and learning and allows students to refer to and reflect on their thoughts, questions, ideas, and annotations.

How do I know if the readability level is appropriate?

Helping students find materials at their individual reading levels can be a major challenge. Readability levels, which are based on text elements such as word choice, sentence length and complexity, and subject matter, provide a very rough guide. But the readability of a text also depends on the reader's interest and prior knowledge. The engaging, high-interest selections in the *Daybook,* as well as helpful background-building activities in the Teacher's Edition, provide the motivation and prior knowledge students need to access the texts. Additionally, the readability of selections throughout the *Daybook* varies so that students will gain experience reading both easier and more challenging texts.

What do you mean by "texts"?

We could call every work by a professional author *literature,* but some people associate that term only with an aesthetic or artistic approach to writing. While we do often use the term *literature* to refer specifically to "imaginative" works such as poems, short stories, and novels, we also use *literature* and *texts* as broader terms that include all written work. *Texts* also includes what students write and is therefore consistent with the *Daybook* philosophy that students are not only consumers but also creators of the written word.

May I photocopy these lessons?

No, unfortunately not. The selections, instructions, and activities are protected by copyright. To copy them infringes on the rights of the authors of the selections and the book. Writers such as Gary Soto, Jacqueline Woodson, Jane Yolen, and Will Hobbs have granted permission for the use of their work in the *Daybook;* to photocopy their work violates their copyright. However, a package that includes a CD-ROM of the *Daybook* is available for purchase. Call 800-259-4490 for details.

WRITING, VOCABULARY, VISUAL LITERACY, AND ASSESSMENT

Writing in the *Daybook*
The writing activities in the *Daybook* emphasize the idea that reading is a "partnership" between author and reader.

Most of the writing activities in the *Daybook* are not intended to take students all the way through the writing process. Rather they allow students to (1) *explore* texts by questioning, analyzing, connecting with, and reacting to literature; (2) *clarify* their understanding of texts by looking at other perspectives and interpreting or reflecting on their initial impressions; and (3) *apply* what they are learning about structure, genre, and craft by modeling professional writers. The types of writing in the *Daybook* include the following:

* **Response Notes** Students keep track of their initial responses to literature by annotating the text as they read. In this way, students develop the habit of recording what they are thinking while they are reading.

* **Graphic Organizers** Students collect writing ideas in lists, charts, clusters, diagrams, and so on, while analyzing particular selections or literary elements in the process.

* **Short Responses** Students summarize themes and main ideas and write paragraphs of description, explanation, evaluation, interpretation, comparison, and persuasion.

* **Personal Narratives** Students write personal stories that connect or relate to what they have read. In some cases, the narratives tell the stories of students' prior reading experiences or how a literary selection relates to their life experiences. Other activities apply and refine students' understanding and use of narrative principles.

* **Creative Texts** Students write poems, character sketches, dialogues, vignettes, and descriptions as a way to apply the knowledge about language and craft they are gaining through their reading. They demonstrate and reinforce their understanding of original texts by writing imaginative reconstructions of gaps in the text—adding scenes, rewriting endings, writing from other characters' points of view, and so on.

Vocabulary in the *Daybook*
The connection between reading comprehension and word knowledge has been clear for many years. The units in the *Daybook* give students the opportunity to use words repeatedly within the context of the same theme over time, applied in different ways about different subject matter. At the beginning of most Teacher's Edition lessons, difficult or significant words from the selection are listed, along with their definitions and an activity for preteaching the words.

Visual Literacy in the *Daybook*
Visual literacy—the ability to produce and read graphics—has become an essential skill in today's media-oriented world. Teachers have long known the value of using graphic organizers, photographs, illustrations, and color-coding to present information, represent ideas metaphorically, and help students see connections.

Graphic aids are especially important for students who are just learning English or whose dominant learning mode is visual-spatial. In the *Daybook,* students read and create visuals and graphic organizers such as sequence maps, word webs, Venn diagrams, charts, and illustrations in order to

- organize ideas and information;
- visualize imagery, details, and form;
- perform close observation, personal association, and analysis;
- stimulate long-term memory by integrating both visual and verbal learning.

Several reproducible graphic organizer templates are provided at the back of the Teacher's Edition for use with the activities in the *Daybook*.

Assessment in the *Daybook*

In assessing students' work, it is important to evaluate students' growing facility with reading and writing, not just their finished products. The *Daybook* must be a safe place for students to think things through, change their minds, make mistakes, and start over. Along the way, the *Daybook* provides multiple opportunities for both teachers and students to monitor progress and identify areas of frustration or difficulty:

- **Assessment Units** Two complete units in the *Daybook,* Units 7 and 14, allow students and teachers to take stock of where students are with respect to the Five Essential Strategies of Critical Reading and Writing. Students read and respond to literature, applying all of the strategies they have learned previously, and then reflect on their achievement and identify areas for improvement. A full writing process activity at the end of each unit provides an opportunity for assessment.

- **Quick Assess** In the Teacher's Edition, suggestions are given at the end of each lesson for informal, observational assessment of students' understanding of lesson concepts.

- **Writing Assessment Prompts** At the back of the Teacher's Edition, writing prompts tied to the texts in each unit address commonly tested modes of writing (expository, narrative, persuasive, expressive-descriptive, interpretive) and assess students' ability to interpret, reflect, evaluate, and connect to experience.

- **Reading Strategy Assessments** The assessments, found at the back of this Teacher's Edition, include a Pretest, four Reading Strategy Assessments, and a Posttest. Each assessment includes passages, based on the types of literature found in the *Daybook,* followed by a set of questions. Both multiple-choice and short answer items are included.

- **Self-Assessment** Throughout the *Daybook,* students engage in informal self-assessment as they write short reflections on what they have learned or how well they are doing.

FIVE ESSENTIAL STRATEGIES OF CRITICAL READING AND WRITING

The *Daybook* is built on a framework of Five Essential Strategies of Critical Reading and Writing.

1. Interacting with the Text
Interacting with text involves physically and mentally engaging with texts. Active readers keep their minds at work throughout reading and writing—they constantly ask questions, make inferences and predictions, and test those inferences and predictions. They write, scratch out, sketch, and rewrite. We use the metaphor of having a "conversation" with a text to describe this process.

2. Making Connections
Making connections means relating the text to oneself, to other texts, and to the rest of the world. Critical readers and writers make relevant connections—a "web of meaning"—between their reading and their experiences, knowledge, memories, and imagination.

3. Exploring Multiple Perspectives
Looking at only one side of an object gives you a limited picture of that object. But when you view it from different angles or points of view, you see the various aspects that make up a whole picture, and you may construct several versions of what the object is or resembles. Likewise, critical readers and writers explore multiple perspectives to generate a more complex understanding of a text.

4. Focusing on Language and Craft
When we take time to focus on how texts work, we analyze how the language and craft of a text—word choice, imagery, style, form, etc.—influence us as readers. This extends our own possibilities as writers. Language has not only meaning but also power, so by understanding how texts work, we gain power to create our own.

5. Studying an Author
Critical readers and writers understand that there is life behind the text and are curious about the author and his or her world. By studying authors—what influences them, where they get their ideas, and how they make decisions about language and craft—students see how they, too, can be authors of works that have personal meaning and relevance.

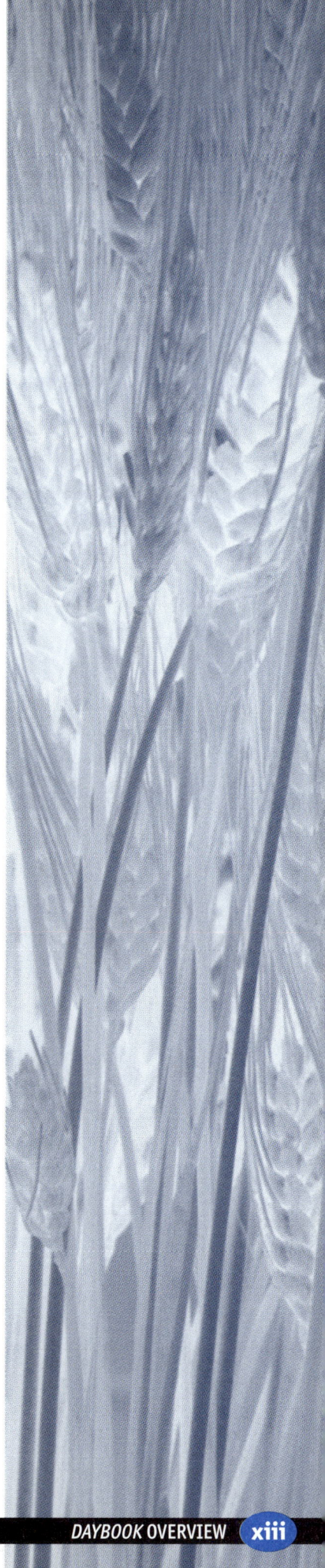

The Essential Strategies in Action

The essential strategies can be applied to any kind of text—fiction, nonfiction, or poetry. Through the lessons in the *Daybook,* students gradually learn which strategies to use when and why. In so doing, students become independent critical readers and writers.

ESSENTIAL STRATEGIES	STRATEGIES (PURPOSEFUL PLANS)	ACTIVITIES (ACTIONS STUDENTS TAKE)
Interacting with the Text	• underlining key phrases • writing questions/comments in the margin • noting word patterns and repetitions • circling unknown words	• Write down initial impressions. • Reread the text. • Write a summary of the text. • Generate two questions and one "certainty." Then discuss in a small group.
Making Connections	• paying attention to the story being told • connecting the story to one's own experience • speculating on the meaning or significance of incidents	• Create a character map to reveal what you have learned about a person in a story. • Make a 3-column incident chart: Incident, Significance, Related incident in your life.
Exploring Multiple Perspectives	• examining the point of view • changing the point of view • exploring various versions of an event • forming interpretations • comparing texts • asking "what if" questions	• Discuss how you might read a text differently if (1) you think the narrator is female (or male) or (2) you live in a different time or place from the narrator. • Rewrite the text from a different point of view.
Focusing on Language and Craft	• understanding figurative and sensory language • looking at the way the author uses words • modeling the style of other writers • studying various forms of literature	• Use a double-entry log to identify metaphors and the qualities implied by the comparison. • Write to model a type of text.
Studying an Author	• reading what the author says about his/her own writing • reading what others say about the author's writing • making inferences about the connections between an author's life and work • analyzing the author's style • paying attention to repeated themes and topics in the work by one author	• Read about an author's life. Make a chart to record events in the author's life, inferences about how the events affected the author, and how they are manifested in the text. • Read what a critic has said about an author's text. Write a short essay agreeing or disagreeing with the critic.

10 WAYS RESEARCH SUPPORTS THE DAYBOOK

The following research-based principles are key to effective literacy instruction and played a critical role in the development of the *Daybook*. Resources for further reading are listed for each principle.

1. **Teach research-based comprehension strategies (i.e. questioning, predicting, connecting, clarifying) and comprehension monitoring strategies (i.e. checking for understanding, reflecting, self-assessing) through direct and explicit instruction.** The *Daybook* provides instruction in these strategies and supports strategy development through reading, writing, and assessment activities.

    Guthrie, J. T. and Taboado, A. (2004). "Fostering the Cognitive Strategies of Reading Comprehension." In J. T. Guthrie, A. Wigfield, and K. C. Perencevich, eds. *Motivating Reading Comprehension: Concept-Oriented Reading Instruction,* pp. 87-112. Mahwah, NJ: Erlbaum.

    Melzer, J. (2002). *Adolescent Literacy Resources: Linking Research and Practice.* (ERIC Document Reproduction Service No.ED466788).

2. **Integrate reading and writing strategy instruction into a wide variety of texts that build both interest and skill.** The *Daybook* provides a wide range of reading and writing activities that help students build habits of mind characteristic of excellent readers.

    Allington, R. L. (2002). You can't learn much from books you can't read. *Educational Leadership, 60*(3): 16-19.

    Alvermann, D. E. (2002, Summer). Effective literacy instruction for adolescents. *Journal of Literacy Research 34(2):* 189-208. (ERIC Document Reproduction Service No. EJ672862).

3. **Use modeling, scaffolding, and apprenticing to demonstrate how proficient readers and writers work strategically.** The *Daybook* provides explicit step by step processing techniques to help students develop conceptual knowledge of the strategies they use.

    Gere, A. R., Fairbanks, C, & Howes, A. (1992). *Language and Reflection: An Integrated Approach to Teaching English.* Upper Saddle River, NJ: Prentice-Hall, Inc.

    Kingen, S. (2000). *Teaching Language Arts In Middle Schools: Connecting and Communicating*. Mahwah, NJ: Erlbaum.

4. **Address the diverse needs of students through targeted instruction with varied reading selections and writing assignments.** The *Daybook* provides a wide variety in text difficulty and genre as well as providing the appropriate background knowledge and scaffolding to support student achievement.

    Allington, R. L. (2005, 2nd edition) *What Really Matters for Struggling Readers: Designing Research-Based Programs.* Boston, MA: Allyn and Bacon.

    Kucer, S. B., (2005). *Dimensions of Literacy: A Conceptual Base for Teaching Reading and Writing in School Settings.* Mahwah, NJ: Lawrence Erlbaum.

5. **Make reading and writing a daily part of literacy instruction to reinforce the common and shared processes of both sending and receiving information.** The *Daybook* provides companion reading and writing activities intended to enhance reading and writing abilities.

    Booth, D. (2001). *Reading and Writing in the Middle Years.* Portland, ME: Stenhouse.

    Fitzgerald, J. (1990). Reading and writing as "mind meeting." In T. Shanahan (Ed.), *Reading and writing together: New perspectives for the classroom*, pp. 81-97. Norwood, MA: Christopher-Gordon.

DAYBOOK OVERVIEW   1

6. Incorporate visual representations and organizing devices to help students represent and organize ideas and information. The *Daybook* provides multiple and varied opportunities for students to visualize and "picture'"what they are reading, organize text graphically, and engage with visual symbols.

   Bustle, L. S. (Ed.). (2003). *Image, Inquiry, and Transformative Practice: Engaging learners in creative and critical inquiry through visual representation.* New York: Peter Lang.

   Bustle, L. S. (2004). "The Role of Visual Representation in the Assessment of Learning." *Journal of Adolescent & Adult Literacy.* 47(5): 416-421.

7. Complement strategy-building instruction with opportunities for students to read at their own pace and make their own decisions about what to read. The *Daybook* provides exposure to a wide range of texts and authors that are meant to entice students to read full length works that are introduced to them in excerpts.

   Guthrie, J. T. and Humenick, N. M. (2004). "Motivating Students to Read: Evidence for Classroom Practices That Increase Reading Motivation and Achievement." In P. McCardle and V. Chhabra, eds., *The Voice of Evidence in Reading Research,* pp. 329-54. Baltimore, MD: Brookes.

8. Conduct multiple types of assessments and self-assessments to monitor student growth that will inform explicit instruction. The *Daybook* provides students with units for self-assessment and many opportunities for teachers to assess both students' reading and writing skills.

   Cohen, J. H. and Wiener, R. B. (2003). *Literacy Portfolios: Improving Assessment, Teaching and Learning.* Upper Saddle River, NJ: Merrill/Prentice Hall.

   William, D., and Black, P. (1996). "Meanings and Consequences: A Basis for Distinguishing Formative and Summative Functions of Assessment?" *British Educational Research Journal 22*(5): 537-48.

9. Determine venues for students to share expertise with one another and foster collaborative literacy projects. The *Daybook* provides opportunities for students to share their thinking and writing, and they are encouraged to do that in more depth through various extension activities suggested in the teachers' edition.

   Vygotsky, L. S. (1978). *Mind in Society. The development of higher mental psychological processes.* Cambridge, MA: MIT Press.

   Wood, K. D., Roser, N. L. and Martinez, M. (2001). "Collaborative Literacy: Lessons Learned from Literature." *The Reading Teacher 55*(2): 102-115.

10. Establish routines that give students ample time to read and write in the classroom, where the teacher can monitor students' progress. The *Daybook* is a resource of multiple and overlapping literacy activities that can support developing and monitoring student understanding.

    Gettinger, M. (1984). "Achievement as a Function of Time Spent in Learning and Time Needed for Learning." *American Educational Research Journal 21*(3): 617-28.

    Lofty. J. (1992). *Time to Write: The Influence of Time and Culture on Learning To Write.* New York: SUNY.

Contents

Focus/Skill		Selection/Author	

UNIT 1 ❄ BUILDING YOUR REPERTOIRE — 9
Critical Approaches to Reading and Writing

Focus/Skill	#	Selection/Author	Page
Interacting with the Text	1	**A Summer Life** by Gary Soto (FICTION) "Seventh Grade" by Gary Soto (SHORT STORY)	10
Making Connections	2	"Seventh Grade" by Gary Soto (SHORT STORY)	13
Exploring Multiple Perspectives	3	"Seventh Grade" by Gary Soto (SHORT STORY)	16
Focusing on Language and Craft	4	"Oranges" by Gary Soto (POETRY)	19
Studying an Author	5	**Living Up the Street** by Gary Soto (NONFICTION)	22

UNIT 2 ❄ INTERACTING WITH THE TEXT — 25
Strategic Reading

Focus/Skill	#	Selection/Author	Page
Making Predictions	6	**The Breadwinner** by Deborah Ellis (FICTION)	26
Questioning the Text	7	**The Breadwinner** by Deborah Ellis (FICTION)	29
Summarizing	8	"Ain't I a Woman?" by Sojourner Truth (SPEECH)	32
Visualizing	9	"Vietnam War Memorial" by Mattie Stepanek (POETRY)	34
Reflecting	10	WRITING ACTIVITY: WRITING AN OPINION PARAGRAPH	37

UNIT 3 ❄ MAKING CONNECTIONS — 39
Story Elements

Focus/Skill	#	Selection/Author	Page
Setting	11	**Year of Impossible Goodbyes** by Sook Nyul Choi (FICTION)	40
Point of View	12	**Year of Impossible Goodbyes** by Sook Nyul Choi (FICTION)	42
Characters	13	"Thank You Ma'm" by Langston Hughes (SHORT STORY)	45
Plot	14	"Thank You Ma'm" by Langston Hughes (SHORT STORY)	48
Theme	15	WRITING ACTIVITY: WRITING ABOUT THEME	51

Focus/Skill		Selection/Author	

UNIT 4 ✳ EXPLORING MULTIPLE PERSPECTIVES — 53
Perspectives on a Person

Focus/Skill	#	Selection/Author	Page
A Biography	16	"Hero on the Ball Field" by Robert Peterson (BIOGRAPHY)	54
An Interview	17	"Henry Aaron Remembers" by Brian Ethier (INTERVIEW)	58
A Personal Account	18	Stealing Home by Sharon Robinson (NONFICTION)	62
A Poetic Portrait	19	"jackie robinson" by Lucille Clifton (POETRY)	65
A Brief Encounter	20	"Lady, That's Jackie Robinson!" by Nan Birmingham (NONFICTION)	67

UNIT 5 ✳ FOCUSING ON LANGUAGE AND CRAFT — 69
Personal Narrative and Poetry

Focus/Skill	#	Selection/Author	Page
People Are Poems	21	Locomotion by Jacqueline Woodson (POETRY)	70
Epistle Poems	22	Locomotion by Jacqueline Woodson (POETRY)	75
Langston Hughes	23	"Mother to Son" by Langston Hughes (POETRY)	77
Finding Ideas	24	"Long Live Langston" from Bronx Masquerade by Nikki Grimes (FICTION)	80
Connecting Through Poetry	25	"Porscha's Journal" from Bronx Masquerade by Nikki Grimes (FICTION)	82

UNIT 6 ✳ STUDYING AN AUTHOR — 85
Yoshiko Uchida

Focus/Skill	#	Selection/Author	Page
A Writer's Heritage	26	"The Princess of Light" by Yoshiko Uchida (FICTION)	86
A Writer's Identity	27	The Invisible Thread by Yoshiko Uchida (NONFICTION)	90
A Writer's Language	28	Journey Home by Yoshiko Uchida (FICTION)	93
A Writer's Themes	29	Desert Exile by Yoshiko Uchida (NONFICTION)	96
A Writer's Intent	30	Interview with Yoshiko Uchida (INTERVIEW) WRITING ACTIVITY: EXAMINING THE AUTHOR'S PURPOSE	99

Focus/Skill		Selection/Author	
UNIT 7		**ASSESSING YOUR GROWING REPERTOIRE**	101
Interacting and Connecting with a Story	31	**"Birthday Box"** by Jane Yolen (SHORT STORY)	102
Using Reading and Writing Strategies	32	**"The Key to Everything"** by May Swenson (POETRY)	106
Studying an Author	33	**Frequently Asked Questions** by Jane Yolen (NONFICTION)	109
Getting Ready to Write	34	**The Call of the Wild** by Jack London (FICTION) **Island of the Blue Dolphins** by Scott O'Dell (FICTION)	112
Revising and Evaluating Your Work	35	WRITING ACTIVITY: REFLECTING ON YOUR WRITING	116
UNIT 8		**EXPANDING YOUR REPERTOIRE**	117
		Reading for Meaning	
Interacting with the Text	36	**Ice Drift** by Theodore Taylor (FICTION)	118
Making Connections	37	**"True Believer"** by Virginia Euwer Wolff (POETRY)	121
Exploring Multiple Perspectives	38	**The Terrorist** by Caroline Cooney (FICTION)	124
Focusing on Language and Craft	39	**"Homeless"** by Anna Quindlen (NONFICTION)	129
Studying an Author	40	WRITING ACTIVITY: WRITING FROM TWO PERSPECTIVES	131
UNIT 9		**INTERACTING WITH THE TEXT**	133
		Reading Visual Texts	
Making Inferences	41	**Bone** by Jeff Smith (FICTION)	134
Characteristics of a Genre	42	**Bone** by Jeff Smith (FICTION)	137
Style and Design	43	**The Borden Tragedy** by Rick Geary (NONFICTION)	140
Dialogue, Narration, and Sound	44	WRITING ACTIVITY: CONVEYING CHARACTERS' FEELINGS	143
Adapting a Text	45	**"Annabel Lee"** by Edgar Allan Poe (POETRY)	145

Focus/Skill		Selection/Author	

UNIT 10 ❋ MAKING CONNECTIONS — 147
Monitoring Your Connections

Connecting to the Facts	46	**America's Great Disasters** by Martin W. Sandler (NONFICTION)	148
Connecting to the People	47	**America's Great Disasters** by Martin W. Sandler (NONFICTION) **Three Fearful Days** edited by Malcolm Barker (NONFICTION)	151
Connecting to Fictional Accounts	48	**Dragonwings** by Laurence Yep (FICTION)	154
Connecting through Photographs	49	WRITING ACTIVITY: DESCRIPTIVE LANGUAGE	158
Connecting to Inform Future Actions	50	"Safety Tips for Earthquakes" by the Rhode Island Red Cross (NONFICTION)	160

UNIT 11 ❋ EXPLORING MULTIPLE PERSPECTIVES — 163
The Art of Persuasion

Problem and Solutions	51	"Are Plastic Bags Harming the Environment?" by Sara Ives (NONFICTION)	164
Convincing Details	52	"Call of the Mall" from *You Are the Earth* by David Suzuki and Kathy Vanderlinden (NONFICTION)	167
Examining the Alternatives	53	"To Drill or Not to Drill" by Steven R. Wills (NONFICTION)	169
Making Connections to Our Lives	54	**Harvest for Hope: A Guide to Mindful Eating** by Jane Goodall with Gary McAvoy and Gail Hudson (NONFICTION)	172
Persuading Others	55	"Save Your Energy" from *You Are the Earth* by David Suzuki and Kathy Vanderlinden (NONFICTION)	175

UNIT 12 ❋ FOCUSING ON LANGUAGE AND CRAFT — 177
Reading, Writing, and Symbols

Reading, in Other Words	56	"Martin Luther King Jr." by Gwendolyn Brooks (POETRY) **A History of Reading** by Alberto Manguel (NONFICTION)	178
Writing as Writing	57	**Symbols of Humankind** by Don Lago (NONFICTION)	182
Writing Goes Extraterrestrial	58	**Symbols of Humankind** by Don Lago (NONFICTION)	184
From Image to Symbol	59	WRITING ACTIVITY: WRITING A POEM	186
Writing a Poem	60	"The Road Not Taken" by Robert Frost (POETRY)	190

Focus/Skill	Selection/Author	
UNIT 13	**STUDYING AN AUTHOR** Will Hobbs	**193**
Stories from Other Stories	61 **The Maze** by Will Hobbs (FICTION)	**194**
Real-Life Stories	62 **The Maze** by Will Hobbs (FICTION)	**197**
Stories in Different Genres	63 **Jason's Gold** by Will Hobbs (FICTION) **Kokopelli's Flute** by Will Hobbs (FICTION)	**200**
Characters in Stories	64 **Downriver** by Will Hobbs (FICTION)	**204**
Revising Stories	65 WRITING ACTIVITY: REVISING	**207**
UNIT 14	**ASSESSING YOUR STRENGTHS**	**209**
Interacting and Connecting with a Story	66 **"Shells"** by Cynthia Rylant (SHORT STORY)	**210**
Studying an Author's Craft	67 WRITING ACTIVITY: MAKING A PREDICTION	**213**
Focusing on Language and Craft	68 **"Shells"** by Cynthia Rylant (SHORT STORY)	**215**
Getting Ready to Write	69 WRITING ACTIVITY: PLANNING AND WRITING A SHORT STORY	**218**
Revising and Reflecting	70 WRITING ACTIVITY: WRITING A FINAL REFLECTION	**221**
	BECOMING AN ACTIVE READER	**223**
	GLOSSARY	**228**
	ACKNOWLEDGMENTS	**235**
	INDEX	**239**

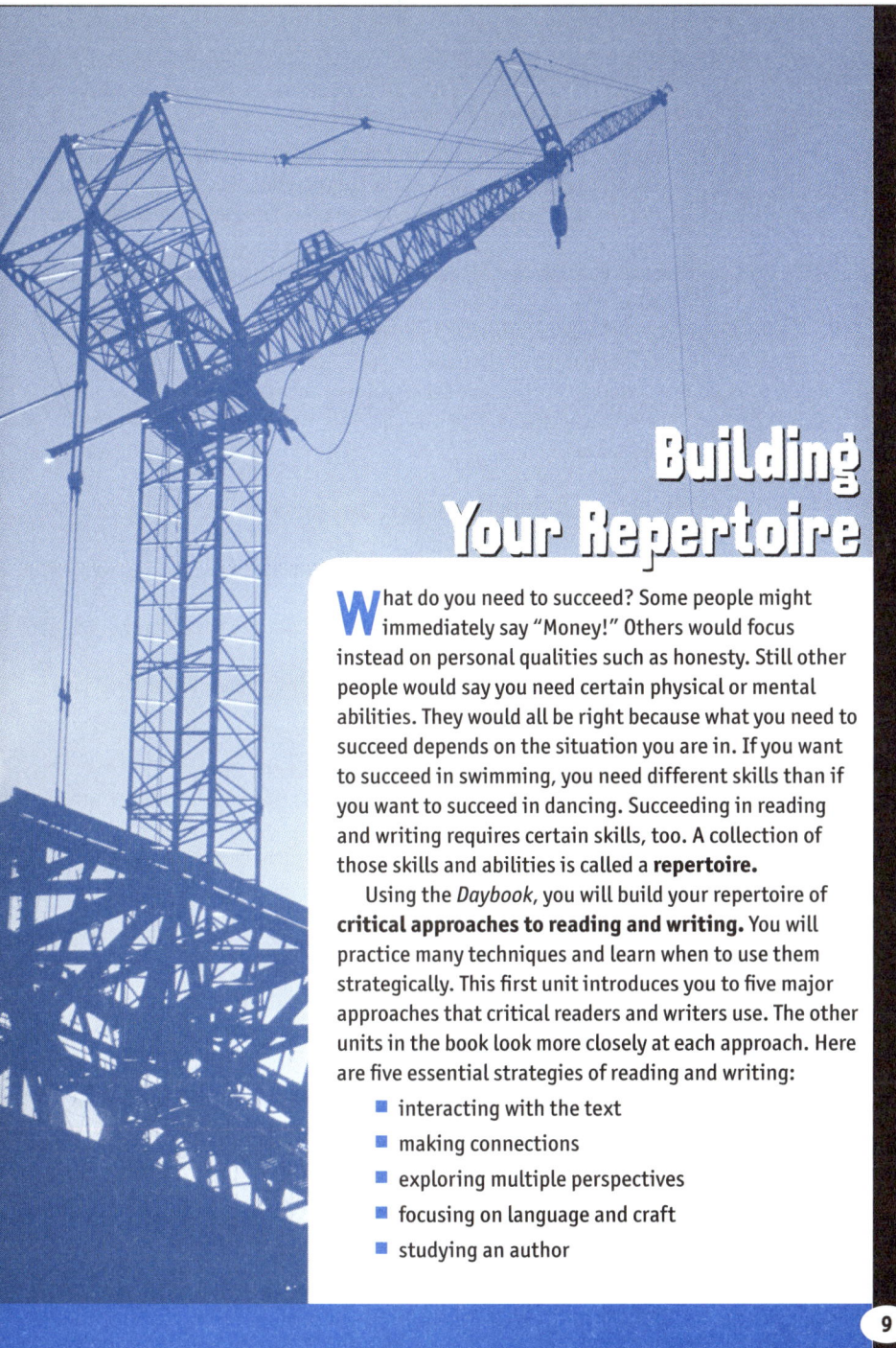

Building Your Repertoire

What do you need to succeed? Some people might immediately say "Money!" Others would focus instead on personal qualities such as honesty. Still other people would say you need certain physical or mental abilities. They would all be right because what you need to succeed depends on the situation you are in. If you want to succeed in swimming, you need different skills than if you want to succeed in dancing. Succeeding in reading and writing requires certain skills, too. A collection of those skills and abilities is called a **repertoire**.

Using the *Daybook*, you will build your repertoire of **critical approaches to reading and writing.** You will practice many techniques and learn when to use them strategically. This first unit introduces you to five major approaches that critical readers and writers use. The other units in the book look more closely at each approach. Here are five essential strategies of reading and writing:

- interacting with the text
- making connections
- exploring multiple perspectives
- focusing on language and craft
- studying an author

UNIT 1 BUILDING YOUR REPERTOIRE

Lessons 1–5, pages 10–24

UNIT OVERVIEW
Reading and writing about four pieces by Gary Soto, students are introduced to five critical reading and writing strategies that will be used throughout the *Daybook*.

KEY IDEA
Good readers develop a repertoire of skills and strategies to help them read and write effectively.

CRITICAL READING SKILLS
by lesson

1. Interacting with the text
2. Making connections
3. Exploring multiple perspectives
4. Focusing on language and craft
5. Studying an author

WRITING ACTIVITIES
by lesson

1. Do a quick-write to explore questions about the stories or the author.
2. Write about how connections help with understanding a character.
3. Retell an episode from another character's perspective.
4. Compare elements of a writer's craft found in a story and a poem.
5. Write an introduction to Gary Soto.

Literature

- ***A Summer Life*** by Gary Soto (short story excerpt)

In this excerpt, the narrator and his friend try, with little confidence, to think of ways to talk to girls.

- ***Seventh Grade*** by Gary Soto (short story)

On the first day of seventh grade, Victor tries various ruses for impressing Teresa, a girl he likes. Despite his clumsiness, she responds, and Victor decides he likes seventh grade.

- ***Oranges*** by Gary Soto (poem)

The narrator in this poem tells of his first walk with a girl and how, thanks to the silent complicity of a compassionate clerk, he buys the girl a candy with only a nickel and an orange.

- ***Living Up the Street*** by Gary Soto (autobiographical excerpt)

The author recounts a discouraging day he spent picking grapes to earn money to buy school clothes.

ASSESSMENT See page 229 for a writing prompt based on this unit.

LESSON 1

Students will read two excerpts by the same author, interact with the text, ask questions, and compare their impressions with other readers.

BACKGROUND KNOWLEDGE
The literature selections in the first four lessons are about boy-girl relationships. Encourage students to share what they have noticed about young people trying to impress each other. For example, ask: *What clothes do teens wear to impress each other? How do teens behave when they want to impress someone? Do these behaviors work? Why or why not?*

VOCABULARY
raza-style   part-Spanish for a handshake style expressive of a Latino culture

saludo de vato   Spanish for a special head nod expressive of a Latino culture

ese   Spanish for 'you.' The use here is similar to saying 'Hello, you!'

quiver   tremble or shake

conviction   a strong belief

After going over the meaning of each term, ask students to circle the words in the passage as they read them in context. Have them think about how the Spanish words add to the meaning of the story.

LESSON 1 — INTERACTING WITH THE TEXT

When you **interact with a text,** you have a conversation with it. The text is one side of the conversation. For your part of the conversation, take your pen and mark up the page as you respond to the text. Make up a code to show how your mind works. Underline parts you like. Use ??? for parts that confuse you, or xxx for parts that upset you, or !!! for parts that surprise you. Add comments such as "Why?" "I don't think so," "I wonder...." Your writing captures your thinking right on the page.

In the *Daybook*, use the **Response Notes** column to help you talk, or converse, with the text as you read. Here's how one reader used the space.

from **A Summer Life** by Gary Soto

In high school, girls were blossoms shaken from a tree and blooming with life. We didn't know how to talk to them, so we rehearsed by the school fountain. "Do you go to this school?" Scott asked, and I punched him in the arm. "Of course they do. Why else would they be here?"

I tried, "I walked by your house and saw that you have a palm tree. I have a palm tree. What a coincidence."

Scott tried: "It's cold for December."

I tried: "A June bug can live on a screen door for days."

Scott tried: "It rains a lot in April, but the funny thing is the rain is either very cold or very warm but never in between." ???

I tried: "My friend Tony said he would take the bullet for the president."

Scott tried: "Chicken is my favorite food."

We needed help. ◆

Response Notes:
- Sounds like a song —I like it.
- What's this about?
- Understatement!

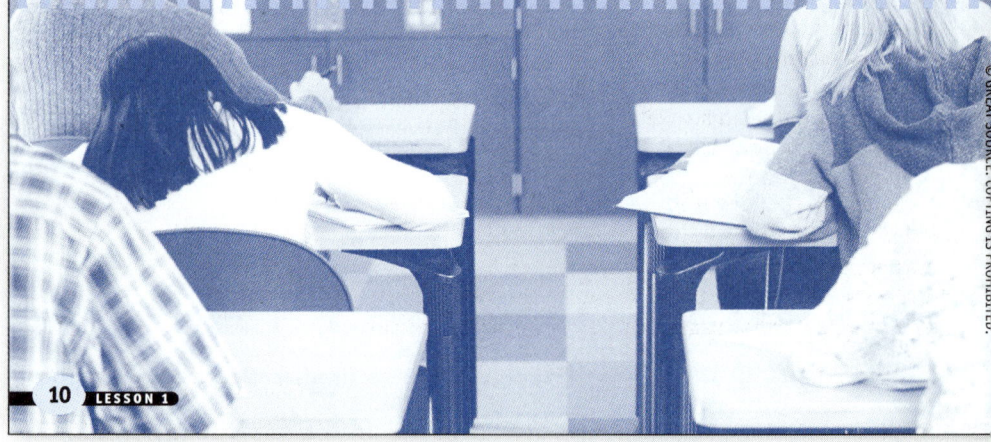

Before

CRITICAL READING SKILL
Interacting with the Text Ask students to define having a conversation (exchanging ideas, asking questions, listening, etc.). Point out that reading is like having a conversation: readers consider and react to ideas presented, ask questions of themselves and of the author, and develop new understandings. Model interacting with the text: *What does this Spanish expression mean? I'll circle it. Why does Victor sock his friend on the arm and scowl if he thinks it's weird? It sounds like he does it to fit in.*

READING PROCESS Explain to students that good readers keep their minds active when they read. They prepare to read by previewing the material and setting a purpose. As they read, they engage with the text and monitor their comprehension. After reading a text, successful readers take time to reflect on what they learned. (See *Daybook* page 223 for more on the Reading Process.)

Gary Soto often writes about boy-girl relationships. As you read the first part of a short story by him, mark it up to show questions, ideas, and any other responses you have.

"Seventh Grade" by Gary Soto

On the first day of school, Victor stood in line half an hour before he came to a wobbly card table. He was handed a packet of papers and a computer card on which he listed his one elective, French. He already spoke Spanish and English, but he thought someday he might travel to France, where it was cool; not like Fresno, where summer days reached 110 degrees in the shade. There were rivers in France, and huge churches, and fair-skinned people everywhere, the way there were brown people all around Victor.

Besides, Teresa, a girl he had liked since they were in catechism classes at Saint Theresa's, was taking French, too. With any luck they would be in the same class. Teresa is going to be my girl this year, he promised himself as he left the gym full of students in their new fall clothes. She was cute. And good at math, too, Victor thought as he walked down the hall to his homeroom. He ran into his friend, Michael Torres, by the water fountain that never turned off.

They shook hands, raza-style, and jerked their heads at one another in a saludo de vato. "How come you're making a face?" asked Victor.

"I ain't making a face, ese. This is my face." Michael said his face had changed during the summer. He had read a GQ magazine that his older brother borrowed from the Book Mobile and noticed that the male models all had the same look on their faces. They would stand, one arm around a beautiful woman, and scowl. They would sit at a pool, their rippled stomachs dark with shadow, and scowl. They would sit at dinner tables, cool drinks in their hands, and scowl.

"I think it works," Michael said. He scowled and let his upper lip quiver. His teeth showed along with the ferocity of his soul. "Belinda Reyes walked by a while ago and looked at me," he said.

Victor didn't say anything, though he thought his friend looked pretty strange. They talked about recent movies, baseball, their parents, and the horrors of picking grapes in order to buy their fall clothes. Picking grapes was like living in Siberia, except hot and more boring.

"What classes are you taking?" Michael said, scowling.

"French. How 'bout you?"

"Spanish. I ain't so good at it, even if I'm Mexican."

"I'm not either, but I'm better at it than math, that's for sure."

A tinny, three-beat bell propelled students to their homerooms. The two friends socked each other in the arm and went their ways, Victor thinking, man, that's weird. Michael thinks making a face makes him handsome.

ABOUT THE AUTHOR

Born in 1952 in Fresno, California, Gary Soto knew both the grueling heat of summer fieldwork and the nurturing warmth of family and community. While not all of his work is strictly autobiographical, Gary Soto's Chicano heritage and experiences growing up in poverty clearly inform much of his writing. Fictional or not, his characters and stories are consistently genuine and familiar, depicting a realistic and ultimately positive view of modern Mexican American culture. Students will likely see bits of themselves and people they know in his writing. For more information, see Mr. Soto's official website: http://www.garysoto.com/.

TEACHING TIP

Collaboration Have students work in pairs to interact with the text. Discussion between partners will help them generate questions and answers, discuss ideas and reactions, and write additional Response Notes.

During

RESPONSE NOTES Encourage students to mark anything they find interesting, important, or puzzling. Model how to circle or highlight the text and jot down quick notes. Advise students that words and phrases are best for note-taking; it is not necessary to write complete sentences. (For more information about marking text, see page 227 in the Daybook.)

SHARING RESPONSES Invite volunteers to share some of their Response Notes with the class. Remind students that there is no right or wrong answer; all responses are personal. Compile the responses in a chart that sorts them into various ways of interacting with text, such as, questioning, circling unfamiliar words, comparing, reacting to something or someone in the text, and so forth.

WRITER'S CRAFT

Show, Don't Tell (Voice) Read aloud the second and third paragraphs on page 11. Point out how the passage sounds like we are inside Victor's head, hearing his thoughts and conversations. This use of internal and external dialogue gives us insight that a mere description cannot impart. Have students jot down ideas about their first day in seventh grade. Remind students to include what they were thinking (internal dialogue) and conversations. Have them save their notes to use later in this unit.

EXTRA SUPPORT

Differentiation To respond to the writing prompts, students who need extra support may benefit from verbal discussion prior to writing. Have them brainstorm questions with you or a partner about the story or the author's style of writing.

Quick Assess

* Do students' Response Notes show a variety of interactions or use coding for questions, new words or phrases, personal comments, etc.?
* Did students mark text that confused them or caught their attention?
* Do students' questions and comments show comprehension of the excerpt?

Response Notes

On the way to his homeroom, Victor tried a scowl. He felt foolish, until out of the corner of his eye he saw a girl looking at him. Umm, he thought, maybe it does work. He scowled with greater conviction.

In homeroom, roll was taken, emergency cards were passed out, and they were given a bulletin to take home to their parents. The principal, Mr. Belton, spoke over the crackling loudspeaker, welcoming the students to a new year, new experiences, and new friendships. The students squirmed in their chairs and ignored him. They were anxious to go to first period. Victor sat calmly, thinking of Teresa, who sat two rows away, reading a paperback novel. This would be his lucky year. She was in his homeroom, and would probably be in his English and math classes. And, of course, French.

* Write your initial impressions of this story. What do you think of it?

* Compare your impressions and your **Response Notes** with a partner or small group. What questions do you have about the story or author? After your discussion, do a quick-write to explore one of your questions about what you've read so far or about Gary Soto's writing.

Interact with the text by marking it up with ideas, questions, and comments as you read.

12 LESSON 1

After

APPLYING THE STRATEGY Provide stories from newspapers, magazines, or other reading materials that students can write on, and have students practice interacting with these texts. Remind students to imagine they are talking to the character or author as they write their questions and notes. Then ask: *How does interacting with the text help you understand what you read? Does it help you stay focused on what you are reading? Does it help you make sense of confusing parts? Are you more or less likely to remember the text?*

MAKING CONNECTIONS — LESSON 2

Often, when you meet someone new, that person reminds you of someone else. Miss Marple, a fictional detective who appears in many of Agatha Christie's novels, often thought about that. She solved crimes by closely observing new people and noticing how they were similar to the familiar residents of her small village. Readers are somewhat like Miss Marple in that way, **making connections** between what they know and what is new. When you read, you can make connections to your ideas and opinions (your life), to other stories you have read or seen on television or the movies (other texts), and to news of world events or places you have visited (the world).

As you read the next part of "Seventh Grade," jot down some connections that you can make between the story's events or characters and events or people in your life.

"Seventh Grade" by Gary Soto (continued)

The bell rang for first period, and the students herded noisily through the door. Only Teresa lingered, talking with the homeroom teacher.

"So you think I should talk to Mrs. Gaines?" she asked the teacher. "She would know about ballet?"

"She would be a good bet," the teacher said. Then added "Or the gym teacher, Mrs. Garza."

Victor lingered, keeping his head down and staring at his desk. He wanted to leave when she did so he could bump into her and say something clever.

He watched her on the sly. As she turned to leave, he stood up and hurried to the door, where he managed to catch her eye. She smiled and said, "Hi, Victor."

He smiled back and said, "Yeah, that's me." His brown face blushed. Why hadn't he said, "Hi, Teresa," or "How was your summer?" or something nice?

As Teresa walked down the hall, Victor walked the other way, looking back, admiring how gracefully she walked, one foot in front of the other. So much for being in the same class, he thought. As he trudged to English, he practiced scowling.

In English they reviewed the parts of speech. Mr. Lucas, a portly man, waddled down the aisle, asking, "What is a noun?"

"A person, place, or thing," said the class in unison.

"Yes, now somebody give me an example of a person—you, Victor Rodriguez."

"Teresa," Victor said automatically. Some of the girls giggled. They knew he had a crush on Teresa. He felt himself blushing again.

"Correct," Mr. Lucas said. "Now provide me with a place."

Response Notes: *I wonder if this will work.*

MAKING CONNECTIONS 13

LESSON 2

Students will respond to a text by making connections to their lives; to other texts; and to other people, places, and events.

BACKGROUND KNOWLEDGE
Invite students to discuss detective characters they know about from the media and books. Ask: *How do these detectives solve crimes? What connections do they make between what they observe at a crime scene and what they know about human behavior?* Point out that a good reader is like a good detective. Good readers make connections between what they read and what they know about people and the world.

VOCABULARY
horizon line where ground meets sky; in this case, the edges of the area that could be seen on the sky secretly

bustled buzzed with activity; was crowded and busy

After going over the definitions, have students write a sentence for each vocabulary word, leaving out the term. Students can trade papers and complete each other's sentences.

Before

CRITICAL READING SKILL
Making Connections Explain that details in a story can trigger memories of something in real life. Such memories help readers connect to the text, relate to the characters, and better understand what they're reading. Have students recall what happened in the previous scene. To help students share how they connect Victor's story with their own lives, other texts they've read, and what they know about the world, ask: *Have you ever been in a similar situation? How did you feel? What were your thoughts? Does Victor remind you of another character or someone you know? In what ways does Victor's situation seem realistic?*

MAKING PREDICTIONS Explain that one way to connect with the text is to predict what may happen next. Have students think about the scene and predict what may happen to Victor. Encourage students to confirm or refute their predictions as they read.

BUILDING YOUR REPERTOIRE 13

Response Notes

Mr. Lucas called on a freckled kid who answered, "Teresa's house with a kitchen full of big brothers."

After English, Victor had math, his weakest subject. He sat in the back by the window, hoping that he would not be called on. Victor understood most of the problems, but some of the stuff looked like the teacher made it up as she went along. It was confusing, like the inside of a watch.

After math he had a fifteen-minute break, then social studies, and, finally, lunch. He bought a tuna casserole with buttered rolls, some fruit cocktail, and milk. He sat with Michael, who practiced scowling between bites.

Girls walked by and looked at him.

"See what I mean, Vic?" Michael scowled. "They love it."

"Yeah, I guess so."

They ate slowly, Victor scanning the horizon for a glimpse of Teresa. He didn't see her. She must have brought lunch, he thought, and is eating outside. Victor scraped his plate and left Michael, who was busy scowling at a girl two tables away.

The small triangle-shaped campus bustled with students talking about their new classes. Everyone was in a sunny mood. Victor hurried to the bag lunch area, where he sat down and opened his math book. He moved his lips as if he were reading, but his mind was somewhere else. He raised his eyes slowly and looked around. No Teresa.

He lowered his eyes, pretending to study, then looked slowly to the left. No Teresa. He turned a page in the book and stared at some math problems that scared him because he knew he would have to do them eventually. He looked to the right. Still no sign of her. He stretched out lazily in an attempt to disguise his snooping.

Then he saw her. She was sitting with a girlfriend under a plum tree. Victor moved to a table near her and daydreamed about taking her to a movie. When the bell sounded, Teresa looked up, and their eyes met. She smiled sweetly and gathered her books. Her next class was French, same as Victor's. ✤

✻ Put a check mark by any **prediction** you made because of a connection between this story and your personal experience or another story. What do you think will happen in French class?

During

RESPONSE NOTES As students read, help them make connections by asking such questions as: *How would you feel if you were Victor right now? What does the math class remind you of?* Model making a connection: *This reminds me of a computer class I took. Nothing made sense! I didn't know half the words the teacher used.*

MAKING PREDICTIONS To model responding to the prompt at the bottom of the page, say, for example: *The way Victor acts reminds me of a girl I knew who always sat by a boy she liked. I predict that Victor will sit by Teresa in French class. I'll put a check mark beside this prediction because I made the connection to my own experience.*

REFLECTING Have students consider how the connections they made helped them understand the passage better. Could they picture the scene more clearly? Could they relate to Victor's nervousness?

❋ Use the connections you made to gain insights about the characters in "Seventh Grade." Fill in the chart below. Support your observations by finding relevant passages in the text. Compare and discuss the connections you made with those of a partner or a small group.

Character in "Seventh Grade"	Description of the character	Connection to my life, other texts, or the world

❋ Select one character from the chart and explain how the connections you made helped you understand that character better.

_____
_____
_____

Making connections to your personal experiences, other texts, or world events and places helps you better understand and remember what you read.

MAKING CONNECTIONS 15

EXTRA SUPPORT

Differentiation Group students heterogeneously. Encourage them to work together to complete the chart. Have students do the following:

❋ List the names of characters for column 1.

❋ Provide the descriptions for column 2.

❋ Explain connections for column 3.

Then, each student can use the chart to respond to the prompt at the bottom of the page.

Quick Assess

❋ Do students' responses to the prompt show a variety of connections, from personal to more global?

❋ Do students' responses explain how making connections helped them understand the character better?

After

WRITING CONNECTION To extend the concept of making connections, have students make notes about their first day in seventh grade. Have them add ideas and details based on reading this excerpt and develop the notes into a short reflection piece. Remind students of the importance of dialogue and description.

BUILDING YOUR REPERTOIRE

LESSON 3

Students will explore multiple perspectives of several fictional characters for a deeper understanding of the story.

BACKGROUND KNOWLEDGE

As students read the next part of "Seventh Grade," they will explore the story's point of view, or perspective. Point out that each person in the classroom has a unique perspective of the room. Describe the perspective you have as the teacher. For example: *I see students facing me and a window to my left. I am standing and the students are sitting.* Then invite volunteers to describe their perspectives.

VOCABULARY

bonjour French word for *hello* or *good day*

Trés bien. Parlez-vous français? French for *Very good. Do you speak French?*

Le bateau est sur l'eau. French for *The boat is on the water.*

sheepishly in an embarrassed way

sprint burst of speed

Review the French terms and their translations. Have students determine the meanings of *sheepish* and *sprint* from using the context of the story.

LESSON 3 — EXPLORING MULTIPLE PERSPECTIVES

A perspective is a way of looking at things: it is a filter made of experiences, education, and emotions, through which a person sees the world. When you read a story, try to see it through the eyes of the author or a character. If you then change the point of view, you will see the story in new ways. Exploring multiple perspectives requires that you keep an open mind while you consider characters and events from different points of view.

As you finish reading "Seventh Grade," think about the point of view you are using. Are you seeing the events through the eyes of Mr. Bueller? Victor? Teresa? Someone else?

"Seventh Grade" by Gary Soto (continued)

They were among the last students to arrive in class, so all the good desks in the back had already been taken. Victor was forced to sit near the front, a few desks away from Teresa, while Mr. Bueller wrote French words on the chalkboard. The bell rang, and Mr. Bueller wiped his hands, turned to the class, and said, *"Bonjour."*

"Bonjour," braved a few students.

"Bonjour," Victor whispered. He wondered if Teresa heard him.

Mr. Bueller said that if the students studied hard, at the end of the year they could go to France and be understood by the populace.

One kid raised his hand and asked, "What's 'populace'?"

"The people, the people of France."

Mr. Bueller asked if anyone knew French. Victor raised his hand, wanting to impress Teresa. The teacher beamed and said, *"Très bien. Parlez-vous français?"*

Victor didn't know what to say. The teacher wet his lips and asked something else in French. The room grew silent. Victor felt all eyes staring at him. He tried to bluff his way out by making noises that sounded French.

"La me vava me con le grandma," he said uncertainly.

Mr. Bueller, wrinkling his face in curiosity, asked him to speak up.

Great rosebushes of red bloomed on Victor's cheeks. A river of nervous sweat ran down his palms. He felt awful. Teresa sat a few desks away, no doubt thinking he was a fool. Without looking at Mr. Bueller, Victor mumbled, "Frenchie oh wewe gee in September."

Mr. Bueller asked Victor to repeat what he had said. "Frenchie oh wewe gee in September," Victor repeated.

Response Notes: I feel embarrassed for Victor!

Before

CRITICAL READING SKILL
Exploring Multiple Perspectives

Explain that an author chooses a specific perspective from which to tell the story. The perspective affects the reader's experience of the story. It often determines the subject matter, style, theme, and other elements of a piece of writing. Explain that, in this story, the author tells how Victor is feeling, what he thinks, and what he notices about other people and events. Telling a story from the point of view of a character, identified by the use of *he* or *she*, is called third-person point of view.

SET A PURPOSE Successful readers have a reason to read; they read for a purpose. Sometimes, good readers read a piece of text twice: the first time, they read just to get a sense of the text, and the second time they read for a particular reason. In this case, students are asked to determine the character with which they have the strongest connection and, therefore, through which point of view they are experiencing the story.

Mr. Bueller understood that the boy didn't know French and turned away. He walked to the blackboard and pointed to the words on the board with his steel-edged ruler.

"*Le bateau*," he sang.

"*Le bateau*," the students repeated.

"*Le bateau est sur l'eau*," he sang.

"*Le bateau est sur l'eau.*"

Victor was too weak from failure to join the class. He stared at the board and wished he had taken Spanish, not French. Better yet, he wished he could start his life over. He had never been so embarrassed. He bit his thumb until he tore off a sliver of skin.

The bell sounded for fifth period, and Victor shot out of the room, avoiding the stares of the other kids, but had to return for his math book. He looked sheepishly at the teacher, who was erasing the board, then widened his eyes in terror at Teresa who stood in front of him. "I didn't know you knew French," she said. "That was good."

Mr. Bueller looked at Victor, and Victor looked back. Oh please, don't say anything, Victor pleaded with his eyes. I'll wash your car, mow your lawn, walk your dog—anything! I'll be your best student, and I'll clean your erasers after school.

Mr. Bueller shuffled through the papers on his desk. He smiled and hummed as he sat down to work. He remembered his college years when he dated a girlfriend in borrowed cars. She thought he was rich because each time he picked her up, he had a different car. It was fun until he had spent all his money on her and had to write home to his parents because he was broke.

Victor couldn't stand to look at Teresa. He was sweaty with shame. "Yeah, well, I picked up a few things from movies and books and stuff like that." They left the class together. Teresa asked him if he would help her with her French.

EXPLORING MULTIPLE PERSPECTIVES 17

WRITER'S CRAFT

Perspective Explain that authors use perspective or point of view to develop characters. For example, readers get to know Victor through Mr. Soto's descriptions of his character's thoughts and feelings.

Read aloud the next to the last paragraph on page 17 and ask: *Whose thoughts and feelings does Mr. Soto tell about here?* (Mr. Bueller's) Explain that the author uses this brief shift in perspective to give the reader a better understanding of the character, Mr. Bueller. Ask: *What did you learn about Mr. Bueller from this paragraph?* (He is empathetic, having had similar experiences.)

EXTRA SUPPORT

Differentiation Visual or spatial learners might benefit from creating cluster diagrams for the characters and listing details that reveal their perspective. Encourage students to add to their diagrams to show other characters' perspectives as the story progresses.

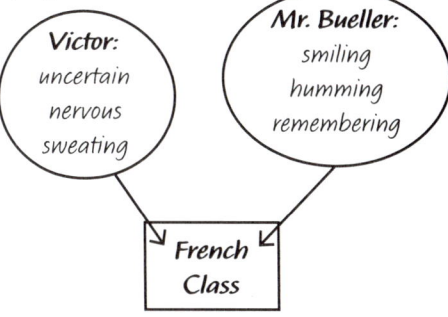

During

RESPONSE NOTES Encourage students to identify specific instances where the author indicates a character's thoughts, feelings, and observations about other people and events. Have them think about how they would write about their own experience from another perspective.

MARKING THE TEXT Suggest that students use a variety of techniques to distinguish various perspectives. For example, they might mark each character's actions, words, and thoughts with a different colored highlighter. Or they might use different handwriting styles (printing/cursive, uppercase/lowercase) for questions or comments about different characters.

BUILDING YOUR REPERTOIRE 17

WRITING SUPPORT

Creating Character Sketches

Before students begin writing from another character's point of view, have them create a character sketch as they imagine the person to be. The sketches should include the following information about the character:

✱ full name and nickname, if desired

✱ physical description (gender, age, physical characteristics, clothing, etc.)

✱ background (family, friends, lifestyle, previous school-related experiences, etc.)

✱ personality (dreams, fears, attitude, sense of humor or lack thereof, favorite sayings or expressions, etc.)

Quick Assess

✱ Do students' retellings focus on the French class episode?

✱ Did students use the first-person point of view?

✱ Did students tell only what the chosen character could think, feel, and know?

"Sure, anytime," Victor said.
"I won't be bothering you, will I?"
"Oh no, I like being bothered."
"*Bonjour*," Teresa said, leaving him outside her next class. She smiled and pushed wisps of hair from her face.
"Yeah, right, *bonjour*," Victor said. He turned and headed to his class. The rosebushes of shame on his face became bouquets of love. Teresa is a great girl, he thought. And Mr. Bueller is a good guy.
He raced to metal shop. After metal shop there was biology, and after biology a long sprint to the public library, where he checked out three French textbooks.
He was going to like seventh grade. ✧

✱ "Seventh Grade" is told from Victor's perspective. How would it be different if the story were told from the perspective of Teresa or Mr. Bueller? Retell this part of the story—the incident in French class—from the point of view of either Teresa or Mr. Bueller. Tell the story in the first person, using *I*, and telling just what that character would know.

Thinking about a text from different perspectives helps you understand the author's message.

WRITING CONNECTION To further develop students' understanding of point of view, have them use their notes about their first day in seventh grade (see page 15) to write from another person's perspective. Remind them to include actions, thoughts, feelings, and dialogue. Encourage them to use third-person point of view referring to themselves by their first names and third-person pronouns (he, she, him, her).

REFLECTING Invite students to share insights gained from writing about their experience. Ask: *Did using another point of view change your version of the experience? What was most difficult about shifting your perspective?*

FOCUSING ON LANGUAGE AND CRAFT — LESSON 4

Gary Soto's first writings were poems. He recalls, "I once worked on a single fourteen-line poem for a week, changing verbs, reworking line breaks, cutting out unnecessary words." He then explains, "Poetry is a concentrated form of writing; so much meaning is packed into such a little space. Therefore, each word in a poem is very important and is chosen very carefully to convey just the right meaning." Choosing the right word is part of Gary Soto's repertoire as a writer. What he says can apply to all writing, not just poetry. Authors craft their work carefully, **choosing words** to create strong images, express ideas, and spark feelings.

Gary Soto sees his readers as his teammates: "You have to concentrate when you read a poem, just as you must concentrate when you're in the batter's box and your team needs you to bring in a player from second base." Take Soto's advice as you read "Oranges." Read it at least twice. Interact with the text as you read—underline words or phrases that strike you. Put a question mark next to anything that you wonder about. Another way to interact with the text is to visualize what you're reading, so use the **Response Notes** for drawings or rough sketches of what you see in your mind as you read.

Oranges by Gary Soto

The first time I walked
With a girl, I was twelve,
Cold, and weighted down
With two oranges in my jacket.
December. Frost cracking
Beneath my steps, my breath
Before me, then gone,
As I walked toward
Her house, the one whose
(Porch light burned yellow)
Night and day, in any weather.
A dog barked at me, until
She came out pulling
At her gloves, face bright
With rouge. I smiled,
Touched her shoulder, and led ▶▶▶

LESSON 4

Students will examine how an author uses sensory language and realistic characterization to convey ideas.

BACKGROUND KNOWLEDGE
To build background for the poem, explain that the poem was written about a time when Soto was twelve, probably in the mid-1960s. At that time, the minimum wage in the United States was just over $1.00 an hour, it cost a nickel to mail a letter, a gallon of gas cost 31 cents, and a candy bar might cost as little as 5 or 10 cents. It would not have been unusual for a boy to take a girl out for candy with far less than a dollar in his pocket. Clearly, though, the boy in the poem is less affluent than many teens today.

VOCABULARY
rouge makeup that reddens cheeks
tiered stacked up

Point out the lines where the words appear, replacing the words with their definitions. Then have students respond to how the rereading changes the sound of the poem.

Before

CRITICAL READING SKILL
Focusing on Language and Craft
In this lesson, students examine the ways an author uses words to develop ideas and create strong images of people, feelings, and situations. Point out that writing is like painting; a good writer paints a picture in your mind. Invite students to draw images that come to mind as you read the poem aloud.

EXTRA SUPPORT

Differentiation To ease some students' anxieties about reading poetry, point out that "Oranges" tells a very simple story. Suggest that they create a pictorial timeline of the story as they read. Then, for each event in the timeline, have students list the words that help the reader "see" the event.

Her down the street, across
A used car lot and a line
Of newly planted trees,
Until we were breathing
Before a drugstore. We
Entered, the tiny bell
Bringing a saleslady
Down a narrow aisle of goods.
I turned to the candies
Tiered like bleachers,
And asked what she wanted —
Light in her eyes, a smile
Starting at the corners
Of her mouth. I fingered
A nickel in my pocket,
And when she lifted a chocolate
That cost a dime,
I didn't say anything.
I took the nickel from
My pocket, then an orange,
And set them quietly on
The counter. When I looked up,
The lady's eyes met mine,
And held them, knowing
Very well what it was all
About.
      Outside,
A few cars hissing past,
Fog hanging like old
Coats between the trees.
I took my girl's hand
In mine for two blocks,
Then released it to let
Her unwrap the chocolate.
I peeled my orange
That was so bright against
The gray of December
That, from some distance,
Someone might have thought
I was making a fire in my hands. ✦

20 LESSON 4

During

LANGUAGE MAP Have students point out words or phrases from the poem that create strong images in their minds (e.g., *face bright with rouge, making a fire in my hands*). Create a web, inviting students to continue adding words and phrases that help them see, feel, and hear the events and mood of the poem. Help students notice how the author's choice of words contributes to the imagery.

RESPONSE NOTES Have students read the poem several times: once to draw sketches of people and scenes, once to ask questions and comments, and once to highlight or underline vivid words or phrases.

20 UNIT 1

✳ What line or small section of the poem was most vivid for you? Put a box around it and then, in the space below, explain why you selected it.

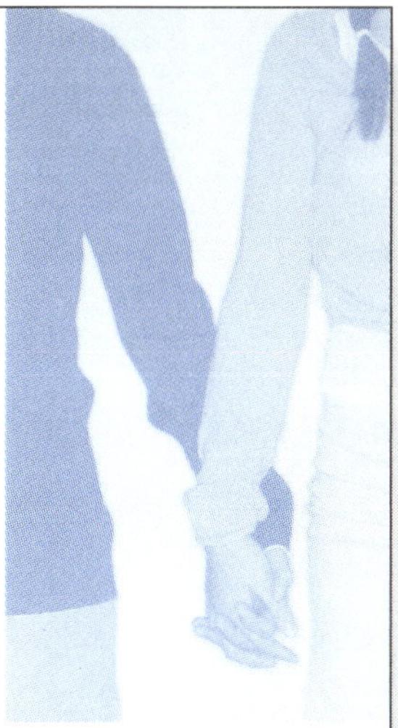

_____
_____
_____

✳ "Oranges" and "Seventh Grade" show boys making friends with girls. Skim both selections again. Fill in the chart to compare some of the elements of craft that you find in each. (Not all of the elements will be present in both pieces.)

Elements of craft	"Oranges"	"Seventh Grade"
strong images		
vivid descriptions of feelings		
humorous phrases or expressions		
realistic characterization		

Focusing on the words and sentences helps you understand an author's ideas and individual style.

WRITER'S CRAFT

Characterization To prepare students for the chart activity, review characterization. Explain that a character's thoughts, feelings, words, and actions reveal the character. For example, you can tell that the saleslady is kind because she doesn't refuse when the boy pays for the candy with a nickel and an orange. Define the term by saying: *Characterization is the method the author uses to show what the character is like. If the character seems like a real person, we say that the characterization is realistic.*

TEACHING TIP

Collaboration Form seven groups. Assign one character to each group: Victor, Michael, Teresa, Mr. Bueller, and the three characters in "Oranges." Have group members work together to identify the characteristics of their assigned character. Then have each group decide whether the characterization is realistic and share their findings with the class.

Quick Assess

✳ Do students' Response Notes include sketches of people and scenes, and comments about the poem?

✳ Do students' charts include at least three entries for each selection?

After

READING/WRITING CONNECTION

Have students revisit the experience they wrote about on page 15. Have them fold a piece of paper into eight sections and label them: *sights, sounds, tastes, smells, thoughts, feelings, people, events*. Encourage students to record several vivid words or phrases in each section. Then challenge them to compose poems using the words and phrases to relate the experience.

LESSON 5

Students will study an author's personal memories to make connections between the author's life and his writing.

BACKGROUND KNOWLEDGE
Explain that Gary Soto grew up in an area in California where many fruit and vegetable crops are grown. Harvesting these crops required manual labor under harsh conditions. The climate in the San Joaquin Valley is very hot and dry in the early fall, the time of year when grapes are harvested. Harvesting grapes is slow, tedious work that involves cutting the clusters of grapes from under the thick leaves of the plant. This job could not be done by machine because grapes are so easily bruised. To set the economic context, tell students that, at the time of this memoir, a pair of new jeans cost about $2.00.

VOCABULARY

groping feeling around with fingers or hands

brimmed filled

recounted reviewed; retold

Ay, Dios Spanish exclamation of surprise or amazement

After discussing the definitions, have students brainstorm synonyms for each term.

LESSON 5 STUDYING AN AUTHOR

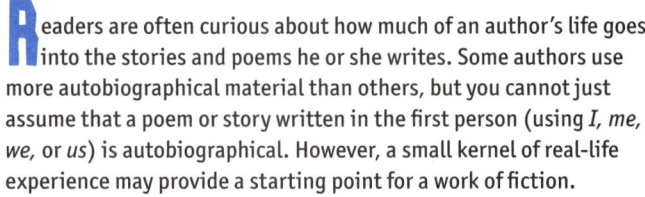

Readers are often curious about how much of an author's life goes into the stories and poems he or she writes. Some authors use more autobiographical material than others, but you cannot just assume that a poem or story written in the first person (using *I, me, we,* or *us*) is autobiographical. However, a small kernel of real-life experience may provide a starting point for a work of fiction.

Read the selection below, which describes Gary Soto's memories of picking grapes to earn money for school clothes. This piece *is* autobiographical, and you may find connections between it and the two selections you have already read—"Oranges" and "Seventh Grade." Read actively by writing your own comments and connections in the **Response Notes**.

from Living Up the Street by Gary Soto

Response Notes

Soto creates images here, as he did in "Oranges."

I cut another bunch, then another, fighting the snap and whip of vines. After ten minutes of groping for grapes, my first pan brimmed with bunches. I poured them on the paper tray, which was bordered by a wooden frame that kept the grapes from rolling off, and they spilled like jewels from a pirate's chest. The tray was only half filled, so I hurried to jump under the vines and begin groping, cutting, and tugging at the grapes again. I emptied the pan, raked the grapes with my hands to make them look like they filled the tray, and jumped back under the vine on my knees. I tried to cut faster because Mother, in the next row, was slowly moving ahead. I peeked into her row and saw five trays gleaming in the early morning. I cut, pulled hard, and stopped to gather the grapes that missed the pan; already bored, I spat on a few to wash them before tossing them like popcorn into my mouth.

So it went. Two pans equaled one tray—or six cents. By lunchtime I had a trail of thirty-seven trays behind me while Mother had sixty or more. We met about halfway from our last trays, and I sat down with a grunt, knees wet from kneeling on dropped grapes. I washed my hands with the water from the jug, drying them on the inside of my shirt sleeve before I opened the paper bag for the first sandwich, which I gave to Mother. I dipped my hand in again to unwrap a sandwich without looking at it. I took a first bite and chewed it slowly for the tang of mustard. Eating in silence I looked straight ahead at the vines, and only when we were finished with cookies did we talk.

"Are you tired?" she asked.

22 LESSON 5

Before

CRITICAL READING SKILL
Studying an Author Remind students that knowing about an author's background can tell a reader a lot about the author's perspective and what he or she values. Ask: *From the writings you've already read (excerpts from* A Summer Life *and* Seventh Grade *and "Oranges"), what do you think is important to Mr. Soto?*

What is his view of the world? Then invite students to read the memoir excerpt for further insights about Gary Soto.

MEMOIR Define memoir as a form of writing that tells about a real experience in a person's life and explains why the experience is important to the writer. Think-aloud about an experience in your life worthy of memoir. For example: *I remember the first time I felt old enough to...*Then ask students to reflect on experiences in their lives that might be important enough for the memoir form.

22 UNIT 1

"No, but I got a sliver from the frame," I told her. I showed her the web of skin between my thumb and index finger. She wrinkled her forehead but said it was nothing.

"How many trays did you do?"

I looked straight ahead, not answering at first. I recounted in my mind the whole morning of bend, cut, pour again and again, before answering a feeble "thirty-seven." No elaboration, no detail. Without looking at me she told me how she had done field work in Texas and Michigan as a child. But I had a difficult time listening to her stories. I played with my grape knife, stabbing it into the ground, but stopped when Mother reminded me that I had better not lose it. I left the knife sticking up like a small, leafless plant. She then talked about school, the junior high I would be going to that fall, and then about Rick and Debra [Soto's brother and sister], how sorry they would be that they hadn't come out to pick grapes because they'd have no new clothes for the school year. She stopped talking when she peeked at her watch, a bandless one she kept in her pocket. She got up with an *"Ay, Dios,"* and told me that we'd work until three, leaving me cutting figures in the sand with my knife and dreading the return to work.

Finally I rose and walked slowly back to where I had left off, again kneeling under the vine and fixing the pan under bunches of grapes. By that time, 11:30, the sun was over my shoulder and made me squint and think of the pool at the Y.M.C.A. where I was a summer member. I saw myself diving face first into the water and loving it. I saw myself gleaming like something new, at the edge of the pool. I had to daydream and keep my mind busy because boredom was a terror almost as awful as the work itself. My mind went dumb with stupid things, and I had to keep it moving with dreams of baseball and would-be girlfriends. I even sang, however softly, to keep my mind moving, my hands moving.

I worked less hurriedly and with less vision. I no longer saw that copper pot sitting squat on our stove or Mother waiting for it to whistle. The wardrobe that I imagined, crisp and bright in the closet, numbered only one pair of jeans and two shirts because, in half a day, six cents times thirty-seven trays was two dollars and twenty-two cents. It became clear to me. If I worked eight hours, I might make four dollars. ❖

EXTRA SUPPORT

Differentiation Students who need extra support might benefit from a roundtable activity. Seat students at a table. Ask students to find words or sentences in *Living Up the Street* that remind them of the boy in "Oranges." Then ask them to find text that reminds them of Victor in *Seventh Grade*. Keep the discussion going until each student finds similarities between the author's own story and details in his writing.

TEACHING TIP

Collaboration Invite students to work in pairs. First, have students read the selection silently and make Response Notes. Then, have partners share their Response Notes and compare ideas to add more details to their notes.

❊ Discuss with a partner any connections you find between Gary Soto's life and his writing. Label the parts of the excerpt from *Living Up the Street* that connect with "Oranges" and "Seventh Grade."

STUDYING AN AUTHOR 23

During

RESPONSE NOTES As students read the memoir, suggest that they include in their notes the following:

❊ questions or comments about Soto's feelings and thoughts

❊ comments about how the experiences in the memoir connect with Soto's fictional writings (*Seventh Grade* and "Oranges")

WRITING SUPPORT

Elements of an Introduction

Invite students to brainstorm a list of information they can use to introduce the author, such as name, biographical information, well-known writings, elements of his writing craft and style, quotes from his writings or memoir, and personal responses to his work. Also invite them to visit his website for additional facts they may want to include in the introduction. (See page 11.)

Quick Assess

* Do students' Response Notes include questions, comments, and connections with fictional writings?
* Do their introductions include information that gives the audience an insight into Soto's work?

The more you know about how an author thinks, the more insight you will have into his or her writing. Read these quotes from Gary Soto. How have you seen his perspective reflected in his writing?

> from an interview in *Contemporary Authors* by Jean W. Ross
> "I like the youth in my poetry, sort of a craziness. For me that's really important. I don't want to take a dreary look at the world and then start writing."

> from *A Fire in My Hands* by Gary Soto
> "I tried to remain faithful to the common things of my childhood—dogs, alleys, my baseball mitt, curbs, and the fruit of the valley, especially the orange. I wanted to give these things life, to write so well that my poems would express their simple beauty."

> from *California Childhood* by Gary Soto
> "Childhood is not only place, but a response toward place. I'm speaking of fear and boredom, the sense of resignation in a poor family, the utter joy of jumping into cold river water, the loneliness of no girlfriend or boyfriend, envy of the rich in 'fresh' clothes, adolescent rebellion—human feelings that move beyond the borders of California to embrace all children."

Gary Soto mentions four elements that make up his perspective:
- a youthful quality, "sort of a craziness"
- an upbeat approach, the opposite of "a dreary look at the world"
- attention to the "simple beauty" of commonplace things and events
- a focus on young people's emotions

* Imagine that you have been asked to introduce Gary Soto to a group of students who will read some of his work. Choose one aspect of Soto's writing that is most interesting to you and write a short introduction.

_____
_____
_____
_____
_____
_____

> Studying an author's life and perspective can give you insights into his or her writing.

After

LISTENING/SPEAKING CONNECTION Have pairs of students role-play introducing Gary Soto to a group of classmates or another class. Then reverse roles and repeat for another group. Continue until every student has introduced the author. You may want to use this activity with other favorite authors from time to time.

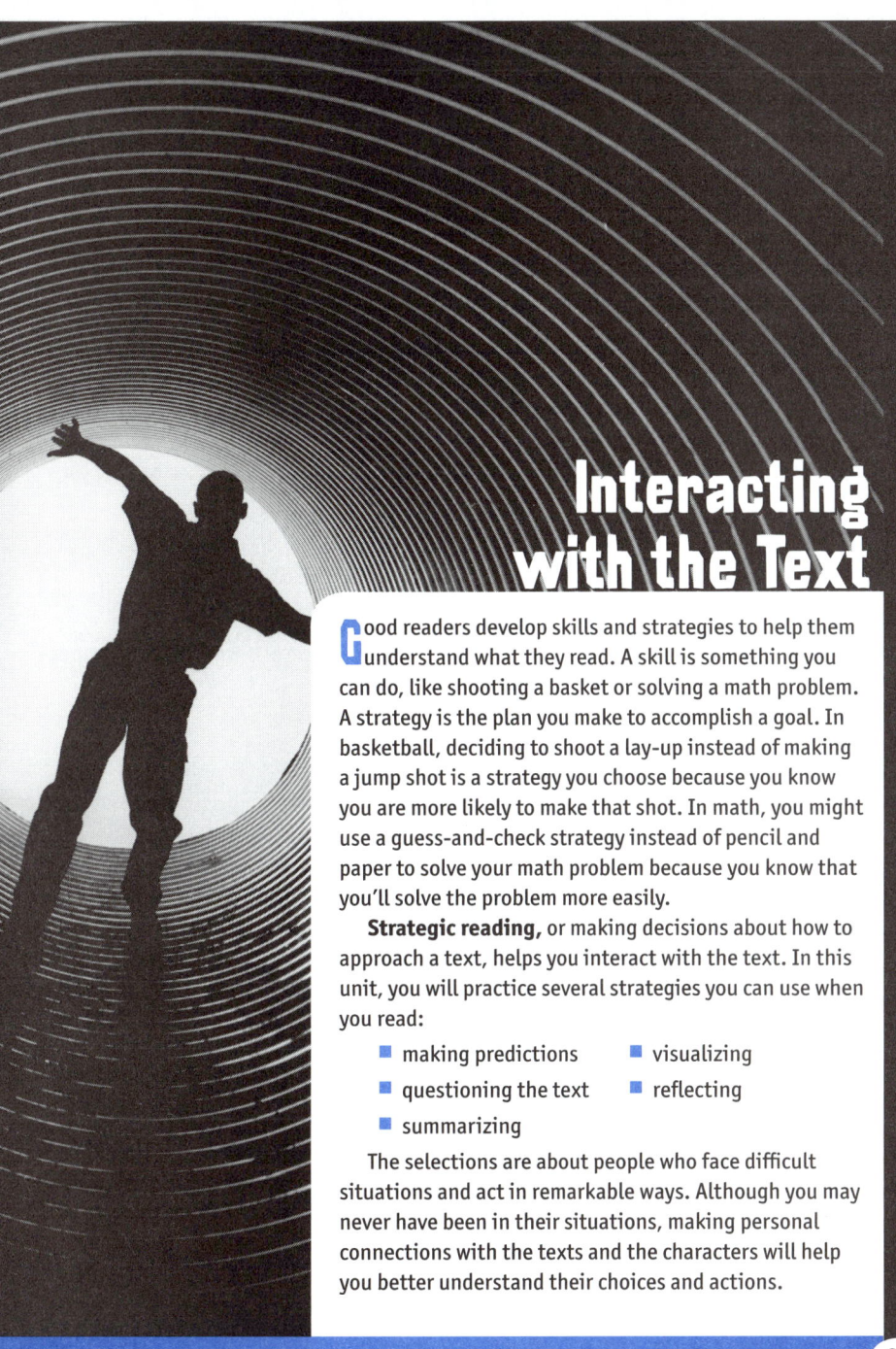

UNIT 2
INTERACTING WITH THE TEXT

Lessons 6–10, pages 26–38

UNIT OVERVIEW
Students learn five critical reading strategies for interacting with texts by and about remarkable people who persevere despite difficult circumstances.

KEY IDEA
Good readers consciously employ certain strategies to understand and evaluate what they read.

CRITICAL READING SKILLS
by lesson

6 Predicting
7 Questioning
8 Summarizing
9 Visualizing
10 Reflecting

WRITING ACTIVITIES
by lesson

6 State and support predictions about a text.
7 Write questions about text and state how they aid understanding.
8 Summarize a speech.
9 Explain a drawing about text.
10 Write reflective paragraphs.

Interacting with the Text

Good readers develop skills and strategies to help them understand what they read. A skill is something you can do, like shooting a basket or solving a math problem. A strategy is the plan you make to accomplish a goal. In basketball, deciding to shoot a lay-up instead of making a jump shot is a strategy you choose because you know you are more likely to make that shot. In math, you might use a guess-and-check strategy instead of pencil and paper to solve your math problem because you know that you'll solve the problem more easily.

Strategic reading, or making decisions about how to approach a text, helps you interact with the text. In this unit, you will practice several strategies you can use when you read:

- making predictions
- questioning the text
- summarizing
- visualizing
- reflecting

The selections are about people who face difficult situations and act in remarkable ways. Although you may never have been in their situations, making personal connections with the texts and the characters will help you better understand their choices and actions.

Literature

- ***The Breadwinner*** by Deborah Ellis (novel excerpts)

Eleven-year-old Parvana, who is living with her family in Afghanistan under the rule of the Taliban, shoulders responsibilities beyond her years.

- **"Ain't I a Woman?"** by Sojourner Truth (speech)

An African American woman makes a profound speech at a women's rights convention in 1851, making the case for equality of men and women.

- **"Vietnam War Memorial"** by Mattie Stepanek (poem)

The young poet reflects on the multiple meanings of a symbol representing a difficult period in American history.

ASSESSMENT To assess student learning in this unit, see pages 230 and 253.

LESSON 6

Students will make predictions based on prior knowledge and textual clues.

BACKGROUND KNOWLEDGE
Point out the location of Afghanistan on a globe or world map. Explain that the Taliban ruled Afghanistan from 1996 to 2001. The group strictly interprets its version of Islamic laws about the roles of men and women, including those laws that prohibit women from participating in such activities as leaving their homes unaccompanied and learning to read and write. For more information, visit http://www.cia.gov/cia/publications/factbook/geos/af.html.

VOCABULARY
breadwinner family member who earns most of the money a family needs to survive

Kabul (KAH bul) capital city of Afghanistan

chador (chah DOR) garment worn by women and girls to cover their hair and shoulders

Taliban (TAL ih bahn) ruling party in Afghanistan from 1996–2001. A member of the party is a **Talib** (TAL eeb).

After going over the definitions, have students correctly use each word in a sentence.

LESSON 6: MAKING PREDICTIONS

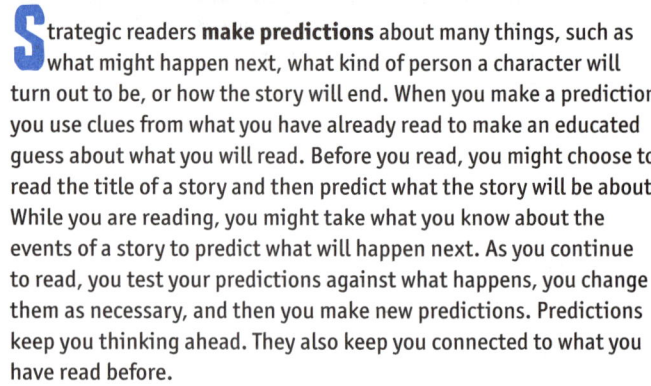

Strategic readers **make predictions** about many things, such as what might happen next, what kind of person a character will turn out to be, or how the story will end. When you make a prediction, you use clues from what you have already read to make an educated guess about what you will read. Before you read, you might choose to read the title of a story and then predict what the story will be about. While you are reading, you might take what you know about the events of a story to predict what will happen next. As you continue to read, you test your predictions against what happens, you change them as necessary, and then you make new predictions. Predictions keep you thinking ahead. They also keep you connected to what you have read before.

As you read the selection below about a girl in Afghanistan, make predictions in the **Response Notes** and test them as you read. When you find something that either supports your prediction or makes you think another way, make a note of that.

If you come across unfamiliar words, circle them and read on to see if the context of the rest of the story helps you make sense of them.

from **The Breadwinner** by Deborah Ellis

"I can read that letter as well as Father can," Parvana whispered into the folds of her chador. "Well, almost."

She didn't dare say those words out loud. The man sitting beside her father would not want to hear her voice. Nor would anyone else in the Kabul market. Parvana was there only to help her father walk to the market and back home again after work. She sat well back on the blanket, her head and most of her face covered by her chador.

Head covering?

She wasn't really supposed to be outside at all. The Taliban had ordered all the girls and women in Afghanistan to stay inside their homes. They even forbade girls to go to school. Parvana had had to leave her sixth grade class, and her sister Nooria was not allowed to go to her high school. Their mother had been kicked out of her job as a writer for a Kabul radio station. For more than a year now, they had all been stuck inside one room, along with five-year-old Maryam and two-year-old Ali.

Parvana did get out for a few hours most days to help her father walk. She was always glad to go outside, even though it meant sitting for hours on a blanket spread over the hard ground of the marketplace. At least it was something to do. She had even got used to holding her tongue and hiding her face.

26 LESSON 6

Before

CRITICAL READING SKILL
Predicting Explain to students that making a prediction is more than just guessing randomly; it means combining what you already know with clues in the text to make an educated guess. Read aloud the first three paragraphs and model making a prediction: *I know that the Taliban doesn't allow women to read or go outdoors unaccompanied. What Parvana whispers tells me that she doesn't like the rules. I think she will get in trouble for reading or being outside.*

RESPONSE NOTES Review with students the final two paragraphs of the Response Notes. Have students underline key words that give them direction for responding (e.g., *make predictions*) as a reminder for when they read.

She was small for her eleven years. As a small girl, she could usually get away with being outside without being questioned.

"I need this girl to help me walk," her father would tell any Talib who asked, pointing to his leg. He had lost the lower part of his leg when the high school he was teaching in was bombed. His insides had been hurt somehow, too. He was often tired.

"I have no son at home, except for an infant," he would explain. Parvana would slump down further on the blanket and try to make herself look smaller. She was afraid to look up at the soldiers. She had seen what they did, especially to women, the way they would whip and beat someone they thought should be punished.

Sitting in the marketplace day after day, she had seen a lot. When the Taliban were around, what she wanted most of all was to be invisible.

Now the customer asked her father to read his letter again. "Read it slowly, so that I can remember it for my family."

Parvana would have liked to get a letter. Mail delivery had recently started again in Afghanistan, after years of being disrupted by war. Many of her friends had fled the country with their families. She thought they were in Pakistan, but she wasn't sure, so she couldn't write to them. Her own family had moved so often because of the bombing that her friends no longer knew where she was. "Afghans cover the earth like stars cover the sky," her father often said.

Her father finished reading the man's letter a second time. The customer thanked him and paid. "I will look for you when it is time to write a reply."

Most people in Afghanistan could not read or write. Parvana was one of the lucky ones. Both of her parents had been to university, and they believed in education for everyone, even girls. ❖

❄ Now that you have read the first few pages of the book, who do you think is "the breadwinner" of the family? Briefly tell why you think so.

_____
_____
_____
_____
_____

ABOUT THE AUTHOR
Born in 1960, Deborah Ellis still lives in the small town in Ontario, Canada, in which she was born. She became interested in oppression around the world at an early age and was a political activist by the time she was 17. Ellis based her novel *The Breadwinner* on the story of a girl in Kabul who cut her hair and donned boys' clothing so that she could support her family by selling items in the marketplace. *Parvana's Journey* is the sequel to *The Breadwinner*.

TEACHING TIP
Graphic Organizer: Prediction Chart Invite students to create three-column charts with these headings: *Predict, Confirm, Revise*. Students can write predictions before reading and then fill in the other columns as they read.

EXTRA SUPPORT
Differentiation Students in need of more support might benefit from a cooperative review of their predictions. Have partners use a Think-Pair-Share format. First, students reflect privately on their predictions. Next, partners work together to identify predictions that were confirmed, those that need revision, and the reasons for revisions (text references or new information). Then, each pair shares its findings with another pair.

During

CONFIRMING PREDICTIONS After students have finished reading page 27, have them review the predictions they have made thus far, reflecting on any predictions that were not confirmed in the text. Ask: *Did you find new information in the text? Did you learn more about a character? Did you remember something related to the events?*

INTERACTING WITH THE TEXT

WRITING SUPPORT

Conflict Before students write their responses to the first prompt, explain that there are several kinds of conflicts in literature. A personal conflict may occur when characters argue or fight because they disagree or have different goals. A conflict with nature may occur when someone is fighting to survive in the elements. A conflict with the world occurs when a character lives in a situation that is harsh because of cultural or political conditions. As students respond to the first prompt, suggest that they think about which kinds of conflicts are likely in *The Breadwinner*.

Quick Assess

* Do students' written responses predict conflicts and other events?
* Do students' written responses explain their thinking?
* Did students label their predictions based on experience and the text?

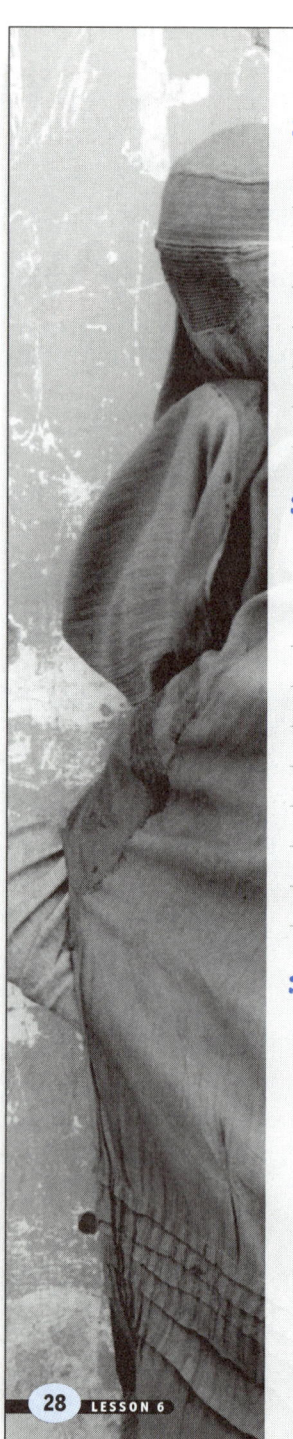

* What conflicts do you predict will occur in this novel? Why do you think so?

  _____
  _____
  _____
  _____
  _____

* Parvana wants to be invisible when the Taliban are around. What do you think would happen if Parvana became separated from her father and a Taliban soldier found her? Explain your reasons for making this prediction.

  _____
  _____
  _____
  _____
  _____

* We make predictions from our life experiences, including information we receive from news, school, and other places. We also make predictions from the words of a text. Go back to the predictions you just made and label your reasons as *E* for those that come from your *experience*. Include what you have learned from news reports or from school. Label predictions that you made from information in the *text* as *T*.

> Making and testing your predictions help you interact with a text to better understand and remember it.

After

APPLYING THE STRATEGY Have small groups of students brainstorm what might happen next in the story, using the Round Robin technique: One student suggests what happens next, the next student adds to the story, and so on.

QUESTIONING THE TEXT — LESSON 7

Another way of reading strategically is to **ask questions** before, during, and after you read. Questions serve different purposes. One purpose is to ask about a fact or definition. For example, in the first lesson, you might have asked "What is a *chador*?" and found out that it is a cloth that women wear to cover their head and shoulders. Asking questions helps to build your understanding as you read. Questions that build understanding usually cannot be answered *yes* or *no*. You ask and answer them based on the information you encounter before, during, and after reading the text.

As you read the next part of the story, ask questions about the characters, the action, the author's reasons for writing as she did, and anything else that you wonder about. Write your questions in the **Response Notes**. The action in this part of the novel takes place in the evening after Parvana and her father return home from the marketplace. The family has had dinner and everyone is laughing at a funny face that Parvana made when she was told to do the dishes.

from The Breadwinner by Deborah Ellis

The whole family was laughing when four Taliban soldiers burst through the door.

Ali was the first to react. The slam of the door against the wall shocked him, and he screamed.

Mother leapt to her feet, and in an instant Ali and Maryam were in a corner of the room, shrieking behind her legs.

Nooria covered herself completely with her chador and scrunched herself into a small ball. Young women were sometimes stolen by soldiers. They were snatched from their homes, and their families never saw them again.

Parvana couldn't move. She sat as if frozen at the edge of the supper cloth. The soldiers were giants, their piled-high turbans making them look even taller.

Two of the soldiers grabbed her father. The other two began searching the apartment, kicking the remains of dinner all over the mat.

"Leave him alone!" Mother screamed. "He has done nothing wrong!"

"Why did you go to England for your education?" the soldiers yelled at Father. "Afghanistan doesn't need your foreign ideas!" They yanked him toward the door.

"Afghanistan needs more illiterate thugs like you," Father said. One of the soldiers hit him in the face. Blood from his nose dripped onto his white shalwar kameez.

Response Notes

How did the author get the information to write about this experience?

LESSON 7

Students will read the next part of a novel and form questions to read strategically.

BACKGROUND KNOWLEDGE
Define a totalitarian regime as a system of government under which the people have little authority and the ruling party wields absolute control. For example, the Nazis (Hitler's party) ruled in Germany in the 1940s. It was common practice for Nazi soldiers to raid private homes in search of Jews. Explain that the Taliban was a totalitarian regime in Afghanistan at the time depicted in *The Breadwinner*.

VOCABULARY
shalwar kameez (SHAHL wahr kah MEEZ) a long, loose shirt and trousers worn by either a man or a woman

Malali (mah LAH lee) legendary young girl who gave Afghani troops the courage to defeat an enemy in 1880

toshak (TOH shawk) a mattress used as a bed, chair, or couch; similar to a futon

Go over the meaning of each term. Have partners write each term in a sentence and then rewrite the sentences, replacing the Afghani terms with similar English ones.

Before

CRITICAL READING SKILL
Questioning the Text Explain that certain types of questions help readers better understand what they read. Effective questions require answers that do the following:

* consist of more than one word (e.g., *yes*, *no*, *true*, or *false*)
* use thinking beyond the text (e.g., questions that begin with *Why* or *How*)
* combine information from various parts of the text

RESPONSE NOTES Model effective questioning: *What do the soldiers think about education? How does the author feel about education? Why is Parvana so concerned about her father's books? What do Parvana's actions tell about her character?* Then encourage students to practice asking these kinds of questions in their Response Notes.

TEACHING TIP

Graphic Organizer: Sequence Chart To support students' understanding of the story, have partners make a sequence chart of the events.

Mother sprang at the soldiers, pounding them with her fists. She grabbed Father's arm and tried to pull him out of their grasp.

One of the soldiers raised his rifle and whacked her on the head. She collapsed on the floor. The soldier hit her a few more times. Maryam and Ali screamed with every blow to their mother's back.

Seeing her mother on the ground finally propelled Parvana into action. When the soldiers dragged her father outside, she flung her arms around his waist. As the soldiers pried her loose, she heard her father say, "Take care of the others, my Malali." Then he was gone.

Parvana watched helplessly as two soldiers dragged him down the steps, his beautiful shalwar kameez ripping on the rough cement. Then they turned a corner, and she could see them no more.

Inside the room, the other two soldiers were ripping open the toshaks with knives and tossing things out of the cupboard.

Father's books! At the bottom of the cupboard was a secret compartment her father had built to hide the few books that had not been destroyed in one of the bombings. Some were English books about history and literature. They were kept hidden because the Taliban burned books they didn't like.

They couldn't be allowed to find Father's books! The soldiers had started at the top of the cupboard and were working their way down. Clothes, blankets, pots—everything landed on the floor.

Closer and closer they came to the bottom shelf, the one with the false wall. Parvana watched in horror as the soldiers bent down to yank the things out of the bottom shelf.

"Get out of my house!" she yelled. She threw herself at the soldiers with such force that they both fell to the ground. She swung at them with her fists until she was knocked aside. She heard rather than felt the thwack of their sticks on her back. She kept her head hidden in her arms until the beating stopped and the soldiers went away.

During

TYPES OF QUESTIONS Explain that some questions ask about information that is stated directly in the text or "on the surface." For example, say: *You can answer "Why did Ali scream?" with "on the surface" information: The slam of the door shocked him.* Other questions ask about information that comes from "under the surface," or inferred from the reader's experience or ideas. For example, say: *You can answer "What is a supper cloth?" with "under the surface" information: Sometimes people cover a dinner table with a tablecloth. The supper cloth must be like a tablecloth.*

RESPONSE NOTES Have students review their questions and identify the types of questions. Then have them mark "on the surface" questions with "O" and "under the surface" questions with "U."

Mother got off the floor and had her hands full with Ali. Nooria was still curled up in a terrified ball. It was Maryam who came over to help Parvana.

At the first touch of her sister's hands, Parvana flinched, thinking it was the soldiers. Maryam kept stroking her hair until Parvana realized who it was. She sat up, aching all over. She and Maryam clung to each other, trembling.

She had no idea how long the family stayed like that. They remained in their spots long after Ali stopped screaming and collapsed into sleep.

❉ Share your questions with a partner and try to answer each other's questions. List two of the questions you would like to discuss in class.

❉ Briefly explain how asking questions before, during, and after you read helped you understand the selection.

> Strategic readers ask questions before, during, and after reading to build their understanding of what they read.

QUESTIONING THE TEXT 31

TEACHING TIP

Collaboration Group students in pairs to share their Response Notes. Encourage partners to "borrow" questions from each other to add to their Response Notes. Suggest that borrowed questions be written in a different color from the original questions.

Quick Assess

❉ Do students' Response Notes include effective questions?

❉ Did students identify both "on the surface" and "under the surface" questions?

❉ Did students explain how asking "how" and "why" questions helped them understand the selection?

After

READING/WRITING CONNECTION
Have students write what might happen in the next scenes of Parvana's story. Have partners exchange papers and write both "on the surface" and "under the surface" questions about the scenes.

SOCIAL STUDIES CONNECTIONS
Have students think of questions they still have about Afghanistan and conduct research into some aspect of Afghanistan's history or culture. Students can then prepare reports to present to the class. Possible topic areas include the following:

❉ art   ❉ geography
❉ music   ❉ religion

INTERACTING WITH THE TEXT 31

LESSON 8

Students will show that they understand main ideas and supporting details by summarizing text.

BACKGROUND KNOWLEDGE
Sojourner Truth (1797 (?) -1883) was born "Isabella" in Ulster County, New York, to parents who were slaves. When she was emancipated in 1828, she began preaching publicly against slavery and in support of women's rights. She delivered her famous speech at the Women's Rights Convention of 1851 in response to words of a clergyman who had warned "if women continued their efforts to obtain 'rights,' they would lose the consideration and deference with which men treated them." Although she was illiterate, Truth was an effective speaker who visited the White House at the invitation of President Abraham Lincoln.

VOCABULARY
out of kilter out of order
in a fix in trouble
bear the lash be beaten
obliged to you thank you

Point out that these terms are informal language, probably reflective of speech more than one hundred years ago. Invite a volunteer to say a sentence using a more contemporary English term.

LESSON 8 SUMMARIZING

Readers show that they understand the main ideas and supporting details when they **summarize** what they read. Finding the main ideas and restating them in your own words is a strategy for you to use when you want to remember key points or ideas.

Sojourner Truth, an African American woman, spoke at a women's rights convention in 1851. Read her speech once to get an idea about the general subject.

❋ When you look at the title and know where and when she gave this speech, what do you predict will be her main point?

"Ain't I a Woman?" by Sojourner Truth

Well, children, where there is so much racket there must be something out of kilter. I think that 'twixt the Negroes of the South and the women at the North, all talking about rights, the white men will be in a fix pretty soon. But what's all this here talking about? That man over there says that women need to be helped into carriages, and lifted over ditches, and to have the best place everywhere. Nobody ever helps me into carriages, or over mud-puddles, or gives me any best place! And ain't I a woman? Look at me! Look at my arm! I have plowed and planted, and gathered into barns, and no man could head me! And ain't I a woman? I could work as much and eat as much as a man—when I could get it—and bear the lash as well! And ain't I a woman? I have borne thirteen children, and seen them most all sold off to slavery, and when I cried out with my mother's grief, none but Jesus heard! And ain't I a woman?

Then they talk about this thing in the head; what's this they call it? ["Intellect," someone in the audience whispers.] That's it, honey. What's that got to do with women's rights or Negro's rights? If my cup won't hold but a pint, and yours holds a quart, wouldn't you be mean not to let me have my little halfmeasure full? Then that little man in black there, he says women can't have as much rights as men, 'cause Christ wasn't a woman! Where did your Christ come from? Where did your Christ come from? From god and a woman! Man had nothing to do with him.

If the first woman God ever made was strong enough to turn the world upside down all alone, these women together ought to be able to turn it back, and get it right side up again! And now they is asking to do it, the men better let them. Obliged to you for hearing me, and now old Sojourner ain't got nothing more to say. ❖

Before

CRITICAL READING SKILL
Summarizing Explain that summarizing involves determining what is most important and stating it fairly briefly. To summarize, students should do the following:

❋ Identify the topic of the text.

❋ Identify the topic's main ideas and supporting details.

❋ Restate the important information in brief form.

Before students begin reading, help them identify the topic of the speech (women's rights). Then have them note each main idea and the supporting details as they read. (Main idea—women are strong. Supporting details—Sojourner has plowed fields and harvested crops.)

✷ After your first reading, what do you think is the main idea of Sojourner Truth's speech?

✷ Now reread the speech so that you can summarize it. As you read, write the main ideas in the **Response Notes** and circle the details in the speech that support what you have written.

✷ Using your annotations, write a summary of Truth's speech. As a challenge, limit your summary to three sentences that contain all of the important points.

Writing a summary of a selection helps you identify and remember the key points.

EXTRA SUPPORT
Differentiation Students who need extra support might benefit from taking notes in a summary chart as they read:

Topic:		
Main Idea #1:	Main Idea #2:	Main Idea #3:
Important Details:	Important Details:	Important Details:

Quick Assess

✷ Are students able to determine the most important information when they read?

✷ Did students write a three-sentence summary of the speech that includes the three main ideas and supporting details?

During

SHARE RESPONSE NOTES
Have students share their Response Notes with a partner and reach consensus regarding which details are important and which are minor. Then they can work together to compose summary statements for the speech.

After

READING/WRITING CONNECTION
For more practice summarizing, have each student select an article from a newspaper or magazine, another speech, or a movie or television documentary about equality and write a summary of it. Have students exchange papers and critique each other's summaries.

INTERACTING WITH THE TEXT

LESSON 9

Students will practice visualizing as a strategy to create mental pictures based on a text, thus making deeper connections.

BACKGROUND KNOWLEDGE
The Vietnam Veterans Memorial in Washington, D.C., honors men and women who served in one of America's most divisive wars. The Memorial grew out of a need to heal the nation's wounds as Americans struggled to reconcile different moral and political points of view. The memorial wall was conceived and designed by Maya Lin as a place where anyone, regardless of opinion, can come to remember and honor those who served in Vietnam. For more information, see the Memorial's website: http://www.nps.gov/vive/home.htm.

VOCABULARY

muscular dystrophy a fatal disease that gradually weakens all muscles in the body

debilitating weakening

fortify strengthen

fortitude strength

Point out the Latin root of *fortify* and *fortitude* (*fort,* which means "strong"). Create a word web or cluster on the board, and ask students to think of other words that stem from the same root (e.g., *fort, fortress, forte*)

LESSON 9 VISUALIZING

If you are like most readers, you see pictures in your mind as you read. **Visualizing** is a way to understand what you are reading by using the author's words and your prior knowledge to make pictures in your mind.

If you read a story or poem about a person who is a lot like a friend, your mental picture will probably look quite a bit like your friend. If you are reading about a subject or person totally unfamiliar to you, your mental pictures will be formed by the words the author uses. Some students have said they see movies in their minds as they read. Being able to "see" what you are reading will help you become a better reader.

In this lesson, you are going to draw some of the pictures you form in your mind as you read about Mattie Stepanek. First, here is some information about Mattie. Use the **Response Notes** to record drawings or quick sketches that show what you are seeing in your mind as you read.

A REMARKABLE BOY
Mattie Stepanek was born with a rare form of muscular dystrophy. His mom, Jeni, also has the disease, which she didn't discover until after she had four children. Mattie's three siblings all died from the disease—but remarkably, Mattie recovered many times from near-fatal episodes. It was only in 2004 that his body was no longer able to survive his debilitating disease. Yet, he had achieved great feats: earning a junior black belt in martial arts, reaching the 11th grade level in home-schooling, and having his poetry published.

THREE WISHES
Mattie always had three wishes: to have his poems published, to meet his hero Jimmy Carter, and to share his message of peace on *The Oprah Winfrey Show.* All three of his wishes were granted. When Oprah asked Mattie why he had chosen those three wishes, he explained, "Because they were things that would last forever. Going to Disney World ends in a week. But being able to talk with Jimmy Carter, being able to have my books published, being able to talk to you here today, lasts forever."

Before

CRITICAL READING SKILL
Visualizing Define visualizing as making pictures in your mind as you read. Explain that this strategy helps readers connect with what they read and enjoy it more. Visualizing can also help readers remember details. To model the process, read aloud "A Remarkable Boy" and then share your visualization. For example: *I see a small boy wearing a martial arts uniform with a black belt. He might look weak on the outside, but his eyes and jaw look determined and strong.*

RESPONSE NOTES
Encourage students to draw as well as write in their Response Notes on this page. Then have them share their notes with a partner and discuss differences in their visualizations. Ask: *What earlier experiences or stories does Mattie remind you of? Do your partner's notes help you remember a detail you missed?*

✳ Compare your visual notes with a partner. What pictures did you see? What is your impression of Mattie?

_____
_____
_____
_____

Mattie wrote about an important monument to fallen soldiers. As you read his poem, jot notes about any connections you make with the poem.

Response Notes

Vietnam War Memorial
by Mattie Stepanek

A wall gives structure.
It can divide and block.
It can support and fortify.
It can be a place to display
Photos, writings, awards,
And memories.
But this is The Wall.
The Wall that gives structure
To the insane losses of a war.
The Wall that represents
A nation divided and blocked.
The Wall that supports too
Many broken hearts and bodies.
The Wall that fortifies the reality
Of dead lives among the living.
The Wall that reflects memories
Of what was, of what is,
Of what might have been,
In photos, in letters and poems,
In medals of honor and dedication,
And in teddy bears, and flowers,
And tears and tears and tears.

This is The Wall,
Born out of pain and anguish
And guilt,
That gives names to the children
Of grieving mothers and fathers
And to the spouses of widows
And to parents of wondering children.
This is The Wall
That echoes sadness and fear,
Yet whispers relief and hope.
This is The Wall.
May we be forever blessed by its
Structure and fortitude and support,
And may we be forever reminded
Of the eternal divisions of war. ✣

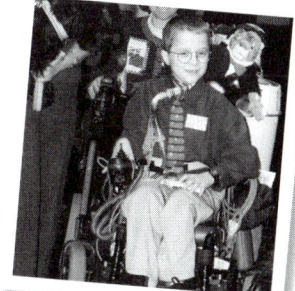

Mattie Stepanek
1990–2004

VISUALIZING 35

ABOUT THE AUTHOR
Mattie Stepanek was born in July of 1990 and lived most of his life in a wheelchair with his service dog, Micah, by his side. Even though he needed a breathing tube, ventilator, and foot braces to survive, Mattie never stopped celebrating life. Not only did he produce volumes of poetry and other writings, but, before succumbing to muscular dystrophy at the age of 14, he also appeared on television with such celebrities as Oprah Winfrey and Larry King and made numerous public speeches about peace efforts and global tolerance. In the span of his short life, he consistently exemplified his message of peace and hope.

EXTRA SUPPORT
Differentiation Students in need of extra support might benefit from practice in visualizing. Read aloud a simple poem or other selection with vivid word choices. Have students close their eyes to listen the first time. Read the selection a second time, pausing frequently for students to describe what they "see" in their minds. Then read the selection a third time, pausing frequently for students to sketch their visualizations.

During

MARKING THE TEXT In addition to writing and drawing visualizations in their Response Notes, have students use colored markers or pencils to mark vivid words or phrases in the poem that inspire pictures in their minds. Suggest that they color-code their marks to remind them of images that specific words inspire.

INTERACTING WITH THE TEXT 35

EXTRA SUPPORT

Differentiation Students who are not visual learners or who feel anxious about having to draw can use alternative means of expression. Provide magazines with colorful photographs or other visual images and explain how to make a collage to express visualization of a passage.

WRITER'S CRAFT

Literary Elements: Theme Point out the repeated use of words about strength in Mattie's poem. Encourage students to speculate about this theme. For example, ask questions, such as this: *Why, do you think, does Mattie emphasize strength?* (*He may focus on it because he is physically weakened by muscular dystrophy, he thinks the war in Vietnam was a time of strength in the U.S., or he wants his readers to gain strength from the poem.*)

Quick Assess

* Do students' drawings or collages represent images related to the poem?
* Did students adequately explain how their representations relate to the poem?

* In the space below, draw the Vietnam War Memorial as you see it from reading Mattie's poem.

* Below your drawing, write a sentence explaining your drawing.

> Making pictures in your mind as you read enriches your understanding by helping you focus on the ideas and details.

36 LESSON 9

After

APPLYING THE STRATEGY Have partners extend their visualizing skills to other poetry by Mattie Stepanek or other poets.

* Partner A reads the poem aloud while Partner B writes vivid words or phrases from the poem.
* Then B reads while A draws visualizations.
* Finally A reads while B draws.

RESEARCH/WRITING CONNECTIONS Invite students to conduct research about either muscular dystrophy or the Vietnam War Memorial. Then they can compose either a poem in Mattie's style or an essay reporting their findings.

36 UNIT 2

REFLECTING — LESSON 10

When you look into a mirror and see your reflection, you think about how you look. You reflect on your reflection!

In the same way, when you think about what you have read, you are **reflecting**. One way to become a stronger reader is to take time to reflect, not just to read the words and then rush to the next activity. Reflecting means slowing down a bit, taking time to think a little longer about what you are reading, and perhaps to write down ideas as they come to you.

Reread the poem in Lesson 9, "Vietnam War Memorial." In the **Response Notes**, add notes about *reflecting* whenever you pause to think about an idea in the poem. You may also indicate places where you use the reading strategies you have practiced in prior lessons: *predicting, questioning, summarizing, visualizing.*

✽ Write a short paragraph telling which reading strategies—*reflecting, predicting, questioning, summarizing,* and *visualizing*—you used to help you understand this poem.

_____
_____
_____
_____
_____
_____
_____

REFLECTING ON REMARKABLE PEOPLE

In this unit, you read excerpts from a novel, a speech, and a poem. You gained insights into a fictional character, an important woman in American history, and a young boy who inspired millions of everyday people as well as notable people such as former President Carter and Oprah Winfrey. As you reflect on these three people, think about how each might be called "remarkable."

Use the questions on page 38 to prompt some ideas. Try to come up with some additional questions of your own.

LESSON 10

Students will reflect on the selections in this unit to make stronger connections with writing by and about remarkable people and the significance of their contributions.

BACKGROUND KNOWLEDGE

Have students look over Lessons 6–9 to refresh their understanding of predicting, questioning, summarizing, and visualizing. Explain that when we read, some strategies may be used more than others, depending on the type of literature we are reading. Encourage students to discuss with partners which strategies they used to understand "The Vietnam War Memorial."

Before

CRITICAL READING SKILL

Reflecting Define reflecting as thinking about ideas that belong to you or someone else. Explain that students will experience two kinds of reflecting in this lesson. First they will reflect on their own thinking in the form of strategies that they use to understand a poem. Then they will reflect on their understanding of an author's thoughts.

Use an analogy to explain: direct students' attention to the picture of the moon and its reflection on the water. Point out that the moon itself looks round, while the reflection looks like streaks or stripes because ripples in the water change the image. Then say: *In a similar way, when readers reflect on what an author writes, they add their thoughts, feelings, memories, beliefs, and ideas to those of the author.*

MODELING THE STRATEGY

Read "Vietnam War Memorial" aloud and model how to reflect on it. For example: *The words* divide *and* block *made me feel sad, but* support *and* fortify *made me feel hopeful.*

INTERACTING WITH THE TEXT

TEACHING TIP

Collaboration Students might benefit from a Jigsaw cooperative learning activity.

※ Form five "question groups."

※ Assign one question from the student page to each group.

※ Each group reaches consensus about answering its assigned question.

※ Rearrange groups so that each new group contains at least one student from each "question group."

※ Have new groups discuss answers to all five questions.

Quick Assess

※ Do students see how the strategies help them when they read?

※ Do students' paragraphs on page 38 explain why the people are remarkable and use text to support ideas?

- What makes a person remarkable?
- What does being famous have to do with being remarkable?
- Does a remarkable person have to do something significant?
- Can a person be remarkable even if no one else knows what he or she has done?
- In what ways can remarkable people have an impact on the world?

※ Write a paragraph reflecting on why you think any one or two of the people listed below might be called *remarkable*. Use quotations from the passages to support your ideas.
- Parvana
- Sojourner Truth
- Mattie Stepanek

Reflecting on your reading gives you time to consider carefully not only the author's words but also the meanings they convey.

38 LESSON 10

During

GRAPHIC ORGANIZER

Create a 2-column chart about the remarkable people in this unit. Write the names in column 1. Allow time for students to reflect silently on the character traits that make each person remarkable. Then invite students to suggest traits for you to record in column 2. Students can then use the chart to write their paragraphs.

Remarkable People	Character Traits
Parvana	determined
Sojourner Truth	confident
Mattie Stepanek	accomplished

After

LISTENING/SPEAKING CONNECTION
For further practice reflecting, have students use the five questions to reflect on a remarkable person they know personally, such as a parent, teacher, minister, counselor, sibling, or friend. Or if they prefer, have them choose someone about whom they have heard or read. Then have them create a character traits chart or present their reflections to the class in an oral report.

38 UNIT 2

UNIT 3
MAKING CONNECTIONS

Lessons 11-15, pages 40-52

UNIT OVERVIEW
In this unit, students will study the basic elements of a story—setting, point of view, characterization, plot, and theme—in two selections.

KEY IDEA
Proficient readers understand the elements of a story and connect them to other texts, others' experiences, and their own lives.

CRITICAL READING SKILLS
by lesson

11 Identifying setting
12 Understanding point of view
13 Analyzing characterization
14 Understanding plot
15 Identifying theme

WRITING ACTIVITIES
by lesson

11 Chart connections between the setting in a story and another setting.
12 Connect with the narrator by writing scene details.
13 Diagram and write about the similarities and differences between two characters.
14 Chart connections between the events in the story and those in another text or experience.

Making Connections

Take a minute to recall one of your favorite stories. It could be a movie, a story you read, a story you heard, or a story of your own.

What comes to mind as you think about this story? Do you picture where it takes place? Do you hear a particular voice telling it? Do you think about the characters? What are they like? What happens to them? Do you think about why the story is meaningful or interesting to you? The answers to all of these questions become the story itself. They are the **story elements**—the essential parts—that make a story.

In this unit, you'll read two stories. The first is an excerpt from a novel. The second is a short story. Both stories explore a common theme: What can we learn from our elders? You will examine how authors combine the following elements to create memorable stories:

- setting
- plot
- point of view
- theme
- characters

You'll also practice making personal **connections** with these elements so that the stories are more interesting and more meaningful to you. You will ask: How do my life experiences relate to this story?

Literature

- **Year of Impossible Goodbyes** by Sook Nyul Choi (excerpt from a novel)

Set in 1945, this novel depicts the struggles of a family living in northern Korea, first under Japanese occupation, then Russian. The ten-year-old narrator, Sookan, tells the story of her family's determination to keep their Korean culture alive despite laws to the contrary.

- **"Thank You, Ma'm"** by Langston Hughes (short story)

Set in Harlem in the 1950s, this short story tells of Roger, an adolescent boy, who learns a lesson about hard times, making connections, and human compassion.

ASSESSMENT To assess student learning in this unit, see pages 231 and 256.

LESSON 11

Students will visualize the setting in order to make connections to other stories and their own experiences.

BACKGROUND KNOWLEDGE
This excerpt from *Year of Impossible Goodbyes* is set in northern Korea in 1945, a year when the region saw a handover from occupation by the Japanese to occupation by the Soviets. Help students understand that living under occupation by another country can be extremely hard. Explain that the narrator of the story is a young girl who looks to her grandfather for comfort and direction.

VOCABULARY

furrow a long, narrow, shallow trench in the ground

menacing threatening

respite a short time of rest or relief

oppressiveness heaviness, burden

benevolent kind, giving

Invite students to brainstorm how the words might be used in the story. Use a think-aloud to model: *I know the girl's life is hard, but the word benevolent means "kind," so maybe she also experiences kindness.*

LESSON 11 SETTING

Think about the most interesting day of your life. If you told the story of that day to a friend, chances are you would include details about the **setting**—when and where the events and actions took place. Knowing the setting would help your friend understand the **context** of your story and picture it more vividly. That's how a setting works in any story. Descriptive details about when and where a story takes place help readers understand and picture the events.

The selection you will read is an excerpt from *Year of Impossible Goodbyes,* a novel by Sook Nyul Choi. It is set in northern Korea at the end of World War II. Concentrate on the images the author creates that help you **visualize** the setting. Circle descriptive words that help create your mental picture of the setting. Remember that setting has to do with both *when* and *where* the story takes place. In your **Response Notes,** write statements that tell both when and where the story takes place.

from *Year of Impossible Goodbyes* by Sook Nyul Choi

Spring 1945

Small clusters of pale green needles emerged from the old weathered pine tree in our front yard. The high mounds of snow in the corner of our yard had begun to melt, the water flowing gently into the furrow of dark earth Grandfather had dug around the base of the tree like a moat. Grandfather's tree stood alone in the far corner of the yard, its dark green-needled branches emanating harmoniously from the trunk, reaching out like a large umbrella. It was a magic tree, holding in the shade of its branches the peace and harmony Grandfather so often talked about.

Despite the warmth of the sun, the air in Kirimni, Pyongyang, was dark and heavy, filled with the sound of gunfire and with the menacing glint of drawn swords. For the people in Kirimni, this day was no different from the bitter gray days of winter. The warmth of the spring sun and the thawing of the icy snow brought no respite from the oppressiveness that engulfed us.

Grandfather, hoping the Korean people might experience the exhilaration and beauty of spring again, had made sure my mother included the word *chun*, or spring, in the names of each of my brothers. My oldest brother's name was Hanchun, meaning "Korean spring"; my second brother, Jaechun, was called "spring again"; my third brother, Hyunchun, the "wise spring"; and my youngest brother, Inchun, the "benevolent spring." Inchun was now almost seven, and a benevolent spring still had not come to our village.

Response Notes: Evidence of war

Before

CRITICAL READING SKILL
Identifying Setting Proficient readers develop an understanding of a story's setting by paying attention to descriptive details in the text, as well as making connections between the setting and other images or settings with which they are familiar.

The lesson begins by asking students to think about the most interesting day of their lives. Invite students to do a quick-write about the day. Then ask them to describe the setting and share their descriptions aloud with the class or with a small group. Ask them to consider the importance of the setting: *If the event were set someplace else, how might the day have been different?*

RESPONSE NOTES
Remind students to note places in the text that indicate *where* (Pyongyang, Korea) and *when* (spring 1945) the story takes place.

✱ Write a few sentences that describe the mental picture in your mind evoked by the author's descriptions.

_____
_____
_____

✱ Compare your notes to a partner's. Discuss how your mental pictures are similar or different.

✱ When the setting of a story reminds you of another setting you are familiar with—an illustration or painting, a place you've been to, the setting of a movie you've seen, or the setting in another book—you can often picture it more vividly. Try to discover your own connections to the setting in the excerpt above. Fill in the Connections Chart below. Working with a partner may help you generate more ideas.

CONNECTIONS CHART

The setting from a movie or other book, place I've been to, or image I've seen . . .	. . . helps me to picture or understand this part of the selection better

Making connections to the setting of a story can help you visualize the time and place, which help you better understand the story.

ABOUT THE AUTHOR
Sook Nyul Choi was born in 1937 in Pyongyang, Korea, now the capital of North Korea. She moved to the United States to attend college, and she now lives in Cambridge, Massachusetts, just outside Boston. Her books are very popular with young people and adults, and Choi is well known for her ability to create characters with whom the reader can connect. She has said that she writes because she wants to share the history and culture of Korea with others. Her books have won numerous awards, including the ALA Best Book for Young Adults and the Judy Lopez Book Award of the National Women's Book Association for *Year of Impossible Goodbyes*. See http://www.scils.rutgers.edu/~kvander/choi.html.

TEACHING TIP
Using a Graphic Organizer: Connections Chart An important part of active reading is making connections with other things we've read. By using the chart, students are encouraged to name those connections and think about how they enhance their understanding of the selection.

Quick Assess
✱ Did students fill in the chart to show their connections to the setting?

During

THE CONTEXT OF SETTING Remind students that the *when* and *where* of setting have to do with the immediate context (such as the particular time of day and particular room), as well as the larger context (such as the historical time period and geographic location).

After students have read the selection in this lesson, have them reflect on the author's description of where the story takes place. Choi includes many details to help the reader picture the yard surrounding the house where the narrator and her family live, but the author also uses the setting to convey a certain mood, a sense of foreboding, with phrases such as, *Pyongyang was dark and heavy, filled with the sound of gunfire.*

After

SOCIAL STUDIES CONNECTION
Have students do some research on the setting, individually or in small groups, around the time that the novel takes place. Encourage them to use multiple sources, such as history books and the Internet, and have them share their findings by creating a report, collage, pamphlet, or oral presentation.

LESSON 12

Students will examine a narrator's vantage point in order to understand how an author uses point of view to tell the story.

BACKGROUND KNOWLEDGE
Some students may not be familiar with the practice of meditation. Explain to students that meditation is when a person is in a state of deep contemplation, deliberately tuning out sensory distractions to reflect on innermost thoughts. Help students understand that Buddha, an important spiritual leader, taught people that meditation can lead to enlightenment, a deeper understanding of yourself and of life. Buddhists pray to Buddha through meditation. The significance to the story is that it's likely the grandfather is deep in meditation. This allows the girl to observe her grandfather without disturbing him.

VOCABULARY
meditation deep reflection
emerged came out
intensity very strong feeling
permeated filled

Use the Word Splash blackline master found on page 272 to help students preview the vocabulary and predict how the words will be used in the story.

LESSON 12 — POINT OF VIEW

Imagine this: you're at a surprise birthday party for your cousin, who hasn't arrived yet. You and your other cousins have spent all day working to make it a really big surprise. No one has let your cousin know that you remember it's his birthday. When he opens the door, the look on his face makes it clear that he's truly surprised.

If you narrated—or told—the story of that day, it would definitely be different than if your cousin narrated it. **Point of view** has to do with the vantage point from which a story is told. It reveals who tells the story and what that narrator can "see"—in other words, how the narrator or the characters "see" the story. There are several possible points of view:

- **First-person point of view** When the narrator is one of the characters and calls himself or herself "I." This point of view often helps readers identify with the narrator.
- **Second-person point of view** When the story is written as if the reader is one of the characters and is the "you" referred to in the story.
- **Third-person point of view** When the narrator is a storyteller who isn't part of the story.
  * A *limited* third-person narrator reveals the thoughts and feelings of only one character. It's as if the storyteller is perched on one character's shoulders and can see inside that character's head.
  * An *omniscient* (all-knowing) third-person narrator reveals the thoughts and feelings of several characters. It's as if the storyteller can fly around, seeing what goes on everywhere, and looking into several characters' minds.

Read another excerpt from *Year of Impossible Goodbyes*. In your **Response Notes**, jot down everything you learn about the narrator.

from Year of Impossible Goodbyes
by Sook Nyul Choi

I saw Grandfather peer out at the yard from his room, and look at the delicate branches of the pine tree playing against the hazy, pale blue sky. He cleared his throat and called out to Mother. "Hyunsuk, today I will do my morning meditation under the tree."

Before

CRITICAL READING SKILL
Identifying Point of View Critical readers are aware of the vantage point from which the story is told and how it affects the reader's perception of the story. Have students read the first two paragraphs of the introduction. Ask them to describe the surprise party from the cousin's point of view and then from their own. Then have students discuss what they learned as they looked at the same party from two different points of view.

RESPONSE NOTES
As students read the selection, ask them to note places in the story that indicate how the granddaughter's physical proximity and emotional state affect the way she views her grandfather. For example, she is excited to see Grandfather meditate in his usual spot, which means that she cares for him.

"It is not all of a sudden. Not a single day has gone by that I haven't thought of it. It has been thirty-six years since I have meditated in the warmth of a spring sun. Today, the Japanese soldiers will not keep me inside. I am too old and too tired to be afraid anymore."

Although Mother let out a heavy sigh, she did not protest. Reluctantly, she brought out a clean straw mat and unrolled it beneath the pine tree, placing the thick cushion in the center of the shade. Grandfather emerged from his room and became part of the peaceful scene. The gentle rays of the April sun flitting through the pine branches played upon his face like dancing fairies.

Excited to see Grandfather meditate beneath his tree, I slid my rice-paper door open a crack and watched. ❖

❋ What do you want to know that you can't learn from the narrator's vantage point? What other points of view are possible besides the narrator's? Write what you would like to know more about.

❋ Get together with a partner and discuss what each of you would like to know more about.

❋ On page 44 is another excerpt from the novel. In your **Response Notes** jot anything you learn about the narrator and the grandfather.

POINT OF VIEW 43

TEACHING TIP

Collaboration Point out to students that one way of understanding different points of view is to make connections with what other readers are getting out of reading the same text. Remind students that as they talk to their partner or share in small groups about what they are reading, they should listen openly and actively to what another person is saying. For example, on page 43, when students share what they would like to know more about from what they've read, encourage them to compare their notes and to add ideas if something another reader says inspires a new question in their own mind.

During

CONNECTING TO THE NARRATOR'S VIEWPOINT In this lesson, students focus on understanding the point of view of the narrator (the granddaughter). They will then explore a personal connection they have made with the narrator's point of view.

After students finish reading the selection, help them get started on their own stories (see page 44). If students struggle to get started, go over the selection with them, and model connecting with their own experience, using a think-aloud: *Notice how the author begins in the middle of an event, with the narrator becoming intrigued and deciding to observe her grandfather as he meditates. Then she finds a place where she can watch without being noticed. I'll start my story in the same way, telling whom I observed and my vantage point.*

MAKING CONNECTIONS 43

EXTRA SUPPORT

Differentiation Help students understand that when we talk about *point of view,* we mean more than just who is telling the story. As in the exercise about the cousin's birthday party, different people will focus on different things when remembering the same event. In the selection, the narrator focuses on what she sees in front of her, the way Grandfather looks as he meditates. But she also expresses how she feels about what she observes, such as how worn and frail her grandfather looks and how worried she is when he doesn't move. Help students see that the narrator's point of view limits how we view the scene. If Grandfather were narrating the same scene, he might tell about how it feels to have his granddaughter watching him, but he would probably also tell about how it feels to meditate in the morning sun after abstaining from this ritual.

Quick Assess

* Were students able to identify places in the text that indicate the narrator's point of view?
* Did they identify things that limit their view?
* Were students able to make a connection to something in their own experience?

Response Notes

from Year of Impossible Goodbyes by Sook Nyul Choi

. . . I crossed my legs, resting my hands on my lap with the palms facing up, just as he did. Though his eyes were closed, I kept mine open to watch him. He sat tall and still, like a statue. He looked peaceful as he prayed, yet there was an intensity, an anticipation, in his expression, as though he were waiting for something special to happen. His wrinkles were deep, and I wished that I could run my fingers along the creases in his forehead as he sat motionless in prayer. I wondered what he had to tell the Buddha this morning.

He was still for so long. I began to worry that my Grandfather had been filled with the spirit of the Buddha and had been turned into a statue. I tiptoed outside, quietly crept up toward him, and put my finger under his nose. I felt his faint breath and he coughed gently to reassure me. I sat next to him and watched, happy to be near him. The smell of the pine permeated the atmosphere, and I breathed deeply.

The sun grew stronger as I watched Grandfather, whose shirt of worn gray cloth hung comfortably from his bony shoulders. His crossed legs looked like two bent chopsticks. His handsome face was sad, peaceful, intent, but always dignified.

. . . Grandfather opened his eyes and looked at me as if he knew I had been staring at him. I was disappointed to see him stir; time would no longer stand still. He looked deep into my eyes, and then smiled, happy that we had celebrated this spring day together in such a special way. We got up and hurried inside to start our morning lessons.

* In the excerpt, the narrator wonders what is going on in her grandfather's mind. Become the narrator of this story, using a third-person limited point-of-view. Perch on grandfather's shoulders and narrate on the writing lines what you imagine is going on in his mind.

> The point of view from which a story is told determines the limits on the type of information or insights that will be revealed.

44 LESSON 12

After

ART CONNECTION After students have finished reading the excerpt from *Year of Impossible Goodbyes,* have them draw a scene depicting the vantage point of the narrator. Students should accompany their scene with a reflection on their choice of scene. If, for example, they choose to draw one of the first scenes, the narrator could be depicted behind her rice-paper door, peeking out at her mother and/or grandfather. If a student chooses to depict the latter part of the selection, the narrator could be tiptoeing outside, touching her grandfather's nose, or sitting beside him.

READING/WRITING CONNECTION Invite students to turn their writing at the end of this lesson into a longer personal narrative. They may want to write about what led up to the moment in which they observed this person and what happened afterwards. Remind them that since this is a personal narrative, it should be told from the first-person point of view, in other words, theirs. First-person point of view is indicated by the use of the pronouns *I* and *me*.

CHARACTERS — LESSON 13

As in a play, a story is populated by a cast of characters. Authors use a range of techniques to reveal details about their story's cast. The way that authors reveal information about their characters is referred to as **characterization.** Some common techniques that reveal a character's personality are the following:

- the narrator's direct descriptions
- the character's words, thoughts, and actions
- other characters' words or thoughts

Characterization allows the people in stories to come alive, enabling us to relate to and interact with them.

Think about the characters you have met in stories. Can you think of characters you could relate to? Ones who have reminded you of someone? Ones you have learned from? Characters you liked? Others you didn't? Often, it is the characters in a story that make it memorable. Making personal connections with characters—connecting them to ourselves, to people we know, or to other characters—makes stories more meaningful.

As you read the first part of the following short story, mark in the text examples of the specific characterization techniques listed above. Record in your **Response Notes** any connections you make with the character. An example is done for you.

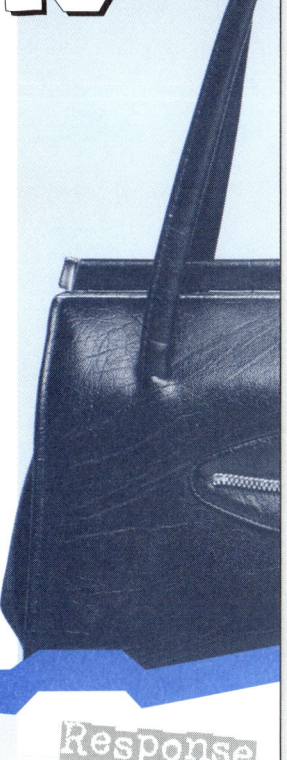

"Thank You, Ma'm" by Langston Hughes

She was a large woman with a large purse that had everything in it but hammer and nails. It had a long strap, and she carried it slung across her shoulder. It was about eleven o'clock at night, dark, and she was walking alone, when a boy ran up behind her and tried to snatch her purse. The strap broke with the single tug the boy gave it from behind. But the boy's weight and the weight of the purse combined caused him to lose his balance. Instead of taking off full blast as he had hoped, the boy fell on his back on the sidewalk and his legs flew up. The large woman simply turned around and kicked him right square in his blue-jeaned sitter. Then she reached down, picked the boy up by his shirt front, and shook him until his teeth rattled.

After that the woman said, "Pick up my pocketbook, boy, and give it here."

She still held him tightly. But she bent down enough to permit him to stoop and pick up her purse. Then she said, "Now ain't you ashamed of yourself?"

Response Notes

Narrator's description makes her seem big and tougher than she might really look.

CHARACTERS 45

LESSON 13

Students will study characterization techniques in a short story to make connections to the characters and to their own personal experiences.

BACKGROUND KNOWLEDGE

"Thank You, Ma'm" was first published in 1958, but there are few clues in the story that tell us when it takes place. The main clue to the time period is the mention of the blue suede shoes. Tell students that blue suede shoes became widely popular after rockabilly star Carl Perkins wrote and recorded a song called "Blue Suede Shoes" in 1955. The song was recorded by rhythm and blues artists, as well as other rock 'n roll musicians, including Elvis Presley. Help students make connections to their own lives by talking about a time when they wanted something that was popular but very expensive, such as a new pair of athletic shoes, but they didn't have the money to buy it. Tell them they're going to read a story about a boy who desperately wants a pair of blue suede shoes.

Before

CRITICAL READING SKILL

Analyzing Characterization Proficient readers learn how to appreciate the characters in a story by analyzing the techniques for creating them.

In this lesson, students will read a short story by Langston Hughes and identify examples of a character's personality revealed through

✻ the narrator's direct descriptions;

✻ the character's own words, thoughts, and actions;

✻ another character's words, thoughts, and actions.

Students will also practice making connections with the characters in the story.

Before they begin reading the selection, have students read the introduction on this page. Invite students to talk about memorable characters from books and stories they've read. Ask students to talk about what made the characters memorable.

RESPONSE NOTES
Remind students to write their responses to and thoughts about the characters as they mark the ways in which Hughes develops his characters. Model the questions a good reader would think about while reading: *In the beginning of the story, Mrs. Jones* ▶▶▶

MAKING CONNECTIONS 45

ABOUT THE AUTHOR

Born in Missouri in 1902, Langston Hughes experienced poverty as a young man. His father, unable to support the family in the United States, moved to Mexico when Langston was young. Langston visited his father in Mexico, but he spent most of his time with his mother and maternal grandmother. The family moved frequently, and eventually Hughes ended up in New York City. During the 1920s, Hughes became one of the key writers in the birth of the Harlem Renaissance, a time unequaled in the gathering of brilliant African American artists, musicians, and writers in one place. From the time he began writing until his death in 1967, Hughes wrote plays, poetry, novels, short stories, and essays.

WRITER'S CRAFT

Dialogue Langston Hughes uses dialogue to convey his characters' personalities. As Mrs. Jones and Roger get to know each other, their words reveal who they are and how they change. For example, point out to students that although Roger was bold enough to try to steal Mrs. Jones's purse, once she grabs him, he is honest and respectful, which says something about his character. Also talk about Hughes's use of dialect, which makes his characters sound real and believable.

Firmly gripped by his shirt front, the boy said, "Yes'm."
The woman said, "What did you want to do it for?"
The boy said, "I didn't aim to."
She said, "You a lie!"
"If I turn you loose, will you run?" asked the woman.
"Yes'm," said the boy.
"Then I won't turn you loose," said the woman. She did not release him.
"Lady, I'm sorry," whispered the boy.
"Um-hum! Your face is dirty. I got a great mind to wash your face for you. Ain't you got nobody home to tell you to wash your face?"
"No'm," said the boy.
"Then it will get washed this evening," said the large woman, starting up the street, dragging the frightened boy behind her.
He looked as if he were fourteen or fifteen, frail and willow-wild, in tennis shoes and blue jeans.
The woman said, "You ought to be my son. I would teach you right from wrong. Least I can do right now is to wash your face. Are you hungry?"
"No'm," said the being-dragged boy. "I just want you to turn me loose."
"Was I bothering *you* when I turned that corner?" asked the woman.
"No'm."
"But you put yourself in contact with me," said the woman. "If you think that that contact is not going to last awhile, you got another thought coming. When I get through with you, sir, you are going to remember Mrs. Luella Bates Washington Jones."
Sweat popped out on the boy's face and he began to struggle. Mrs. Jones stopped, jerked him around in front of her, put a half-nelson about his neck, and continued to drag him up the street. When she got to her door, she dragged the boy inside, down a hall, and into a large kitchenette-furnished room at the rear of the house. She switched on the light and left the door open. The boy could hear other roomers laughing and talking in the large house. Some of their doors were open, too, so he knew he and the woman were not alone. The woman still had him by the neck in the middle of her room.
She said, "What is your name?"
"Roger," answered the boy.
"Then, Roger, you go to that sink and wash your face," said the woman, whereupon she turned him loose at last. Roger looked at the door—looked at the woman—looked at the door—*and went to the sink.*

46 LESSON 13

During

sounds mean or intimidating. I wonder if she will stay this way or if she will change as the story progresses. I'll have to watch for what she says and does. I should also notice how Roger reacts to her.

MAKING PERSONAL CONNECTIONS
This story is especially good for making connections to students' own experiences. You may want to have students read the first part of the selection and then talk about how they feel about the characters so far. Ask them whether they can relate to them in any way. Then have students continue reading the next part of the story, found on the following page.

After students have finished reading, have them review their Response Notes and compare them with a partner's notes in order to build a more complete picture of the characters.

✼ Take a moment to look over your **Response Notes.** Compare what you wrote with a partner's notes. Help each other decide the strongest connections you made with each of the characters.

✼ Write a character sketch that describes the qualities of the character you most strongly connect to. Is it Roger or Mrs. Jones? Explain why you made this connection.

_____
_____
_____
_____
_____
_____
_____
_____
_____

✼ How does this connection contribute to your understanding and response to the characters in the story?

_____
_____
_____
_____
_____

Making connections to characters can enhance your understanding and strengthen your response to their viewpoints and actions.

TEACHING TIP

Using a Graphic Organizer: Venn Diagram Venn diagrams help students visualize comparisons and contrasts. Remind students to put the things that are different between the two characters in the outer part of each circle and the things that are the same in the middle, where the two circles overlap. Once they've thought about how the characters are the same and how they are different, students can use their Venn diagrams to reflect on how this exercise helped them make stronger connections to the characters in the story.

Quick Assess

✼ Did students mark places in the story where they connected with the characters?

✼ Were students able to evaluate how making connections to the characters added to their understanding of the story?

After

APPLYING THE STRATEGY

Have students look at the three basic techniques of characterization listed on page 45. Have students work in small groups to create a characterization chart, illustrating the use of each technique for stories with which they are familiar. Post students' charts in the classroom. Encourage students to talk about how effective the characterizations are and why.

LESSON 14

Students will examine the pattern of plot development to connect important events in the story.

BACKGROUND KNOWLEDGE
Tell students that every story is told differently, but most plots follow a certain pattern. Draw a large pyramid shape on the board or on chart paper or use a copy of the Plot Diagram on page 271. Review the events from a simple, familiar story and plot them along the pyramid, beginning at the bottom left corner. Explain that most stories begin with an *exposition,* or background, which introduces the setting and the characters to the reader. Next chart the events in the *rising action* along the left side of the triangle. These events build the conflict in the story. At the apex, record the *climax,* or turning point, of the story, when the conflict reaches its peak and must be resolved. Record the events in the *denouement or falling action,* in descending order along the right side of the triangle. It contains the action or dialogue necessary to lead the story to the resolution. Identify the *resolution* as the end of a story—the last part in which the problems are resolved or the story gets "wrapped up" at the bottom right corner of the diagram.

LESSON 14 PLOT

Think back to the example of the birthday party described in Lesson 12. If you were to tell the story of that day, what events would you choose to share? Certainly you wouldn't tell *everything* that happened that day. Instead, you would choose interesting, important, or relevant events. An author has to make similar decisions to create the **plot** of a compelling story. Each event is carefully chosen to work with the other events.

Recall the first part of "Thank You, Ma'm" as you read the rest of the story. In the **Response Notes,** summarize plot events as you read. An example is done for you.

"Thank You, Ma'm" by Langston Hughes (continued)

"Let the water run until it gets warm," she said. "Here's a clean towel."

"You gonna take me to jail?" asked the boy, bending over the sink.

"Not with that face, I would not take you nowhere," said the woman. "Here I am trying to get home to cook me a bite to eat and you snatch my pocketbook! Maybe, you ain't been to your supper either, late as it be. Have you?"

"There's nobody home at my house," said the boy.

"Then we'll eat," said the woman, "I believe you're hungry—or been hungry—to try to snatch my pocketbook."

"I want a pair of blue suede shoes," said the boy.

"Well, you didn't have to snatch *my* pocketbook to get some suede shoes," said Mrs. Luella Bates Washington Jones. "You could of asked me."

"M'am?"

The water dripping from his face, the boy looked at her. There was a long pause. A very long pause. After he had dried his face and not knowing what else to do, dried it again, the boy turned around, wondering what next. The door was open. He could make a dash for it down the hall. He could run, run, run, *run!*

The woman was sitting on the day-bed. After a while she said, "I were young once and I wanted things I could not get."

There was another long pause. The boy's mouth opened. Then he frowned, but not knowing he frowned.

The woman said, "Um-hum! You thought I was going to say *but,* didn't you? You thought I was going to say, *but I didn't snatch people's pocketbooks.* Well, I wasn't going to say that." Pause. Silence. "I have done things, too, which I would not tell you, son—neither tell God, if he didn't already know. Everybody's got

Response Notes

Roger washes his face as he tells Mrs. Jones why he tried to steal her pocketbook.

Before

CRITICAL READING SKILL
Understanding Plot In order to make meaning from the text, readers need to understand the plot—the story events as they relate to one another.

Point out to students that some stories follow the pattern explained above more than others. Some writers jump right into the story, with little or no exposition.

Other writers leave the resolution up to the reader's imagination. Students need to understand that how the plot develops is up to the writer; a good writer will do what works best for the story.

In this lesson, students will connect the main events in the plot to understand how the author develops the message of the story.

RESPONSE NOTES Ask students to highlight the main events of the story and to circle the climax, or turning point. Tell them they will use these notes later on in the lesson.

something in common. So you set down while I fix us something to eat. You might run that comb through your hair so you will look presentable."

In another corner of the room behind a screen was a gas plate and an icebox. Mrs. Jones got up and went behind the screen. The woman did not watch the boy to see if he was going to run now, nor did she watch her purse which she left behind her on the day-bed. But the boy took care to sit on the far side of the room where he thought she could easily see him out of the corner of her eye, if she wanted to. He did not trust the woman *not* to trust him. And he did not want to be mistrusted now.

"Do you need somebody to go to the store," asked the boy, "maybe to get some milk or something?"

"Don't believe I do," said the woman, "unless you just want sweet milk yourself. I was going to make cocoa out of this canned milk I got here."

"That will be fine," said the boy.

She heated some lima beans and ham she had in the icebox, made the cocoa, and set the table. The woman did not ask the boy anything about where he lived, or his folks, or anything else that would embarrass him. Instead, as they ate, she told him about her job in a hotel beauty-shop that stayed open late, what the work was like, and how all kinds of women came in and out, blondes, red-heads, and Spanish. Then she cut him a half of her ten-cent cake.

"Eat some more, son," she said.

When they were finished eating she got up and said, "Now, here, take this ten dollars and buy yourself some blue suede shoes. And next time, do not make the mistake of latching onto *my* pocketbook *nor nobody else's*—because shoes got by devilish ways will burn your feet. I got to get my rest now. But from here on in, son, I hope you will behave yourself."

She led him down the hall to the front door and opened it. "Good-night! Behave yourself, boy!" she said, looking out into the street as he went down the steps.

The boy wanted to say something else other than, "Thank you, Ma'm," to Mrs. Luella Bates Washington Jones, but although his lips moved, he couldn't even say that as he turned at the foot of the barren stoop and looked up at the large woman in the door. Then she shut the door. ❖

PLOT 49

WRITER'S CRAFT

Element of Surprise Sometimes writers provide surprise endings to their stories. Ask students to talk about what they thought would happen at the end of "Thank You, Ma'm." Were they surprised by what happened? For example, did they expect Mrs. Jones to ask Roger to stay? Did they think she was going to lecture him on never stealing again? What did they think of her giving Roger money to buy the shoes? How does that affect their view of her? Ask students how the plot twist makes the story a better one. Have them give reasons for their opinions.

During

IDENTIFYING KEY EVENTS After students have finished reading the rest of the story, have them list the story events in the space provided at the top of page 50, or if they prefer, draw a plot diagram (see page 271). Remind students to include the parts of the story they read in Lesson 13.

Then invite students to talk about the events they listed and to answer these questions.

❖ Why is each event important?
❖ What does each event tell us about the characters?

Then have students complete the Connection Chart activity at the bottom of page 50.

(Suggested answers: (1) a boy tries to snatch a woman's purse, (2) the woman caught the boy and demanded her pocketbook back, (3) Mrs. Jones brought Roger home and made him wash his face, (4) Roger makes the decision not to run, (5) Mrs. Jones fed Roger and gave him $10, (6) Roger left, unable to say "Thank you, Ma'm.")

MAKING CONNECTIONS 49

TEACHING TIP

Collaboration As students complete the first two activities on page 50, you may want them to use the Think-Pair-Share technique.

1. **Think** Ask students: What are the main plot events in this story? (Have them review their Response Notes from the lessons and their list of events at the top of page 50.)
2. **Pair** After they have identified the main events, have students work with a partner to discuss those events they identified. Point out that their lists may differ. Encourage them to talk about why they had different answers.
3. **Share** Have each pair report to the class on their discussion. Invite students to discuss what they've learned. Ask: *What do you think the author is saying in "Thank You, Ma'm"?* Their answer should reflect that an act of kindness that could not be repaid gave a troubled boy another chance.

❋ Look over your **Response Notes** for the whole story (beginning with Lesson 13) and consider the events Hughes chose as he wrote the story. List them in the space provided.

1. _____   2. _____
3. _____   4. _____
5. _____   6. _____

❋ Share your list with a partner and compare the events each of you chose. Why is each event important? What does each event tell us about the characters?

❋ At any point while you were reading "Thank You, Ma'm," did you find yourself thinking, "Hey! That reminds me of a time when . . ." or "Oh, that's kind of similar to what happened in . . ."? If you did, you made a connection with the plot of the story. Talk with a partner or a group about connections you made with the story.

❋ Think about one connection you made with the events of "Thank You, Ma'm." Use it to fill in the Connection Chart below.

CONNECTION CHART

This part of the plot of "Thank You, Ma'm"	. . . connects to this

❋ How does this connection influence your understanding of the story? How does it influence your response?

Identifying the plot helps you to understand and make connections with stories.

After

VISUALIZING Have students create a storyboard for the story events they identified. Explain that a storyboard is a visual representation of the scenes in a story, often used by film directors to plan the plot of a movie. You may want to provide students with a roll of butcher paper so they can create one continuous storyboard to display in the room.

POETRY CONNECTION Invite students to find collections of poems by Langston Hughes at the library or on the Internet. Ask them to share the poems they find and make connections between the meanings of those poems and what they feel Hughes is saying in "Thank You, Ma'm."

THEME LESSON 15

Stories play an important role in our lives. In addition to entertaining, they often prompt us to think about new things or to think about things in new ways. They sometimes teach us lessons, and they frequently help us understand others and ourselves better.

A **theme** is the main topic or message that is explored through the characters and the plot. Most stories have several themes. Some stories have clear messages, while others simply illuminate or explore topics. One way, then, to describe a theme is as a "topic *plus*." For example, the topic of a text could be "growing up." Ask yourself, what does the text *say* about growing up? The answer could be that the theme is "the struggles of growing up" or that "positive role models are important for teenagers." To understand a story's theme, ask: What does this author lead me to think about or understand?

One common theme in *Year of Impossible Goodbyes* and "Thank You, Ma'm" is *what we can learn from our elders*. What do you think each selection says about what we can learn from people older than ourselves? Fill in the Theme Chart below with your response. Include evidence from the text to support what you say.

THEME CHART

What Sookan learns from her grandfather in *Year of Impossible Goodbyes*
Evidence from story that makes me think so

What Roger learns from Mrs. Luella Bates Washington Jones in "Thank You, Ma'm"
Evidence from story that makes me think so

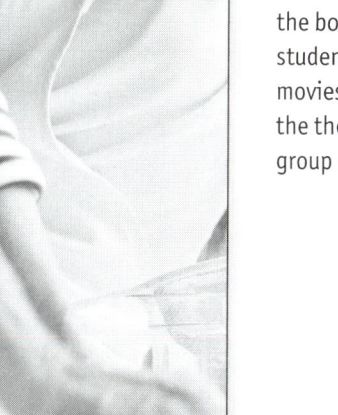

THEME 51

LESSON 15

Students will study the element of theme to understand a story's message and to make personal connections to the work and its author.

BACKGROUND KNOWLEDGE
Help students explore the concept of *theme* by reading the first three paragraphs on this page and then talking about themes in books the class has read together or movies students are likely to have seen. Sample themes: *working together will get the job done; don't judge people until you get to know them; older people have a lot to teach us; young people can make a difference; believing in yourself can help you accomplish great things.*

You may want to write some themes on the board or chart paper, and invite students to talk about books and movies they've seen that share one of the themes. Summarize by creating a group definition of what theme means.

Before

CRITICAL READING SKILL
Identifying Theme Often, a story's theme is not stated directly, and readers need to infer it on their own. One way proficient readers can understand the theme is to make personal or textual connections.

Have students think about the themes they shared in the Background Knowledge section. Then have them focus on the last two stories they have read by completing the Theme Chart at the bottom of page 51.

MAKING CONNECTIONS 51

WRITING SUPPORT

Using a Graphic Organizer Remind students of the importance of planning what they're going to write. Talk about some of the different graphic organizers writers use to plan their writing, such as clusters, charts, diagrams, timelines, storyboards, and outlines. Have students look at the Theme Chart they completed on page 51. Then have them draft what they're going to say, using the examples from the Theme Chart.

Quick Assess

- Were students able to show their understanding of the theme by noting examples from both stories?
- Were students able to make a personal connection to the themes explored in *Year of Impossible Goodbyes* and "Thank You, Ma'm"?

✳ Write a short essay describing how the stories *Year of Impossible Goodbyes* and "Thank You, Ma'm" help you think about what you can learn from your elders. Use your Theme Chart to provide specifics.

Title: _____

✳ Make a personal connection with the theme you explored in your essay. Does it relate to anything in your own life? To the life of someone you know? Or does it relate to the theme in another text you're familiar with? Explain the connection.

Identifying and making personal connections with themes deepens your understanding of a story.

During

CONNECTING TO THE THEME
Before completing the Theme Chart, facilitate a class discussion that addresses the question, *What does each author want to teach me?* It may help students to look closely at the lessons learned by the characters. Be sure students find evidence from the texts to support their entries in the Theme Chart.

You may want to model creating a thesis statement before students draft their essays on the theme. Model with a think-aloud: *Both authors wrote about relationships between young people and old people. My opening statement is going to be: "Thank You, Ma'm" and Year of Impossible Goodbyes both explore the theme of what young people can learn if they listen to older people.*

After

READING/WRITING CONNECTION
Have students write theme statements for other books or stories. Remind students to examine the lessons learned by the characters to help them write their statements. You may want to collect them in a class book or post them on a class website for students to use when selecting new reading material.

UNIT 4
EXPLORING MULTIPLE PERSPECTIVES

Lessons 16-20, pages 54-68

UNIT OVERVIEW
Reading about one subject—Jackie Robinson—from different perspectives helps students understand how to evaluate information from different sources.

KEY IDEA
The way information is presented and by whom determines what facts, details, and impressions the reader receives.

CRITICAL READING SKILLS
by lesson

16 Evaluating information from an outside perspective
17 Evaluating information from an inside perspective
18 Evaluating information from a personal account
19 Understanding a poetic portrait
20 Evaluating information from someone's brief encounter

WRITING ACTIVITIES
by lesson

16 Complete a chart.
17 Write interview questions.
18 Write a short paragraph.
19 Write an original poem.
20 Defend the selection of key words to characterize Jackie Robinson

Exploring Multiple Perspectives

"A life is not important except in the impact it has on other lives."
—Jackie Robinson

When you hear the name "Jackie Robinson," whom do you picture? A gifted athlete who excelled in sports as varied as baseball, tennis, football, and golf? The first African American to play major league baseball? A man devoted to his family? A tireless worker for civil rights? Those are all aspects of Jackie Robinson.

In this unit, you will explore different views, or **perspectives,** of this famous man. No single text can reveal everything about Jackie Robinson, but each one will add insight to the overall picture. You will also learn that *who* tells the story has a lot to do with *what* the story says.

Literature

- **"Hero on the Ball Field"** by Robert Peterson (magazine article)

The author describes Jackie Robinson's challenges and triumphs as a baseball player in this biographical article.

- **"Henry Aaron Remembers"** by Bryan Ethier (interview excerpt)

A sportswriter interviews Henry "Hank" Aaron and focuses on Aaron's recollections of Jackie Robinson.

- *Stealing Home* by Sharon Robinson (autobiography excerpt)

Jackie Robinson's daughter recalls her father's explanation of prejudice and his support for the students involved in integrating Central High School in Little Rock, Arkansas, in 1957.

- **"jackie robinson"** by Lucille Clifton (poem)

Clifton uses powerful images to portray Robinson in a short poem.

- **"Lady, That's Jackie Robinson!"** by Nan Birmingham (nonfiction article)

In this first-person story of a chance meeting on an airplane, Nan Birmingham reveals additional qualities of Jackie Robinson.

ASSESSMENT To assess student learning in this unit, see pages 232 and 259.

LESSON 16

Students will read a biographical account to analyze an author's perspective on his subject.

BACKGROUND KNOWLEDGE
Explain to students that Jackie Robinson was the first African American to play modern major league baseball. From 1947 to 1956, Robinson batted .311 in 1,382 games. In 1962, he was elected to the Baseball Hall of Fame, the first African American player so honored. In "Hero on the Ball Field," students will read a biography that slants positively toward its main character through the use of selected facts and clearly expressed opinions. Peterson's biography is written in third-person point of view, and his individual perspective is clearly one of strong appreciation for this baseball pioneer.

VOCABULARY
acrobatic able to move like an acrobat, exceptionally agile

taunts ugly remarks intended to anger

Ask questions to check students' understanding: *What players today would you call "acrobatic"? Why? What taunts have you heard at a game? How would you feel if you were the victim of a taunt?*

LESSON 16 — A BIOGRAPHY

Interpretation—everyone does it. We take the facts as we know them and, in writing them, add our own understanding. A biographer examines the facts of a person's life. Some biographers try to present an impartial view by focusing only on the facts. Others reveal their feelings about the subject in the way they select and interpret the facts. They may include facts that make the person look better or worse than he or she really was. Or a writer might select only the incidents from a person's life that illustrate a certain point.

Robert Peterson combines facts and his own commentary, or interpretation, in "Hero on the Ball Field." As you read, use a highlighter of one color to mark the places where Peterson **draws conclusions,** such as "It was a tough time to be black, and not just for baseball players." Use a highlighter of a different color to mark the **facts,** such as "In Southern states, black kids went to separate schools."

Response Notes

"Hero on the Ball Field" by Robert Peterson

As a baseball player, Jackie Robinson won over the fans, his teammates—and his own hot temper.

Robinson was a line-drive hitter, an acrobatic fielder and the best base runner of his time. He was also the first African-American player in the big leagues in [the last] century.

In Robinson's rookie year, 1947, baseball topped the sports world. Pro football and basketball were far less popular 50 years ago.

It was a tough time to be black, and not just for baseball players. In Southern states, black kids went to separate schools. Black people had to ride in the backs of buses. There were even separate drinking fountains for blacks and whites. In the North, things were a little better, but not much. There had not been a black player in the major leagues in more than 60 years.

Blacks—even those good enough to play major-league baseball—had their own teams and leagues.

Jackie Robinson was a fiery competitor. "This guy didn't just come to play," an old baseball man once said. "He came to beat you!"

When the Brooklyn Dodgers signed Robinson, the club president, Branch Rickey, told Robinson he would have to curb his temper if he was abused or taunted by white players or fans. Rickey worried that if Robinson answered back, people who did not want blacks in baseball would say, "See, we told you blacks and whites should not compete."

Robinson asked, "Mr. Rickey, do you want a player who's afraid to fight back?"

Before

CRITICAL READING SKILL
Evaluating Information from an Outside Perspective In this lesson, students will discuss the concept of a writer's objectivity. To help students understand objectivity, read aloud a sports article from a local newspaper or magazine. Have students discuss whether it contains more facts or opinions. Help students understand that something objective has verifiable facts, words with neutral connotations, and no evidence of the writer's opinion.

RESPONSE NOTES
Using two different highlighter colors is a good technique to help students read closely and see the contrasting details in the text. Visual learners especially benefit from this strategy. Some students may be tempted to highlight just about everything, but caution them that they should limit their highlighting only to information that fits the criteria.

"I want a player with guts enough not to fight back," Rickey said. "You've got to do this job with base hits and stolen bases and fielding ground balls, Jackie. Nothing else."

Jackie Robinson was the loneliest man in baseball in 1947. During spring training a half-dozen Dodgers players said they would not play if he joined the team. Branch Rickey put down that mutiny with stern words. Soon most Dodgers warmed up to Robinson. They saw he was helping them win games.

Opponents were not so friendly. Some made it as tough as they could for the black pioneer. A few tried to spike Robinson as they crossed first base, Robinson's position that year, on a close play. He was hit by pitches nine times. Once he was kicked as he slid into second base.

Many players and fans screamed racial taunts at him.

"Plenty of times I wanted to haul off when somebody insulted me for the color of my skin," he said later.

Robinson was not even safe from hate at home. The mail brought letters threatening his life. Some letter writers said they would kidnap his infant son, Jackie Jr., or attack his wife.

Despite the great pressure on him, Robinson had a fine season. He batted .297, led the Dodgers in runs scored with 125 and hit 12 home runs. He led the league with 29 stolen bases. That may not seem like a lot today, but baseball was not a running game in 1947.

As a base runner, Robinson was constantly in motion. Pitchers worried more about him than the batter. Often the batter got a fat pitch to hit because the dancing Robinson distracted the pitcher.

Robinson sometimes "stole" bases after the ball was hit. He would race from first to third when the safe thing to do was stop at second.

But here is a fact that tells you how daring the muscular, pigeon-toed Robinson was on the bases: He stole home 19 times in his career, more than anyone since the early years of this century.

Fans—black and white—flocked to see Jackie Robinson play. In his first year, the Dodgers and four other National League teams set attendance records. He became a hero in black communities.

That year the Dodgers won the National League pennant but lost the World Series to the New York Yankees. Robinson was named National League Rookie of the Year.

Even before the 1947 season ended, Robinson's success paved the way for other black players. In July the Cleveland Indians signed Larry Doby, a slugging young outfielder, who became the first black player in the American League. A month later, pitcher Dan Bankhead, who had been with the Memphis Red Sox in the Negro American League, joined Robinson on the Dodgers.

Jackie Robinson's best position was second base, but he played all four infield positions and some in the outfield.

A BIOGRAPHY 55

ABOUT THE AUTHOR
Robert Peterson was born December 19, 1925, in Warren, Pennsylvania. A reporter and editor for major newspapers and a contributing editor for *Scouting* magazine, Peterson also edited books about subjects other than sports. His most famous book is *Only the Ball Was White* (1970), a history of the Negro Baseball Leagues. A research award given by the Society for American Baseball Research is named for him. Peterson died in 2006.

WRITER'S CRAFT
Organization Ask students to identify the order that Peterson has used to organize his information. They will quickly see that he has used *chronological order,* or time order, putting events in the sequence they occurred. Another way to organize information is *order of importance.* Explain to students that writers make decisions about how to present material and ask them to speculate why Peterson would use chronological order in this case. Students will likely suggest that Peterson is using significant events of Robinson's life to show that he was a "hero off the baseball field as well as on." They might suggest that organizing the details in chronological order helps the reader remember them as part of a story.

During

SHARING RESPONSES After students have read the selection, make two columns on the board. Label one "Fact" and one "Opinion." Invite students to write phrases from the selection under the appropriate heading. Facts they might list include *signed with the Brooklyn Dodgers, stole 29 bases in 1947, retired in 1957, elected to the Hall of Fame in 1962.* Commentary that shows Peterson's opinion could include *acrobatic fielder, best base runner of his time, daring, hero in black communities, a leader.* This chart will help them answer the questions on page 56.

Fact	Opinion

EXPLORING MULTIPLE PERSPECTIVES 55

EXTRA SUPPORT

Differentiation Provide oral support for students before they complete the writing prompts on *Daybook* page 56. Work with individuals or a small group to find evidence to support their answers. Remind students of the following information:

* A fact is something that can be proved.
* Commentary, or an opinion, is a person's belief.
* Consider the title of the biography.

TEACHING TIP

Collaboration Students' opinions may differ in response to the question on page 56 about why Peterson wrote the biography as he did. Students can consider any number of perspectives by discussing their answers in small groups. At the end of the discussion, ask students to write one sentence telling how the discussion reinforced or changed their initial opinion.

From 1949 to 1952 he was one of the two or three best players in baseball. In 1949 he led the National League in batting with a .342 average and in stolen bases with 37. He was third in triples and runs scored. That performance earned him the league's Most Valuable Player award.

Robinson retired from baseball in 1957, the year before the Dodgers moved to Los Angeles. Five years later he was elected to the Baseball Hall of Fame.

He became an outspoken leader in the fight for equality for black people. Jackie Robinson proved himself a hero off the baseball field as well as on.

❋ Does Peterson use more facts or more commentary? Why do you think he wrote Robinson's biography this way?

❋ Look back at the commentary you highlighted. What does Robert Peterson think of Jackie Robinson? How can you tell?

✳ Fill out the chart below to help you understand how Peterson uses incidents to express his perspective on Jackie Robinson.

Incident	What the incident reveals about Robinson
Robinson receives hate mail	Robinson was able to perform well even under intense pressure and stress.

Biographers often select and present facts about a person that reveal the biographer's point of view about that person.

WRITER'S CRAFT

Revealing a Person's Characteristics Point out to students that writers often reveal characteristics of a person gradually through *showing* rather than *telling*. When Peterson tells us that Jackie Robinson chose to ignore hate mail and played well, we know that he was an extraordinary player because he did not let the pressure affect his game. Students might also include that opponents tried to spike him at first base and some fans screamed racial taunts at him.

Completing the chart on page 57 will support students' thinking about the connections between the incidents (*showing* details) and what they reveal about the man.

Quick Assess

✳ Were students able to differentiate between fact and opinion?

✳ Did students cite evidence to assess the author's view of Jackie Robinson?

✳ Were they able to identify ways in which the incidents the author recounts reveal what Robinson was like?

After

APPLYING THE STRATEGY Have students research the experiences of some of the other early African American major league stars, such as Willie Mays, Hank Aaron, or Ernie Banks. In their research, they should look for how the biographer or interviewer presents fact and commentary. Ask them to evaluate the author's credibility based on these details.

INTERDISCIPLINARY CONNECTIONS Encourage students to read articles in other disciplines to identify an author's perspective. What conclusions can they make about the writing? Help them to consider the author's background and bias toward the topic.

LESSON 17

Students will read and respond to an interview that has an inside perspective on Jackie Robinson.

BACKGROUND KNOWLEDGE

Explain to students that when Jackie Robinson was breaking the race barrier in major league baseball, it was a frightening and courageous thing to do. Prejudice was so strong that fans of the game would often yell racial slurs at Robinson and taunt his teammates as well, not just in the southern states, where segregation was still in effect, but in the northern states as well. In this interview, students will learn more about Jackie Robinson through the recollections of another great African American baseball player, Henry "Hank" Aaron.

VOCABULARY

discrimination act based on class or category rather than individual merit

farm team a minor-league team

embittered to harbor feelings of anger and resentment

Ask students to talk about how the words *discrimination* and *embittered* might be related in the story of Robinson's career. After they read the selection, have them check their sentence to see if the words were used the same way in the selection.

LESSON 17 — AN INTERVIEW

In reading or listening to an **interview,** we get information and impressions about a person. The information is filtered through the people participating in the interview, though. The questions the interviewer asks will determine the information the interviewee gives. The interviewee will put his or her own interpretations on the facts, based on previous experiences.

In 1997, Bryan Ethier interviewed Henry "Hank" Aaron about Jackie Robinson. Aaron himself was famous. When the Atlanta Braves player hit home run 715 on April 8, 1974, Aaron shattered Babe Ruth's 39-year record. Although many people applauded this accomplishment, others were upset that a black man had broken a white man's record. According to Ethier, Aaron received death threats and "had even feared for his children's safety. But through it all, Aaron had kept his emotions to himself, letting his bat do his talking; it was a policy he had followed throughout his career."

As you read, think about what Aaron reveals about Jackie Robinson. In the **Response Notes,** mark the places where you learn something about Robinson's influence and his personal qualities.

from "Henry Aaron Remembers" by Bryan Ethier

AMERICAN HISTORY [the name of the magazine in which the interview was published]: As a young black ballplayer, what was your reaction when you learned of Jackie Robinson signing with the Dodgers?

HENRY AARON: Well, I guess it was kind of like putting it in the same perspective as the signing of the bill that ended discrimination as far as drinking fountains and railroads and bath facilities, and things like that. Kind of taking a burden off your back, when you felt like Jackie Robinson had done something to give every black kid a chance to live his dream.

AH: Do you recall the time, as a young player, when you first met Jackie?

AARON: When I was in high school—when I was in Mobile, Alabama—I remember Jackie Robinson. They had a farm team in Mobile, and teams always used to come through there to play the Mobile Bears. And Jackie came there to make a speech, and I remember that I stayed out of school to listen to him speak.

AH: Did that speech, and meeting him at that time, set your career on its course?

AARON: Well, he certainly did affect me when I listened to him. But even before then he affected me, just knowing that Jackie Robinson was the

---

Before

CRITICAL READING SKILL

Evaluating Information from an Inside Perspective In this lesson, students read an interview that reveals more information about Robinson. By exploring an insider's perspective and comparing it with the outsider's perspective in the previous lesson, students can develop an understanding of how multiple perspectives contribute to what we learn about a subject.

RESPONSE NOTES

Have students reread Robinson's own words on page 53 and then mark places in this interview where Aaron explains the influence Robinson had on him.

58 UNIT 4

first black man that ever played professional baseball certainly inspired me to go ahead and fulfill my dream.

• • •

AH: There was some comment at the time that Jackie was brought up by Branch Rickey more because of his personality, his upbringing, and his intelligence than for his baseball ability. Perhaps there were more athletic players who could have been brought up?

AARON: I'm sure some of that was true. I'm sure they probably could've brought in a lot more, many more, players that had more talent than Jackie Robinson. But that wasn't the only criteria at that time. You had to have somebody who could deal with the pressure; you had to have somebody who had the outlook of a Dr. Martin Luther King, who could turn the other cheek at times, and also be able to play baseball so that people would appreciate it. So, I'm sure the things mentioned, all of that was true.

• • •

AH: Over his career, Jackie began to change and became more embittered, did he not?

AARON: He had proven himself, that if given the opportunity he could play baseball. He had proven that to himself, but he was a man, and he had a temper just like everyone else. He felt like he had done all of these things, and he just needed to be his own man. He had a lot of pressure stored up in him from when people would slide into him, slap him, call him names, and all that other stuff. He just felt like he didn't need to take that anymore. ❖

❋ What is your first reaction to this interview? Jot down a few notes about your impressions of Jackie Robinson and Hank Aaron.

❋ Explain how Aaron answers the reporter's questions about Robinson's playing ability and about Robinson becoming embittered. How does Aaron stress the positive side of Robinson?

TEACHING TIP

Reading Critically To answer the second writing prompt, students will need to read the interview carefully. They must get into the mind of Hank Aaron to see two strategies he uses. First, he agrees with the interviewer that there might have been players who were more talented. But then he goes on to praise Robinson for all of the other qualities he brought and suggests how important those were. His second strategy is to avoid using the interviewer's word *embittered*. Instead, he explains that Jackie was a man just like everyone else with a temper like everyone else who had had to put up with a lot. In this way, he does not agree that *embittered* is the right word to use.

During

UNDERSTANDING FIRST-PERSON POINT OF VIEW As students read and respond to the interview, have them keep in mind that Aaron revealed things that an outsider could not. However, only Robinson himself could tell us exactly what it felt like to be a pioneer in breaking the race barrier in sports.

Have students think about interview questions they would like to ask Robinson if he were alive today. After students have finished the writing on page 60, encourage them to research more about Jackie Robinson to see if they can find answers to their questions, especially those in Robinson's own words.

TEACHING TIP

Collaboration Encourage students to work in pairs or in small groups to brainstorm their interview questions. After choosing their subject, they should focus on who they will interview about their famous person. Have them write questions that will uncover facts as well as personal opinions. Ask them to consider if they will want to pose the same questions to both interviewees. Have them reread the Ethier interview as a model for writing their own.

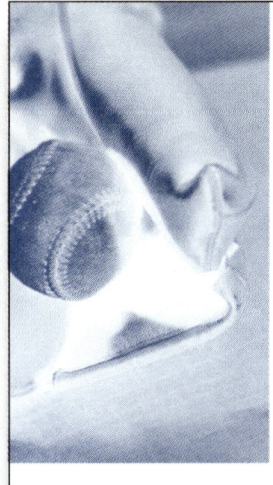

❈ Think of a famous person. Write three questions that you could ask someone about that person.

Name of Person _____

❈ Now imagine two different interviews. The first one will be with someone who admires the person. The second one will be with someone who does not. Organize your questions and answers below.

Famous Person _____
Interview with person who admires him/her

Q
A

Q
A

Q
A

Interview with person who does not admire him/her

Q (same as above)
A

Q
A

Q
A

✳ Look at the introduction to "Henry Aaron Remembers." Review what you marked in the **Response Notes,** and re-read the excerpt from *Hero on the Ballfield* in Lesson 16. Use a Venn diagram to compare these two views of Jackie Robinson.

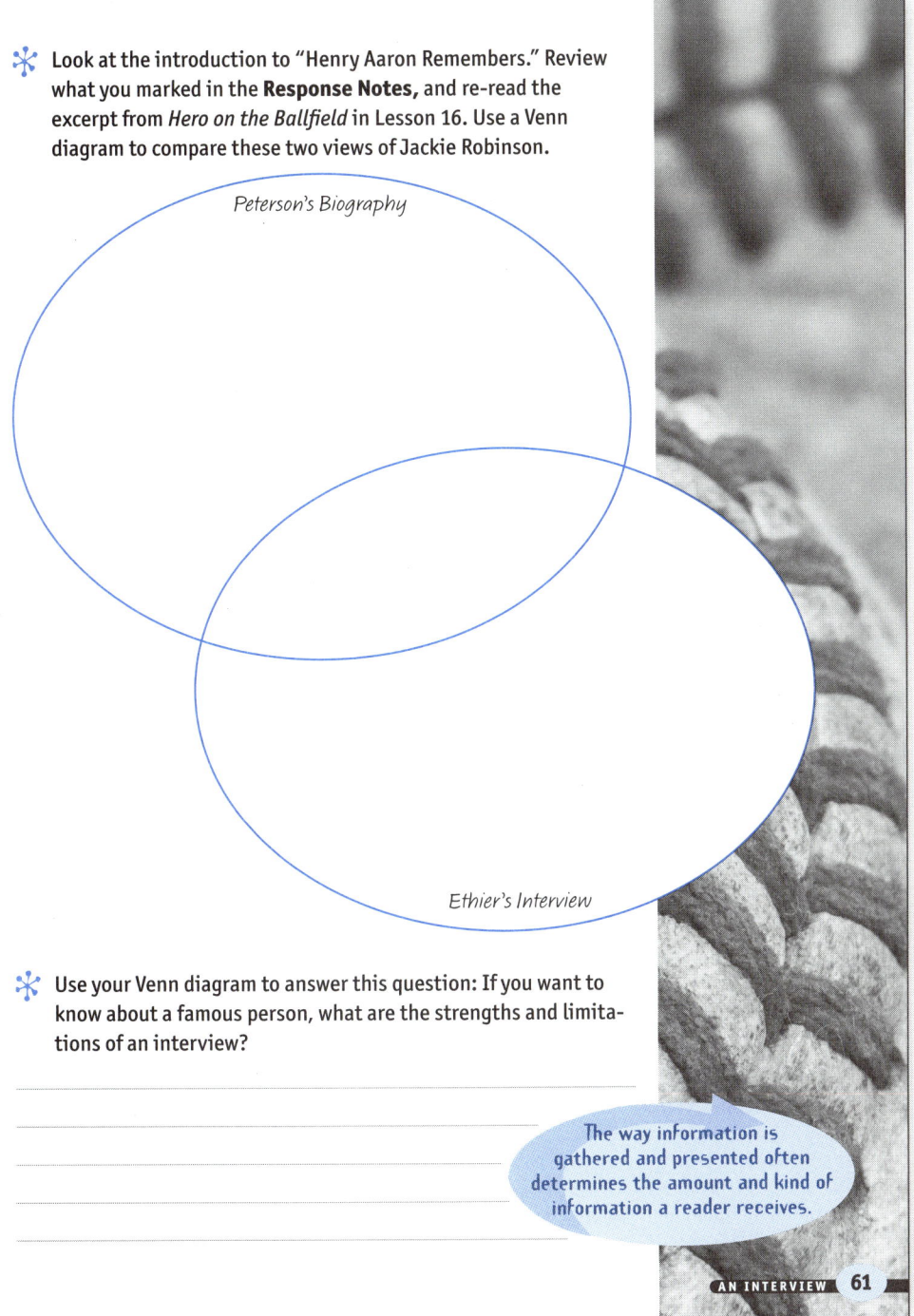

Peterson's Biography

Ethier's Interview

✳ Use your Venn diagram to answer this question: If you want to know about a famous person, what are the strengths and limitations of an interview?

_____
_____
_____
_____

The way information is gathered and presented often determines the amount and kind of information a reader receives.

AN INTERVIEW

TEACHING TIP

Using a Graphic Organizer Students use a Venn diagram to compare two views of Robinson. By comparing what the two accounts have in common and contrasting how the two accounts differ, students will get a clearer understanding of how point of view can influence their understanding of the subject.

Quick Assess

✳ Were students able to identify places in the text where Aaron shares his thoughts and feelings about Robinson?

✳ Did students write interview questions that would reveal their subject?

✳ Did students provide details from the two accounts in Lessons 16 and 17 to compare and contrast the two perspectives?

After

READING/WRITING CONNECTION

Ask students to imagine that they are in the shoes of someone who has been mistreated because of some characteristic such as race, ethnicity, disability, and so on. Have them write about their feelings and experiences in a short monologue or poem from the perspective of that person to a sympathetic audience.

EXPLORING MULTIPLE PERSPECTIVES

LESSON 18

Students will read and respond to a personal narrative in order to reach a deeper understanding of the author's viewpoint.

BACKGROUND KNOWLEDGE

Sharon Robinson describes an incident in which nine black teenagers from Little Rock, Arkansas, began the court-ordered integration of schools. Arkansas Governor Orval Faubus called out the Arkansas National Guard to prevent the integration of the all-white Little Rock Central High School. President Dwight D. Eisenhower then sent federal troops to enforce the law, and the black students were admitted. Have students speculate about how this incident connects with what they know about Jackie Robinson's life.

VOCABULARY

discrimination unfair rules and attitudes based on prejudice

tremendous great

rebellious likely to go against the rules

defiant defying or showing resistance to authority

impenetrable unbreakable

Discuss how certain defiant or rebellious actions might be seen positively and negatively, depending on the perspective of the person observing them.

LESSON 18 — A PERSONAL ACCOUNT

Another perspective on a person's life can come from someone close to that person—a relative or good friend. Sharon Robinson, Jackie's daughter, has a perspective that allows her to know some details that a biographer with an outside perspective might not. However, as a family member, her depiction of her father will undoubtedly be filtered through her thoughts about and feelings for him.

In her **autobiography**, *Stealing Home,* Sharon Robinson tells about her childhood in a famous family. In this excerpt, she recounts a dinner-table conversation. Jackie Robinson is talking about an incident in Little Rock, Arkansas, in 1957. When nine black teenagers began the court-ordered integration of schools, they faced jeers, taunts, and humiliation. Four of the children had spoken with Robinson about the ordeal. As you read this personal account, mark places where Sharon Robinson reveals her own thoughts.

from Stealing Home by Sharon Robinson

Without talking down to us, Dad used this opportunity to explain prejudice. Generally, he moved quietly around the house, but it was obvious that this situation had him worked up and he wanted my brothers and me to understand the situation.

"I suppose we all fear the unknown—the strange, the different. The natural fears of parents are made worse by ignorance, and unfortunately they pass them down to their children. In the process, the stories get more and more distorted and eventually become fact in the minds of the storyteller. The sad part for everyone is that prejudice prevents people from sharing talents which could benefit the whole community. The only way racial discrimination can have a hope of being erased is through exposure. The more people understand each other the less they will fear the differences."

"What did you say to the children, Daddy?" I asked, trying to picture their faces.

"Were they boys or girls?" David added.

"How old were they?" Jackie wanted to know.

Dad smiled and continued with the story of his phone conversation. He reminded us that the boys and girls were high school students. I felt somewhat relieved to know that they were much older than we were. I wondered how the children could possibly learn under such tremendous pressure.

I looked questioningly at Jackie, who was ten at the time, trying to picture him as a teenager going to high school. I figured my rebellious brother, Jackie

62 LESSON 18

Before

CRITICAL READING SKILL

Evaluating Information from a Personal Account Critical readers evaluate the information they get by looking at the source of the information. Help students see that there are multiple perspectives on events. It doesn't mean that one perspective is right and another is wrong. What's important to keep in mind as a reader is how an author's perspective may affect or shape what information is presented.

RESPONSE NOTES

In this lesson, students will read an account of an incident told from the point of view of Sharon Robinson, Jackie Robinson's daughter. Encourage students to mark places in the text that reveal Sharon Robinson's feelings about her father, as well as what her father is telling her. For example, the opening phrase *(without talking down to us)* indicates that Jackie Robinson respected his children.

Junior, would arrive at school and when he was told he couldn't go inside, he would drop his books right in front of the soldiers (because he'd have to do something defiant), turn around, and go to the movies with his friends. I started to laugh at that image but then the sound of Dad's voice reminded me that we were discussing something serious. I took another bite of the baked chicken on my plate and chewed it, quietly listening to Dad.

"One of the girls I talked to this morning was named Gloria Ray and another was Minnie Brown. I told the girls that they were doing a tremendous job that made us swell up with pride. I wanted them to know that there were people throughout the country supporting them," Dad went on. "I couldn't believe Minnie's response. She said that they were following in my footsteps. Can you imagine?"

Dad's voice had faded. I had to strain to hear him. He was staring straight ahead not really focused on any one person, but I could still see the tears building in his eyes. I watched as he blinked several times. His expression said more than his words: a sadness because the children were so young; a pride in their courage and determination. I am sure that he also felt good playing a role, and grateful that the school experiences of his own children did not include such extreme displays of hatred.

I went to bed that night and dreamed of linking arms with Gloria, Minnie, Thelma, and Melba. We formed an impenetrable barrier. Our faces conveyed an unstoppable message. The National Guard offered no resistance. They parted their ranks and we entered Central High School. As far away as Arkansas was from Connecticut, I felt a bond with the children in Little Rock.

※ How would you describe Sharon Robinson's attitude toward her father in this excerpt? Write two quotations that support your description.

A PERSONAL ACCOUNT

During

UNDERSTANDING ANOTHER PERSON'S PERSPECTIVE After students write about Ms. Robinson's attitude toward her father, have them complete the activity at the top of page 64. Students might find it helpful to divide the work space into three columns, one for each of the selections. (Accept answers that students can support with evidence from the text, for example, these suggestions: Biography—athletic, persevering; Interview—inspirational, balanced; Personal Account—rebellious [as a child], respectful.)

EXTRA SUPPORT

Differentiation If students are having difficulty identifying how Ms. Robinson feels about her father, review the selection and model finding clues to her feelings: *The image of Jackie Jr. defying the soldiers makes Sharon start to laugh, but she stops herself. She doesn't seem afraid, but she clearly wants to hear what her father has to say. She must have been very proud of him. She seems to respect him so much.*

EXPLORING MULTIPLE PERSPECTIVES

TEACHING TIP

Collaboration You may want to have students work in groups of three to do the activity at the top of page 64. Each member can be responsible for collecting information from one of the selections they've read on Robinson so far. Have students make a master list of what they've found, labeling the source of the characteristic. Let students know that some characteristics may show up in more than one source. Once the group has finished, have students write the characteristics in the *Daybook*.

Quick Assess

* Were students able to identify Sharon Robinson's thoughts and feelings?
* Did students describe Ms. Robinson's attitude toward her father and provide supporting quotations?
* Did students come up with a labeled list of characteristics for Jackie Robinson?
* Did they describe a recommendation for someone wanting to read about Robinson? Did they give reasons for their recommendations?

✻ You have read three different pieces of writing about Jackie Robinson. Brainstorm a list of Robinson's personal characteristics based on what you have learned from these pieces of writing. Then identify the source or sources for each characteristic by marking it B (Biography), I (Interview), or PA (Personal Account).

✻ Imagine that a friend wants to learn more about Jackie Robinson and has asked you to recommend a resource. You might not have a specific title in mind, but what kind of writing would you tell your friend to look for? Which perspective would you recommend that your friend begin with and why?

A personal account or memoir can provide readers with insights and details that may be absent from accounts with a more distant perspective.

64 **LESSON 18**

After

READING/WRITING CONNECTION

Linda Rief, in *Seeking Diversity*, offers an exercise in which students map across a timeline the five best events of their lives. Have students map their events on a timeline before selecting one event. Next, instruct students to write one scene of the event from two points of view. For example, they may describe a time when they felt proud of themselves from their own point of view and again from the point of view of an observer.

UNIT 4

A POETIC PORTRAIT — LESSON 19

A poet can provide another perspective on a person. Although this poem doesn't provide information about Jackie Robinson, it does give you another way to think about him. It adds another perspective to consider as you create an image of Jackie Robinson.

In a few lines, Lucille Clifton uses **powerful images** to portray Jackie Robinson. Her impression of him becomes clearer each time you read the poem. Read it two or three times, each time adding questions or insights to your **Response Notes.** Mark the images that strike you.

jackie robinson by Lucille Clifton

> ran against walls
> without breaking.
> in night games
> was not foul
> but, brave as a hit
> over whitestone fences,
> entered the conquering dark.

✳ Lucille Clifton's language in this poem is distilled to present the essence of Jackie Robinson as she sees him. If the poem seems too condensed, try this: Rewrite the poem as two sentences, each starting with "Jackie Robinson" and ending with the periods that are already in the poem.

✳ What characteristics of Robinson does Clifton emphasize?

LESSON 19

Students will read a short poem about Jackie Robinson to gain another perspective about him.

BACKGROUND KNOWLEDGE
Review with students what they like about poetry. Discuss how poetry often uses vivid images to carry its message. Many times, readers need to think about the images and reread the poem to get at its meaning. Also talk about the oral tradition of poetry, how it is a genre of writing that is meant to be spoken aloud and often meanings are revealed through hearing the poem.

Select two or three striking images from previous selections. For example, from Sharon Robinson's account, use "He was staring straight ahead not really focused on any one person, but I could still see the tears building in his eyes." Ask students to shorten this image to the least number of words needed. After volunteers read aloud their revision, discuss the effects created by distilling an image in this way.

Before

CRITICAL READING SKILL
Understanding a Poetic Portrait
Strategic readers use different skills to read poetry. Poems are condensed expressions of meaning and tend to be filled with images and poetic language. In this lesson, students will explore a poetic portrait of Jackie Robinson to gain another way of understanding him.

CAPTURING THE ESSENCE
Read the poem aloud several times to students. While the poem uses no capital letters, its punctuation helps carry the meaning the author intends. Pause after each period and comma to help students grasp the meaning of the ideas. Then have students read or recite the poem again independently.

You may want to do the activities on page 65 with the whole class and then have students complete the activity on page 66 independently.

EXPLORING MULTIPLE PERSPECTIVES

ABOUT THE AUTHOR

Lucille Clifton was born in 1936 in Depew, New York. She has written many books and poems for adults and children over the years. Her poetry is known for its minimalist style, spare but powerful choice of words, and strong images. She has received many honors for her work, including being named Maryland's Poet Laureate in 1979. Two of her books of poetry were chosen as finalists for the Pulitzer Prize.

Quick Assess

* Did students follow Clifton's word pattern in their poem?
* Do students understand how a poet can convey a perspective on a subject?

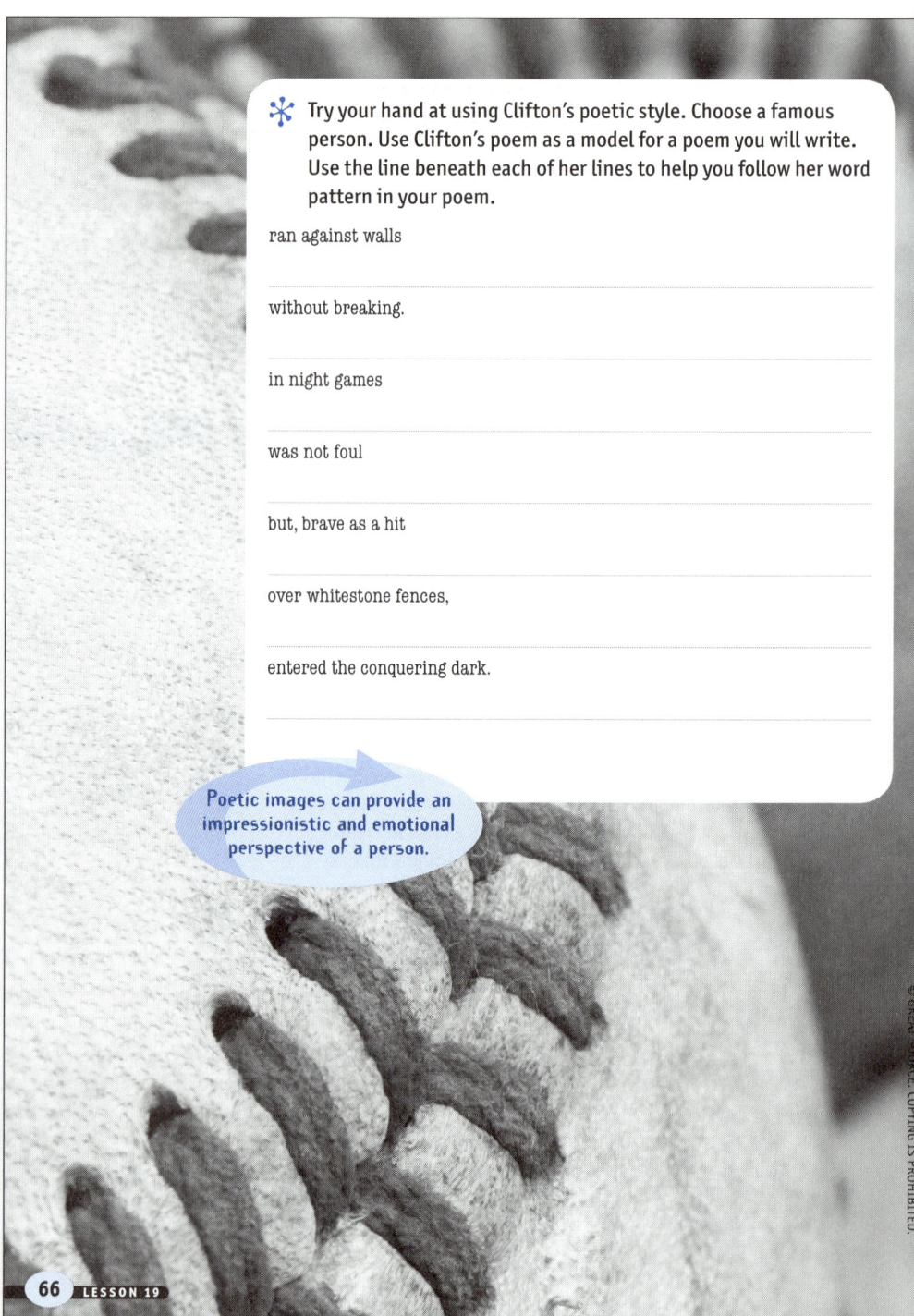

❊ Try your hand at using Clifton's poetic style. Choose a famous person. Use Clifton's poem as a model for a poem you will write. Use the line beneath each of her lines to help you follow her word pattern in your poem.

ran against walls

without breaking.

in night games

was not foul

but, brave as a hit

over whitestone fences,

entered the conquering dark.

> Poetic images can provide an impressionistic and emotional perspective of a person.

After

VISUAL ARTS CONNECTION Have students find another poem in this book or another collection that has a poetic image that they like. Have them draw or find a picture to represent the strongest image from the poem. Display students' pictures with copies of the poems that inspired them. For an additional challenge, separate the poems and pictures and ask students to match them.

Ask them to write a short explanation on an index card of why they matched the poems and pictures as they did. Post their explanations near the picture displays.

A BRIEF ENCOUNTER — LESSON 20

One incident can reveal much about a person. Nan Birmingham briefly met Jackie Robinson when she sat next to him on an airplane in the late 1960s. He had been retired since 1957, but he was still well known. As you read Ms. Birmingham's story, think about how your impression of Jackie Robinson is enhanced or changed.

"Lady, That's Jackie Robinson!" by Nan Birmingham

I was bone-tired by 2 a.m., when I boarded the plane for home after criss-crossing six southern states in five days on the lecture circuit. Gradually, I became aware that passengers shuffling with fatigue along the aisle perked up when they passed the man seated next to me.

"I should be asleep at home by now," he said quietly. "I only flew south for dinner." "Dinner?" I asked, searching for clues to his identity. "I was the speaker at the National Conference of Christians and Jews," he explained. I wrestled with famous names and came up empty.

Before dawn the PA [on the airplane] announced that Kennedy was again socked in. We were to land in Newark and be bused to JFK. My seatmate gave in to annoyance. "I still have to drive to Connecticut."

"Do you take the thruway?" I asked. "I live in Westchester just off the thruway. You wouldn't have to stop. Just slow down. I'll jump."

"You wouldn't have to do that," he said with a smile.

When he left his seat briefly, the man across the aisle whispered, "What a great guy is giving you a ride."

"Yes," I agreed knowingly. Then I chanced, "He is Elston Howard, isn't he?"

"Elston Howard?" the fellow bellowed. "Lady, *that's* Jackie Robinson!" he added in utter amazement.

Jackie Robinson refastened his seatbelt. I wanted him to know I knew and exploded enthusiastically. "My sister, Marion, was at UCLA when you played for the Bruins."

"Really," he said calmly. "That was some time ago. I'm Jackie Robinson, and what is your name?"

When the bus pulled up at Kennedy on that gray morning, Jackie Robinson stood up in front and shouted, "If anyone needs a ride to Westchester or Connecticut, I'm driving up the New England Thruway."

A young soldier spoke up, "Sir, I'm going to Waterbury."

"Come along," said Robinson.

As the soldier and I waited for Robinson to come with his car I said with a certain know-it-all smugness, "Young man, are you aware of just *who* is giving us a ride?"

Response Notes

LESSON 20

Students will read an author's recollection of a chance meeting to gather more information about the subject.

BACKGROUND KNOWLEDGE

A couple of references in this selection need explanation. Tell students that Jackie Robinson may have been spurned by those who opposed integration, but he was a sought-after speaker by groups who were working on behalf of civil rights. In the selection, Robinson mentions that he's returning from speaking at the National Conference of Christians and Jews, a group that sought to break down barriers that divided people. Elston Howard was the first African American to play for the Yankees. The reference to the Bruins alludes to the fact that Robinson played football for the UCLA Bruins.

VOCABULARY

bellowed yelled
pretense pretending something isn't what it is
candidly honestly
ventured tried, said
brouhaha huge fuss

Use the Word Splash activity found on page 272.

Before

CRITICAL READING SKILL
Evaluating Information from Someone's Brief Encounter In this lesson, the author creates word pictures, like a series of snapshots, to capture small moments that reveal the subject. Like Sharon Robinson's account, Nan Birmingham's recollections reveal as much about the author herself as Jackie Robinson. Birmingham does not recognize Robinson and mistakes him for another ballplayer. As students begin reading, tell them to think about what it would be like to meet Jackie Robinson for the first time.

During

MAKING INFERENCES As students read, they will be hearing about things Jackie Robinson said and did, as told from the point of view of a woman he sat next to on a plane. Tell students that there's more to be revealed about Robinson than just what the narrator tells us. Encourage them to "read between the lines" and draw conclusions from his words and actions about his character.

EXTRA SUPPORT

Differentiation Help students who are having difficulty making inferences about Robinson by going over the selection together. For example, ask students to review his response to the author's plea for a ride to Westchester on page 67 *("You wouldn't have to do that," he said with a smile.)* Ask students what this "snapshot" reveals. (Robinson readily helped others, in spite of the circumstances or inconvenience.)

Write students' responses on the board or on chart paper. Then have them go back and mark the examples in the text before they answer the first question on page 68.

Quick Assess

* Were students able to identify clues to Jackie Robinson's character in this selection?

* Did they come up with three words to describe Robinson based on the selections in this unit? Did they give reasons for choosing those words?

Response Notes

"Man, am I!" he beamed. "I can't wait to tell my mama. She's in the hospital. This is going to make her feel real good."

The morning light and exhaustion stripped away pretense, and we spoke candidly about our families and children as the car nosed north. "It's funny," Robinson said with a touch of sadness, "you think you're doing things right and it all goes wrong. One of my kids has a knack for trouble. I don't know why. He's going to be all right. I know that. But he's rebelled against everything my wife and I have stood for."

"Mr. Robinson," I ventured, "weren't you a rebel? A rebel with a cause?"

"No," he said. "I just wanted to play ball."

Home, finally. Jackie Robinson carried my suitcase to the door and wished me well. He motioned to the soldier to move up front, and both waved goodbye as the car edged out of sight.

Sitting with a cup of coffee I wondered how to explain to my kids who this hero was; how to explain the brouhaha 40 years ago over a black man playing in the major leagues. Then I thought about the courage it took for that young man to walk into that stadium and face a hostile crowd—alone. I'll tell my children about that man.

The perspective of a stranger can focus attention on the details of the story rather than on the person who tells it.

✳ What is your impression of Jackie Robinson after reading this story?

_____
_____
_____

✳ With a partner, select three key words that could characterize Jackie Robinson, based on the perspectives you have read in this unit. Write those words with a brief reason for each one here.

_____
_____
_____
_____
_____

After

SOCIAL STUDIES CONNECTION

Have students find other anecdotal stories from the Civil Rights Era, such as accounts of the Freedom Riders or articles that tell about the integration of schools in Arkansas, Alabama, or Boston. Students can pick one particular account to analyze or they can pick multiple accounts of an incident and compare and contrast the points of view for a more complete picture.

UNIT 5
FOCUSING ON LANGUAGE AND CRAFT

Lessons 21–25 pages 70–84

UNIT OVERVIEW
Students learn about poetry's form and techniques as well as its power to express feelings and connect people.

KEY IDEA
Poets draw inspiration from the world around them and use poetic techniques to communicate their message.

CRITICAL READING SKILLS
by lesson
21 Interacting with the text
22 Focusing on audience
23 Understanding metaphor
24 Identifying allusion
25 Connecting to the text

WRITING ACTIVITIES
by lesson
21 Complete a questionnaire about personal writing habits and write a poem.
22 Write an epistle poem.
23 Draw and write about a metaphor in a poem.
24 List ideas for a poem.
25 Use a journal entry to inspire a poem.

Focusing on Language and Craft

In this unit, you will read **personal narrative and poetry** in which writers express personal thoughts and make connections. You will hear the voices of contemporary teenagers and established poets, like Langston Hughes. As you read, you will also be writing. Sometimes you will write back to the writers themselves; sometimes you will write to people you want to hear you, to know you for who you are, inside.

The poet e. e. cummings said, "To be nobody but yourself—in a world which is doing its best, night and day, to make you like everybody else—means to fight the hardest battle which any human being can fight; and never stop fighting." All the narrators in this unit are trying to be "nobody but" themselves.

Literature

- from *Locomotion* by Jacqueline Woodson (novel excerpt)

Lonnie C. Motion, a young poet, describes conflicting influences that encourage and discourage him to write poetry in his own true voice.

- "Mother to Son" by Langston Hughes (poem)

This famous poem presents sharp, metaphoric images while communicating the reality of a mother who has faced unending challenges.

- "Long Live Langston" from *Bronx Masquerade* by Nikki Grimes (novel excerpt)

Poetry student Wesley Boone praises Langston Hughes for inspiring pride and self-worth during the Harlem Renaissance.

- "Porscha's Journal" from *Bronx Masquerade* by Nikki Grimes (novel excerpt)

Through making a connection with a new friend, a young student is able to express her innermost feelings about a personal loss.

ASSESSMENT To assess student learning in this unit, see pages 233 and 262.

LESSON 21

Students will analyze a poem's language, structure, and meaning to articulate their writing persona and write an original poem.

BACKGROUND KNOWLEDGE

Students will read a poem about writing poetry. To help students connect to the piece, solicit their impressions of reading and writing poetry. For example, ask: *Have you ever written a poem? What was it about? Was it easy or hard? Why?*

List students' answers on the board. Explain that poetry is a demanding writing form. Compared to other forms, it relies on few rules yet requires masterful use of language. Therefore, initial reactions to poetry can range from excitement to the bewildered "I don't get it." Tell students that they are going to read a poem about someone who discovers what poetry can do for him.

VOCABULARY

locomotion the ability to move around from place to place

Explain that the excerpt is from a book titled *Locomotion,* after the nickname of the main character Lonnie Collins Motion. Why might someone be named Locomotion? (He might be energetic or he might move from place to place.)

LESSON 21 PEOPLE ARE POEMS

In Jacqueline Woodson's book *Locomotion,* we learn that Lonnie Collins Motion, nicknamed "Locomotion," lost both his parents when he was seven years old. Now eleven, he's learning how to put his feelings on paper, into poems.

Here's Locomotion's first poem. Read it once just to find out what it says.

Response Notes

Who's Miss Edna?

from *Locomotion* by Jacqueline Woodson

This whole book's a poem 'cause every time I try to
tell the whole story my mind goes *Be quiet!*
Only it's not my mind's voice,
it's *Miss Edna's* over and over and over
Be quiet!

I'm not a really loud kid, I swear. I'm just me and
sometimes I maybe make a little bit of noise.
If I was a grown-up maybe Miss Edna
wouldn't always be telling me to be quiet
but I'm eleven and maybe eleven's just noisy.

Maybe twelve's quieter.

But when Miss Edna's voice comes on, the ideas in my
head go out like a candle and all you see left is this little
string of smoke that disappears real quick
before I even have a chance to find out
what it's trying to say.

So this whole book's a poem because poetry's short and

this whole book's a poem 'cause Ms. Marcus says
write it down before it leaves your brain.
I tell her about the smoke and she says
Good, Lonnie, write that.
Not a whole lot of people be saying *Good, Lonnie* to me
so I write the string-of-smoke thing down real fast.
Ms. Marcus says *We'll worry about line breaks later.*

Write fast, Lonnie, Ms. Marcus says.
And I'm thinking Yeah, I better write fast before Miss
Edna's voice comes on and blows my candle idea out.

Before

CRITICAL READING SKILL

Interacting with the Text First, recall that to interact with the text is to become involved with it: listening to what it says, asking questions about it, rereading it, and marking it. Then, read aloud the poem, which is called "Poem Book," reminding students that it is written in the voice of an eleven-year-old boy.

Explain that, although most poetry is shorter than prose, it should be read multiple times to gain understanding. Tell students that when they first read a poem they don't have to think about its message or figure out its meaning. Instead, they should focus on the words that reveal the subject.

RESPONSE NOTES Have students highlight the words, phrases, and lines in the poem that form the strongest mental pictures. They should also jot down questions (Who's Miss Edna?) about anything they don't understand.

❄ Now go back and read the poem again, this time using the **Response Notes** column to write what you're thinking or wondering as you read.

❄ With a partner or group, talk about the poem. Here are some questions to get you started:
- What do you know about Lonnie so far?
- What do you think Lonnie means about the "string-of-smoke thing"?
- Can you guess yet who Miss Edna is? If so, who is she to Lonnie?

❄ In this unit, along with reading the thoughts, ideas, and personal stories of teenagers, you're also going to write your own pieces. Before starting to write, here is a questionnaire that will help you picture yourself as a writer. Jot down your responses in the space provided.

Myself as Writer

1. When I write, the things I need to have around me are . . .

2. If there is one thing I can't stand when I'm writing, it's . . .

3. When I have to write assignments for school, generally, I . . .

4. When I have to write quickly, as in an essay test, I usually . . .

5. If I were ever going to get serious about writing, it would probably be about this kind of writing (tell what it is):

6. I (always or never) outline before I write. (Tell which and explain.)

7. If I had to classify myself as one kind of writer, it would be . . .

ABOUT THE AUTHOR
Jacqueline Woodson was born in 1963 in Ohio and raised in South Carolina and Brooklyn, New York. The ethnic and socioeconomic diversity of her Brooklyn neighborhood provided inspiration for her novels and picture books, and Woodson's works for young adults have been praised for addressing difficult issues. *Locomotion,* which is excerpted here, is the recipient of a Coretta Scott King Author Honor. Students might be interested to know that Woodson did not like to read poetry when she was young! See http://www.jacquelinewoodson.com.

TEACHING TIP
Collaboration To complete the discussion prompt collaboratively, separate students into groups of three to create a response triangle.

❄ Distribute a large sheet of paper to each group and have students draw a large triangle on it.

❄ Have each student write a bulleted question from the *Daybook* prompt at their nearest triangle corner.

❄ Next each student writes an answer to the question.

❄ Then the group rotates the triangle. Each student answers the question that is nearest him or her.

❄ Have each group share its completed triangle with the class.

During

WRITING SUPPORT
Discovering My Writing Identity
Remind students that people often use poetry as a process of self-discovery. Encourage students to answer the questions to learn more about their personal style.

You may want to lead students through the questionnaire, explaining the questions and giving time for students to respond.

❄ For Questions 1 and 2, ask: *What makes it easy or hard to write—having a phone to call someone, a comfortable chair, a snack, or a drink? What else?*

❄ For Question 3, ask: *Do you start right away or put it off? Do you feel challenged or afraid?*

❄ For Question 4, ask: *Does your mind freeze up or do you try to relax?*

❄ For Question 5, give examples of kinds of writing: investigative reporting, poetry, novels, interviews, screenplays and so on.

❄ For Question 6, explain that outlining is a kind of prewriting.

❄ For Question 7, offer examples of kinds of writers: funny, serious, imaginative, honest, and so on.

EXTRA SUPPORT

Differentiation Students who feel limited by this space or overwhelmed by drawing should use other materials such as a digital camera, poster board, pictures from magazines or the Internet, markers, or colored pencils.

❋ Look for some connections among the answers you wrote on page 71. Do one or two aspects of you as a writer emerge? Draw a picture of yourself as a writer. The drawing might be symbolic, impressionistic, or realistic.

❋ Explain your picture and tell how it represents you as a writer.

_____
_____
_____
_____
_____
_____
_____
_____

WRITING SUPPORT

Visual Representation For the first prompt on page 72, help them make connections between their answers and their representation. Say: *Use your answers for adding details to your drawing. Try to picture yourself as you write.*

Using think-alouds, offer examples for each type of drawing given in the prompt.

❋ For symbolic, you might say: *I could draw an animal that goes with my personality. I'm quiet and I like to write by myself, so I'm kind of like a turtle in its shell.*

❋ For realistic, you might say: *I am an impatient writer, so I could show myself crossing my arms and tapping my foot, like I'm waiting for an idea.*

❋ For impressionistic, you might say: *I get excited when I have a good idea, so I could draw myself with a lot of squiggly lines to make the viewer feel my high energy.*

At the beginning of the book *Locomotion,* Lonnie writes,

> Name all the people
> You're always thinking about
> People are poems.

In this lesson, you will write a poem about the people "you're always thinking about." They can be family, friends, teachers, celebrities, sports figures, whoever captures your attention.

To plan your writing:

- Begin by just clustering their names in a web.
- In the same oval, write a word or phrase that describes that person.
- Then write the name of something you associate with that individual on a spoke.

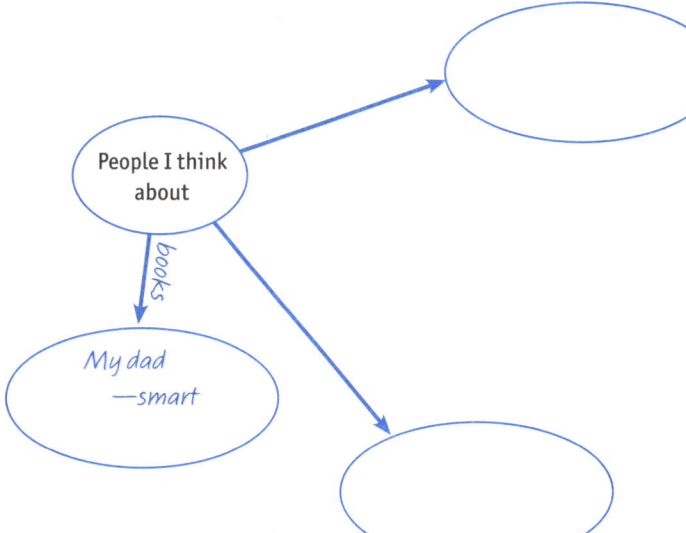

TEACHING TIP

Collaboration Have students work in pairs to brainstorm their clusters. If students get "stuck" trying to find associations, encourage them to question each other. For example: *Picture yourself with the person. Where are you? What things are in the picture? Or, of what does this person make you think? How does he or she act?*

Quick Assess

* Can students use details to describe themselves as writers? Do students' clusters:

  - have at least three names?
  - have descriptive words for each name?
  - have something that is associated with each person?

WRITING SUPPORT

Creating Associations Model the prewriting steps for the people poem (page 73).

* Explain that "people you're always thinking about" could be someone you know now, have known in the past, or are interested in (such as a famous person).

* Make your own list of a few people on the board. To help students follow your thinking, include someone the students would know, e.g., a school staff member or community leader. As you list each person, explain the association you have made.

* Model thinking of a descriptive word or phrase for one person. For example: *Karl, the custodian, always helps me when I lock myself out of the classroom. I'll write, "Helps with a smile."*

* Model creating an association with the person. For example: *When I think of Karl, I think of a key, because that's what he uses to help me. Karl's association is a key.*

FOCUSING ON LANGUAGE AND CRAFT

WRITER'S CRAFT

Line Breaks Before students discuss their poems, briefly point out line breaks in the poem from *Locomotion*.

❉ Ask a volunteer to read the excerpt on *Daybook* page 74. Have the volunteer pause briefly between each line.

❉ On the board, copy the poem, but break the lines in a different way. For example:

*Ms. Marcus says line breaks
help us figure
out what
…*

❉ Ask another volunteer to read the reconfigured poem. Then ask: *Is the poem different this time? Why?* (Possible answers: it looks or sounds different, its rhythm is different)

❉ Return to the excerpt and point out the third line "line breaks help." Ask: *How do the line breaks help readers understand the poet's meaning?*

❉ Direct students to experiment with altering the line breaks in their own poems.

Writers can use poetry to express their thoughts and feelings.

❉ Using some of the names and words from your list or cluster, write a poem about the people you think about often. You might title it "People Are Poems" or another title you choose.

❉ Share your poem with your partner or group. Notice how different people chose to write their poems. Remember to frame your comments in positive ways. Talk about the decisions you each made about what to write. Did you all break your poems up into lines? Here's what Lonnie says about that:

> Ms. Marcus
> says
> line breaks help
> us figure out
> what matters
> to the poet
> *Don't jumble your ideas*
> Ms. Marcus says
> *Every line*
> should count.

Ask yourself: does every line in my poem count? If not, you can always change it. That's the beauty of writing. You can always make changes when you think of a way to make it say more clearly what you mean.

APPLYING THE STRATEGY Have students choose one person from their people poem as the sole subject of a new poem. Direct students to do additional prewriting, adding description and building on previous associations. After students have revised their work, invite them to give or send a finished copy to their subject.

FURTHER READING Encourage students to search for poetry by and about young adults. Some possible sources are:

❉ www.teenink.com

❉ www.merlynspen.org

❉ www.thewritesource.com/publish

❉ Aguado, Bill (Ed.). *Paint Me Like I Am: Teen Poems from WritersCorps.* Harper-Tempest, 2003.

❉ Soto, Gary. *A Fire in My Hands.* Harcourt, 2006.

Students can create a notebook section or computer file to copy and keep titles and reviews of poems that they like.

LESSON 22: EPISTLE POEMS

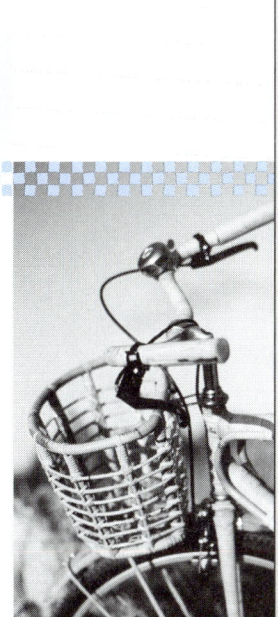

Ms. Marcus, Lonnie C. Motion's teacher, taught the class about a different kind of poem. It's called an **epistle poem**, which means a letter written as a poem. Here's how Lonnie describes it in a letter to his father. (His father and mother had both died in a fire.)

from *Locomotion* by Jacqueline Woodson

Hey Pops,
Today our teacher showed us this poem by this poet guy named Langston Hughes. It made me remember something. That long time ago when you read us that goodnight poem about that guy who loved his friend…

Lonnie goes on to explain to his father that an epistle poem is written as a letter. In his letter, he says,

I didn't know a letter could be a kind of poem. So now I'm writing one to you to say that even though we can't do stuff like go to the park on our bikes…even though we can't do that kind of stuff no more, I haven't forgot none of it. I'm gonna go see if I can find that poem about the guy loving his friend. I hope it's by Langston Hughes.
Love, Locomotion

❄ Read Lonnie's epistle poem to his father again and use the **Response Notes** column to respond to such questions as these:
- Where is it suggested that Lonnie's father is dead?
- Are there any places in the poem where Lonnie's use of nonstandard English or spelling makes it hard to understand? If so, mark them.

❄ Talk with your group about Lonnie's epistle poem. Use these suggestions to get started.
- Talk about your Response Notes.
- Talk about whether you think Lonnie's epistle poem is a poem.
   What makes it seem like a poem?
   What makes it seem like ordinary prose?
- Talk about whether you ever "talk" to someone who isn't right there with you.

EPISTLE POEMS 75

LESSON 22

Students will read and analyze an epistle poem and use it as a model to write an original poem.

BACKGROUND KNOWLEDGE

Ask students to share an occasion when they wrote and sent a letter to someone. Ask students why they sent a letter instead of using e-mail or a telephone. (Possible answers: wanted to give something handwritten; needed to use a formal format)

Tell students that they will be reading an epistle. Explain that an epistle is a type of literary composition, such as a poem, written in the form of a letter. Lonnie, the main character in *Locomotion*, has endured much in his short life: his parents died in a fire, his sister was sent to live with a wealthy family, and Lonnie was sent to live with Miss Edna. Writing poetry is how Lonnie expresses his feelings and copes with his ever-changing life.

VOCABULARY

Langston Hughes (1902-1967) a poet who was an influential presence in the Harlem Renaissance, a movement based in New York City that celebrated African American life and culture

Point out that *Locomotion* makes a reference to "this poet guy named Langston Hughes," about whom they will read in Lesson 23.

Before

CRITICAL READING SKILL

Focusing on Audience Ask a volunteer to read the letter poem aloud. Then explain how to make inferences about this poem's audience. Say: *You can make inferences about the audience, or to whom a poem is written.* Then ask students: *Can you tell anything about Lonnie's father from this poem?* (Possible answers: He read poetry, he is missed by Lonnie)

RESPONSE NOTES

Before directing students to complete the **Response Notes**, explain each bulleted question.

❄ Tell students to mark the words that suggest that Lonnie's father is dead.

❄ Explain that nonstandard English is what some people call any variety of English that does not follow all of the grammar and spelling rules we expect to see and hear in formal situations. English has many *registers* or *levels* that we use depending on audience and purpose. When you're speaking with your friends, you might use *colloquial* language or *slang*. For example, the expression "Sup?" is a nonstandard contraction of "What's up?" and slang for "How are you?"

FOCUSING ON LANGUAGE AND CRAFT 75

TEACHING TIP

Collaboration Have partners read each other's poems aloud so students can hear their work. Tell students that if their voice doesn't sound natural, the way they would talk to their audience, they can revise it.

Quick Assess

* Do students' poems follow the conventions of a letter?
* Do students give clues about the intended audience?
* Do students use natural-sounding language?
* Do students' revisions show thoughtful changes?

WRITING YOUR OWN EPISTLE POEM

* Write an epistle poem. You might write to a grandparent, your mother, your father, a friend, or a coach. When you write your epistle poem, keep these tips in mind:
  - Write it in the form of a letter.
  - Make clear to whom you're writing and whether the person is alive or not.
  - Write as Lonnie did, from the heart.
  - Use the language that you use in everyday speech—comfortable, informal language like Lonnie used in his poems.

* Share your poem with a partner or your group. See how it feels to read your poem aloud. Does it sound as if it is in your own voice? Does it sound like you are speaking, or does it sound artificial or false?

REVISING

* As you read your work aloud, you might find that there are words or phrases that you'd like to change. **Revising** your work is part of the act of writing. Look carefully at your epistle poem and make any changes you think would make it a stronger letter poem. Use these suggestions for revising:
  - Look for places where you could be more specific.
  - Add sensory language when it is appropriate.
  - Mention your relationship with the person you are writing to.
  - Be sure you are writing honestly; remember that Ms. Marcus told her class "every line should count."

* When you have made the changes you want to make, copy your poem and sign it.

An epistle poem helps you focus on your audience because it is written to a specific person.

76 LESSON 22

During

WRITER'S CRAFT

Written Conventions Briefly review the features of a letter:

* The salutation is usually "Dear," but it can be informal.
* The body paragraphs contain the message.
* The closing is the writer's personal farewell or "goodbye."

After

ART CONNECTION After students have completed their poems, invite them to draw a picture of the recipient of the letter reading the letter poem. Students should also write a reflection on the relationship between the epistle poem and the drawing. Display the epistles and drawings together.

ALTERING THE POINT OF VIEW Invite students to pretend that they are the recipient of the epistle they wrote. Students can then write an epistle back to themselves. Remind students that an epistle should reflect the true voice of its writer, so they must imagine they are the other person. They should consider the person's background, age, health, education, and experience to help them develop a realistic voice.

LESSON 23: LANGSTON HUGHES

In *Bronx Masquerade* by Nikki Grimes, Wesley "Bad Boy" Boone explains that his teacher, Mr. Ward, had the class reading poetry from the Harlem Renaissance for about a month. "Then Mr. Ward asked us to write an essay about it. Make sense to you? Me neither. I mean, what's the point of studying *poetry* and then writing *essays*? So I wrote a bunch of poems instead."

That was the beginning of the poetry revolution. Wesley not only wrote "a bunch of poems," he wanted to read them to the class. The first poem he wrote was about one of the most important of the Harlem Renaissance poets, **Langston Hughes.** Remember that Lonnie mentioned "this poet guy" Hughes in his epistle poem to his father.

Before you read Wesley's poem in Lesson 24, however, read a poem by Langston Hughes. That way you will share with Wesley and the other students what they had been reading in class. Note images of what life has been like for the mother in your **Response Notes.**

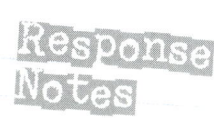

Mother to Son by Langston Hughes

Well, son, I'll tell you:
Life for me ain't been no crystal stair.
It's had tacks in it,
And splinters,
And boards torn up,
And places with no carpet on the floor—
Bare.
But all the time
I'se been a-climbin' on,
And reachin' landin's,
And turnin' corners,
And sometimes goin' in the dark
Where there ain't been no light.
So, boy, don't you turn back.
Don't you set down on the steps.
'Cause you finds it's kinder hard.
Don't you fall now—
For I'se still goin', honey,
I'se still climbin',
And life for me ain't been no crystal stair.

LANGSTON HUGHES 77

LESSON 23

Students will read "Mother to Son" by Langston Hughes to analyze the poet's use of everyday language and metaphor.

BACKGROUND KNOWLEDGE

Ask students if they remember, from the previous lesson, the meaning of *colloquial* or any examples of colloquial language. If necessary, remind students that colloquial language is informal and reflects the way that people speak.

Then explain that students will read a colloquial poem that reflects the way African Americans spoke in New York City in the 1920s. This historic period was known as the Harlem Renaissance, and one of its most famous writers was Langston Hughes. Like the epistle poem in the previous lesson, this poem involves a child and parent, but it is written from mother to son.

VOCABULARY

crystal high quality glass

Explain that crystal objects, such as fancy water glasses, jewelry, or knick-knacks, can be very beautiful and expensive. Make a list of the qualities of crystal: smooth or sharp-edged (cut crystal), clear, colorless, sparkling.

Before

CRITICAL READING SKILL

Understanding Metaphor Before reading the poem, tell students that it contains a metaphor. Then define the term. Say: *A writer is using a metaphor when he or she describes one thing as being something else.* For an example, you may want to return to "Poem Book" on *Daybook* page 70, noting that Lonnie used a candle as a metaphor for his ideas.

Then read the poem aloud. Ask: *What is the metaphor, or the comparison of two things, in the poem?* (life, a staircase) If students don't immediately volunteer answers, ask questions to elicit clues, such as: *What images are in the poem?* (stairs, floor, landings) *What do all of these things describe?* (a staircase) *About what is the mother talking to her son?* (life, as stated in the second line)

RESPONSE NOTES As students reread the poem, direct them to think about what each part of the metaphor says about the mother's life. For example: *The first image is a crystal stair. What could stairs symbolize?* (moving up) *The mother's stairs are not crystal. What does the image say about the mother's life?* (Her life is difficult and full of obstacles.)

FOCUSING ON LANGUAGE AND CRAFT 77

ABOUT THE POET

Langston Hughes was born in Joplin, Missouri, in 1902 and raised in Cleveland, Ohio. He started writing poetry in the eighth grade and eventually moved to New York City to attend Columbia University. Throughout his life, he wrote poems, novels, short stories, and musicals, mostly about the African American experience. Though he lived until 1967, Hughes's work is most often associated with the Harlem Renaissance period of the 1920s (which students will learn about in more detail in *Daybook* Lesson 24).

TEACHING TIP

Collaboration Pair or group students who need extra support with on- or above-level students. Each student can contribute an image to the drawing. Then have the students collaborate to form the descriptive sentence. Students can share their drawings and sentences with the class.

DRAWING THE POEM

* Using the images in the poem as guidelines, draw what life has been like for the mother in this poem. Under your drawing, write a sentence that you think describes the mother.

During

IMAGERY Discuss how the poem's individual images give hints to the mother's life. Read the first five lines of the poem aloud, pausing after each image. When you pause, have a volunteer draw the image. Then ask: *How do you picture the woman? Can you imagine her trying to climb the steps? Does she look energized or tired?* Direct students to complete the drawing and description.

DISCUSSION

- What do you think Hughes means by the terms *splinter* and *crystal stair*?
- In your group, talk about how life has been for the mother in the poem. Use the images of *splinters* and *crystal stair* in your discussion.
- What do you think is the most important thing the mother tells the son?
- ✱ Write a paragraph in which you talk about some of the *splinters* or *crystal stairs* in your own life or in the lives of your parents.

Poetic metaphors can convey powerful thoughts in everyday language.

WRITING SUPPORT

Analyzing Metaphors Guide students through the first discussion question (page 79). Brainstorm associations with *tacks* and *splinters*, such as painful or sharp shards of glass, and *crystal*, such as finely faceted, translucent and costly. Then ask: *Where would you find crystal stairs? What is the mother saying about her experience?*

EXTRA SUPPORT

Differentiation If students are having difficulty speculating about the mother's life, focus the discussion on contemporary life. For example: *Splinters, tacks, and darkness make it hard for someone to move around. Have you known someone who wanted to "get somewhere" in life but found it hard? What challenges did he or she have?* (Possible answers: lack of money or education.) Then have the students consider which challenges the mother may have faced.

Quick Assess

- ✱ Do students' drawings use images from the poem?
- ✱ Do students' descriptions reflect the message of the poem—that life has been hard for this woman?

After

PERFORMING A POEM Have groups perform "Mother to Son." Encourage creativity in performance, as long as it emphasizes or supports the message: a varied number of voices on each line, sound effects or rhythmic accompaniment, movement, and so forth.

READING/WRITING CONNECTION The challenges of life is a common discussion topic between parents and children. Ask students what messages their parents or elders give them about life. For example: be serious and focused, life was harder for me when I was your age, etc.

Then have students think about what they would like to tell their elders about their own life. Is it harder than their parents think? Easier? Have students choose a metaphor for their own lives and write a poem in the style of "Mother to Son." Students should use imagery and be attentive to line breaks and conciseness.

LESSON 24

Students will analyze a poem's subject, language, and rhythm to generate a list of topics for writing original poems.

BACKGROUND KNOWLEDGE

Students will read a tribute to Langston Hughes and the Harlem Renaissance. If possible, convey the mood of the times by playing jazz of the era, such as Duke Ellington's "Echoes of Harlem" (at PBS's website: www.pbs.org). Or, display fine art from the era, such as William Johnson's *Street Life, Harlem* (at the Smithsonian's Web site: www.si.edu/resource/).

VOCABULARY

Lenox and 7th Harlem streets

Jesse Semple a character in many of Hughes's stories

Sweet Flypaper of Life a book of Harlem photographs by Hughes and photographer Ray DeCarava

Apollo a theater in Harlem

Renaissance man a person who is accomplished in many areas, both arts and sciences. This has a double meaning because Hughes was active during the Harlem Renaissance.

Speculate with students on the possible significance of each term in a poem about this era. For example: *Perhaps the Apollo was where exciting new music was played.*

LESSON 24 FINDING IDEAS

Every Friday, Mr. Ward, the teacher in *Bronx Masquerade,* holds an Open Mike session for his students to read their poems. Here's the poem Wesley "Bad Boy" Boone read after the class studied Langston Hughes's poems. In your **Response Notes,** list wording and images you find interesting. Tell why.

Long Live Langston from *Bronx Masquerade*
by Nikki Grimes

Trumpeter of Lenox and 7th
Through Jesse B. Semple,
you simply celebrated
Blues and Be-bop
and being Black before
it was considered hip.
You dipped into
the muddy waters
of the Harlem River
and shouted "taste and see"
that we Black folk be good
at fanning hope
and stoking the fires
of dreams deferred.
You made sure
the world heard
about the beauty of
maple sugar children, and the
artfully tattooed backs of Black
sailors venturing out
to foreign places.
Your Sweet Flypaper of Life
led us past the Apollo and on
through 125th and all the other
Harlem streets you knew like
the black of your hand.
You were a pied-piper, brother man
with poetry as your flute.
It's my honor and pleasure to salute
you, a true Renaissance man
of Harlem.

Before

CRITICAL READING SKILL

Identifying Allusions Read the poem aloud, paying careful attention to the rhythm. Then ask volunteers to reread it, each one reading a sentence aloud. Explain that poets often use images from the world around them to express their thoughts and feelings. This poet was inspired by reading Langston Hughes and wrote a poem about him and the Harlem Renaissance.

Say: *When a writer makes a reference to something famous, he or she makes an allusion.* Then point out an allusion to Harlem, such as "Trumpeter of Lenox and 7th/Through Jesse B. Semple" in the first two lines. Explain: *Someone who is familiar with the Harlem Renaissance will read this allusion and know that the poem is about Hughes and this era.*

RESPONSE NOTES
As students read, encourage them to underline allusions with which they have become familiar and to circle images that they don't understand. When students are finished responding, list phrases they didn't "get" and brainstorm or research possible meanings based on context clues in the poem.

✳ Notice how Wesley Boone got **ideas** from reading. Make a list of things you think could trigger a poem for you. Include things you've read, things you've seen, or encounters with other people.

Save this list for the next lesson.

Poets find inspiration for their poems from the world around them—from their friends and family, from their reading, from the experiences they have had.

FINDING IDEAS 81

ABOUT THE AUTHOR
Nikki Grimes was born in 1950 and raised in New York City. Besides writing numerous novels, picture books, and children's radio shows, she has also taught students about poetry all over the world. In 2006, she received the Coretta Scott King Author Honor for her novel, *Dark Sons,* as well as the Award for Excellence in Poetry for Children from the National Council of Teachers of English.

TEACHING TIP
Harlem Renaissance Note New York City on a U.S. map. Explain that, in the early 1900s, African Americans migrated from southern to northern U.S. cities for better jobs and housing. In Harlem, a New York City neighborhood, many African Americans flourished and a whole new movement of artists, writers, and musicians emerged. Pride was the theme of the times as African Americans were "reborn"—a synonym for *renaissance*—from their previous identity as slaves or oppressed field workers.

Quick Assess
✳ Do students understand that poets get their ideas from the world around them?

During

WRITING SUPPORT
Brainstorming Model using clusters to group types of influences: places, people, books, music, movies and TV, etc. Then use a think-aloud to model how to generate items. For example: *I went to Chinatown for the first time last month. I could write about the interesting things I saw. Or, the first book I read more than once was* The House on Mango Street *because I loved the Esperanza character, etc.*

Students might choose to write about how they are perceived by others versus what they are really like. (See page 83.)

After

WRITING/ART CONNECTION
Have students research an artistic figure from the Harlem Renaissance and create a word and image collage about the artist's life and works.

✳ Literature: Countee Cullen, Zora Neale Hurston
✳ Music: Cab Calloway, Duke Ellington
✳ Visual Arts: Roy DeCarava, Aaron Douglas

FOCUSING ON LANGUAGE AND CRAFT 81

LESSON 25

Students will read a journal excerpt about sharing poetry to make connections with other writers and read their poems in class.

BACKGROUND KNOWLEDGE

Students will read a journal entry by Porscha, another character in *Bronx Masquerade*. Tell students the journal entry is about two girls who don't like each other but don't really know much about each other. Discuss why certain students become quick friends and why others immediately dislike each other. Ask: *Why do some students form friendships and others dislike students they barely know?* Some possible answers are: students judge each other by how they look and act; students feel comfortable with others who have the same kinds of lives; students are competitive and may be threatened by someone who appears smarter, richer, stronger, better-looking, etc.

VOCABULARY

bold fearless; brave

Use the Word Splash blackline master, found on page 272.

LESSON 25 — CONNECTING THROUGH POETRY

Two of the students in Mr. Ward's class, Leslie and Porscha, discovered when they ran into each other in the locker room that they had both lost their mothers. Although they had not liked each other before, they unexpectedly became friends. Their **connection** led them to sharing their poetry in Mr. Ward's class and changed not only how they felt about school, but how they felt about themselves. Read this section of Porscha's journal, written toward the end of the school year.

"Porscha's Journal" from *Bronx Masquerade* by Nikki Grimes

Leslie says I've got to learn to let people in, and I know she's right. Poetry just may be a way to do that. I mean, it worked for Devon, didn't it? And Tyrone. We all got to see another side of them. Even Janelle gets up there—Miss Shyness herself! I've never seen her turn so **bold**, although the boldness only seems to last as long as she's up front reading her poems. Still, that's something. Tyrone was the biggest surprise, though. Who would have guessed he wrote poetry? And he knows his poems by heart, no less.

The first time he got up there, I rolled my eyes like half the sisters in class, certain he was going to spout something lame.... But there was nothing lame about this poem.... It was about what's going on in the world, and about trying to make sense of it. It was a poem by somebody who really thinks about things, and that somebody turned out to be Tyrone. He made me change my mind about him that day. Maybe I can change people's minds about me too. It's worth a shot. I better do it quick, though. There are only a few Open Mike Fridays left before school's out, and the last one will be at assembly, and I don't plan on getting up in front of a whole group of strangers my first time out.

Friday is two days away, and I know exactly what poem I'm going to read.

In Leslie's journal, she recounted her conversation with Porscha. Porscha told Leslie how she was ashamed of her mother and how she died. She had never said good-bye to her mother or forgiven her for dying. The poem that Porscha read to her class during that Friday's Open Mike session ended with the line, "Mom, I finally forgive you. Good-bye, Love, Porscha."

Before

CRITICAL READING SKILL

Connecting with Poetry Discuss the power of making connections. Ask students how they feel when they discover that someone else shares their interests or opinions. When people find that they have something in common, they are more accepting of each other; they are no longer strangers. Explain that these connections also work with fictional characters, both from one character to another and from the character to the reader.

RESPONSE NOTES

Remind students that successful readers read for a purpose. In this case, the purpose is to make connections with Porscha. Does she have the same thoughts that they have? Do they think she is brave? Students can record their feelings in their Response Notes.

What you discover when you read the poems from the sophomores in Mr. Ward's class is that writing and sharing their poetry created a class bond that was powerful. For the first time they saw each other honestly, through the masquerade that had kept them apart before. They saw each other change, growing in understanding of themselves and each other.

* Imagine that you are getting ready to read a poem to your class. Think about the relationships you have with your friends. Think about how you might like to get to know some of the other students whom you don't know too well.

* Look back at the list you made at the end of the last lesson. Feel free to add to it now. Then choose one event from your list—something you did with another person, something you read, something you viewed in a special way—and write about it as a journal entry.

Journal entry for _____ date _____

EXTRA SUPPORT

Differentiation Students may not know what an Open Mike Friday is. In the book *Bronx Masquerade,* students share their poetry with an audience. The event becomes very popular with students. Porscha plans to use the open mike as a way to get her message out in public.

During

PRESENTING A DIFFERENT PERSPECTIVE Prompt students to think about what assumptions others, whom they don't know very well, may make about them based on the way they act or look.

Post these questions on the board:

* What might someone who doesn't know me very well say or think about me?

* What do I wish people knew about me? How could I show that side of me more?

Then encourage them to choose a topic for their journal entry that challenges assumptions about them. Use a think-aloud to model the thought process. For example: *My students might think I'm straight-laced because I dress conservatively. But there's another side of me they don't know, such as when I was in high school, I was in a rock band. I think I'll write about that.*

TEACHING TIP

Classmate Consideration Remind students that sharing poetry can make writers feel vulnerable because they are exposing personal thoughts and feelings. If you are planning on having students read or post their poems, tell them ahead of time. Caution them against writing about a topic that, if shared with others, would make them uncomfortable. Also, direct peer reviewers to always treat each other's work with respect.

Quick Assess

Do students' journal entries:

* have the date recorded?
* focus on one event from the list they compiled in *Daybook* Lesson 24?
* convey their thoughts and feelings about the event?
* use natural language that reflects their everyday speech?

Do students' poems

* use natural language?
* focus on one event or emotion?
* use concrete images and sensory language?

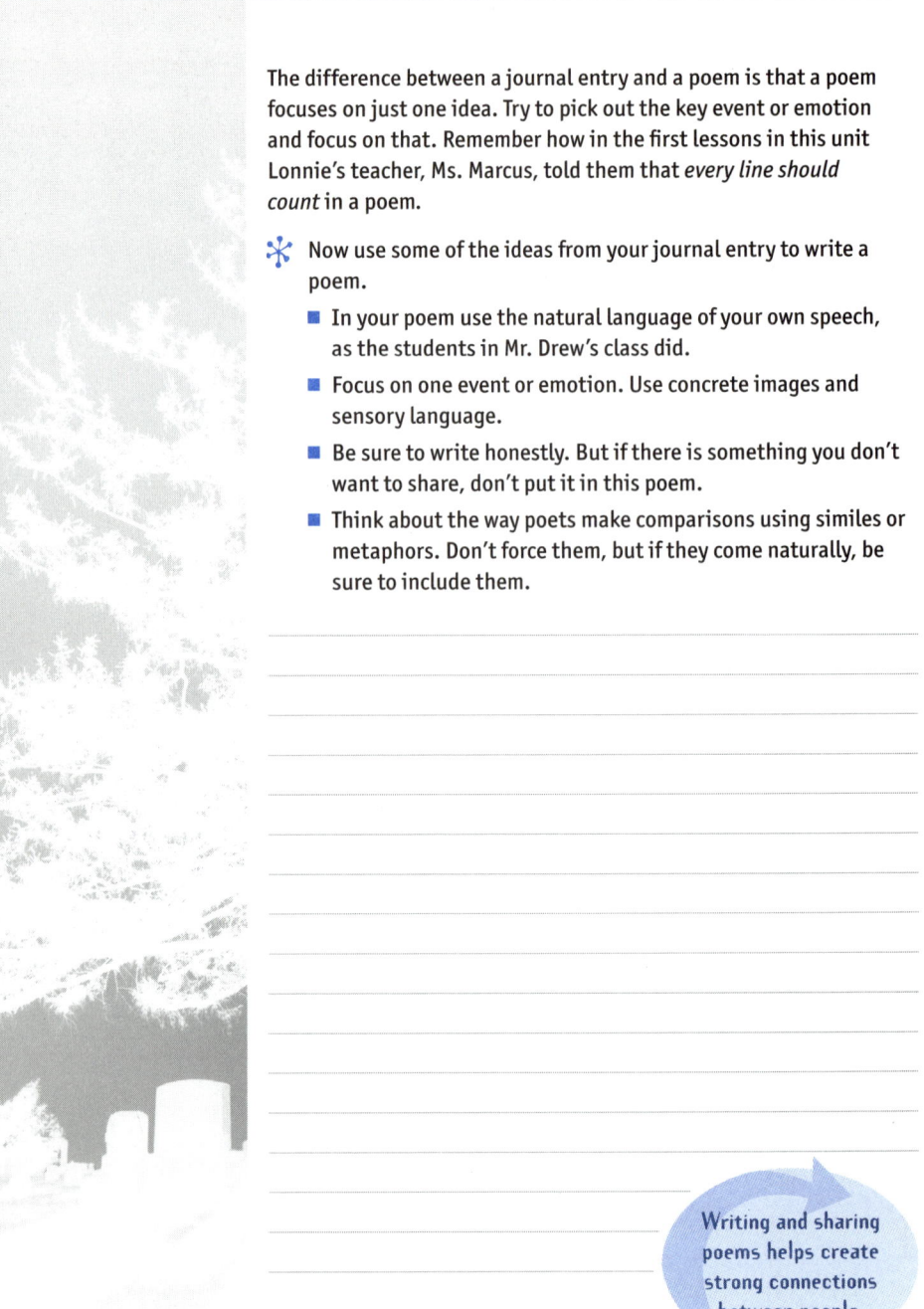

The difference between a journal entry and a poem is that a poem focuses on just one idea. Try to pick out the key event or emotion and focus on that. Remember how in the first lessons in this unit Lonnie's teacher, Ms. Marcus, told them that *every line should count* in a poem.

❋ Now use some of the ideas from your journal entry to write a poem.
  ▪ In your poem use the natural language of your own speech, as the students in Mr. Drew's class did.
  ▪ Focus on one event or emotion. Use concrete images and sensory language.
  ▪ Be sure to write honestly. But if there is something you don't want to share, don't put it in this poem.
  ▪ Think about the way poets make comparisons using similes or metaphors. Don't force them, but if they come naturally, be sure to include them.

Writing and sharing poems helps create strong connections between people.

After

LISTENING/SPEAKING CONNECTION Hold a Poetry Friday in the class. Invite volunteers to read their poems aloud. Afterward, have students discuss what they learned from each other's poems. Or, have students respond in a journal entry about what it was like to read and/or hear other students' poems.

PUBLISHING Encourage students to submit their poems for online or print publishing. See page 74 for ideas.

UNIT 6
STUDYING AN AUTHOR

Lessons 26-30, pages 86-100

UNIT OVERVIEW
In this unit, students examine the impact of Yoshiko Uchida's life experiences on her writing.

KEY IDEA
Writers draw on their experiences in life. Exploring an author's life experiences helps readers appreciate the author's themes and craft.

CRITICAL READING SKILLS
by lesson

26 Analyzing a writer's heritage
27 Exploring a writer's identity
28 Studying a writer's language
29 Identifying a writer's themes
30 Discovering a writer's purpose

WRITING ACTIVITIES
by lesson

26 Write a letter from the author's perspective.
27 List information about the author's identity.
28 Respond to the author's use of sensory language.
29 Write a journal entry that connects the author's theme to personal experience.
30 Summarize an author's purpose and use a graphic organizer to summarize an author's work.

Studying an Author

For a good part of her childhood, **Yoshiko Uchida** felt very much alone. She was born in Alameda, California, the daughter of two Japanese immigrants. Because her parents were Japanese and she was American, she sometimes felt as if she didn't belong. To avoid getting bored, young Yoshiko turned to writing. She started out writing stories about Japanese and Japanese American children. When she was in her early twenties, she published many of her articles and folk tales about Japan. Later, she switched her focus and began writing about Japanese Americans and their experiences before, during, and after World War II.

In this unit you'll explore the works of Yoshiko Uchida. As you read, watch for questions, experiences, and feelings that remind you of yourself. How is your search for an identity similar to that of Uchida?

Literature

■ **"The Princess of Light"** by Yoshiko Uchida (folk tale excerpt)

This story tells of the miraculous arrival of a child and riches to an elderly, childless couple.

■ *The Invisible Thread* by Yoshiko Uchida (autobiography excerpt)

This excerpt recounts the author's early experiences of being torn between two cultures.

■ *Journey Home* by Yoshiko Uchida (novel excerpt)

This brief excerpt tells about a young girl's terrifying experience in a desert internment camp.

■ *Desert Exile* by Yoshiko Uchida (memoir excerpt)

As an American-born child of Japanese parents, the author relates her mixed feelings as she departs from a Japanese internment camp.

ASSESSMENT See page 234 for a writing prompt based on this unit.

LESSON 26

Students will read a Japanese folk tale to identify the author's beliefs and values about two cultures.

BACKGROUND KNOWLEDGE
Remind students that folk tales are very old stories that have been told and retold for many years. Most folk tales were handed down from generation to generation before they were ever written down as a way of teaching the younger generation the values and beliefs of their culture. Have students recall folk tales they have heard before, particularly ones from their own culture. Invite volunteers to recount the tales as classmates guess at the values and traditions that the folk tale might pass down. Explain that the folk tale they are about to read is from the Japanese culture and the two main characters embody aspects of life greatly valued by the Japanese. Invite students to reflect on those aspects of life as they read "The Princess of Light."

VOCABULARY
thicket a place where plants grow very close together

shrine a place for worship

Oya-oya! Japanese exclamation meaning "my goodness!"

After discussing the definitions, have students use each word in a sentence.

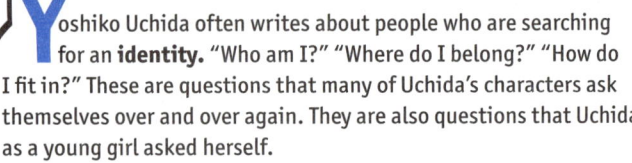

LESSON 26 A WRITER'S HERITAGE

Yoshiko Uchida often writes about people who are searching for an **identity**. "Who am I?" "Where do I belong?" "How do I fit in?" These are questions that many of Uchida's characters ask themselves over and over again. They are also questions that Uchida as a young girl asked herself.

For Yoshiko Uchida, the search for an identity began some two thousand miles from home. Determined to find her identity, Uchida traveled to Japan. While there, she spent most of her time learning everything she could about Japan—its customs, its history, and its people. During this period she found part of the answer to the question, "Who am I?"

Read this excerpt from the folk tale "The Princess of Light." As you read, underline words and phrases that show Uchida's respect for Japanese customs and history. In your **Response Notes**, mention any personal connections you can make to this story.

from "The Princess of Light" by Yoshiko Uchida

Once upon a time, there was an old man and an old woman who lived in a small village in Japan. Their little wooden house with the low thatched roof stood nestled against a hillside covered with trees. Each day the old man strapped his straw sandals on his feet and went out to the nearby bamboo thicket to cut down long, slender stalks of bamboo. When he brought them home, the old woman would help him cut and polish the smooth stalks. Then together they would make bamboo vases, baskets, flutes, and many beautiful ornaments which they could sell in the village.

They were good, kind, and honest people, and they worked very hard. They were happy, but they were lonesome, for they had no children. Both of them wanted a child more than anything else in the world.

"Oh, if only we had a little boy or a little girl, how happy we would be," sighed the old man.

"Yes, wouldn't that be wonderful!" answered the old woman. "I would rather have a child than all the riches on earth!"

And so each day they both knelt at the little shrine in the corner of their room, and prayed that some day they would be granted a child.

Now one day when the old man went out into the bamboo thicket, he saw one stalk which was shining so brightly it looked as though it were made of gold. He hurried toward it and looked at it closely, but he could not tell what made it shine.

Response Notes: This reminds me of another folk tale I've read.

Before

CRITICAL READING SKILL
Analyzing a Writer's Heritage Have students speculate why a writer might want to write stories about his or her cultural heritage. (Possible answers: to celebrate one's own cultural beliefs and values; to reconnect with those values; to share those values with others) Point out that for the author, Yoshiko Uchida, it was probably "all of the above." Explain that in this lesson, however, students will be looking at different aspects of the Japanese culture that are reflected in the tale, and paying attention to the ways in which the author shows her deep and abiding respect for those aspects of her cultural heritage.

RESPONSE NOTES Remind students to underline the parts of the selection that show the author's respect for her Japanese heritage. Suggest that they explain what they've underlined in their Response Notes. (For example, the name of the child has a very positive connotation.)

"My, what a strange bamboo," said the old man to himself. "Perhaps I'd better see what is inside." So he began to cut it down with the saw which he carried at his side. But suddenly he stopped, for he heard something very strange!

"What was that?" asked the old man. "It sounded like the crying of a baby!"

He straightened his back and looked all around, but he did not see anyone. All he could see were the stalks of bamboo swaying gently in the breeze.

He shook his head slowly and said, "My, I must be getting old to be hearing such strange sounds in a bamboo thicket."

He was turning again toward the shining bamboo when he heard the sound once more. He was sure this time that it was a baby crying, and the sound came right from inside the strange shiny stalk. Quickly he cut down the bamboo and looked inside the hollow of the stalk. There he saw a tiny baby girl! She looked up at the old man and smiled sweetly. And the old man was so surprised at this strange sight, he blinked hard and touched the little girl to see if she were real.

"My goodness! Good gracious! Oya-oya!" was all the old man could say. "This child must have been sent to us straight from heaven," he thought, as he picked her up very carefully. Then he quickly started homeward, for he could scarcely wait to show her to the old woman.

When the old woman saw the beautiful child, she threw up her hands in surprise. "God has been good to us!" she exclaimed. "We must take very good care of our little girl." Then she hurriedly set about spreading a quilt on the floor where she gently laid the new baby.

The next morning the old man was up bright and early. He whistled gaily as he walked toward the bamboo thicket. As he came closer to the spot where he had found the little baby the day before, he saw another bamboo which was shining brightly.

"I wonder if I will find another little baby," thought the old man, as he prepared to cut down the bamboo. He listened for any sound that might be the crying of a child, but he heard only the song of a sparrow as it flew into the thicket. This time, when he cut down the shiny bamboo stalk, a shower of gold coins fell to the ground. They glittered and sparkled, and seemed to tell

ABOUT THE AUTHOR

Yoshiko Uchida was born in California in 1921 and lived there with her family for twenty years. During World War II, when the United States was at war with Japan, President Franklin D. Roosevelt called for the imprisonment of 120,000 Japanese Americans. Yoshiko and her family were forced to leave their home to live in a Japanese internment camp in Utah. Eventually, she and her sister were allowed to leave the camp to further their education. In 1952, Yoshiko received a fellowship to collect folk tales in Japan. Of the experience, she says, ". . . my years in Japan had made me aware of a new dimension to myself as a Japanese American and deepened my respect and admiration for the culture that had made my parents what they were."

EXTRA SUPPORT

Differentiation Support comprehension for visual learners by inviting them to draw storyboards for the folk tale. Invite auditory learners to perform the tale as Readers' Theater. Suggest that kinesthetic learners act out the story with simple props and costumes.

During

MAKING INFERENCES By examining what the author writes, the reader can make inferences about the author's intent for writing. Use this think-aloud to model how to make inferences about the author's intent: *Sometimes writers explicitly state their values in their writing, for example,* I admire my grandmother's bravery in coming to America on her own. *At other times, writers show us what they value through the story they choose to tell and the types of characters and events they portray.* Ask: *Why would Uchida choose to tell this particular folktale? What are the qualities of the characters? What does the story say about the values of the author and her heritage?* (The author tells us that the elderly couple ". . . were good, kind, and honest people, and they worked very hard." Later in the story, when they are rewarded with the child they have always wanted, we understand through story events that this is a value that both the author and the Japanese culture admire.)

WRITER'S CRAFT

Folk Tale Remind students of the common characteristics of a folk tale:

❋ The main character has a problem.

❋ The solution is often magical.

❋ Good characters are rewarded.

Invite students to provide examples of these characteristics in "The Princess of Light." Then, have students work in pairs to choose a folk tale from another culture, identify similar characteristics in it, and share their findings with the class.

EXTRA SUPPORT

Fluency Uchida's folk tale lends itself to reading aloud and developing oral fluency. Divide the reading tasks so that one individual (or group) reads the words of the old man and another reads the words of the old woman. You, or another experienced reader will read the narration. Be sure students have ample time to practice their parts so that their reading is smooth and expressive.

Response Notes

the old man, "Take us home. We are yours!" The old man gathered up the coins and filled his moneybag. Then he hurried home once more, chuckling softly to himself to think how he would again surprise his wife.

When the old woman saw the coins, she said, "My, how lucky we are! Perhaps this is God's way of helping us provide for our little daughter. We must be grateful and take good care of her."

"Yes, yes, we shall always work hard and take good care of our child," said the old man.

From that day on, each time the old man went out to the bamboo thicket, he found one shiny golden stalk. When he cut it down, he always found the hollow filled with gold coins. Before long, the old man and woman became rich, but they continued to work hard.

The little baby of the bamboo was a wonderful child indeed. Each night she seemed to grow a whole year older, instead of just a day older. Each morning she surprised the old man and woman by being able to do or say something new.

"My, but she is a bright child," said the old woman.

"And see how much more beautiful she becomes each day," added the old man.

As she grew older, they discovered something even more wonderful about her. A beautiful, bright light seemed to glow all around her, just like the light which the old man had seen around the bamboo in which he found her. So the old man and woman decided to call their lovely daughter Kaguya Hime, which means Princess of Light. Their little home seemed to be filled with golden sunlight day and night, and they no longer had to use the lamps in the evening.

Kaguya Hime continued to grow in beauty each day, until soon the whole countryside had heard of her loveliness and of the radiant glow which she cast about her.

"She is like a lovely golden sunbeam," said some. "She is like sunshine on a rainbow," said others. "She is an angel from heaven," said still others; and everyone who knew her came to love her dearly. ❖

❋ Based on what you've read, what would you say is Uchida's attitude toward Japan?

88 LESSON 26

88 UNIT 6

❉ What connection can you make between "The Princess of Light" and the questions "Who am I?" and "Where do I belong?"

❉ Imagine you are twenty-year-old Yoshiko Uchida on an extended stay in Japan. Write a letter home to your parents. In your letter, explain your answers to the questions "Who am I?" and "Where do I belong?"

Authors, like many people, explore questions such as "Who am I?" and "Where do I belong?"

TEACHING TIP

Graphic Organizers To help students move from the cultural elements of the story to the identity questions (page 89), explain: *One purpose of a folk tale is to pass cultural values from one generation to the next. This helps young people learn how they fit into the culture. For example, when children hear "They were good, … and they worked very hard," they learn that, to fit in with their culture, they must work hard. In this way, being a hard worker becomes one part of a child's answer to the question "Who am I?"*

Have students think of other folk tales they have heard or read, and analyze them, using a three-column chart such as the following:

Folk Tale Element	Cultural Value	Who Am I?
• They were good … people, and they worked very hard.	• Good people work hard.	• I am a hard worker.

Quick Assess

❉ Can students make an inference about the author's message?

❉ Did students make connections between the folk tale and the author's identity questions?

❉ Did students' letters explain answers to the questions?

After

LISTENING/SPEAKING CONNECTION Have students recall such experiences as family traditions and special times with family or friends. Say: *These are the kinds of experiences that connect a person with his or her cultural heritage.* Invite students to reflect on why they remember these events and then write or draw about them and explain to a group or the class the insights about their cultures that they gained from the experiences.

LESSON 27

Students will read an excerpt from an author's autobiography to find clues that reveal the author's identity.

BUILD BACKGROUND

Remind students that an autobiography is a writer's personal story. In the excerpt from *The Invisible Thread*, Yoshiko Uchida expresses her feelings of alienation and exclusion as a young Japanese-American. Uchida writes about longing to be like other California children, with blonde hair and blue eyes. During the summer of her eleventh year, on a rail trip to the East Coast with her family, she realizes that no matter how much she wants to belong, some Americans will always consider her a foreigner.

VOCABULARY

pass a permission form

barge a large, flat-bottomed boat used to carry heavy loads

impelled moved or urged to do something

relish a feeling of enthusiasm or delight

Discuss each definition, pointing out that students may be familiar with different meanings the words *pass* and *relish* have in other contexts. Then have students think of a synonym for each term. See also the Word Splash blackline master on page 272.

Before

CRITICAL READING SKILL

Exploring a Writer's Identity Have students recall a time and place when they felt out of place, such as moving to a new neighborhood, or making friends at a new school. Model expressing feelings of uncertainty about belonging, for example: *When I went to a new friend's home, I didn't know whether to wear my shoes inside the house or leave them at the door. I felt nervous and unsure of myself.* Then invite students to share their experiences of not fitting in and express how they felt.

LESSON 27 — A WRITER'S IDENTITY

Because she was an American, Uchida wrote about Japan from an American perspective. For example, in *The Forever Christmas Tree*, Uchida tells the story of a Japanese boy who longs for a Christmas tree, even though his family does not celebrate Christmas:

> It was too cold to play outside, so Takashi sat where he could watch the road. He waited and waited for Kaya to come home from school. When at last he saw her, she was running, and Takashi knew she had something special to tell. As soon as she was in the house, the words came tumbling out.
>
> "Today we learned about Christmas!" she said, and the bright glow of her excitement quickly spilled out to fill Takashi too.
>
> Takashi did not know much about Christmas for no one celebrated it in Sugi Village. It was the New Year that mattered.

At times, Uchida felt torn between these two different cultures. In her **autobiography**, she describes how, as a child, she often felt as if she were being pulled in two completely different directions, never quite knowing who she was, or how she fit in. As you read this excerpt from Uchida's autobiography, underline or highlight information about the author's sense of identity. Note the connections to your life in the **Response Notes** column.

from The Invisible Thread by Yoshiko Uchida

I was born in California, recited the Pledge of Allegiance to the flag each morning at school, and loved my country as much as any other American—maybe even more.

Still, there was a large part of me that was Japanese simply because Mama and Papa had passed on to me so much of their own Japanese spirit and soul. Their own values of loyalty, honor, self-discipline, love, and respect for one's parents, teachers, and superiors were all very much a part of me.

There was also my name, which teachers couldn't seem to pronounce properly even when I shortened my first name to Yoshi. And there was my Japanese face, which closed more and more doors to me as I grew older.

How wonderful it would be, I used to think, if I had blond hair and blue eyes like Marian and Solveig. Or a name like Mary Anne Brown or Betty Johnson.

If only I didn't have to ask such questions as, "Can we come swim in your pool? We're Japanese." Or when we were looking for a house, "Will the neighbors object if we move in next door?" Or when I went for my first professional haircut, "Do you cut Japanese hair?"

Response Notes: I hate when teachers mispronounce my name!

Still, I didn't truly realize how different I was until the summer I was eleven. Although Papa usually went on business trips alone, bringing back such gifts as silver pins for Mama or charm bracelets for Keiko and me, that summer he was able to take us along, thanks to a railroad pass.

We took the train, stopping at the Grand Canyon, Houston, New Orleans, Washington, D.C., New York, Boston, Niagara Falls, and on the way home, Chicago, to see the World's Fair.

Crossing the Mississippi River was a major event, as our train rolled onto a barge and sailed slowly over that grand body of water. We all got off the train for a closer look, and I was so impressed with the river's majesty, I felt impelled to make some kind of connection with it. Finally, I leaned over the barge rail and spit so a part of me would be in the river forever.

For my mother, the high point of the trip was a visit to the small village of Cornwall, Connecticut. There she had her first meeting with the two white American pen pals with whom she had corresponded since her days at Doshisha University. She also visited one of her former missionary teachers, Louise DeForest, who had retired there. And it was there I met a young girl my age, named Cathy Sellew. We became good friends, corresponded for many years, and met again as adults when I needed a home and a friend.

Everyone in the village greeted us warmly, and my father was asked to say a few words to the children of the Summer Vacation Church School—which he did with great relish.

Most of the villagers had never before met a Japanese American. One smiling woman shook my hand and said, "My, but you speak English so beautifully." She had meant to compliment me, but I was so astonished, I didn't know what to say. I realized she had seen only my outer self—my Japanese face—and addressed me as a foreigner. I knew then that I would always be different, even though I wanted so badly to be like my white American friends.

❋ What are three things you learned about Uchida from reading this excerpt?

1. _____

2. _____

3. _____

A WRITER'S IDENTITY 91

WRITER'S CRAFT

Word Choice Point out Uchida's expressive word choices, such as "...my Japanese face, which closed more and more doors for me..." To model explaining why the example is effective, say: *Those words create an image of doors slamming in my face. That makes me feel shut out and unwanted.* Invite students to identify other examples of powerful language and explain why they are so effective.

EXTRA SUPPORT

Differentiation Help students go beyond the literal text to make inferences about Uchida's identity. Read aloud the first paragraph on page 90 and then say the following: *When I read the first paragraph of* The Invisible Thread, *I see facts about the author. But what does Uchida really mean? Since I have read a little bit about the author and I have read this excerpt before, I think she uses this information to tell her audience that, even though she has a Japanese name and comes from Japanese ancestry, she is American.*

Have students finish the excerpt to note how the events contribute to Uchida's sense of herself as an American. (Each event either establishes her identify as an American or shows that other people assumed she was Japanese, not American.)

During

RESPONSE NOTES
Have students review portions of the selection that they underlined or highlighted and reflect on how they connect with students' own experiences of not fitting in. Then have students write Response Notes that explain their markings. Encourage them to add notes about how they connect with these portions of the excerpt.

CHARACTERIZATION
Define character as a person's personality, beliefs, and standards for behavior. Explain that what an author tells about personal thoughts, actions, and words reveals the writer's character. Have students highlight Uchida's thoughts, actions, and words throughout the excerpt.

WRITING SUPPORT
Prewriting Facilitate a discussion of attributes the excerpt reveals about Yoshiko's character as a child. Then students can use their highlighting to plan their response to the prompt on page 92.

STUDYING AN AUTHOR 91

TEACHING TIP

Collaboration Form groups for a Team Word Web activity. Give each group a large piece of paper and a different colored marker for each group member. Have students write "Who am I?" in the center of the web. Then have each student add to the web ideas that are inspired by questions, such as:

✻ What made Yoshiko feel like she belonged to her family or group?

✻ When did she feel like she did not belong to or was different from some group?

✻ Which of her attributes closed doors?

✻ Which of her attributes opened doors?

Then invite groups to share their webs with the class.

Quick Assess

✻ Did students write about three things they learned about Yoshiko as a child?

✻ Did students clarify the "three children" in their diagrams?

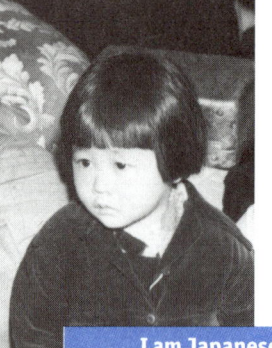

✻ As a child, Uchida felt as if she were three children rolled into one. Sometimes she was Japanese, sometimes she was American, and sometimes she was Japanese American. Review the notes you made while reading the excerpt from *The Invisible Thread*. Complete the chart below by listing some of the ways Uchida felt as if she were three little girls in one.

YOSHIKO UCHIDA AS A CHILD

I am Japanese	I am Japanese American	I am American
My name is Japanese		

> When you read an autobiography, watch for the ways the author answers the questions "Who am I?" and "How do I fit in?" These questions will help you see how the author views himself or herself.

92 LESSON 27

After

WRITING CONNECTION Have students reflect on times in their lives when they have gained a sense of their personal identities. Invite them to create their own chart to reflect different periods in their lives. Then have them write brief autobiographical incidents similar to the excerpt from *The Invisible Thread*.

A WRITER'S LANGUAGE — LESSON 28

During World War II, more than 120,000 West Coast Japanese Americans were uprooted from their homes and sent to U.S. government detention camps in the desert. Men, women, and children were imprisoned for as long as three years, for no other reason than that they were of Japanese ancestry. The majority of those imprisoned were U.S. citizens.

In 1942, Yoshiko Uchida and her family were "relocated" to a horse stall at Tanforan racetrack in San Bruno, California. Later they were moved to Topaz, a Japanese American internment camp in Utah. The Uchida family spent many long, frightening months at Topaz.

For years after she was released, Yoshiko kept quiet about the alienation and rejection she felt as a result of her internment. In the early 1970s, however, she decided she would remain silent no longer. She wrote a series of books—fiction and nonfiction—that describe the experiences of her family and friends.

In her books about the detention camps, Uchida uses **sensory language** (words that can help you see, hear, touch, smell, or taste the thing described) as a way of giving readers a "you are there" feeling. As you read this excerpt from *Journey Home*, underline words and phrases that help you see, hear, feel, smell, and even taste what it was like at the detention center in Topaz. Record your reactions to her experiences in your **Response Notes**.

from *Journey Home* by Yoshiko Uchida

I can't see, Yuki thought frantically. I can't breathe.

The screaming desert wind flung its white powdery sand in her face, stifling her and wrapping her up in a smothering cocoon of sand so fine it was like dust. It blinded her and choked her and made her gag as she opened her mouth to cry out.

The black tar-papered barracks on either side of the road had vanished behind the swirling dust, and Yuki was all alone in an eerie, unreal world where nothing existed except the shrieking wind and the great choking clouds of dust. Yuki stumbled on, doubled over, pushing hard against the wind, gasping as she felt the sting of sand and pebbles against her legs.

Suppose she never got back to her barrack? Suppose the wind simply picked her up and flung her out beyond the barbed wire fence into the desert? Suppose no one ever found her dried, wind-blown body out there in the sagebrush?

A cry of terror swelled up inside her. "Mama! Papa! Help me!"

LESSON 28

Students will examine how sensory language helps to recreate an emotional experience.

BACKGROUND KNOWLEDGE
While the United States was fighting World War II in Europe, in part to liberate Jews and other groups from Nazi concentration camps, the American government was running detainment camps of its own on U.S. soil. While the internment camps were not death camps, they did imprison people whose only "offense" was that they were of Japanese ancestry.

The internment camp to which Yoshiko's family was relocated in 1942 was situated in a high desert area of Utah, south of Salt Lake City. The region was very dry and subject to constant winds that frequently caused blinding dust storms.

VOCABULARY

cocoon a protective cover or case, such as shelter larvae during the pupa stage

barracks a large, plain, temporary building

barbed wire fence wire with many sharp points along it

Use the Word Splash activity on page 272.

Before

CRITICAL READING SKILL
Studying a Writer's Language
Remind students that writers use sensory language to create vivid images that help their readers connect with the writer's ideas. Explain: *The word* sensory *comes from the word* sense. *Sensory language is language that connects with your five senses: sight, sound, smell, taste, and feel.* Compare these two sentences, asking which is more effective and why: The wind blew sand in her face. "The screaming desert wind flung its white powdery sand in her face …"

RESPONSE NOTES
As students mark sensory language in the selection, have them write in their Response Notes which sense is connected to each marked portion. (See page 227 for tips on marking text.)

STUDYING AN AUTHOR

WRITING SUPPORT

Prewriting Remind students of the previous lesson about the impact of sensory language. Facilitate a discussion about how this writing technique causes emotional responses in the reader. Model how to express an emotional response. For example, say: *The passage made me feel (afraid and overwhelmed) by the power of the storm. I could feel how (helpless and lonely) the child felt.* Invite students to share emotional responses orally to prepare for writing in response to the prompt.

EXTRA SUPPORT

Differentiation Students who need extra support might benefit from a more detailed introduction of the excerpt: *In this passage, Yuki, the narrator, describes being out in a windstorm. The wind is so strong that it shrieks loudly and covers Yuki in very fine sand. Yuki becomes afraid as she wonders if she will be lost in the desert.*

❋ What is your reaction to the passage you just read? Explain your feelings.

During

SENTENCE FLUENCY In addition to sensory language, Ms. Uchida employs long, complex sentences in this excerpt. Point out how these sentences move the action rapidly forward and help create a sense of panic so that the reader can appreciate the child's experience. Invite students to read the passage aloud, pausing at commas and periods. Then have them reread it rapidly to emphasize the sense of panic. Facilitate a discussion of how the use of sensory language and long, complex sentences help readers understand the mood of the story.

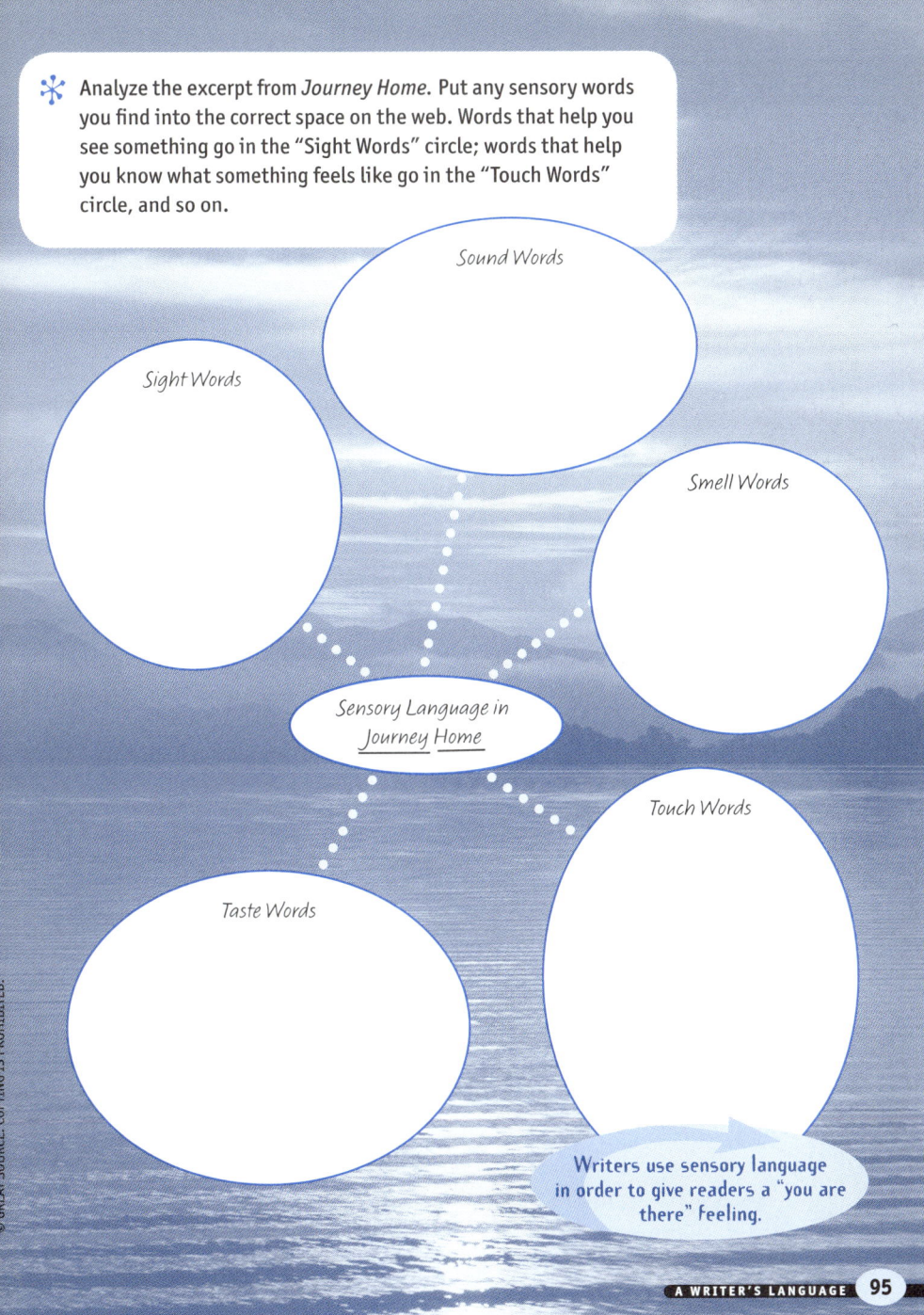

After

WRITING/SPEAKING CONNECTION

Propose a frightening or otherwise emotionally charged experience, such as being caught in a powerful thunderstorm or becoming lost in a strange place, and make a five senses chart about the experience. Then have students write brief passages about their own experience in a style similar to that of the excerpt from *Journey Home*. Suggest that they begin their story in the middle of the action, using the excerpt as a model. Encourage them to use sensory language to describe the setting and their feelings at the time. Provide short lessons on combining sentences to create longer, more complex sentences in the style of the Uchida excerpt. Invite volunteers to read their finished story aloud to the class.

STUDYING AN AUTHOR 95

LESSON 29

Students will determine the author's themes and make connections to their own life.

BACKGROUND KNOWLEDGE
After a year in the internment camp, Yoshiko and her sister were allowed to leave the camp to further their education. Yoshiko had been accepted at Smith's College in New York. Her freedom came at a high price, however. It meant leaving her parents behind in the camp. This excerpt recounts the girls' departure from the camp. The children mentioned in the first paragraph were those Yoshiko had taught during her time in the camp.

VOCABULARY
ventured forth set out on a new adventure

trauma emotional shock

financial security having enough money to live a comfortable life

tangible something that can be touched

steadfast firm, constant, unwavering

Form five groups and assign one term to each group. Have groups find the terms and use context clues and dictionaries to define them. Finally, have each group share its findings with the class.

LESSON 29 — A WRITER'S THEMES

Readers who are familiar with Uchida's work know that she explores two **themes** over and over again in her writing. The first theme—pride in one's ancestry—is a reflection of Uchida's own feelings about herself and her family. Her second major theme—courage during times of trouble—is especially apparent in her books about Japanese American internment camps.

As you read this excerpt from Uchida's memoir *Desert Exile*, watch for ideas that relate to these two themes. Does Uchida give the two themes equal weight in this selection? Write notes in the **Response Notes** column. (*Issei* is a term for people born in Japan who live in America; *Nisei* are the American-born children of Issei parents.)

from Desert Exile by Yoshiko Uchida

On my last day at school, the children of my class presented me with a clay bowl one of them had made, and they stood together, giggling and embarrassed, to sing one last song for me.

On our last Sunday, my sister and I went to say goodbye to all our friends, especially the older Issei who we knew would probably remain in camp until the end of the war.

It was hard for us to go, leaving behind our Issei parents in the desolation of that desert camp. And I imagine other Nisei felt as we did as they ventured forth into the outside world.

Because we Nisei were still relatively young at the time, it was largely the Issei who had led the way, guiding us through the devastation and trauma of our forced removal. When they were uprooted from their homes, many had just reached a point of financial security in their lives. During the war, however, they all suffered enormous losses, both tangible and intangible. The evacuation was the ultimate of the incalculable hardships and indignities they had borne over the years.

Before

CRITICAL READING SKILL
Identifying a Writer's Themes Define *courage* as facing one's fear and not letting it stop one from reaching a goal. Ask students to recall books, movies, or TV shows with characters who, in the face of difficult situations, persevered or took action. Students might recall Brian (from *Hatchet*), Stanley Yelnats (in *Holes*), Martin Luther King, Jr., or a sports hero, for example. Ask students to identify the courageous character and explain what the character did that proved his or her courage.

RESPONSE NOTES
Suggest that students make notes about the two themes separately. First, look for ideas that relate to pride in one's ancestry. Then, look for ideas that relate to courage during times of trouble.

And yet most of our parents had continued to be steadfast and strong in spirit. Our mothers had made homes of the bleak barrack rooms, just as my own mother, in her gentle, nurturing way, had been a loving focal point for our family and friends.

Deprived of so much themselves, the Issei wanted the best for their Nisei children. Many had sacrificed to send their children to college, and they encouraged them now to leave camp to continue their education.

As my sister and I prepared for our departure, thoughts of gratitude toward our Issei parents still lay unspoken deep within us, and it was only in later years that we came to realize how much they had done for us; how much they had given us to enrich and strengthen our lives.

※ Look over the notes you made about ancestry and courage while reading the selection. In the diagram below, list the ways that Uchida explores these themes in *Desert Exile*.

Taking Pride in One's Ancestry
She is respectful of the sacrifices of the Issei.

Showing Courage in Times of Trouble
She bravely leaves her parents behind.

TEACHING TIP

Graphic Organizers Remind students that a writer's identity can be revealed through a character's thoughts, words, and actions. Invite students to diagram these three attributes as Yoshiko reveals them in the excerpt.

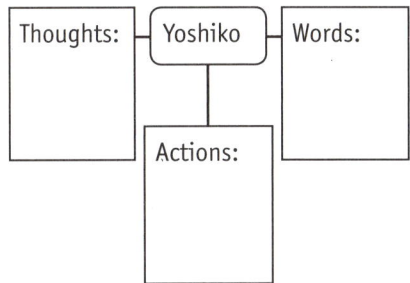

Then have students label each entry with an A, for those that show pride in ancestry, or a C, for those that show courage.

During

WORD CHOICE Point out that Ms. Uchida uses very powerful terms to express her feelings about both themes during this episode. Invite students to make two lists of words or phrases: one for happy feelings related to pride of ancestry, and one for sad or frightened feelings related to situations that require courage. To model distinguishing the two, say: *The phrase* ventured forth *sounds exciting, so I'll list it under happy terms; the words* trauma *and* uprooted *sound like hard times, so I'll list them under sad terms.*

After students have listed as many terms as they can, invite them to discuss their lists with a partner. Allow students to use both lists to respond to the writing prompt.

WRITING SUPPORT

Journals Ask students to explain what they know about on-line blogs. Explain that the word blog comes from two words, *Web* and *log*. They are similar to journals in that they record a writer's experiences and opinions. Explain that there are other kinds of journals. For example, say: *Some people keep travel journals to track places they've seen and money they've spent. A scientist keeps a journal of experiments and their results. Many people keep private journals to record their experiences, reflections, and other thoughts. This kind of journal can be similar to a diary.* Invite students to share what they know about various types of journals. Then facilitate a discussion of personal journals: reasons for keeping one, privacy considerations, etc. Tell students that the journal entry they will write on this page should be a kind of personal journal entry, but one written for others to read, like a blog.

❋ Now connect one of Uchida's themes to your own life. Write a journal entry describing a time you showed courage or a time you demonstrated pride in your heritage.

Journal entry for _____ date _____

Understanding an author's themes can help you connect your reading to your own life.

98 LESSON 29

After

CONTENT AREA CONNECTION

Invite each student to conduct research about a person who exemplifies pride in ancestry or courage in difficult times. Have students use at least two different sources of information, such as books and the Internet, and create visual aids to use in presenting oral reports about the people they chose.

A WRITER'S INTENT — LESSON 30

Some authors write to entertain their readers. Others write in order to argue or persuade. Still others write so that they can teach readers about something that is important or meaningful. Many writers try to do a little bit of each.

What is Uchida's **purpose**, or intent? Read this excerpt from an interview with Yoshiko Uchida. Underline any clues about her purpose. Be sure to note your questions in the **Response Notes**.

from an interview with Yoshiko Uchida

I hope to give young Asians a sense of their own history. At the same time, I want to dispel the stereotypic image still held by many non-Asians about the Japanese Americans and write about them as real people. I hope to convey as well the strength of spirit and the sense of hope and purpose I have seen in many of the first generation Japanese Americans. Beyond that, I write to celebrate our common humanity, for I feel the basic elements of humanity are present in all our strivings.

Response Notes

* Summarize in your own words Uchida's purpose for writing.

* Think about this passage and other writings by Yoshiko Uchida. What have you learned from reading Uchida's works?

A WRITER'S INTENT 99

LESSON 30

Students will summarize an author's purpose for writing her own story, use a graphic organizer to relate common themes and messages, and reflect on their own purpose for writing.

BACKGROUND KNOWLEDGE
Have students think about the last time they sent an e-mail or text message, telephoned, or otherwise contacted a friend. Once each student has a message in mind, ask: *Why did you contact the other person? What did you hope to accomplish by contacting the person? Did you achieve your purpose?* Explain that the person's purpose for contacting another is his or her intent. Similarly, a writer's purpose for writing is his or her intent. Most professional writers can explain their intents very specifically. The interview excerpt tells how Ms. Uchida once explained her intent.

VOCABULARY
dispel to scatter; drive away
stereotypic not original or having no individuality; trite
humanity human qualities
strivings trying hard

Ask students how they can use related words to figure out the meanings: *dispel/disperse, stereotypic/stereotype, humanity/human,* and *strivings/strive*.

Before

CRITICAL READING SKILL
Discovering a Writer's Intent Have students identify key words and phrases in Ms. Uchida's interview statement and list them on the board. Then facilitate a discussion about her statement by asking questions, such as: *What does the author hope to change about the world or society? What feelings does she want her readers to have? What values does she hold?*

RESPONSE NOTES Have students write their questions in the Response Notes and answer the questions during class discussion.

STUDYING AN AUTHOR 99

Quick Assess

✳ Do the summaries include all the important ideas in the interview excerpt?

✳ Do students clearly explain what they have learned about the author?

✳ Are the graphic organizers complete?

✳ Reflect on what you know about Yoshiko Uchida—her life and her works. Use the graphic organizer below to make notes about her stories, themes, and messages.

YOSHIKO UCHIDA: WRITER, STORYTELLER, TEACHER

What she writes about	In what selection?	What lesson does she want to teach?

Some authors write with the intention of conveying to you, the reader, something they believe is important or meaningful.

100 LESSON 30

During

YOSHIKO UCHIDA'S WORK To help students distinguish the columns of the graphic organizer, explain that the first column asks for the topic of a specific work, the middle column asks for the title, the last column asks about the author's intent for that work. Suggest that students first write the titles of the selections in this unit in the middle column:

"The Princess of Light," *The Invisible Thread, Journey Home,* and *Desert Exile*. Then have them skim each selection to recall the topics and write the topic of each work in the first column. Finally, allow time for students to study each selection in more depth before they complete the last column.

After

APPLYING THE STRATEGY
Discovering a Writer's Intent Have students write a statement about the author's intent for a particular piece of writing, such as a novel, a poem, an editorial, or a short story.

Assessing Your Growing Repertoire

At this point in the *Daybook*, you have been introduced to a number of ways to become a better reader and a better writer. You have learned different strategies for interacting and connecting with the stories or essays you have read. You have experimented with multiple perspectives. You have examined language and craft. You have focused on one particular author.

Now you are going to combine those skills and strategies in one unit. In this unit, you will read a short story by Jane Yolen, and then participate in a number of reading and writing activities designed to show how well you organize and express your ideas. You will demonstrate how you use the skills and strategies presented in the *Daybook*. You will work both individually and in groups as you read, talk, draw, and write.

After you have written and revised your essay, you will evaluate your own work. You will consider what you need to do to improve your skills as you continue to strengthen your use of **critical reading and writing strategies**.

UNIT 7
ASSESSING YOUR GROWING REPERTOIRE

Lessons 31-35, pages 102-116

UNIT OVERVIEW
Students will use the strategies they have learned in Units 1-6 in reading and writing activities.

KEY IDEA
Good readers and writers use multiple strategies to effectively interact with the material.

CRITICAL READING AND WRITING SKILLS
by lesson

31 Interacting and connecting with the text
32 Using reading and writing strategies
33 Studying an author
34 Getting ready to write
35 Revising and evaluating an opinion essay

WRITING ACTIVITIES
by lesson

31 Write about a personal connection.
32 Write a paragraph analyzing a poem.
33 Write questions to ask Jane Yolen.
34 Write a persuasive essay.
35 Write a reflection.

Literature

- **"Birthday Box"** by Jane Yolen (short story)

In this story, a young girl celebrates her birthday at her dying mother's bedside. In time, she comes to realize the meaning of her mother's puzzling gift to her.

- **"The Key to Everything"** by May Swenson (poem)

This enigmatic poem explores the topic of trying to comprehend another person, or another side of one's self.

- *Frequently Asked Questions* by Jane Yolen (interview)

Yolen gives insights into her writing process and why she writes.

- *The Call of the Wild* by Jack London (novel excerpt)

In this excerpt from London's classic, Buck, the half-dog/half-wolf encounters a wolf and feels the stirrings of his wilder instincts.

- *Island of the Blue Dolphins* by Scott O'Dell (novel excerpt)

In this excerpt from O'Dell's well-known novel about survival, a young girl tries to leave the solitude of the island for the mainland.

LESSON 31

Students will interact with a story that contains symbolism and make connections to their personal experiences.

BACKGROUND KNOWLEDGE
Tell students they're going to read a story in which one of the characters has said that it's not the gift but the thought that counts. Discuss this idea. Do students agree with the statement? Why or why not?

NOTE: This story is about a girl whose mother dies of cancer. Use your judgment about presenting this story if cancer is a sensitive subject in your classroom.

VOCABULARY
oncologist a doctor who specializes in cancer diagnosis and treatment

Remind students that words are sometimes defined within the text. Locate the word *oncologist* on page 103. Ask students to explain how they can tell what the word means. (It is defined in the text.) Then ask what prediction they can make about the story, knowing that it contains *oncologist*. (It will probably be about someone who has cancer.)

LESSON 31 — INTERACTING AND CONNECTING WITH A STORY

Ten children's authors were asked to write a story based on the idea that one beautifully wrapped birthday gift is empty. Here is Jane Yolen's response to that challenge. As you read "Birthday Box" by Jane Yolen, use the **Response Notes** column. Remember you can draw or write, make predictions, ask questions, comment on what surprises you, and **make connections** to what you already know or have experienced. Show how well you have learned the strategies in the previous lessons by making your annotations as complete as you can.

"Birthday Box" by Jane Yolen

I was ten years old when my mother died. Ten years old on that very day. Still she gave me a party of sorts. Sick as she was, Mama had seen to it, organizing it at the hospital. She made sure the doctors and nurses all brought me presents. We were good friends with them all by that time, because Mama had been in the hospital for so long.

The head nurse, V. Louise Higgins (I never did know what that V stood for), gave me a little box, which was sort of funny because she was the biggest of all the nurses there. I mean she was tremendous. And she was the only one who insisted on wearing all white. Mama had called her the great white shark when she was first admitted, only not to V. Louise's face. "All those needles," Mama had said. "Like teeth." But V. Louise was sweet, not sharklike at all, and she'd been so gentle with Mama.

I opened the little present first. It was a fountain pen, a real one, not a fake one like you get at Kmart.

"Now you can write beautiful stories, Katie," V. Louise said to me.

I didn't say that stories come out of your head, not out of a pen. That wouldn't have been polite, and Mama—even sick— was real big on politeness.

"Thanks, V. Louise," I said.

The Stardust Twins—which is what Mama called Patty and Tracey-lynn because they reminded her of dancers in an oldfashioned ballroom—gave me a present together. It was a diary and had a picture of a little girl in pink, reading in a garden swing. A little young for me, a little too cute. I mean, I read Stephen King and want to write like him. But as Mama always reminded me whenever Dad finally remembered to send me something, it was the thought that counted, not the actual gift.

"It's great," I told them. "I'll write in it with my new pen." And I wrote my name on the first page just to show them I meant it.

102 LESSON 31

Before

CRITICAL READING SKILL
Interacting and Connecting with a Story This is a story that most readers can connect with on some level. However, the story might touch on a sensitive issue for students who have experienced the death of a loved one. Tell your students that the story is told by the narrator of the story, a girl named Katie, who spends her tenth birthday in her mother's hospital room. Katie's mother has cancer and is close to death. You may prefer to read the story aloud to monitor the reactions of your students.

RESPONSE NOTES Encourage students to draw on what they've learned in previous units about how to interact with the text and make connections. Remind them to use their Response Notes as a place to question, predict, and react as they read. If necessary, review the tips for marking text on page 227.

They hugged me and winked at Mama. She tried to wink back but was just too tired and shut both her eyes instead.

Lily, who is from Jamaica, had baked me some sweet bread. Mary Margaret gave me a gold cross blessed by the pope, which I put on even though Mama and I weren't churchgoers. That was Dad's thing.

Then Dr. Dann, the intern who was on days, and Dr. Pucci, the oncologist (which is the fancy name for a cancer doctor), gave me a big box filled to the top with little presents, each wrapped up individually. All things they knew I'd love— paperback books and writing paper and erasers with funny animal heads and colored paper clips and a rubber stamp that printed FROM KATIE'S DESK and other stuff. They must have raided a stationery store.

There was one box, though, they held out till the end. It was about the size of a large top hat. The paper was deep blue and covered with stars; not fake stars but real stars, I mean, like a map of the night sky. The ribbon was two shades of blue with silver threads running through. There was no name on the card.

"Who's it from?" I asked.

None of the nurses answered, and the doctors both suddenly were studying the ceiling tiles with the kind of intensity they usually saved for X rays. No one spoke. In fact the only sound for the longest time was Mama's breathing machine going in and out and in and out. It was a harsh, horrible, insistent sound, and usually I talked and talked to cover up the noise. But I was waiting for someone to tell me.

At last V. Louise said, "It's from your mama, Katie. She told us what she wanted. And where to get it."

I turned and looked at Mama then, and her eyes were open again. Funny, but sickness had made her even more beautiful than good health had. Her skin was like that old paper, the kind they used to write on with quill pens, and stretched out over her bones so she looked like a model. Her eyes, which had been a deep, brilliant blue, were now like the fall sky, bleached and softened. She was like a faded photograph of herself. She smiled a very small smile at me. I knew it was an effort.

"It's you," she mouthed. I read her lips. I had gotten real good at that. I thought she meant it was a present for me.

"Of course it is," I said cheerfully. I had gotten good at that, too, being cheerful when I didn't feel like it. "Of course it is."

I took the paper off the box carefully, not tearing it but folding it into a tidy packet. I twisted the ribbons around my hand and then put them on the pillow by her hand. It made the stark white hospital bed look almost festive.

Under the wrapping, the box was beautiful itself. It was made of a heavy cardboard and covered with a linen material that had a pattern of cloud-filled skies.

I opened the box slowly and . . .

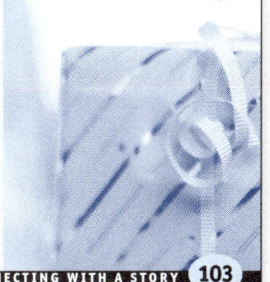

ABOUT THE AUTHOR

Jane Yolen (born 1939), the award-winning author of many stories for children and young teens, wrote "Birthday Box" in response to a challenge. Ten children's authors were asked to write a story based on the premise that one beautifully wrapped birthday gift is empty. "Birthday Box" is Yolen's story of a dying mother who plans a birthday party at the hospital for her daughter. The stories are published in *Birthday Surprises: Ten Great Stories to Unwrap,* collected by Johanna Hurwitz (1997 Morrow). The collection is not only a great source of stories for reading aloud, but it will also inspire students to create their own stories about a mysterious gift. See http://www.janeyolen.com for more information.

During

SHARING CONNECTIONS After students have read the selection, talk about the connections they made to the story in their Response Notes. These may range from how to deal with a serious illness in the family, to getting unusual birthday presents, to the symbolism of the birthday box. Then have students work in small groups to talk about inferences they can make about Katie and her relationship with her mother. Have the groups use the questions on page 105 to prompt discussion.

Finally, ask students to respond to the prompt at the bottom of page 105.

WRITER'S CRAFT

Voice Ask students to think about the character Katie. Can they relate to how she feels? Point out that Jane Yolen has written this story from Katie's point of view, in Katie's voice. Discuss how a grown woman is able to write as if she's a young girl. What might help an author to do this? Help students understand that good writers draw on their own experiences to develop realistic characters.

Response Notes

"It's empty," I said. "Is this a joke?" I turned to ask Mama, but she was gone. I mean, her body was there, but she wasn't. It was as if she was as empty as the box.

Dr. Pucci leaned over her and listened with a stethoscope, then almost absently patted Mama's head. Then, with infinite care, V. Louise closed Mama's eyes, ran her hand across Mama's cheek, and turned off the breathing machine.

"Mama!" I cried. And to the nurses and doctors, I screamed, "Do something!" And because the room had suddenly become so silent, my voice echoed back at me. "Mama, do something."

I cried steadily for, I think, a week. Then I cried at night for a couple of months. And then for about a year I cried at anniversaries, like Mama's birthday or mine, at Thanksgiving, on Mother's Day. I stopped writing. I stopped reading except for school assignments. I was pretty mean to my half brothers and totally rotten to my stepmother and Dad. I felt empty and angry, and they all left me pretty much alone.

And then one night, right after my first birthday without Mama, I woke up remembering how she had said, "It's you." Not, "It's for you," just "It's you." Now Mama had been a high school English teacher and a writer herself. She'd had poems published in little magazines. She didn't use words carelessly. In the end she could hardly use any words at all. So—I asked myself in that dark room—why had she said, "It's you"? Why were they the very last words she had ever said to me, forced out with her last breath?

I turned on the bedside light and got out of bed. The room was full of shadows, not all of them real.

Pulling the desk chair over to my closet, I climbed up and felt along the top shelf, and against the back wall, there was the birthday box, just where I had thrown it the day I had moved in with my dad.

I pulled it down and opened it. It was as empty as the day I had put it away.

"It's you," I whispered to the box.

And then suddenly I knew.

Mama had meant *I* was the box, solid and sturdy, maybe even beautiful or at least interesting on the outside. But I had to fill up the box to make it all it could be. And I had to fill me up as well. She had guessed what might happen to me, had told me in a subtle way. In the two words she could manage.

I stopped crying and got some paper out of the desk drawer. I got out my fountain pen. I started writing, and I haven't stopped since. The first thing I wrote was about that birthday. I put it in the box, and pretty soon that box was overflowing with stories. And poems. And memories.

And so was I.

And so was I.

✻ Work with a small group to share some of your questions and ideas about the story. As you talk, use your **Response Notes** to read lines from the story that support your ideas. You can also add notes as you discuss the story.
  - What do the presents Katie receives on her birthday tell you about her?
  - What do you think about the "birthday box" at first?
  - How would you describe the relationship between Katie and her mother?
  - What do you think of the way Katie acted after her mother died?
  - What do you know about Katie's dad?
  - What did Katie's mother mean when she said, "It's you"?

MAKING CONNECTIONS

When you make connections, you are reaching beyond the story itself. Think of stories in your own life or from books, movies, or television shows that relate in some way to "Birthday Box." Your connection might be in experiencing the death of someone close to you, in remembering a memorable birthday celebration, or in finally understanding why you acted as you did at a particular time.

✻ Have you ever received a gift you did not appreciate or understand until later? What personal connection did you make to this story? Write your ideas about it here.

When you interact and connect with a story, you get more meaning out of it.

INTERACTING AND CONNECTING WITH A STORY

TEACHING TIP

Collaboration Have students work in small groups to discuss the questions at the top of page 105. Have each group assign a note-taker to record responses. After the groups have answered the questions, ask for a volunteer from each group to report what the group learned from its discussion.

Quick Assess

✻ Did students make connections to the story in their Response Notes?

✻ Did students respond to the questions regarding the selection in the group discussion?

✻ Did students write about a personal connection they made with the story?

✻ Do students understand how making connections enhances a reader's response to a story?

After

READING/WRITING CONNECTION

Ask students to write a letter to Katie. In the letter, ask them to write about the ways in which they understand what she is going through and any advice they may have for her. Invite volunteers to read their letter to the class.

ASSESSING YOUR GROWING REPERTOIRE

LESSON 32

Students will put themselves in the place of a character to interact and connect with a story.

BACKGROUND KNOWLEDGE

In this lesson, students try to imagine they are Katie, from "Birthday Box," as they think about what she would put in her Birthday Box. From the clues they've gathered from the story, they draw conclusions about her interests and her tastes. Ask students to talk about their impressions of Katie's personality and values. Invite students to give examples that support the conclusions they draw. Let students know that they will read a poem in this lesson called "The Key to Everything" in which the narrator is trying to connect with the person she's addressing. Challenge students to ask who that person might be. Remind them that viewing something from someone else's perspective can help us see things in new ways.

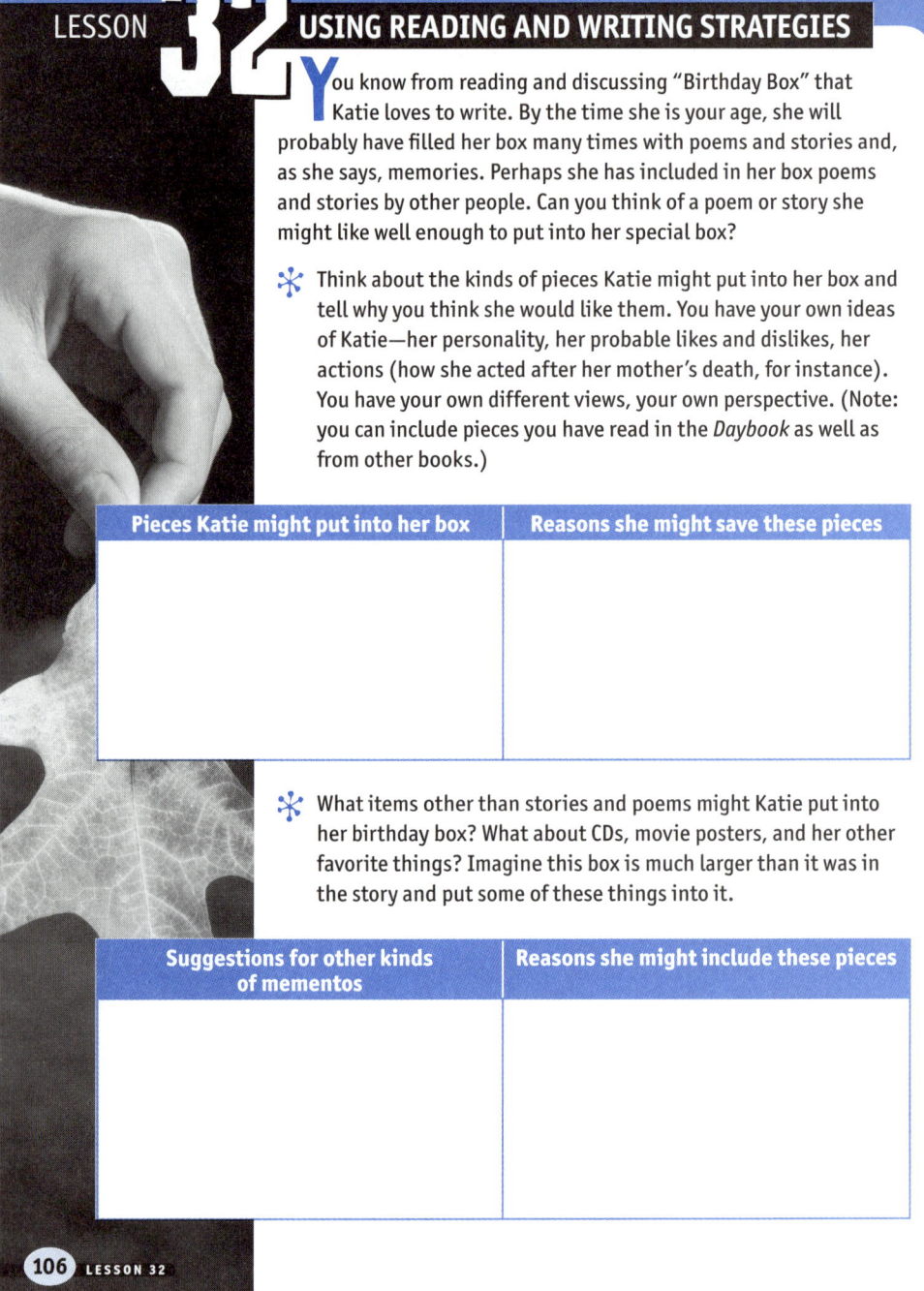

LESSON 32 USING READING AND WRITING STRATEGIES

You know from reading and discussing "Birthday Box" that Katie loves to write. By the time she is your age, she will probably have filled her box many times with poems and stories and, as she says, memories. Perhaps she has included in her box poems and stories by other people. Can you think of a poem or story she might like well enough to put into her special box?

❋ Think about the kinds of pieces Katie might put into her box and tell why you think she would like them. You have your own ideas of Katie—her personality, her probable likes and dislikes, her actions (how she acted after her mother's death, for instance). You have your own different views, your own perspective. (Note: you can include pieces you have read in the *Daybook* as well as from other books.)

Pieces Katie might put into her box	Reasons she might save these pieces

❋ What items other than stories and poems might Katie put into her birthday box? What about CDs, movie posters, and her other favorite things? Imagine this box is much larger than it was in the story and put some of these things into it.

Suggestions for other kinds of mementos	Reasons she might include these pieces

106 LESSON 32

Before

CRITICAL READING SKILL

Using Reading and Writing Strategies Review with students what they have learned so far about interacting and connecting with a text. (Both strategies help the reader establish a personal investment in a story, which helps the reader understand and remember the story better.) Review, also, the idea of exploring multiple perspectives. Talk about how authors express the viewpoints of a character or narrator. Also talk about the way an author chooses the best form to make those viewpoints compelling. In "Birthday Box," Yolen tells a story from Katie's point of view, one shaped by the loss of her mother. In "The Key to Everything," Swenson creates an "I" poem to ask questions about impending loss. Both authors are writing from their perspective, but the reader's own experience and perspective will influence how the selections are interpreted.

Have students work in groups to discuss the kinds of keepsakes Katie might put into her box and tell why they think each choice reflects who she is and who she is becoming.

FOCUSING ON LANGUAGE AND CRAFT

Read May Swenson's poem "The Key to Everything," using the **Response Notes** column as you read. Make notes about the questions the poem raises for you.

"The Key To Everything" by May Swenson

Is there anything I can do
or has everything been done
or do
you prefer somebody else to do
it or don't
you trust me to do
it right or is it hopeless and no one
    can do a thing or do
you suppose I don't
really want to do
it and am just saying that or don't
you hear me at all or what?

You're
waiting for
the right person the doctor or
the nurse the father or
the mother or
the person with the name you keep
mumbling in your sleep
that no one ever heard of there's no one
named that really
except yourself maybe
If I knew what your name was I'd
prove it's your
own name spelled backwards or
twisted in some way the one you
keep mumbling but you
won't tell me your
name or
don't you know it
yourself that's it
of course you've
forgotten or
never quite knew it or
weren't willing to believe it

Then there *is* something I
can do I
can find your name for you
that's the key to everything
    once you'd
repeat it clearly you'd
come awake you'd
get up and walk knowing where
    you're
going where you
came from

And you'd
love me
after that or would you
hate me?
no once you'd
get there you'd
remember and love me
of course I'd
be gone by then I'd
be far away ❖

Response Notes

ABOUT THE AUTHOR

May Swenson was born in Logan, Utah, in 1913. As a poet May Swenson liked to explore the unknown and the unknowable. Swenson once said that her experience of poetry is "based on a craving to get through the curtains of things as they appear, to things as they are, and then into the larger, wilder space of things as they are becoming." During her long career, Swenson's poetry was highly regarded by her readers as well as her fellow writers. She left a legacy of nearly fifty years of writing when she died in 1989.

WRITER'S CRAFT

Multiple Levels of Meaning For first-time readers of this poem, the lines may seem to run together and lose their impact or meaning. Have students imagine that the "I" persona of the poem is in a hospital room, sitting next to the bed of someone who is dying and unresponsive. The patient could be a friend or family member who can't remember the narrator.

Then talk with students about how poems can often be read on several levels. Another level of meaning could be that the narrator is actually the patient and is addressing her inner self. Ask students how this reading also might be true. Help students understand that sometimes we have conversations with our inner selves, and Swenson could be exploring this idea in her poem.

During

READING POETRY After students have completed the activities on page 106, introduce the poem "The Key to Everything."

Read aloud "The Key to Everything," once all the way through and then a second time, stopping occasionally to voice ideas about the poem as you read. For example:

❖ Emphasize where punctuation marks are missing by the way you read the lines.

❖ Set up a dialogue between the "I" and the "you." Ask students to think about whether or not these might be two viewpoints of the same person.

TEACHING TIP
Collaboration—Choral Reading
To help students read the poem effectively, divide the poem into four or five parts. Then divide the room into an equal number of sections and assign groups of students to each section. Give each group one part of the poem. Allow time to practice reading their part all together. Finally put the groups in sequence and read through the whole poem. Ask students whether the experience of hearing the poem read chorally helps them understand the poet's message better than reading it on their own.

Then have students answer the questions on page 108 within their groups.

Quick Assess

* Did students choices for the birthday box reflect an understanding of Katie?
* Were students able to write an effective paragraph about the poem?
* Did they express an opinion on whether or not Katie would include the poem in her box?

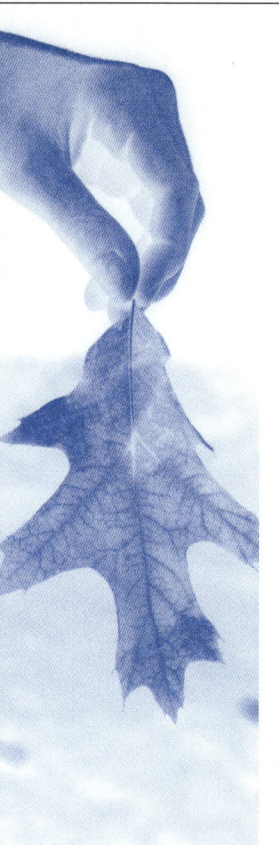

Sometimes you need to know the right word to help you explain a poem. The word *enigmatic* is one that could apply to May Swenson's poem "The Key to Everything." *Enigmatic* means "puzzling, or difficult to figure out." To figure out this poem, talk with a partner or group about these questions. You and your partner do not need to agree on your responses to these questions.

DISCUSSION
1. Who is the "I" of the poem? What makes you think so?
2. Who is the audience? How can you tell?
3. What might be the situation in which the speaker is saying these things?
4. Can you explain what this poem is about or what you think after reading it?
5. What is the dominant tone/mood of the poem (funny, sad, somber, questioning, etc.)?
6. How is that tone achieved?
7. How would you describe the language of the poem? What is an example?
8. How important is the title in conveying the main idea?

* After your discussion, choose three or more of the questions and write a paragraph explaining what you think about this poem. End your paragraph with a statement about whether you think Katie would or would not include this poem in her birthday box.

Using critical reading strategies can help you understand and remember what you read.

After

ART CONNECTION Have students bring in a box. Tell students that the boxes symbolize who they are and who they will become. Using colored markers and/or pictures from magazines or newspapers, have them decorate their own box:

1. Suggest that the outside of the box should reflect the image they present outwardly. For example, they might draw or write words to represent how they think other people see them.
2. Suggest that they fill the box with items that represent the way they see themselves. For example, they might include pictures of themselves, their family, and their pets; poems they have written; lyrics of songs they like; pictures of their favorite foods; pictures of movie stars or musical groups they like, and so on.
3. Invite students to write or talk about what they've included and why.

STUDYING AN AUTHOR — LESSON 33

You may have read some of Jane Yolen's books, but you may not know a lot about her. Here is an interview she compiled from frequently asked questions. In the **Response Notes** column, note **connections** between Yolen's life and her writing.

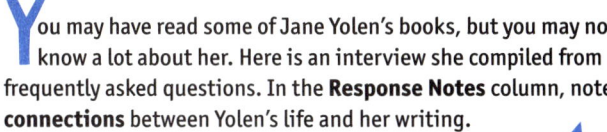

Frequently Asked Questions by Jane Yolen

When did you start writing?
I love writing and have always been good at it. I started as a poet and a writer of songs. I still do both. My first big success as a writer was in first grade where I wrote the class musical. It was all about vegetables and I played the chief carrot. We all ended up in a salad together! In junior high I wrote my big class essay about New York State manufacturing in verse, with a rhyme for Otis Elevators I have—thankfully—forgotten. In college I wrote my final exam in American Intellectual History in rhyme and got an A+ from a very surprised teacher.

Who were your parents?
Both my parents were writers. My father was a journalist, my mother a short story writer who also created crossword puzzles and acrostics for magazines and books. So I just assumed all grownups were writers! Since my brother is a journalist, and my three grown children all write well, in our family—at any rate—that is true.

What kind of a family do you have?
My husband and I have three children (Adam, Jason, Heidi); though they're all grown up now, they still give me ideas. And now that I have five granddaughters and a grandson, I am sure they will give me ideas as well!

Where do you get your ideas?
I am always asked where I get my ideas from. That is a very difficult question to answer, since I get my ideas from everywhere: from things I hear and things I see, from books and songs and newspapers and paintings and conversations—and even from dreams. The storyteller in me asks: what if? And when I try to answer that, a story begins.

What awards have you won?
My books have won any number of awards—the Caldecott, the Golden Kite, the Christopher Medal, the Nebula, etc. And I have won a number of body-of-work awards—the Kerlan, the Keene State, the Regina Medal. But awards just sit on the shelf gathering dust. The best awards are when young readers love my books.

LESSON 33

Students will read an interview with author Jane Yolen to understand how her own experiences influence and inform her writing.

BACKGROUND KNOWLEDGE
Explain that the expression "body of work" refers to everything an author has written. Activate prior knowledge by sharing your favorite books by Jane Yolen (*Briar Rose, The Devil's Arithmetic,* or *Dear Mother, Dear Daughter*). Ask students to talk about which is their favorite and why. Yolen has been writing for many years. It's what she does for a living. Invite students to talk about whether or not they'd like to write for a living. Ask them to give their reasons.

VOCABULARY

persistent keeping at it

naysayers people who say you can't do something

scholars people who make a living studying things

critics people who write reviews of other people's work

Talk about the words and their meanings. Ask students to predict how the words will be used in the interview with Jane Yolen that they're about to read. Use the Word Splash activity on page 272.

Before

CRITICAL READING SKILL
Studying an Author Talk with students about what they have learned previously about how studying an author will help them understand the author's writing. Help them understand that knowing the author's background and experience can often make the author's work more meaningful.

RESPONSE NOTES
Have students note places in the interview that give them insight into who Jane Yolen is and how she sees herself as a writer. Students should mark places that show a connection between Yolen's life and her writing. One example is the paragraph about her parents, which seems to explain Yolen's choice of items for the birthday box.

ABOUT THE AUTHOR

Jane Yolen, an author of children's books, is also a poet, a teacher of writing and literature, and a reviewer of children's literature. Jane Yolen's books and stories have won numerous awards, including the Caldecott Medal, two Nebula Awards, two Christopher Medals, and the World Fantasy Award. Visit Yolen's website to learn more about her: http://www.janeyolen.com.

Response Notes

Q: What are you writing now?
A: I'm always working on something, usually several somethings. At times I am working on as many as ten projects: stories, books, poems, songs.

Q: What advice do you have for young writers?
A: I have three pieces of advice for young writers. One: read, read, read! You must read every day, and try to read a wide range of books. Two: write, write, write! Keep a journal, write letters, anything to keep the "writing muscles" in shape. Three: don't let anyone stop you from writing. Be persistent no matter what "naysayers" or critical editors have to say about your writing.

Q: Which is your favorite book you have written?
A: I don't actually have a favorite book except whatever I am working on at the moment that question is asked. That's because all the books of mine that you can read are well in my past. *Owl Moon*, for example, was published in 1987, and written at least three years earlier than that. You may have just read it, but it's a dim memory for me. So my favorite is what I am currently obsessed with, a story or poem or book which you—the reader—might not see for years yet.

Q: Who inspired your writing?
A: All the books that I have ever read inspire my own writing. My parents, both of whom were writers, were very supportive of my writing and that helped to inspire me as well.

Q: What do you do in your spare time?
A: I love to read and walk, I love traveling to foreign countries, I love to watch movies. I love to listen to music on tape and hear live music as well.

Q: What is your favorite food?
A: Chocolate cake: but alas, I can no longer eat chocolate cake. And nuts—but alas, I cannot eat them either. I can, however, eat salads of all kinds, salmon, lemon chicken, lamb chops, and carrot soup—all favorites.

During

WHO IS THE AUTHOR? As students read the interview, have them characterize Jane Yolen. Ask students to note adjectives to describe her, such as *friendly, funny, down-to-earth,* and so on.

Then have students reflect on what they've learned about Yolen and how that affects their understanding of "Birthday Box." Finally, ask students to list questions they would like to ask the author.

Q: What is your favorite animal?
A: My favorite animal is the cat. My favorite cat was named Pod. Pod was a gentle, loving, golden-orange tom cat with double paws. Pod was the nicest cat we ever had. Now I share my granddaughter's cat, a lovely, feisty female black-and-white cat named Sammy.

Q: Do you ever have an idea and then lose it?
A: Every time I get an idea, I write it down and file it in my Idea File. There is no organization to it; all the ideas are jumbled together.

Q: What makes a good book?
A: Scholars and critics have been debating that question for decades. I like books that touch my head and my heart at the same time.

Q: How do you develop a style?
A: Find those narratives that you like in your favorite books. Then try to mimic those effects in your own writing.

* Thinking of what you know about Jane Yolen now, do you have any additional insights into Katie, the main character in "Birthday Box"?

* What three questions would you like to ask Jane Yolen? List them here.

Learning about a writer's life can give you new insights into his or her writing.

STUDYING AN AUTHOR 111

EXTRA SUPPORT

Differentiation If students are having difficulty connecting what they've read about Yolen with Katie's story, go over the interview with the author and talk about specific statements Yolen makes. For example: *Jane Yolen says she gets her ideas from lots of places. She asks the question "What if...?" I think she probably asked herself, "What if someone gave an empty box as a gift? What would happen?"*

Quick Assess

* Did students mark places in the interview that told them more about Jane Yolen's personality?

* Were they able to apply insights about Jane Yolen to their understanding of "Birthday Box?"

* Did they write questions they would like to ask Jane Yolen?

After

READING/WRITING CONNECTION

Have students write about their own experience as a writer. They can write an essay about what writing means to them, or they may want to work with a partner to interview each other, following the model of the Yolen interview. Here are some additional questions students could ask to help plan their writing:

* What kind of writing do you prefer? Why?

* Did the work of any particular author influence your writing? How?

* What do you like best/least about your writing?

* Do you prefer to work on the computer or with pencil and paper?

ASSESSING YOUR GROWING REPERTOIRE 111

LESSON 34

Students will compare and evaluate author's style.

BACKGROUND KNOWLEDGE

The first selection is about a character named Buck. What is unusual about this story, which is told from Buck's point of view, is that Buck is an animal: half dog and half wolf. The second selection in this unit is about a girl alone on an island. Based on real events, *The Island of the Blue Dolphins* is the story of Karana, a young American Indian girl who lives on the Island of the Blue Dolphins. She and her brother are marooned on this island when all the villagers leave to live on another island. As time passes, Karana struggles to survive on her own.

VOCABULARY

unwonted unusual
commingled mixed
pivoting turning around
flank side
at bay cornered
pertinacity ability to stick with it
half-coy acting shy
belie misrepresent
lope run with a steady rhythm
somber darkening
gorge deep narrow passage

Preview the words by discussing their meanings in context.

Before

CRITICAL READING SKILL

Getting Ready to Write Preview the chart on page 114. Tell students that they will be reading to examine and compare the writing styles of Jack London and Scott O'Dell. Make sure that students understand the terms *point of view*, *figurative language*, and *tone*.

RESPONSE NOTES As they read, students should mark examples of the writer's style in the text, using the questions on page 112 as a guide. Remind students that they can circle or underline phrases and/or write notes about style in the Response Notes column.

LESSON 34 — GETTING READY TO WRITE

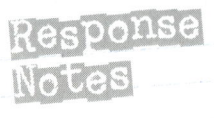

Using what you have learned in all of the units so far, demonstrate your best reading and writing skills. Read two short prose excerpts. You will complete an exercise to help you think about the excerpts and then write an essay about them.

Think about the authors you enjoy reading. What draws you to them? Is it the subject matter they write about? Is it the form (story, poem, or novel)? Or is it the style? You know about style when it refers to the kinds of clothes you choose or the way you wear your hair. Writers have styles that depend on the choices they make in diction (word choice) and sentence structure, as well as their subject matter and point of view. You have a writing style, too, one that is changing as you develop as a writer.

When you read the following excerpts, make notes about style choices such as these:

- Does the writer use mostly short, simple sentences, more complex sentences, or a combination?
- Is the narrator directly involved in the story or on the outside?
- Is the language informal or formal?
- Are the words simple or complex?
- Does the writing include much description? Does it include action?

In the following excerpt from *The Call of the Wild* by Jack London, Buck, who is a wolf and dog hybrid, encounters a wolf.

from The Call of the Wild by Jack London

He had made no noise, yet it ceased from its howling and tried to sense his presence. Buck stalked into the open, half crouching, body gathered compactly together, tail straight and stiff, feet falling with unwonted care. Every movement advertised commingled threatening and overture of friendliness. It was the menacing truce that marks the meeting of wild beasts that prey. But the wolf fled at sight of him. He followed, with wild leapings, in a frenzy to overtake. He ran him into a blind channel, in the bed of the creek, where a timber jam barred the way. The wolf whirled about, pivoting on his hind legs after the fashion of Joe and of all cornered husky dogs, snarling and bristling, clipping his teeth together in a continuous and rapid succession of snaps.

Buck did not attack, but circled him about and hedged him in with friendly advances. The wolf was suspicious and afraid; for Buck made three of him in weight, while his head barely reached Buck's shoulder. Watching his chance, he darted away, and the chase was resumed. Time and again he was cornered, and the thing repeated, though he was in poor condition or Buck could not so easily have overtaken him. He would run till Buck's head was even with his flank, when he would whirl around at bay, only to dash away again at the first opportunity.

But in the end Buck's pertinacity was rewarded; for the wolf, finding that no harm was intended, finally sniffed noses with him. Then they became friendly, and played about in the nervous, half-coy way with which fierce beasts belie their fierceness. After some time of this the wolf started off at an easy lope in a manner that plainly showed he was going somewhere. He made it clear to Buck that he was to come, and they ran side by side through the somber twilight, straight up the creek bed, into the gorge from which it issued, and across the bleak divide where it took its rise.

On the opposite slope of the watershed they came down into a level country where were great stretches of forest and many streams, and through these great stretches they ran steadily, hour after hour, the sun rising higher and the day growing warmer. Buck was wildly glad. He knew he was at last answering the call, running by the side of his wood brother toward the place from where the call surely came. Old memories were coming upon him fast, and he was stirring to them as of old he stirred to the realities of which they were the shadows. He had done this thing before, somewhere in that other and dimly remembered world, and he was doing it again, now, running free in the open, the unpacked earth underfoot, the wide sky overhead. ❖

ABOUT THE AUTHOR

Jack London was born in 1876 in San Francisco, California. London loved adventure and held many jobs during his life, including sailor, railroad hobo, journalist, and gold prospector in the Klondike. London wrote much in his short life (he died at age forty). *The Call of the Wild* is one of his most famous novels.

Scott O'Dell was born May 23, 1898, in Los Angeles, California. After working as a camera operator for movies and as a book editor for the *Los Angeles Times,* he became a full time writer of children's books.

O'Dell wrote *The Island of the Blue Dolphins* in 1960. He won the Newbery Medal for this book, a classic example of young adult literature. The book was even made into a motion picture.

In the following excerpt, a young girl named Karana is alone on an island after all the members of her tribe leave. In this section, Karana tries to leave the island for the mainland.

from Island of the Blue Dolphins by Scott O'Dell

At dusk I looked back. The Island of the Blue Dolphins had disappeared. This was the first time that I felt afraid.

There were only hills and valleys of water around me now. When I was in a valley I could see nothing and when the canoe rose out of it, only the ocean stretching away and away. Night fell and I drank from the basket. The water cooled my throat.

The sea was black and there was no difference between it and the sky. The waves made no sound among themselves, only faint noises as they went under the canoe or struck against it. Sometimes the noises seemed angry and at other times like people laughing. I was not hungry because of my fear.

During

COMPARING AND EVALUATING TEXTS Students are asked to compare the selections and then pick one to recommend as required reading for seventh grade. Make sure that students understand that they can think both books are worth reading, but they should pick one of them to recommend as required reading. Let them know that required reading is usually based on the following criteria:

Is it a book most students will enjoy? Does the book have important lessons to teach students at that age? Is the author someone students should study to learn more about the craft of writing?

TEACHING TIP

Using a Graphic Organizer: Comparison/Contrast Chart As students fill in the chart on page 114, have them think about what the two selections have in common and how they are different. If students need help, model filling in one of the entries in the chart: *In the last paragraph of O'Dell's selection, he says that "the canoe made a path in the black water like a snake." I'll put that down in the Scott O'Dell column, next to "Use of figurative language."*

Collaboration You may want to have students work with a partner or in small groups to find examples from the selections. Students can split up the selections, or they can divide the style choices.

The first star made me feel less afraid. It came out low in the sky and it was in front of me, toward the east. Other stars began to appear all around, but it was this one I kept my gaze upon. It was in the figure that we call a serpent, a star which shone green and which I knew. Now and then it was hidden by mist, yet it always came out brightly again. Without this star I would have been lost, for the waves never changed. They came always from the same direction and in a manner that kept pushing me away from the place I wanted to reach. For this reason the canoe made a path in the black water like a snake. But somehow I kept moving toward the star which shone in the east.

What style choices did Jack London and Scott O'Dell make? Use the chart below to compare and contrast their styles. Under the authors' names, give specific examples from the two excerpts.

Style Choice	Jack London	Scott O'Dell
Point of View (who is telling the story)		
Length of sentences		
Type of language (formal or informal, simple or complex)		
Use of figurative language (imagery, similes and metaphors)		
Tone (how the writing sounds: suspenseful, scary, exciting, and so on)		

You are now ready to write the first draft of your essay.

WRITING PROMPT:

Imagine you are on a planning committee for next year's seventh-grade English class. Based on the excerpts, which book—*The Call of the Wild* or *Island of the Blue Dolphins*—do you think should be required reading? Why? You may choose the criteria on which you base your answer, but consideration of style should be one of your points. Other criteria might be subject matter, compelling story, action, description, and so on. Remember, it is not enough to say you just liked one better. You need to explain why.

- Meet with your partner or group to share the first draft of your paper. Before you read each other's papers, it is important for you to know what your teacher will look for when he or she reads your story.

An outstanding paper will

- tell which book you would recommend.
- explain why you recommend that book by dealing with a comparison of important features such as style, subject matter, plot, and description.
- show how well you are able to
  - express your ideas
  - organize your ideas
  - write clear sentences that flow when read aloud
  - make good word choices (specific nouns, vivid verbs)
  - spell words correctly
  - punctuate and capitalize correctly

- Each of you will now read your paper aloud to a partner or members of a small group. When each person finishes reading, the other members should tell the reader what they liked about the paper. Then they should use the criteria in the box to offer constructive criticism. As your group members talk about your paper, make notes so that when you revise it, you will remember what they suggested.

Reading your paper with your group will help you make decisions about what you want to revise.

WRITING SUPPORT

Evaluation Criteria Review the list for writing an outstanding paper on page 115. Explain to students that this list serves as a guideline for evaluating their writing. Before they write their first draft, ask them to refer to this list. Then have them use the list when they revise their essay.

After

COMPARING TEXTS Have students compare two other texts and think about whether or not they should be required reading for students in the seventh grade. Their selections can be nonfiction or fiction, persuasive or factual. Encourage students not only to include their personal feelings about the text but also to explain why their selection would be important for seventh graders to read.

LESSON 35

Students will learn that self-assessment is valuable.

LESSON 35: REVISING AND EVALUATING YOUR WORK

Reread the list of the traits of an outstanding paper in Lesson 34. Then, using your notes, go over your draft carefully to decide how you can improve it. Make a clean copy of the final draft of your paper. Remember to give it a title.

REFLECTION

As you have worked through the lessons in this book, you have had many opportunities to learn and practice skills and strategies to become a better reader and writer. You have learned and practiced five essential critical reading and writing strategies:

- interacting with the text
- making connections
- exploring multiple perspectives
- focusing on language and craft
- studying an author

In this reflection, consider how much you have improved as a reader and writer during your work with the *Daybook*. Think about the areas in which you need more practice to become a more effective and confident reader and writer.

❋ Write a paragraph reflecting on how you have improved and what you can do to become a stronger reader and writer.

Self-assessment is an important part of learning how to strengthen your reading and writing skills.

Before

CRITICAL READING SKILL
Revising and Evaluating Your Work
Self-assessment allows students to think about their learning and to notice where they have improved and where they need to strengthen their efforts. It is worth taking time to reflect on one's own learning.

During

REVISING AND EDITING
Have students go over their draft carefully to decide where they can improve it, using the checklist on page 115 and feedback from their peers. Remind them to carefully edit and proofread their essay for spelling, punctuation, and usage errors before handing it in for your review.

After

APPLYING THE STRATEGY
Have students select another piece of their writing to revise based on the following criteria:

How well have they

❋ organized their ideas;
❋ written clear sentences;
❋ made good word choices;
❋ spelled words correctly;
❋ punctuated and capitalized correctly.

UNIT 8 EXPANDING YOUR REPERTOIRE

Lessons 36–40 pages 118–132

UNIT OVERVIEW
Students strengthen the basic strategies they have learned in order to gain deeper meaning from the texts.

KEY IDEA
A good writer uses techniques to be understood. A good reader works with the author's techniques in order to evaluate the message and meaning.

CRITICAL READING SKILLS
by lesson
36 Interacting with the text
37 Making connections
38 Exploring multiple perspectives
39 Focusing on language and craft
40 Studying an author

WRITING ACTIVITIES
by lesson
36 Write to monitor understanding.
37 Complete sentences that cite personal connections to a text.
38 Evaluate the effectiveness of presenting two perspectives.
39 Write a paragraph to evaluate an author's use of language in supporting a point of view.
40 Write paragraphs that show multiple perspectives of one event.

Expanding Your Repertoire

You probably lead an active life. Think of the activities you are involved with each week, or even each day—school, sports, clubs, friends, and performances—your life is action-packed. Successfully navigating your day and your schedule requires focus. You have to pay attention. You may find there's little time for sitting back and doing nothing at all.

Imagine now that you apply to your reading the same type of focus you give to the other activities of your life. It takes energy to read. Two of the main reasons for reading are to get information and to entertain yourself. When you read, you give meaning to the individual words on the page. This makes the reading personal.

In this unit, you will expand your repertoire of reading strategies by focusing on **reading for meaning.** Authors write to be understood, and with focus and effort you can discover what the author is trying to say and what the message means.

Literature

- ***Ice Drift*** by Theodore Taylor (novel excerpt)

An Inuit boy is seal hunting on the frozen sea when the ice begins to recede from land, throwing him and his dog into a desperate panic.

- ***True Believer*** by Virginia Euwer Wolff (novel excerpt)

Through narrative verse, LaVaughn, a fifteen-year old girl, gives running commentary on helping her mother prepare for a date.

- ***The Terrorist*** by Caroline Cooney (novel excerpt)

Events leading up to a terrorist bombing are recounted from the perspectives of its victim and his older sister.

- **"Homeless"** by Anna Quindlen (personal narrative)

A journalist recalls meeting a homeless woman and reflects on comfort and belonging.

ASSESSMENT See page 235 for a writing prompt based on this unit.

LESSON 36

Students will learn to monitor their understanding by becoming engaged with the text.

BACKGROUND KNOWLEDGE
Students will read part of a story about two brothers who live on an island off Greenland. Locate Greenland on a map, and ask what students know about the Arctic. Explain that, even though the weather changes with the seasons, most places have temperatures above freezing for only one month during the year. Also, because winter has stretches of days with little or no sunlight, there is not a lot of vegetation.

Explain that the characters in *Ice Drift* are Inuit, or native to the Arctic region. Ask: *What would it be like to live in the Arctic?*

VOCABULARY

char fish; a kind of trout

aglus hole in a piece of ice where a seal comes up for air

floe a large piece of floating ice

kayak a kind of canoe

Have students draw pictures of each vocabulary word. Groups can discuss what each individual item would look like, or students can create a small scene that incorporates all three.

LESSON 36 — INTERACTING WITH THE TEXT

Imagine two baseball teams in the middle of a game: the pitcher on the mound, watching the catcher's signs; the shortstop hunched over, glove in hand and the batter watching the pitcher. Everyone is interacting. But team sports are not the only games that involve interaction—think of your favorite board game or video game. Even these, like baseball, require that players pay attention to details in order to form winning strategies. Each move a player makes is determined by an earlier move. In all of these cases, the participants must **interact** with the game in order to play it effectively.

Interacting with a text also requires strategy. Instead of players on a field, there are words on a page; rather than characters on a screen, the words come to life in your mind. Your job is to pay attention and to make meaning from the words.

Interacting with the text requires you to establish *what* is happening, *when* and *where* it is happening, *why* it is happening, and *who* it is happening to. As you read the following excerpt from the novel *Ice Drift* by Theodore Taylor, use your **Response Notes** to record important details about *who, what, when, where,* and *why* as you best determine them in a very brief moment in the novel.

from *Ice Drift* by Theodore Taylor

The time was mid-October 1868, on the (eve of the long winter darkness.) The shallow noon light was already fading. Snow had fallen a week earlier and would stay until almost June. The caribou were mating, char were spawning, and the sea ice was forming. All over the arctic, inhabitants, both human and animal, were preparing for the frozen siege.

Response Notes: What does this mean?

❄ Interacting with the text requires you to focus on *who* is involved and what you are learning about the characters. As you continue reading, use your **Response Notes** to record details about the *who* in the novel.

Jamka, the lead sledge dog, had sniffed out the small hole where he expected a ringed seal would soon surface to breathe, and Alika had prepared for the day's hunt by building a windbreak of snow blocks and a snow-block seat next to the *aglus* that he covered with a square of polar bear hide to keep his

---

Before

CRITICAL READING SKILL
Interacting with the Text Briefly review strategies to interact with text: questioning, commenting, noticing, circling, highlighting, etc. Suggest that students use the 5 Ws (who, what, when, where, why) to construct questions to monitor their understanding. Then read the first paragraph aloud, modeling an interaction: *When did this story take place? Right away, I know this story took place more than 100 years ago.* Then ask students to find the supporting text (the first sentence). Model an interaction with the text by saying this: *I wonder if the ways of life there have changed much since 1868, a time when the United States was recovering from the Civil War.*

SETTING A PURPOSE Good readers identify a purpose for their reading. As students read, they should continue with the rest of the 5 Ws.

bottom warm. An indicator rod of caribou bone was in the hole. When a seal came up, it might touch the thin rod, wiggling it and alerting him.

Descendants of the Thule people who had first settled in the north a thousand years before, fourteen-year-old Alika and his brother, ten-year-old Sulu, were Inuit, meaning "mankind," and their diet was mostly from the sea, mostly cooked.

Alika said to Jamka. "You promised me a seal a long time ago."

The Greenland husky, dark eyes always seeming to have an intelligent expression, stared back as if to say, "But I didn't tell you when."

Alika sighed.

When Alika was seven years old, he and Jamka had bonded in an emergency, and they had been almost inseparable ever since. One September day, when the ice was still thin on a lake two miles from Nunatak, Alika was fishing for char when the crust broke. Into the water he went. Jamka pulled him out by the parka hood and dragged him home. Alika well remembered looking up at Jamka's wet belly as he slid on his back along the snow. He was convinced that Jamka thought like a human, and he trusted the dog with his life.

❄ Interacting with the text requires that you keep track of what is going on. Remember, you are reading for meaning. Use your **Response Notes** to keep track of what is happening.

Alika rose and called to the other dogs that were half buried in the snow. It was past time to go home.

Jamka stood up, also looking at the quickly darkening, threatening sky. Very experienced, Jamka seemed to sense danger in guiding the team, as if he knew exactly where hidden crevasses were; where the thin ice was. He'd fought polar bears and been wounded by them. He was the best lead dog Kussu had ever owned.

Then suddenly, unexpectedly, the floe shook and a loud crack shattered the stillness. Alika watched in horror as the dark expanse of water between the ice floe and the shore began to widen. *Three feet! Five feet! Seven feet!* Alika's body stiffened with fear and helplessness. The same thing had happened to several villagers without kayaks to reach shore. Their floe had split off, and they were never seen again. ❖

Now that you have interacted with the text, think about what you have learned so far.

ABOUT THE AUTHOR
Theodore Taylor was born in 1921 and raised in North Carolina. His careers in the U.S. Navy and the film industry took him to remote locales all over the world, providing inspiration and setting for many of his adventure-themed novels. Taylor started his writing career as a sports writer for radio news. After serving in World War II and the Korean War, he published over 25 novels for young adults, along with screenplays and other novels. His most famous work *The Cay*, published in 1969, is still widely read today.

EXTRA SUPPORT
Differentiation As the setting may be unfamiliar for students, some individuals will benefit from hearing the excerpts read aloud by you or an on- or above-level partner. Have readers adjust their reading rate according to the needs of their partners and allow them time to jot down their responses. To provide a visual context, see http://www.arctic.noaa.gov/gallery.html.

During

RESPONSE NOTES Regroup after students read each excerpt and model an interaction for the next one. For example:

❄ For the second excerpt, say: *Jamka expects a seal to come out of the hole. He must be good at hunting, and he probably goes hunting all of the time.*

❄ For the third excerpt, say: *Jamka senses danger and knows about thin ice. I wonder if he thinks they're going to fall through the ice!*

After students have finished each excerpt, solicit responses. Discuss the clues that students are finding in the text as well as their comments. Then sum up what's been learned about the story in the excerpt.

(Alika and his dog are very close, the setting plays a crucial role in the action, the author builds tension through the action.) Have students save their questions for the chart on *Daybook* page 120.

WRITER'S CRAFT

Point of View To respond to the second prompt on page 120, students are asked to write the next paragraph in the story. Students should note that the story is written from the third-person point of view. Contrast this style of writing with a first-person narrative, such as the excerpt from *Island of the Blue Dolphins* on page 113. Pronouns such as *he* and *they* are a clue to a third-person vantage point. The author tells only what an observer would see, not what the characters actually think and see. Discuss the differences in the two perspectives: what kind of information is in one but not the other? Which style of narrative do you prefer? Why?

Quick Assess

* Did students fill in the chart with what they know and what they don't understand about the excerpt?

* Were students able to reflect their understanding of the excerpt by writing a paragraph that is a logical extension of it?

✳ Use the chart below to organize your thinking about what you know and what you don't understand.

What is going on?	What don't I understand?
It's winter and very cold.	Why will snow stay until June? Is the Arctic always cold?

✳ Another way to monitor your understanding is to try to step into what you are reading and "walk around" in the action and events. In the space below, write the next paragraph in the story. Predict what will happen next.

Interacting with the text requires that you pay attention to what is going on, give meaning to what you read, and monitor your understanding as you read.

120 LESSON 36

After

APPLYING THE STRATEGY Choose another story the class has read for which making a connection was difficult, perhaps due to its unfamiliar setting or events. Read an excerpt from the story to the class. Draw the chart that appears on *Daybook* page 120 on the board or overhead, and complete it together. Have students reflect on how asking questions can help them understand the story better.

READING/WRITING CONNECTION Challenge students to create a cumulative story to continue the excerpt. Have students copy their completed paragraphs and form groups of three. Then, each student can take the paragraph from the person to the left and add another paragraph. When students are finished, have them repeat the process, writing an ending to the story. Groups can choose their favorite ending to the story and read it aloud to the class. Encourage interested students to read the novel and compare their ending with Taylor's.

MAKING CONNECTIONS — LESSON 37

As a reader, you are a very important player in the text. That's right. Even though you may not be the narrator, a character, or the author, you are involved. Sometimes what we read helps us understand ourselves better. Other times, we learn about other people and understand them better. Your knowledge and experience bring the story to life and allow the words on the page to become the ideas in your head.

Great writers are experts at creating people and situations that remind us of ourselves. Although we might not identify with everything a character does, we often see a little of ourselves or someone we know in the hopes, actions, and fears the author writes about.

In the following excerpt from *True Believer* by Virginia Euwer Wolff, look for something of yourself in the character, LaVaughn. Or perhaps the events and situations remind you of a friend or a family member instead. Use your **Response Notes** to keep track of places in the story where you **make connections**.

from True Believer by Virginia Euwer Wolff

31.

On Saturday night
I watched my mom making herself too pretty,
too detailed for just a night out with those women
she takes the job stress off with once in a while.
They go to a movie, a real laugher, and they howl together,
or a real crier, and they sob together,
and they have Chinese food after,
and they make a fuss over the movie for hours,
changing the ending to make it better, or even the middle,
till I wonder why they saw it in the first place.
Once I went along. But their voices
were too drowning out for me.

But this night my mom is not just
going with those women, I could tell.
It wasn't just pants and old shoes and a jacket.
It was a dress.

My mom can really wear a dress.

Something was up.

LESSON 37

Students will read a narrative written in free verse to make personal connections with the main character.

BACKGROUND KNOWLEDGE

Post this statement: *When I grow up, I want a good life.* Then discuss what it might mean. Ask: *What circumstances can contribute to a "good" life?* Answers may surround the issues of money, jobs, education, travel, or where one lives. Explain that students will read a novel excerpt about a teenage girl who lives amid urban poverty and violence but wants a better life in the future.

VOCABULARY

stitching a decoration made from thread

cooing talking in an overly happy way; similar to "baby talk"

queasy having nausea

grudge feelings of anger or bitterness

ceramic made from clay

Discuss the words by asking questions: *What objects are ceramic?* (a flower vase; a knick-knack) *What sound does someone make when he or she coos?* (soft, bird-like, baby sounds) *What does it mean to hold a grudge?* (you believe a person has offended you and you hold it against the person).

Before

CRITICAL READING SKILL

Making Connections Read aloud the first four lines of the excerpt and ask students how this excerpt looks different from other fiction excerpts. Elicit that it is written in free verse form, and emphasize that it should be read as a story. Students will be familiar with this form if they have read the excerpts from Jacqueline Woodson's *Locomotion* in Unit 5.

Then briefly review ways to make connections to a text. It might be helpful to post these questions on the board:

✻ Are any of these people similar to me or someone I know?

✻ Can I relate to what LaVaughn is thinking or feeling?

Remind students that asking questions as they read is a good strategy for making personal connections with the story. Remind students that whether or not they relate to LaVaughn, they should use their Response Notes to record questions and reactions.

ABOUT THE AUTHOR

Virginia Euwer Wolff was born in 1937 in Portland and raised in a log cabin in rural Oregon. Wolff started out as a high school English teacher, having her first novel published when she was in her 40s. *True Believer,* which is excerpted here, is the winner of the American Library Association's Printz Award for Excellence in Young Adult Literature, among other prestigious awards. It is a sequel to Wolff's *Make Lemonade*—the first book in a planned trilogy about LaVaughn.

WRITER'S CRAFT

Free Verse Point out that although *True Believer* is written as poetry, it neither rhymes nor follows a rhythm. Explain that this kind of poetry is called *free verse*.

Use the last two sentences of the excerpt to illustrate the difference between free verse and prose. First write the sentences on the board as a paragraph. Then write the sentences as they appear in the excerpt. Ask a volunteer to read both examples aloud, pausing at the line breaks for the verse form. Then ask: *The words are the same, but what is different about reading it each way?*

Point out that line breaks help the reader pause between bits of information. Also, they isolate important phrases, such as *and it is sacred*.

Response Notes

33.

His name is Lester.
He is at her new job, he is in charge of something there.
And he is coming to our house to eat supper.
My mom is a good cook, she brags
she never has those packages like at Jolly's house.
"Things with sauce" she calls them
and she insists, "We need sauce, I'll make sauce."
Now Lester is coming and I'll see what he looks like.

I still have my mind on Jody
And it's hard to concentrate on the rest of life
And now we get Lester. My throat goes lumpy.

My mom tells me to climb on the kitchen stool
and get down the good plates, three of them,
plus three more for dessert plus one for the rolls.
She tells me to move the stool to the other cupboard
to get the glasses we only use on holidays
when the aunts are here.

This Lester has some special stomach
to need all these special plates and holidays glasses.
Is it because he has a good job?
Is it because my mom is lonely?
I'm lonely, and I eat on the regular plates
every single time.

"Oh, and La Vaughn, you'll wear something nice, won't you?
How about that green sweater with pretty stitching?"
I honestly believe I hear my mom cooing.
Ick.
It makes me queasy.

I sit on the stool and tear up the lettuce
wondering what will happen
and resenting dressing up for Lester
when it's Jody I dress for everyday,
all the time sneaking and hiding from wherever he might be
to make sure he won't see me.

It's just a mouth.
Two mouths.
Jody's mouth and mine.
Just mouths, that's all.
Just the thought can take me out of whatever room I'm in.

122 LESSON 37

During

RESPONSE NOTES Help students make connections to the text as they read by encouraging them to ask themselves the posted questions. Remind them to explain their answers in the Response Notes.

TEACHING TIP
Collaboration Have students work in pairs in order to support each other's comprehension of the text. Use the Think-Pair-Share technique:

1. **Think** Have individuals write down connections and comments in the Response Notes as they read.

2. **Pair** Have students discuss their responses with a partner and choose one to share with the rest of the class.

3. **Share** Have pairs take turns sharing and discussing their responses with the class.

122 UNIT 8

34.

Lester arrives in person,
he is carrying live flowers in paper.
I feel bad immediately for my grudge on him.
He leans forward, he shakes my hand, his hand is soft.

My mom exclaims so bright over the flowers
and tells me almost in a song voice
to get the blue patterned ceramic pot and put them in.
Only she says "arrange," not put.

If Lester could read minds
he would see the history going between my mom and me.
That blue patterned pot
was a wedding gift. She always keeps it on that shelf
and it is sacred.

❋ Two of the main characters in this section are LaVaughn and her mother. Try to think of instances in the story when one of these characters reminds you of yourself or some part of your own experience. How do the characters remind you of people you know well? How do they and the situation LaVaughn describes make you feel?

Example from the story: *when her mother goes out with her friends for a movie or Chinese food.*

Makes me feel: *like my mother should do more of that. She works too hard and needs to enjoy herself more.*

Example from the story:

Makes me feel:

Example from the story:

Makes me feel:

Connecting the characters to your own experiences helps you understand yourself and the text better.

EXTRA SUPPORT

Differentiation Support students who struggle to make connections by asking questions such as the following after each numbered section:

❋ *What do you picture as you read? Do you see anything familiar?*

❋ *What is this section about? What do you think about as you read?*

Remind students that they don't necessarily have to agree with the character in order to find a connection to the text; their feelings can be different from what LaVaughn is feeling. Adjust the number of examples for students' reading level.

Quick Assess

❋ Do students find at least three meaningful connections to the text?

❋ Can students elaborate on why they do (or don't) relate to what is happening in the story?

❋ Do students' examples reflect the story? Do they explain their feelings?

After

APPLYING THE STRATEGY
Encourage students to read more of *True Believer*, looking for connections with the events of LaVaughn's life. Students may want to compare her life to a main character in another story. Have them complete a Venn diagram to compare and contrast the characters' circumstances. Have students present their diagrams to the class, using details from each story to support their comparisons.

READING/WRITING CONNECTION
Tell students to connect details from the story (for example, the good plates, special food, a gift of flowers) to a similar event in their lives. Then, have students write about the moment in free verse, imitating Wolff's style.

❋ Point out that, in free verse, authors try to mimic the natural rhythm of speech, breaking the lines where a speaker might pause. Encourage students to read their writing aloud to hear where to break the lines.

❋ Remind students that their narrative should describe the event, incorporating who was there and what was happening.

❋ Have volunteers practice and revise their verse with partners before reading it to the class.

LESSON 38

Students will read a story about a tragic event from two perspectives and determine how different points of view affect their understanding.

BACKGROUND KNOWLEDGE
Locate London on a map. With over 8 million people, London is about as populated as New York City. Briefly discuss students' knowledge of living in a large city and using public transportation. Explain that many people in London travel by underground subway.

The excerpt ends in a rather startling way: the package that Billy picks up explodes in his arms. Consider whether all students in your class are mature enough to handle this situation. This work is fiction; however, in a tragic coincidence, the London subway system suffered a major terrorist attack in 2005.

VOCABULARY
Scotland Yard/MI 5 security forces of the British government

funneled came from various directions toward one point

Underground formal name for London's subway system, also called the tube

Have students underline context clues and suggest possible definitions.

LESSON 38 EXPLORING MULTIPLE PERSPECTIVES

Each single moment in time is unique for each person. Each moment of your life is shaped by where you are and what you are doing. Think about a recent significant event. Maybe it was the birth of a new cousin, or the death of an older relative; maybe it was a natural disaster in a far-off place. Think about what you were doing at that moment. Now think about what that moment might have been like for someone who was personally involved.

Multiple perspectives allow a reader to look at a moment or event from more than one angle. From each **point of view,** the reader gains insight. In the following two excerpts from the same novel, you will see how an author weaves a moment together from two different perspectives.

Begin by reading Billy's perspective of the events. Use your **Response Notes** to record your reactions and questions.

from The Terrorist by Caroline Cooney

Once on the train, none of them sat. It would be unthinkable to take a seat when you could stand by the doors, swaying, feet spread, refusing to hold a metal post and too short to reach a hanging strap. Billy prided himself on never having fallen into anybody.

He gazed with superiority at the businessmen and women whose briefcases were hugged between their knees. Leather cases always made him think of his family's arrival at Heathrow Airport. Signs everywhere said not to leave baggage unattended. "Are they worried somebody will steal my pajamas?" Billy had asked his father.

"No, they're worried about bombs," explained his father. "Terrorists."

Billy's mother was so horrified by that, she reacted like a shepherd whose flock is surrounded by wolves. Constantly watching their dozen suitcases and tugging to make the pile more compact, she eyed innocent strangers for signs of evil intent.

Billy yearned to abandon a suitcase and see what happened next. Either Scotland Yard or MI 5 would seize it, which would be worth the whole flight, or else a terrorist would steal it and Billy could seize the terrorist, which would be worth any two flights.

Annoyingly, his parents had refused to leave a suitcase.

The train pulled into Baker Street, where they would change lines. The three boys hurled themselves out into the belowground corridors and sets of stairs.

Before

CRITICAL READING SKILL
Exploring Multiple Perspectives
Use the op-ed pages of a newspaper (including editorials, letters to the editor, cartoons) to illustrate various perspectives and points of view. Understanding multiple perspectives of an event helps to shape one's own thinking.

RESPONSE NOTES
Let students know that they will be reading two perspectives of one event. As the first excerpt is dense with action, encourage students to read slowly and ask questions about parts they don't understand. Model reading the first paragraph and making an interaction. For example: *Who are the people on the train? Why don't they like to sit?*

A train was waiting, doors open, car packed. They crammed themselves in. No need to hang on to anything this time: other bodies would keep them upright.

At the third stop, they leaped from the car, and began the race to see who would get outside to the fresh air first. It was another five pence for the winner. Billy firmly believed that pennies added up, even British pennies.

But he got caught by passengers swarming onto the train, so Chris and Georgie got way ahead. Chris yelled triumphantly over his shoulder, "I'm gonna win this time!"

Billy sprinted after them, slithering among the Indians, Asians, and Africans who made up the English population that he had thought would look like Robin Hood and Maid Marian.

Passengers funneled toward the only working escalator. Tired people stood on the right side, clutching briefcases, handbags, and shopping trolleys, little wire suitcases on wheels that Londoners used to bring their groceries home. Energetic people ran up the left edge as the steps moved under their feet.

Chris and Georgie were almost out of sight.

Billy tried to elbow past some old ladies, but somebody caught his arm. Expecting to be yelled at, Billy prepared to hide his American accent. Billy didn't mind being yelled at, but he hated it when somebody inevitable muttered, "Oh, those rowdy American children!"

If there was one thing English children were not, it was rowdy. Sometimes Billy wondered if they were even alive.

Actually at London International Academy, he was in classes with every nationality *except* the English. They had their own schools to go to. He was living right here in England and had tons of friends and none of them were English.

Billy decided on another new page in his notebook. He'd have a Nationality List. A Country Collection. Just in his sixth-grade homeroom were kids from Denmark, Iran, Syria, Argentina, Israel, Hong Kong, and America. He was pretty sure Juan was from somewhere else entirely, and Priya might be from India.

But the man who caught his arm actually smiled, saying, "Your friend dropped this."

Billy was amazed and pleased by this unusual helpfulness. "Oh gee, thanks a lot," he said. He grabbed the package and tore up the escalator.

Stopped by a woman who was awkwardly balancing a stroller with a baby across the width of the rising stairs, he glanced down at the package.

Funny.

He didn't remember Georgie or Chris carrying anything. Just book bags slung on their shoulders.

There was something very British about the package.

Not American.

The whole way it was wrapped. The cheapness of the cellophane tape. The texture of the brown paper.

EXPLORING MULTIPLE PERSPECTIVES 125

ABOUT THE AUTHOR
Caroline Cooney was born in 1947 and raised in Connecticut. She wrote eight novels before her first one was published—the result of a short story that appeared in *Seventeen* magazine. Cooney is a nonstop researcher and writer and has written over 75 books, including historical fiction, mystery, and suspense. She earned acclaim for her series of books about Janie Johnson, a teenager who discovers she may have been kidnapped from her family when she was a young girl.

EXTRA SUPPORT
Visual Learners To help students follow the events, encourage them to create a map of the subway station per the author's description. Include the following: the escalator; passengers moving toward, riding, and walking up or down the escalator; the woman with the stroller; and Billy. If possible, you may want to display photos of stations, available at the London Underground website: www.tfl.gov.uk/tube/arts/filming/filming-brochure.asp.

During

MONITORING UNDERSTANDING
Have students stop before completing the writing prompt on *Daybook* page 126. Briefly discuss the story and students' responses to assure that they have a full understanding of the story so far. Ask questions such as these:

❋ *Where did Billy begin?* (in the train) *Where is he right before the excerpt ends?* (the escalator)

❋ *Who is he with?* (his friends)

❋ *What was he thinking about on the train?* (his parents, reactions to signs at the airport that warn against leaving baggage unattended)

❋ *From where did he get the package?* (a friendly stranger)

Ask students to point out where they got the information for the answers they gave. Give students additional time to add or adjust their responses in light of anything they learned from the discussion.

EXPANDING YOUR REPERTOIRE

Response Notes

He remembered the signs and warnings at Heathrow. Do Not Leave Any Luggage Unattended. He remembered the fire drills at school, which the big kids said were really bomb drills.

There was a sickening moment of knowledge.

He could not throw the package into the innocent crowd.

There was no place to set it down.

Nor could he give it back.

In front of him was a sleeping baby.

Oh, Mom! thought Billy, turning away from the stroller and wrapping himself around the package.

The package exploded. ❖

✳ Take a moment to think about your strongest images and reactions to this scene. What are your impressions of Billy? What is the strongest image in your mind of what he is seeing and feeling throughout this scene? Do a quick-write to get all your thoughts and reactions down on paper.

WRITING SUPPORT

Forming Impressions Explain writing about impressions. Say: *When you give your impression of someone, you make judgments about what that person is like.* Then briefly discuss what influences personal impressions: what the person says and does, how the person reacts to situations, and so forth.

Use a think-aloud to model giving an impression of Billy. For example: *My first impression based on when he was thinking about leaving a suitcase at the airport as a joke was that he was a show-off and a troublemaker. Violating security rules could have caused a lot of problems! But when he wrapped himself around the package to protect the sleeping baby, my impression changed. Not everyone would make an unselfish, noble choice.*

Tell students that because impressions are based on personal opinion, there is no right or wrong answer to the prompt. However, students should connect their impressions to the events in the story.

✱ Now read another section of the novel that tells about the same moment in time, but from Billy's sister's **perspective.** Use your **Response Notes** to keep track of where you see similarities and differences in Billy's and Laura's perspectives.

Laura often thought that when her brother, Billy, grew up, he was going to be the heartthrob of his entire school. You could see in his arms the muscles that were going to come. And his thick, dark hair, which he never combed or brushed after a shower (assuming you could shove him into a shower with the water on in the first place), was going to lie around on his forehead, and girls would want to sweep it away from his flirty eyes…

Laura loved London. She was from a small suburb and, like everybody else in America, considered a car the only way to move, and she was correct: at home, public transportation was a trial and a joke. But in London she could hop on a bus, take the tube, or flag down a taxi. From Shakespeare to sweatshirt shopping, she was free the way no kids at home were until they had their own car.

The 113 appeared with Eddie waving insanely.

She got on, said "Hi" to Eddie and three other L.I.A. students, and the five of them sorted out with whom they would have lunch, whether anybody was going on the London Walk that afternoon, and had Laura heard about the escaped terrorists?

At L.I.A., they had bomb practice, the way in Massachusetts they had fire drills. L.I.A. students marched out the door and lined up on the sidewalk while London police timed them and teachers checked lockers and possible bomb-hiding spots. Everybody was happy, especially the people who got out of math…

"No, I didn't hear anything," said Laura. "What terrorists?" She wondered how the embassies would handle privacy once *Caller I.D.* appeared in London.

The five teenagers changed buses. They were disgusted with Laura. Hadn't she watched the morning news? Hadn't she read the morning paper?…

The bus halted with a lurch at their stop, which was in front of the tube exit and a mere three-block walk to L.I.A.

Laura was thinking that maybe terrific blond Andrew (a Ten) would talk to her after history. Maybe in the cafeteria she'd finally be in line next to that splendid hunk Mohammed (as opposed to Muhamet, who was sleazy, and Mohammet, who dated Jenny), and then—

Ambulances and fire trucks filled the sidewalks.

People were screaming and sobbing.

Police and teachers from L.I.A. were rushing back and forth

Her friends—Andrew, Con, Mohammed, Jehran, Bethany—were clinging to one another.

EXPLORING MULTIPLE PERSPECTIVES 127

WRITER'S CRAFT

Character and Perspective As students track differences in Billy's and Laura's perspectives, they will also notice differences in their characters. Point out that authors use characters' personal thoughts as a way to convey what the characters are like. Cooney fills this excerpt with Laura's thoughts. Pose questions for students to answer. For example:

✱ *In the beginning, what are Laura's thoughts about Billy?* (that he will be handsome some day)

✱ *Why does she like living in London?* (because she enjoyed the freedom of getting around the big city on her own)

✱ *How is Laura different from her friends?* (she is an American who did not have bomb drills in school)

✱ *What is on Laura's mind most of the time?* (her life in London, her friends, and meeting boys)

✱ *How do Laura's character traits affect her interpretation of the events around her?* (she is rather self-centered and unaware of danger)

Emphasize that Laura's perspective is not as visually detailed as Billy's because the immersion in her thoughts hinders her from comprehending what is happening. Therefore, her perspective could even be vastly different from her companions' view.

EXPANDING YOUR REPERTOIRE 127

EXTRA SUPPORT

Differentiation For the first prompt, some students may have difficulty generating parallel images, ideas, and actions from each excerpt. Students may want to start the task by creating separate timelines for Billy's and Laura's excerpts. As an intermediary step, students can draw connections between thoughts, images, and events that are on the timelines. Finally, they can use the chart to sum up their comparisons.

Quick Assess

* Do the charts show direct comparisons of the excerpts?
* Does the information in the chart correctly reflect the events of the story?
* Can students articulate how reading two different perspectives of the same event can affect their understanding of the event?

What had happened? Who was hurt? It must be very bad, it must be somebody from school, it must be—

Laura's clothing shivered on top of her skin.

Billy took the Underground.

Billy could be such a jerk. He liked to play with the car doors. He'd stick his head out, or his foot, and yank himself back in the nick of time. Laura was always yelling at him.

But of course it couldn't be Billy, because Billy was the kind of person who survived. Billy would always land on his feet. ❖

❋ You probably noticed several parallel events in time, and yet Laura is focusing her attention on very different things than Billy was. Use the space below to compare the images, ideas, and actions that contribute to their different perspectives of the same period of time. Refer back to your **Response Notes**.

Billy	Laura
* Billy gets on the subway with his friends.	* Laura is still waiting for the bus.
* Billy is thinking about the businessmen and focuses on their leather briefcases.	* Laura is thinking about Billy as a person.

❋ Compare your chart with a partner. Discuss how reading the two different perspectives affected your reactions to the events. Why or why not is it an effective technique to give more than one perspective?

_____
_____
_____
_____

Exploring multiple perspectives allows you to gain additional insight and understanding.

After

CHARACTER DEVELOPMENT

Ask students to speculate how Laura's life will be different after the events in these excerpts. Have them write a paragraph or two from Laura's perspective.

FOCUSING ON LANGUAGE AND CRAFT — LESSON 39

One of the ways authors appeal to readers is through the language they choose. **Emotional language** can evoke feelings. You might feel angry or scared or happy after reading a passage. The words and phrases can evoke strong mental pictures.

Read the excerpt that follows. Use your **Response Notes** to keep track of ideas that appeal to your emotions. Circle words and phrases or sentences that cause particular reactions.

from "Homeless" by Anna Quindlen

Her name was Ann, and we met in the Port Authority Bus Terminal several Januarys ago. I was doing a story on homeless people. She said I was wasting my time talking to her, she was just passing through, although she'd been passing through for more than two weeks. To prove to me that this was true, she rummaged through a tote bag and a manila envelope and finally unfolded a sheet of typing paper and brought out her photographs.

They were not pictures of family, or friends, or even a dog or cat, its eyes brown-red in the flashbulb's light. They were pictures of a house. It was like a thousand houses in a hundred towns, not suburb, not city, but somewhere in between, with aluminum siding and a chain link fence, a narrow driveway running up to a one-car garage and a patch of backyard. The house was yellow. I looked on the back for a date or a name, but neither was there. There was no need for discussion. I knew what she was trying to tell me, for it was something I had often felt. She was not adrift, alone, anonymous, although her bags and her raincoat with the grime shadowing its creases had made me believe she was. She had a house, or at least once upon a time had had one. Inside were curtains, a couch, a stove, pot holders. You are where you live. She was somebody.

I've never been very good at looking at the big picture, taking the global view, and I've always been a person with an overactive sense of place, the legacy of an Irish grandfather. So it is natural that the thing that seems most wrong with the world to me right now is that there are so many people with no homes. I'm not simply talking about shelter from the elements, or three square meals a day or a mailing address to which the welfare people can send the check—although I know that all these are important for survival. I'm talking about a home, about precisely those kinds of feelings that have wound up in cross-stitch and French knots on samplers over the years. ❖

Response Notes: I don't always think of homeless people as "somebody."

LESSON 39

Students will read a story and evaluate how a writer uses language to appeal to a reader.

BACKGROUND KNOWLEDGE
Solicit students' associations with *homeless*.

❖ What would be the hardest thing about being homeless?

❖ If you were homeless, what would you carry with you?

❖ Would anyone choose to be homeless? Why or why not?

Explain that students will read a personal narrative about one woman's encounter with a homeless person.

VOCABULARY
anonymous without an identity

global view having a broad perspective

cross-stitch a kind of embroidery handicraft

French knots on samplers an allusion to a common symbol of home—the words "Home, Sweet Home" cross-stitched in a wall hanging; French knot is a particular type of stitch

Speculate with students on the possible significance of each term in an essay about homelessness.

Before

CRITICAL READING SKILL
Focusing on Language and Craft

Explain that part of evaluating a writer's message is paying attention to how the words and phrases affect your emotions. To illustrate this, point out the title of the selection and ask students: *Does this make you think the topic will be happy, fun, or serious? Does it make you want to read on or not?*

As students read the excerpt, have them circle words or phrases that appeal to the emotions. Students can use the Response Notes column to list their reactions to the language in the excerpt.

SHARING RESPONSES
When students are finished reading and responding, have pairs of students share their examples from the text, along with their reactions.

ABOUT THE AUTHOR

Anna Quindlen was born in 1953 in Philadelphia and attended college in New York City. She first wrote for the *New York Post* and eventually penned a regular column for the *New York Times*, winning the Pulitzer Prize for Commentary in 1992. Besides commentary, Quindlen has published novels and children's books. Both her fiction and nonfiction center on themes of simplicity, values, and the struggle to live a thoughtful life in a materialistic world. This excerpt comes from Quindlen's 1989 compendium of newspaper columns, *Living Out Loud*.

Quick Assess

* Were students able to create a word picture that depicts their strongest feelings about "Homeless"?

* Did students comment clearly on the effectiveness of Quindlen's use of language?

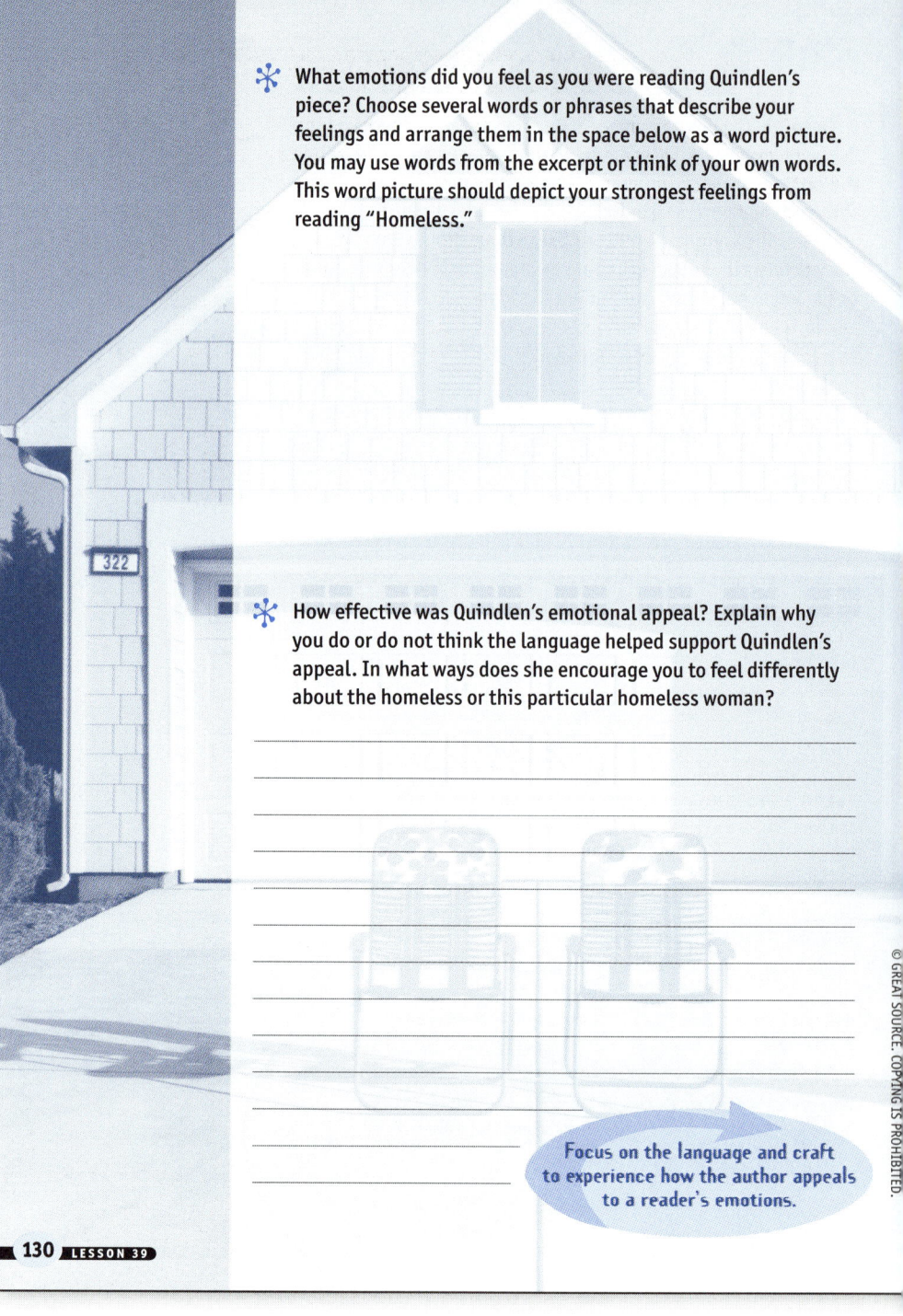

* What emotions did you feel as you were reading Quindlen's piece? Choose several words or phrases that describe your feelings and arrange them in the space below as a word picture. You may use words from the excerpt or think of your own words. This word picture should depict your strongest feelings from reading "Homeless."

* How effective was Quindlen's emotional appeal? Explain why you do or do not think the language helped support Quindlen's appeal. In what ways does she encourage you to feel differently about the homeless or this particular homeless woman?

_____
_____
_____
_____
_____
_____
_____
_____
_____
_____

Focus on the language and craft to experience how the author appeals to a reader's emotions.

130 LESSON 39

During

WRITING SUPPORT

Evaluating To prepare students for the second prompt, clarify Quindlen's appeal: people need more than shelter; they need a place to belong. Then use a think-aloud to model an evaluation. For example: *The author says, "She was somebody." She gets right to the point. This made me want to read more.* Or: *The author uses a lot of imagery, but I'd rather that she suggest what I can do about the issue.*

After

LISTENING/SPEAKING CONNECTION
Have the class brainstorm other social topics they might want to investigate such as crime, poverty, gangs, etc. Then, have students form groups and choose one topic to research. Have the groups formulate interview questions to ask family members or friends regarding the topic.

When students have gathered their information, have each group create a word picture poster that uses the most powerful words and phrases from their interviews. As groups present their posters, they should explain:

* how each word relates to the topic;
* how they represented their interviewees' ideas on the topic.

Afterward, have each student write a short reflection on what they learned from doing the research.

STUDYING AN AUTHOR — LESSON 40

The meaning you get from your reading determines how you react to what you read. What are some reasons that you were drawn to the writing of one author more than another in this unit? Discuss this with a partner.

In this lesson, you will analyze the meaning you took from each excerpt as a way of thinking about your reaction to each author. Each writes about a different subject with flair and style. But the work you did *with* the author determines what you will take away. By *monitoring* your reading of each author, you will figure out why that author appeals to you.

❋ Use the chart below to help you sort out the meaning you took from each piece. In each box, answer the questions asked.

Author	Did you make a personal connection to this piece? Why or why not?	What did you notice about the language and craft in this writing?	What did you learn from this author?
Theodore Taylor, *Ice Drift*			
Virginia Euwer Wolff, "True Believer"			
Caroline Cooney, *The Terrorist*			
Anna Quindlen, "Homeless"			

STUDYING AN AUTHOR 131

LESSON 40

Students will review the excerpts in this unit and rank their preference based on what they learned from the writing of each author.

BACKGROUND KNOWLEDGE
Briefly review how authors crafted the previous four selections.

❋ In *Ice Drift,* Theodore Taylor used action and dialogue to convey danger and suspense.

❋ In *True Believer,* Virginia Euwer Wolff used narrative verse to help readers connect with her character's inner thoughts.

❋ In The *Terrorist,* Caroline Cooney used multiple perspectives to provide a broad view of one moment in time.

❋ In "Homeless," Anna Quindlen used description of one moment to make a point about an issue.

Then invite students to share which selection they thought was the most meaningful or memorable. Use questions to provoke input, such as these: *Which character or viewpoint did you relate to? Which selection made you feel like you were right there, in the middle of the scene?*

Before

CRITICAL READING SKILL
Studying an Author Explain that good readers pay attention to the meaning and connections they draw from a text. Then say: *Sometimes, the way that something is written can influence how meaningful it is to you.*

Have students complete the chart. Read through each question and, as necessary, model finding examples from the selections. For example: *When I was younger, I had a dog who protected my home. So, I connected to Alika's feelings about Jamka.* Or: *Even though it was interesting, I didn't connect to* Ice Drift *because my life circumstances are so different from Alika's.*

SHARING RESPONSES
After students have completed their charts, compose a chart together as a class. Invite students to share their responses.

TEACHING TIP
Acknowledging Contributions Write down students' names next to their additions to the class chart. This acknowledges contributors and helps build their confidence in reviewing text.

EXPANDING YOUR REPERTOIRE 131

EXTRA SUPPORT

Differentiation Use modeling to help students who may have difficulty creating multiple perspectives.

1. Choose an event, preferably one at which students were also present, such as a school performance or assembly.
2. Choose a viewpoint in addition to your own—such as a performer or an audience member.
3. Chart a few actions, images, and thoughts for each viewpoint.

WRITING SUPPORT

Portraying Multiple Perspectives
Remind students that they must be able to describe with detail the event they choose. Brainstorm possible events with multiple perspectives, such as the following: weddings, ceremonies, sports events, or world events witnessed on television.

Have students return to their Response Notes and written work for this unit. Review how to formulate a timeline for different viewpoints, using it to draw comparisons and contrasts in the two perspectives.

Quick Assess

- Did students complete the chart on author's language?
- Do students' paragraphs each reflect the perspective of a character in the story excerpts?

※ Now think about what you can learn from the author that will be useful in your own writing. Use Cooney's crafting of multiple perspectives as a guide, for example. Think of an event in your life that can be told from two different viewpoints. Use the space below to outline the events from each viewpoint, just as you did when you charted Billy's and Laura's perspectives.

Viewpoint #1	Viewpoint #2

※ Using the chart above, draft an opening paragraph from each perspective. Share your paragraphs with a partner.

PARAGRAPH #1

PARAGRAPH #2

One way of studying an author is to monitor the connections and meaning you make from reading that author's work.

During

READING/WRITING CONNECTION
Have students choose two authors from the unit's selections and write a comparison of their style and craft. Students can use the information in the charts on *Daybook* page 131, as well as a Venn diagram, for planning their writing. Encourage students to expand on their points by returning to the selections and finding additional examples of language, craft, and personal connections.

After

APPLYING THE STRATEGY
Have students read additional works by their favorite author. While reading, have students use interactive strategies to monitor whether or not the author uses the same style and whether or not they continue to enjoy the author's work, especially if it's a sequel. Students can also focus on meaning, tracking whether or not the author continues to focus on the same topics and themes.

Interacting with the Text

We are surrounded by **visual information**, some designed to entertain and some designed to persuade. Knowing how words and pictures work together to communicate messages will help you understand and question the content of the messages. To **interact** with **visual text**, you can use many of the strategies you have already learned for interacting with print text. You will also learn new strategies for reading visual images, and you will create visual text of your own.

UNIT 9 INTERACTING WITH THE TEXT

Lessons 41–45, pages 134–146

UNIT OVERVIEW
Through excerpts from graphic novels, students learn the importance of interpreting visual text.

KEY IDEA
Comprehending visual texts requires learning a new set of skills and applying previously learned skills to assist with reading words and pictures.

CRITICAL READING SKILLS
by lesson
41 Making inferences based on visual clues
42 Identifying characteristics of a visual-text genre (graphic novel)
43 Comparing style and design
44 Analyzing visual elements
45 Adapting a poetic text to visual form

WRITING ACTIVITIES
by lesson
41 Complete an inference chart.
42 Explain how an author uses visual characteristics to communicate ideas.
43 Compare styles of two authors.
44 Identify ways visual text conveys sound.
45 Create visual text for a poem.

Literature

- *Bone* by Jeff Smith (graphic novel excerpts)

The novel relates the adventures of the three Bone cousins, Fone, Smiley, and Phoney. In these excerpts, Fone, rescued and befriended by Thorn, finds himself in conflict with a honey vendor at a fair who attempts to woo Thorn.

- *The Borden Tragedy* by Rick Geary (graphic novel excerpt)

This retelling, based on unpublished memoirs of an unknown woman from Massachusetts, brings a new perspective to the historic tale of Lizzie Borden, who was tried for the axe-murder of her parents. In this excerpt, Lizzie tells a neighbor of her concerns about her family's safety.

- "Annabel Lee" by Edgar Allan Poe (poem)

The speaker describes the rare love he shared with Annabel Lee and deeply mourns her death.

ASSESSMENT To assess student learning in this unit, see pages 236 and 253.

LESSON 41

Students will read an excerpt from the Bone series by Jeff Smith to interact with visual text and make inferences about meaning.

BACKGROUND KNOWLEDGE

Smith's Bone cousins are creatures that have some human characteristics and special powers:

✳ Phoney Bone often concocts scams that result in chaos.

✳ Fone Bone has the ability to cope with most any situation. He consistently saves his cousin Phoney from the results of his schemes.

✳ Smiley Bone has a penchant for participating in outlandish plots that have no hope for success.

Thorn, a girl who befriends Fone, is one of several human characters the Bone cousins meet in the course of their adventures and escapades.

VOCABULARY

combs honeycombs; the waxy structures in which bees store honey

whiff a light breath; the phrase "take a whiff" means to smell something

Discuss the meanings and then have students use each term in a sentence that confirms understanding of the term.

LESSON 41 MAKING INFERENCES

Readers **make inferences** by reading "between the lines," filling in what is not stated directly by making a reasonable guess that is based on what is stated. You use what you read in a text and what you know to make an inference. When you read dialogue in a story, you might put yourself in the character's place. When the text includes visual information, you are given additional clues as to how a character feels and speaks the words in the story, similar to stage directions in a play.

Bone is a nine-volume series that tells the epic adventures of the three Bone cousins—Fone, Smiley, and Phoney. They are run out of Boneville, get separated in an uncharted desert, and slowly find each other again in a forested valley populated by strange and wonderful creatures. Thorn rescues and befriends Fone. She hopes to help him find his cousins and then send them all home, but there are terrifying adventures ahead that will interfere with their plans. In the excerpt that follows, Thorn and Fone go to the spring fair. As you read the story, see what you can infer about the characters.

Before

CRITICAL READING SKILL

Making Inferences Read the explanatory text aloud. Remind students that making an inference about the characters involves adding what they know to their reading of new text. Explain that in visual texts, much of the story can be inferred by studying the pictures first.

Point out the hearts drawn around Fone's head and his facial expression in the first two frames. Then point out the vertical lines over his head and his facial expression in the third frame.

Ask students to add what they know about these symbols to infer what Fone is feeling (attraction, infatuation). Then invite students to infer his feelings from the pictures in rows two and three, noting such details as facial expressions, gestures, and posture and proximity of the characters.

When they are finished making inferences, invite students to read aloud the words to verify their inferences.

from **Bone** by Jeff Smith

ABOUT THE AUTHOR
Born in the American Midwest, Jeff Smith began learning about cartooning at an early age from the comic strips, comic books, and animated shorts on TV that so captivated him. He started the Bone cousin stories while he was still in kindergarten! During his four years at Ohio State University, Jeff drew comic strips for the student newspaper, and in 1986 he co-founded the Character Builders animation studio. In 1991, he launched a company called Cartoon Books to publish his *Bone* books. Currently printed in thirteen languages, *Bone* has earned several European awards. See http://www.boneville.com/cartoonbooks/drawingboard/.

TEACHING TIP
Collaboration Have students work in triads to read aloud the dialogue in the excerpt. Allow time for the groups to practice the excerpt several times so that each person's reading is fluent and expressive. The text contains some humor and exaggerated personalities, so students can certainly "ham" it up!

EXTRA SUPPORT
Differentiation Some students may have trouble understanding the referents for pronouns in the last two frames of the excerpt. *A nose like that* refers to Fone's nose, which in the illustration is a bit large. *It's not that big* also refers to Fone's nose.

During

DETERMINING SEQUENCE Explain that authors of graphic novels use several ways to suggest the passage of time and sequence of events. They can use the shape of a panel (a wider rectangle might seem to indicate a longer period of time), the white space around a panel, and the words within the panel. It is still up to the reader to fill in the gaps by making inferences.

Point out that in this excerpt, panels two and three in the top row are linked by the two parts of Thorn's sentence, showing a short time. The gap in action that occurs between the last panel in the first row and the first panel in the second row is longer. In row one, Thorn and Fone have just arrived at the fair. In row two, they are shown at Tom's booth at the fair.

Ask students to imagine what happened in between, draw a panel, and write speech bubbles to convey what probably occurred. After reading the last row of frames in this excerpt, challenge students to predict what will happen next.

WRITING SUPPORT

Prewriting Invite students to review the inferences they made as they read the excerpt. Then ask them to mark the visual details and text in each panel they used to make inferences. Ask students to identify two or three inferences that they feel are strongly supported in the pictures or text of the story. Then have them choose from these inferences to complete their chart. Encourage students to add more rows to the chart.

Quick Assess

* Did students mark details in both text and pictures to interact with the text and make inferences?

* Did they complete both columns of the inference chart?

 Use the inference chart to record your conclusions about the characters and the story. In the right-hand column describe or draw the word and visual clues writer/artist Jeff Smith provided. There is space for you to add another inference and other techniques.

Inference	Technique
Fone Bone has a crush on Thorn.	hearts around his word bubble dreamy-eyed look created by adding a line at the top of his eyes
Thorn is protective of Fone Bone.	She holds his hand and leads him. She defends him against Tom's insult.

Reading the pictures and the text together helps you make better inferences about the story.

136 LESSON 41

After

APPLYING THE STRATEGY

Making Inferences Ask students to bring in examples of visual texts they have read outside school. Encourage them to create inference charts similar to the one in the *Daybook* and use pictorial and textual clues to make inferences and fill in the gaps in sequence in each example. Then have them share their observations in their reading groups or class.

CHARACTERISTICS OF A GENRE — LESSON 42

One way of understanding a **genre,** or a type of writing, is to look at its **characteristics.** Characteristics are the features that define a genre. In fantasy, for example, you might find talking animals or a battle between good and evil. Visual texts have their own characteristics, such as ways to show emotion or emphasis. Knowing the characteristics can help you get more out of a text.

As you finish reading the scene with Thorn, Tom, and Fone Bone at the fair, think about the characteristics of **graphic novels.**

from **Bone** by Jeff Smith

Response Notes

CHARACTERISTICS OF A GENRE 137

LESSON 42

Students will use the characteristics of a genre to make inferences.

BACKGROUND KNOWLEDGE
To build background for Tom's and Fone's comments about bees and smoke, explain how beekeepers utilize a smoker (a portable firebox with a spraying nozzle and bellows) to extract honeycombs from beehives. The beekeeper blows smoke into the hive. The smoke has two effects: it dulls the guard-bees' receptors so they don't warn the colony of an invasion; it also causes bees to gorge themselves on honey, which makes them drowsy. Once the bees are subdued by the smoke, the beekeeper can safely remove the honeycombs from the hive.

VOCABULARY

cupie-doll a variation in spelling of Kewpie doll, an early 1900s doll with a rotund body and a wisp of hair

toddle to walk unsteadily

freak show a display of unusual creatures, such as a two-headed dog, commonly found at a fair

carnie mildly insulting slang term for "carnival worker"

runt a small creature. The runt of a litter of puppies is the smallest.

Discuss the meanings and have students highlight each term in the text as they read.

Before

CRITICAL READING SKILL
Identifying Characteristics of a Genre Explain that writers employ specialized techniques to convey meaning. In textbooks, for example, writers often incorporate visual information in graphs and charts to clarify concepts. Ask: *How would you describe this visual text to someone who has never seen one? What characteristics would you mention?* Help students develop a list, such as:

✤ panels (individual pictures) with white space around them

✤ speech balloons to show what characters say

✤ word balloons to show what characters think

✤ facial expressions, symbols, and gestures

Suggest that students circle examples of these techniques and explain their purpose in the Response Notes.

INTERACTING WITH THE TEXT 137

EXTRA SUPPORT

Differentiation Point out textual characteristics, such as informal or conversational English (*th'* for "the," *an'* for "and," etc.), punctuation marks, and oversized copy. Explain that authors of visual text use special techniques to provide information to the reader. In the last panel, for example, Fone challenges Tom when he says "HEY!" The techniques used (large letters and exclamation point) convey Fone's emotions loudly.

Invite pairs of students to prepare Readers' Theater presentations of one or more panels, using the techniques as their stage directions. Encourage supportive feedback to the performers for their interpretations of the text.

Response Notes

✳ Before you write about the characteristics of this genre, think about the inferences you made about the characters in Lesson 41. What do you you think about them now? What will they do next?

_____
_____
_____

138　LESSON 42

During

CRITICAL READING SKILL

Examining the Setting Explain that Jeff Smith set his story in the past and created visual and print details to support the setting:

✳ a country fair in a long-ago village

✳ Thorn's clothing, Tom's bare chest and hat, the honey booth

✳ words like *cupie-doll* and *freak-show*

Remind students to watch for these and other techniques the author adds to communicate the setting and record them in the Response Notes.

138　UNIT 9

❋ To help you think about characteristics of visual texts, answer the following questions.

- In what order did you read the panels of *Bone*?

- Where is Fone Bone placed in relationship to Tom and Thorn in this scene compared to the panels in Lesson 41? How much power does he seem to have to separate Tom and Thorn?

- What are the different ways that Smith uses lines to show anger?

> Sequence, layout, and expression lines are three characteristics of graphic art that convey meaning.

WRITING SUPPORT

Organizing Ideas Explain that artists position their characters within each frame to show how they relate to each other. To illustrate the concept, invite one student to stand in front of another. Point out that the student in front appears to be the leader and the second student in line appears to be the follower. Invite students to fill in a chart with notes about the relative positions of Tom, Thorn, and Fone:

Page	In front	Between	Close/Far
134			
135			
137			
138			

Have students use this chart to formulate their responses to the second prompt on page 139.

Quick Assess

❋ Do students explain the order in which they read the panels?

❋ Do students discuss how Fone's power is expressed?

❋ Do students comment on several ways that Smith shows anger?

After

APPLYING THE STRATEGY

Create a Setting Suggest that pairs or small groups of students brainstorm how the story would be different if set in modern times and which techniques would communicate a modern-day setting. For example, Thorn and Tom would wear modern clothes and Thorn and Fone might visit a candy shop in a mall or a fast food restaurant. Have students work together to rewrite one episode of the story, set in modern day. Then have them share their story with the class.

LESSON 43

Students will compare visual texts by two different authors to explore how style and design influence the readers' experience.

BACKGROUND KNOWLEDGE
Students will read part of a perspective on the story of the Borden murders. Lizzie Borden was 32 years old when she reported that her father and stepmother, with whom she lived, had been killed. Lizzie was charged with the murders, and the circumstantial case against her was strong. The decisive facts presented at trial included the following: both Bordens had been slain by multiple blows of an axe; although witnesses saw no trace of blood on Lizzie moments after the murders, three days later a friend saw Lizzie burning a dress that Lizzie claimed was paint stained. No other relatives, residents, or servants in the home were charged in connection with the crime. Lizzie was acquitted of the crime, but she lived the rest of her life under its shadow.

VOCABULARY
maiden an unmarried woman
foreboding a feeling that something dreadful is about to happen
grim serious, gloomy
adjacent to next to, connected to

Discuss the meanings and conduct the Word Splash activity on on page 272.

LESSON 43 STYLE AND DESIGN

Artists who write and illustrate **graphic novels** use such elements as lines, depth of field, and space to convey their ideas. The choices artists make about the design of the visual images contribute to their individual **styles**.

In *The Borden Tragedy,* Rick Geary presents the story of Lizzie Borden, who was accused of using an axe to kill her father and stepmother in 1892. Although she was ultimately found not guilty, suspicion remained, especially since the murderer was never found. Geary claims that his story has been "excerpted and adapted from the unpublished memoirs of a (thus far) unknown lady of Fall River, Massachusetts." As you read about Lizzie's visit to Alice Russell on the night before the murders, pay attention to the art as well as the words.

from The Borden Tragedy by Rick Geary

Before

CRITICAL READING SKILL
Style and Design Explain that within the general genre of movies, there are many sub-genres, such as romantic comedies, documentaries, horror films, and adventure movies. Similarly, there are sub-genres within the genre of graphic novels, including fantasy stories, historical fiction stories, nonfiction stories, and superhero stories. Explain various style elements of that are typical of each sub-genre. For example, nonfiction graphic novels tend to use more straight lines and subdued colors, while superhero comics usually use more curved lines and bright colors.

If available, distribute examples of a variety of graphic novels and invite groups of students to discuss the uses of lines, space, and depth of field in each sample. Then invite groups to share their observations with the class.

ABOUT THE AUTHOR

Rick Geary, born in 1946, is known primarily for his nonfiction comic books. He often uses unusual narrative devices, such as the period diary excerpts that tell the Lizzie Borden story. Geary began working in comics in 1977, contributed to the *National Lampoon* for thirteen years, and illustrated for *The New York Times Book Review* for four years. For more information, see the author's website: www.rickgeary.com.

EXTRA SUPPORT

Differentiation Demonstrate how to read the visual details. Model how to mark up a frame to draw attention to specific elements. For example, circle a historically accurate detail, a realistic facial expression, an accurately drawn object, a deep shadow, and a spatial element. Explain how each creates an impression of realism.

During

AUTHOR'S STYLE Point out artistic style and design elements that Rick Geary uses for this nonfiction story: realistic facial features, historically accurate details of the house exterior and interior, dark background, and captions for narration. Ask: *How do these drawings differ from those in the Bone excerpt? Why do you think Mr. Geary uses this style for this story?* Facilitate a discussion of how the design elements also present a serious, factual tone: the straight lines create realism, the deep shadows show depth of field, and the use of space all contribute to the realism.

TEACHING TIP

Collaboration Form groups of three. Have group A complete the first row of the chart, group B complete the second, and group C complete the third. As each group shares its findings with the class, have the other students take notes to use in completing their own comparison charts.

Quick Assess

* Do students' Response Notes include style and design elements?
* Are students' comparison charts complete?
* Do students' comparisons address all the notes in their comparison charts?

✳ Use the following chart to compare the design of the panels in *The Borden Tragedy* to the panels in *Bone*.

	The Borden Tragedy	**Bone**
Kinds of lines and how they are used		
Depth of field (impression of depth, having a foreground and a background)	Art seems 3-dimensional. The characters stand out from the background.	
Use of space		Each panel includes a lot of detail. There is often some white space near the center, where nothing is drawn.

✳ Compare Jeff Smith's style in *Bone* to Rick Geary's in *The Borden Tragedy*. Which style do you prefer? Why? Use the chart to support your thinking.

> Authors and artists create a distinctive style, which determines how the reader experiences their work.

LESSON 43

After

CONNECTIONS TO CURRENT EVENTS Explain that the tale of Lizzie Borden is one of the most intriguing tales in U.S. history. Encourage students to compare the story to modern-day trials that have received a great deal of media and public attention. Discuss media treatment of serious issues today.

Invite students to discuss possible reasons for continued curiosity in the tale. Suggest such factors as the violent nature of the crime, the fact that the accused was a woman, and the fact that the crime has never been solved.

UNIT 9

DIALOGUE, NARRATION, AND SOUND — LESSON 44

Where do the words go in graphic novels? You have already seen two techniques for placing words in a visual text. Jeff Smith used just **dialogue** in word balloons. His word balloons take on different shapes, such as the wavy boundary around "Hello, small mammal!" and the hearts around the first part of Fone Bone's conversation with Thorn. These details help the author convey a character's feelings. Rick Geary used both a **narrator**, whose words are not in a balloon, and dialogue in word balloons for Alice and Lizzie. The word balloons seem almost formal with their similar shape and dark lines, which would fit the atmosphere Geary was trying to re-create.

Sound also has to be conveyed visually. How does the reader know that a character is shouting or whispering? How does the reader know which words to emphasize or how fast or slow the character is speaking? How does the reader know when a speaker pauses?

❉ Imagine that you want to draw a conversation between two people. You can use the techniques that Jeff Smith and Rick Geary used, such as word balloons of different shapes, a bold font to emphasize certain words, and other techniques that you noticed.

Draw that conversation in the space provided on page 144. You can add drawings of characters, if you like, or you can let the word balloons stand alone. Readers of your conversation should be able to tell immediately how the two characters feel by looking at how their words are displayed.

LESSON 44

Students will examine conversations in graphic novels to understand how dialogue, narration, and sound are conveyed in visual text.

TEACHING TIP

Collaboration Students may find it easier to find examples with a partner. Partners should agree on which story to examine. Encourage them to read one excerpt aloud, taking the parts of the narrator and characters. Allow enough time for them to read their selection several times. Then have them identify and record the techniques the author used in a chart. In a paragraph, have students explain which techniques helped them read the dialogue and interpret characters' feelings.

Before

CRITICAL READING SKILL
Analyzing Visual Elements Remind students that visual text artists often try to make printed words look like they sound by employing such techniques as:

❉ boldface letters

❉ italics

❉ onomatopoetic words, such as *Bam!* or *Whoosh!*

❉ ellipses and dashes

Ask students which techniques they think are effective and why.

Tell students to choose from these techniques when they draw their own conversation.

During

USING VISUAL ELEMENTS
Invite students to circle or highlight examples of visual sound techniques in the excerpts in Lessons 41-43. Then discuss what each technique indicates in each excerpt. Ask: *How does the author show a pause, a voice trailing off, or interrupted speech? How does he show emphasis or volume? How does he reveal aspects of a character's personality?*

INTERACTING WITH THE TEXT

TEACHING TIP

Collaboration Encourage students with advanced abilities to create an entire conversation using a single word, such as *yes* or *what* in a meaningful variety of ways.

Quick Assess

* Did students use different techniques for conveying sound visually?

Knowing how authors and artists convey dialogue, narration, and sound helps readers better understand both the art and the words in a visual text.

After

WRITING/SPEAKING CONNECTION

Display several short sentences, showing emphasis on the word *you,* such as:

* *You* look nice today.
* Where have *you* been?
* *You* don't care.

Invite groups of students to write each sentence a different way, emphasizing a different word in each sentence. Then have volunteers speak the lines aloud, emphasizing the word they chose.

Discuss the differences in meaning that are created by the various emphases. For example: How does "Where have *you* been?" differ from "*Where* have you been?" Then invite groups to continue practicing the technique with new pairs of sentences.

ADAPTING A TEXT — LESSON 45

In *The Borden Tragedy*, Rick Geary claimed to be adapting a text that he had found. When artists adapt a text, they use the author's words and ideas and their own art. They may shorten the text or set it in a different time and place, but they do not significantly change the meaning of the original.

In this lesson, you will have a chance to adapt a poem by Edgar Allan Poe, "Annabel Lee." As you read or listen to the poem, visualize. Create pictures in your mind of the setting, of Annabel Lee, and of the speaker. You might even want to doodle in the **Response Notes**.

Annabel Lee by Edgar Allan Poe

It was many and many a year ago,
In a kingdom by the sea,
That a maiden there lived whom you may know
By the name of Annabel Lee;
And this maiden she lived with no other thought
Than (to love) and (be loved) by me.

I was a child and she was a child,
In this kingdom by the sea:
But (we loved) with (a love) that was more than (love)—
I and my Annabel Lee—
With (a love) that the winged seraphs of heaven
Coveted her and me.

And this was the reason that, long ago,
In this kingdom by the sea,
A wind blew out of a cloud, chilling
My beautiful Annabel Lee;
So that her highborn kinsmen came
And bore her away from me,
To shut her up in a sepulcher
In this kingdom by the sea.

The angels, not half so happy in heaven,
Went envying her and me—
Yes!—that was the reason (as all men know,
In this kingdom by the sea)
That the wind came out of the cloud by night,
Chilling and killing my Annabel Lee.

Repeating love and loved—shows speaker's strong feelings

ADAPTING A TEXT 145

LESSON 45

Students will use what they have learned about visual texts to create one of their own.

BACKGROUND KNOWLEDGE
Edgar Allan Poe was born in 1809 in Boston, Massachusetts, to parents who were itinerant actors and died before Edgar reached the age of three. The boy was taken in by the family of a merchant named John Allan whose surname Edgar took as his middle name. Usually associated with the horror genre, Poe also composed intensely moving poetry. "Annabel Lee" is Poe's tribute to his wife from whose loss he never recovered. The overall mood of the poem is melancholy; however, the repeating rhymes and sing-song rhythm create a rather upbeat feeling, which may cause readers to experience it differently.

VOCABULARY
seraphs angels, heavenly beings
coveted longed for, desired
kinsmen relatives, members of one's family
sepulcher a grave or tomb
dissever to separate, to cut apart

Ask students to look for word parts they know, such as *kin*, *men*, *sever*, or *covet* to determine the meaning of each word. Then present the definitions above and have students compare them to their definitions.

Before

COMPARING GENRES Present or ask students to compare how a story is presented in different genres, such as the adventures of superheroes in comic books and the portrayal of them in movies. Ask students to compare the effectiveness of the visual elements of the genres: *Which genre expresses motion best? Which gives a clearer understanding of the characters?* Have students support their opinions with reference to specific elements of each genre.

Invite students to create Venn diagrams to compare two interpretations of the same story. Have them write the name of the story as the title of the entire page, then label each circle with each genre, as the example at right shows.

Encourage students to work with partners or in groups to complete their comparisons.

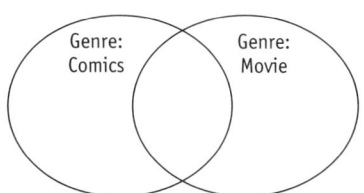

Story: Spider-Man

Genre: Comics / Genre: Movie

INTERACTING WITH THE TEXT 145

WRITING SUPPORT

Peer Conferences To help them plan, have students draft rough sketches of one or two panels. In peer conferences, have students provide feedback regarding each other's sketches, with respect to the use of various techniques and their effectiveness in conveying an appropriate mood for the story.

Quick Assess

* Do students' Response Notes reflect the mental images the poem inspires?
* Do students' visual poems adapt and depict the tale?

But our love it was stronger by far than the love
Of those who were older than we—
Of many far wiser than we—
And neither the angels in heaven above,
Nor the demons down under the sea,
Can ever dissever my soul from the soul
Of the beautiful Annabel Lee—

For the moon never beams, without bringing me dreams
Of the beautiful Annabel Lee;
And the stars never rise, but I feel the bright eyes
Of the beautiful Annabel Lee;
And so, all the night-tide, I lie down by the side
Of my darling—my darling—my life and my bride,
In the sepulcher there by the sea,
In her tomb by the sounding sea.

* In the space below, plan your new visual text for the poem. Decide on the effect you want to achieve—humorous, solemn, "dark," "light," formal, informal, modern, and so on. Then select two techniques that were discussed in this unit that you could use. For example, do you want to use a narrator and dialogue or just the words of the poem? How much detail will be in the art? How much white space will you leave in your design?

* After you have made a plan, draw your visual poem on a separate sheet of paper. If you do not want to draw, you can use computer graphics or magazine cutouts for the visuals, as long as you can make them consistent with your intended effect.

A good way to understand how visual texts work is to create your own.

146 LESSON 45

During

VISUAL ELEMENTS Review the visual elements studied in Lessons 41–44:

* symbols
* facial expressions, gestures, positions and proximity of subjects
* lines
* shadows
* speech balloons, thought bubbles
* captions
* clothing
* special fonts and letter sizes

Facilitate a discussion of how each of the elements was used in *Bone* and *The Borden Tragedy* to create specific moods. Encourage students to consider all these style and design elements as they plan their visual texts to adapt the story of Annabel Lee.

After

APPLYING THE STRATEGY
Adapting a Text Invite students to adapt other poems they have read. Remind them to recreate the same mood, story line, and characterization, and use style and design techniques to do so.

UNIT 10 MAKING CONNECTIONS

Lessons 46-50, pages 148-162

UNIT OVERVIEW
As they learn about the San Francisco earthquake of 1906, students learn to make connections with what they are reading.

KEY IDEA
Depending on his or her perspective, a reader will make different kinds of connections.

CRITICAL READING SKILLS
by lesson

46 Connecting to the facts
47 Connecting to the people
48 Connecting to fictional accounts
49 Connecting through photographs
50 Connecting to inform future actions

WRITING ACTIVITIES
by lesson

46 Write questions.
47 Create a flier.
48 Write the next scene of a story.
49 Write three similes based on details from a photograph.
50 Write a family guidebook on earthquake preparedness.

Making Connections

If you have experienced a hurricane firsthand, you probably remember the hearing the roaring winds or feeling the sheets of rain pounding against your face. You have a personal connection to the meaning of a hurricane.

A scientist who studies hurricanes makes different kinds of connections. She connects her learning to current weather patterns and can make predictions about the path and strength of the hurricane. When you read an article she has written, you have the opportunity to connect what you know with the knowledge she is sharing.

If you see a hurricane on television, you might connect to the visual images—noticing the damage, the floodwaters, or the downed power lines. You connect these images to what you have read or seen before and to your own personal experience.

Each of the **connections** described above emphasizes different aspects of hurricanes. Each connection is stored in your memory and becomes part of what you have learned about hurricanes. The next time you hear "hurricane," all these connections will come back. In this unit, you will make a series of connections to one event—the San Francisco earthquake of 1906.

Literature

- **America's Great Disasters** by Martin Sandler (nonfiction excerpt)

This nonfiction selection takes a factual look at the background of the 1906 San Francisco earthquake and provides an eyewitness account of the quake itself.

- **Three Fearful Days: San Francisco Memoirs of the 1906 Earthquake and Fire** compiled by Malcolm E. Barker (contemporary eyewitness accounts)

These eyewitness accounts of the events of the 1906 earthquake offer a fascinating viewpoint of the disaster.

- **Dragonwings** by Laurence Yep (novel excerpt)

In this excerpt from Yep's novel, Moonshadow tells of his experience during the 1906 quake while living with his father in San Francisco's Chinatown.

- **"Safety Tips for Earthquakes"** from the American Red Cross (excerpt from a website)

This guide provides a practical checklist for earthquake preparedness.

ASSESSMENT To assess student learning in this unit, see pages 237 and 256.

LESSON 46

Students will chart details about an event, make connections to what they know about the topic, and form questions to understand the topic better.

BACKGROUND KNOWLEDGE
This selection introduces the reader to conditions that lead to earthquakes and to a view of San Francisco before the historic quake of 1906. Ask students what they know about earthquakes. What mental pictures do they have? Brainstorm words they associate with earthquakes, such as *earth's crust, liquid rock,* and *faults*. Create a cluster around the word *earthquake* on an overhead or on the board. Help students locate San Francisco on a map. Talk about its precarious position in relation to earthquake fault lines and its susceptibility to quakes. Create a cluster for the word *San Francisco*.

VOCABULARY
convulsion violent upheaval
fractures breaks
erupted released suddenly

Go over the vocabulary words and their meanings. Talk about how the words might be used in a selection about earthquakes.

LESSON 46 CONNECTING TO THE FACTS

Think for a moment about this scenario: A powerful city sits on the edge of the Pacific Ocean. The location gives it access to the sea and to other major cities. Think of a city with a fun-loving spirit—one filled with elegant hotels, opera, and theater. See hilly streets packed with tourists, traders, business operators, and immigrants. The narrow alleyways of Chinatown reveal restaurants, kite shops, and teahouses. But beneath the city, the earth trembles. Then it shifts. You probably know what will happen next.

As you read the following excerpt, circle information that confirms what you already know about earthquakes or about San Francisco. In your **Response Notes**, jot down surprises, record your questions, and list topics you want to discuss.

from *America's Great Disasters* by Martin W. Sandler

One of the things that we take for granted is the fact that the earth will remain solid and stable beneath our feet. When the earth begins to move violently and splits apart, those who are caught up in an earthquake experience a terror unlike any other.

Although it may be hard to believe, more than ten thousand earthquakes take place around the globe every year. Most are mild and go practically unnoticed. Some quakes are caused by the movement of the mixture of solid and liquid rock that lies under volcanoes. The most violent and most disastrous earthquakes, however, are those set into motion by movements that take place within the earth's "crust."

The crust is the layer of rock underneath the earth's soil. It contains many breaks, known as faults. The crust on either side of these faults moves very slowly. If two sections of crust become locked together and can't move, enormous pressure steadily mounts along that section of the fault. When the pressure is suddenly released by a shift of the crust on either side of the fault, it triggers a gigantic convulsion in the earth's surface, known as an earthquake....

San Francisco, California, has been a city both blessed and cursed by its location. Perched on high hills overlooking the Pacific Ocean on one side and one of the world's loveliest harbors on the other, it is a beautiful place to live.

It is also a city that grew almost overnight. At the start of 1848, San Francisco was a tiny village containing about thirty-five houses. Its number of residents was so small that, according to one visitor, "not more than twenty-five persons would be seen in the streets at any one time."

Response Notes

!!!

Before

CRITICAL READING SKILL
Connecting to the Facts In this lesson, students learn to connect new information with information they know and then come up with questions about what else they would like to learn on the topic. Remind students that when they read nonfiction, they are constantly engaged in linking what they know, what they have learned, and what they want to learn.

RESPONSE NOTES
Have students underline the last sentence of the introductory text as a reminder of how to respond in the Response Notes. (See page 227 for more about marking text.)

Then, on January 24, 1848, gold was discovered in the area. People everywhere dropped whatever they were doing and headed for the goldfields, hoping to strike it rich. Most made the long journey by ship, landing in San Francisco's wide harbor.

As millions of gold-seekers and thousands of merchants, anxious to sell supplies, poured into San Francisco, its population exploded. Even after the goldfields had been mined dry, tens of thousands who had fallen in love with the region remained and settled there. By 1906, the once-tiny village had become a booming city of more than four hundred thousand people. . . .

But although few were aware of it at the time, the same physical location that made San Francisco so attractive to its residents, its growing number of visitors, and its businessmen also placed everyone in the city in great danger. Unfortunately for San Francisco, the city had sprung up within a few miles of one of the greatest hidden earth fractures in the world. Known as the San Andreas Fault, this break in the earth's crust runs parallel to the California coastline for about 800 miles. By 1906, pressure had been building up along the fault near San Francisco for years. Early in the morning of April 18, 1906, all this pressure finally erupted and unleashed the greatest earthquake America has ever experienced.

The quake began out at sea, some ninety miles north of San Francisco. Traveling southward at an incredible two miles per second, it tore up the coastline in its path and headed directly toward the city. It hit San Francisco at 5:13 A.M.

✱ One way to monitor your connections is to think about what you learned through the reading. In the following chart, list some examples of information that is new to you.

What I Learned About San Francisco
1.
2.
3.
4.
5.

YOU

What I Learned About Earthquakes
1.
2.
3.
4.
5.

CONNECTING TO THE FACTS 149

ABOUT THE AUTHOR
Martin W. Sandler has written many nonfiction books, including *Pioneers, Cowboys, Immigrants,* and *Presidents*. He is an Emmy-Award-winning television producer and has been twice nominated for the Pulitzer Prize.

TEACHING TIP
Using a Graphic Organizer: Reflection Chart Using a chart to record what they learn helps students organize and reflect on their reading and the connections they make. Model filling in an entry on the chart, using a think-aloud: *I didn't know San Francisco grew in population so fast. It says at the bottom of page 148 that San Francisco had only about 35 houses at the beginning of 1848. I'll write that fact in the chart under "What I learned about San Francisco."* Tell students that the information they record in this chart will help them complete the activities on page 150.

During

THINKING THROUGH CONNECTIONS As students read, they are asked to circle information that confirms what they already know and then jot down surprises, questions, or topics they want to discuss. Model making connections with known and new information: *I know that earthquakes make splits in the earth's crust. I wonder why pressure builds. I'd like to know what the crust is made of and what that has to do with how pressure builds up.*

MAKING CONNECTIONS 149

TEACHING TIP

Collaboration After students have completed the chart about what they have learned on page 149, have them discuss the information in pairs or in small groups. Then they can work together to generate questions and record those questions and speculations. Ask: *What do you want to know more about?* Students can then work collaboratively or independently to complete the last activity on page 150. Writing the paragraph after they complete the chart will encourage them to use the strategy of making connections.

Quick Assess

* Did students write down the facts they learned about the 1906 earthquake and about San Francisco?
* Were students able to generate three questions about the topic and speculate on possible answers?
* Were students able to list additional information they would like to know about the topic?

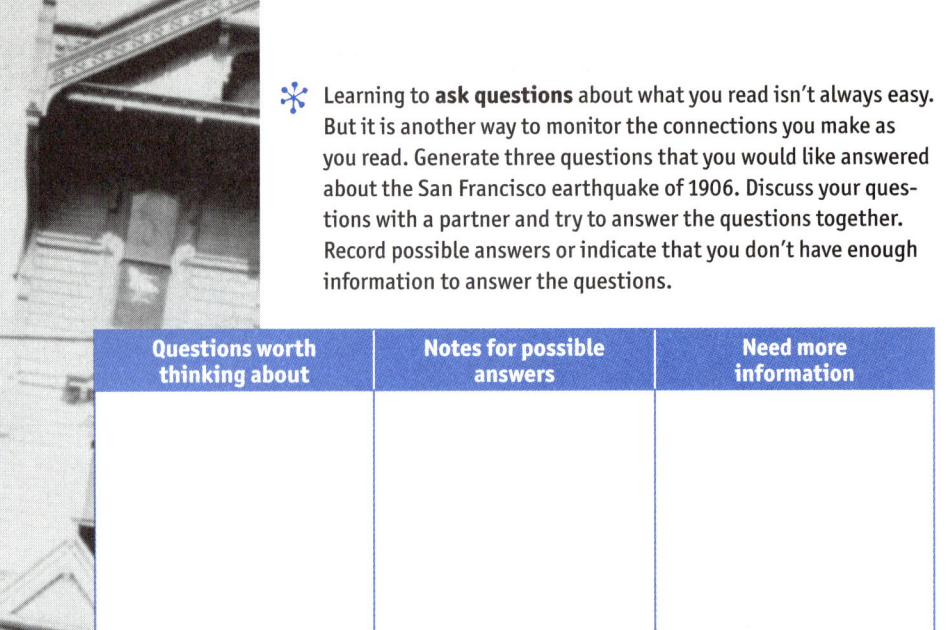

❋ Learning to **ask questions** about what you read isn't always easy. But it is another way to monitor the connections you make as you read. Generate three questions that you would like answered about the San Francisco earthquake of 1906. Discuss your questions with a partner and try to answer the questions together. Record possible answers or indicate that you don't have enough information to answer the questions.

Questions worth thinking about	Notes for possible answers	Need more information

❋ If you want to know more about a subject, you will probably have questions about it. Write a paragraph indicating what you would like to learn about the San Francisco earthquake that you didn't learn through your reading so far.

Connect what you already know to what you are learning or want to know.

After

RESEARCH Provide students with additional materials and Internet access to research the 1906 earthquake. You may want students to work in teams to explore a specific, related topic, such as (1) the San Andreas Fault, (2) twentieth-century earthquakes in the United States, (3) statistics on the 1906 earthquake in San Francisco, (4) the 1906 earthquake in photographs, and (5) earthquake preparedness. Each group could then make a short report to classmates or create posters showing key information about their topic.

CONNECTING TO THE PEOPLE — LESSON 47

What if the focus of our attention shifts from the earthquake to the people who experienced it? An eyewitness provides a first-hand account. An eyewitness is someone who experiences an event and sees the effects of it. What did eyewitnesses feel and see?

Several eyewitness accounts follow. In your **Response Notes,** keep track of your reactions to what you learn from each person about the earthquake's effects on people's lives. Record questions that arise as you read.

from America's Great Disasters by Martin W. Sandler

Account #1: John Bartlett, a news editor: "Of a sudden," Bartlett later wrote, "we found ourselves staggering and reeling…then came the sickening sway of the earth that threw us flat upon our faces…We could not get on our feet. I looked in a dazed fashion around me…Big buildings were crumbling as one might crush a biscuit in one's hand…Storms of masonry rained into the street. Wild, high jangles of smashing glass cut a sharp note into the frightful roaring… Trolley tracks were twisted, their wires down, wriggling like serpents, flashing blue sparks all the time…From the south of us, faint, but all too clear came a horrible chorus of human cries of agony. Down there, in a ramshackle section of the city, the wretched houses had fallen in upon sleeping families…"

Response Notes

from Three Fearful Days Malcolm Barker, editor

Account #2: James Hopper, a review writer: …I got up and walked to the window. I started to open it, but the pane obligingly fell outward and I poked my head out, the floor like a geyser beneath my feet. Then I heard the roar of bricks coming down in cataracts and the groaning of twisted girders all over the city, and at the same time I saw the moon, a calm, pale crescent in the green sky of dawn. Below it the skeleton frame of an unfinished sky-scraper was swaying from side to side with a swing as exaggerated and absurd as that of a palm in a stage tempest.

Just then the quake, with a sound as of a snarl, rose to its climax of rage, and the back wall of my building for three stories above me fell. I saw the mass pass across my vision swift as a shadow. It struck some little wooden houses in the alley below. I saw them crash in like emptied eggs and the bricks pass through the roof as through tissue paper.

The vibrations ceased and I began to dress. Then I noted the great silence. Throughout the long quaking, in this great house full of people I had not heard a

CONNECTING TO THE PEOPLE 151

LESSON 47

Students make connections between paired texts and form a personal response.

BACKGROUND KNOWLEDGE
Ask students: *What does eyewitness mean?* Explain that an "eyewitness account" is information told from the point of view of someone who saw an event with his or her own eyes. Students will be reading eyewitness accounts of the San Francisco earthquake of 1906, which devastated most of the city. For photos of the earthquake, try a website such as http://quake.wr.usgs.gov/info/1906/.

VOCABULARY
masonry bricks and stones
jangles harsh metallic sounds
ramshackle rundown, not sturdy
wretched badly made
geyser a hot spring that shoots water or steam into the air
cataracts waterfalls
girders big beams that support a building or bridge
tempest storm
apathy a feeling of not caring

Assign one or two words to individuals or groups. Have them determine each word's meaning and then share the definitions with the class.

Before

CRITICAL READING SKILL
Connecting to the People Explain that creating a connection to people portrayed in any story or event is one way to become more involved in what you are reading. Before reading, ask students to imagine what it must have been like for the people living in San Francisco on the morning of the earthquake. Let them spend some time talking about whether or not they have been in a similar situation. Ask them to speculate about the experience based on their experience or their reading about other disasters. Read Account #1 together, reminding students that these accounts were written in 1906, pointing out some of the differences in phrasing, language usage, and so on.

RESPONSE NOTES   Model how to record thoughts in the Response Notes: *In the first paragraph of John Bartlett's account, he says that he felt a "sickening sway of the earth" and was thrown flat on the floor. I would be really scared if the earth suddenly heaved beneath my feet and threw me to the floor! I'll write that I would be scared.*

MAKING CONNECTIONS 151

EXTRA SUPPORT

Differentiation The eyewitness accounts in this lesson contain powerful and immediate images of what it was like to be in the middle of such a terrifying disaster. Some students may struggle with the accounts, however, due to unfamiliar vocabulary and the style of the period. Read each account aloud and summarize what the narrator is describing as you move through the excerpt.

WRITER'S CRAFT

Figurative Language These accounts are filled with the vivid imagery of metaphors and similes. Review with students the meaning of metaphor *(when one thing is described as something else)* and *simile* (a comparison using *like* or *as*). Invite students to find examples in the text. (Metaphors: "through smoking canyons of red-hot twisted girders," "great tongues of fire." Similes: "the bricks pass through the roof as through tissue paper," "only a brick was falling here and there like the trickle of a spent rain.") Talk about how the writer uses figures of speech to create vivid mental pictures for the reader.

cry, not a sound, not a sob, not a whisper. And now, when the roar of crumbling buildings was over and only a brick was falling here and there like the trickle of a spent rain, this silence continued, and it was an awful thing. But now in the alley someone began to groan. It was a woman's groan, soft and low. ✤

Account #3: Harry Coleman, newspaper photographer: I saw miles of flames raging as smoke-blackened firemen stood helplessly by dry hydrants, watching their useless hoses curl up in the fire. With my cheeks almost blistered and my hair singed with the terrific heat, I shot pictures down Market Street past the Palace and Grand Hotels, through smoking canyons of red-hot twister girders, down to the wrecked ferry building, into Front Street and along the twisted rails of the Belt Line railroad, where the fire tugs Active and Leslie were pumping feeble streams of bay water on the roofs of wooden wharves, while excited seamen and stevedores trampled out sparks as they fell from the sky.

Threading my way over hot, cobbled streets, through swarms of stampeding rats, I continued my photographing up Mission Street into the lodging-house district, where great tongues of fire and clouds of smoke were everywhere, and the injured were trying to bandage each other's wounds with handkerchiefs and shreds of cloth. I pictured the frenzied crowds, standing aquiver, afraid to re-enter their houses to gather up what remained of their belongings. Frantic men separated from their families, pitiful mothers dragging frightened children, and sailors pulling sea-chests formed a human tide of refugees which flooded past my lens as they struggled toward the waterfront. ✤

Account #4: Mary Edith Griswold, assistant editor of *Sunset Magazine*: The fire is within two blocks of my house—everyone in my block had been told to leave. Our house has been ordered dynamited. The apathy of the last two days has given way. The firemen are frantic. If they don't stop the fire now the whole Western Addition will go—the policeman with a red face is running up and down in front of the house. A dead Italian lies in the middle of the street opposite my house. Members of his family sit around his body in a circle. I got so scared I couldn't swallow a glass of water. The heat on the balcony was intense—too hot to stay out there. The paint on the woodwork was blistering. Everyone was fire mad. My home will surely go. ✤

During

COMPARING ACCOUNTS
Once students have finished reading the eyewitness accounts, talk with students about how they are similar and how they are different. Talk about who the narrators are (a news editor, a review writer, a newspaper photographer, and an assistant editor at a magazine) and why their accounts differ. (For example, since it's written in the present tense, Mary Edith Griswold's account appears to have been written as the disaster was occurring.) Have students consider why she might have written this in the present tense.

After the class has discussed the accounts, have students complete the activities on page 153.

MULTIPLE PERSPECTIVES
Each person who wrote an account wrote from his or her perspective, or point of view. Recall that by piecing together multiple perspectives, a reader is able to have a more complete picture of an event. Caution students, however, that eyewitness accounts are limited by what the eyewitnesses actually saw. It is doubtful that an eyewitness will have all the facts about an event.

❉ Based on the connections you are making to the accounts of the earthquake, write a response to each question:

1 What would I do if I were in this situation?

2 What would be my greatest fear during the earthquake?

3 What would I do to help others during and after the earthquake?

❉ Now imagine that you have decided to head a relief effort to help the people who have survived the earthquake in San Francisco. On a separate sheet of paper, design a flier that is intended to recruit volunteers to support relief efforts in San Francisco. Use any details from the reading that will help convince people to support your cause.

Volunteer! Volunteer!
EARTHQUAKE RELIEF

 WE NEED VOLUNTEERS TO HELP THE PEOPLE WHO HAVE SURVIVED THE EARTHQUAKE IN SAN FRANCISCO.

SAN FRANCISCO
APR 1906
CALIFORNIA

Connect what people are feeling and experiencing to your feelings.

CONNECTING TO THE PEOPLE 153

TEACHING TIP

Collaboration Ask students to share their responses to the questions with a partner. Once students have had time to discuss their responses, invite the class to discuss what they learned in their discussions.

WRITING SUPPORT

Planning Your Writing Before students create their fliers, ask them to brainstorm the types of help people would need following the earthquake. Remind them to think about what they have learned from the eyewitness accounts about the effects of the disaster. Once students have created a list of what type of help would be needed, they can work individually or in groups to create fliers.

Quick Assess

❉ Were students able to express the connections they made with the eyewitness accounts?

❉ Were students able to put themselves in the place of those who experienced the earthquake?

❉ Did students' fliers reflect an understanding of what would be needed after the earthquake?

After

READING/WRITING CONNECTION

Ask students to write a first-person fictional account of the 1906 earthquake. They can write it as if they were a witness, or they may prefer to tell the story through a fictitious character. Encourage students to choose one account to use as their model. They may even want to include the writer in their story. Students should research the earthquake so that they can include believable details in their writing.

ART CONNECTION
Ask students to work together in groups to create a mural depicting the 1906 quake. They could include words and phrases on the mural that explain the emotions felt by those who experienced it firsthand.

REFLECTING
Ask students to write a short paragraph discussing how the eyewitness accounts in Lesson 47 helped them make connections to the factual information in Lesson 46. Have them review their Response Notes and include any questions they still have about the disaster.

MAKING CONNECTIONS 153

LESSON 48

Students will read a fictional account of the San Francisco earthquake and make connections to what they have learned about the event.

BACKGROUND KNOWLEDGE
Ask students what they know of San Francisco's Chinatown. Talk about how San Francisco's Chinatown was founded by Chinese workers and immigrants in the 1800s. By 1906, Chinatown was a mixture of old-world Chinese traditions and the emerging Chinese American culture. When the earthquake hit Chinatown, the area was devastated. After the quake, some religious and political leaders tried to keep people from returning to Chinatown. In the end, the Chinese leaders prevailed and returned to build the thriving community that exists today.

VOCABULARY
tenement rundown buildings
undulate roll like a wave
ominously in a threatening way
queue a ponytail once worn by Chinese men
steeples pointed towers on churches
debris remains of something that's been destroyed
eerie spooky, scary

Have students do the Wordsplash blackline master on page 272.

LESSON 48 — CONNECTING TO FICTIONAL ACCOUNTS

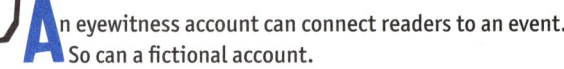

An eyewitness account can connect readers to an event. So can a fictional account.

Works of fiction often use places, events, and people from actual events. *Dragonwings* is a novel set in San Francisco in the early 1900s, and it depicts the 1906 earthquake. Moonshadow and his father are Chinese immigrants. In 1906, Chinatown was a newly developed neighborhood in San Francisco.

As you read, **connect** factual information you have learned about the events to the fictional account. In the **Response Notes,** keep track of any connections you make to information from Lessons 46 and 47.

from Dragonwings by Laurence Yep

I had gotten dressed and gone out to the pump to get some water. The morning was filled with that soft, gentle twilight of spring, when everything is filled with soft, dreamy colors and shapes; so when the earthquake hit, I did not believe it at first. It seemed like a nightmare where everything you take to be the rock-hard, solid basis for reality becomes unreal.

Wood and stone and brick and the very earth became fluidlike. The pail beneath the pump jumped and rattled like a spider dancing on a hot stove. The ground deliberately seemed to slide right out from under me. I landed on my back hard enough to drive the wind from my lungs. The whole world had become unglued, Our stable and Miss Whitlaw's house and the tenements to either side heaved and bobbed up and down, riding the ground like ships on a heavy sea. Down the alley mouth, I could see the cobblestone street undulate and twist like a red-backed snake.

From inside our stable, I could hear the cups and plates begin to rattle on their shelves, and the equipment on Father's worktable clattered and rumbled ominously.

Suddenly the door banged open and Father stumbled out with his clothes all in a bundle. "It's an earthquake, I think," he shouted. He had washed his hair the night before and had not had time to twist it into a queue, so it hung down his back long and black.

He looked around in the back yard. It was such a wide, open space that we were fairly safe there. Certainly more safe than in the frame doorway of our stable. He got into his pants and shirt and then his socks and boots.

"Do you think one of the mean dragons is doing all this?" I asked him.

"Maybe. Maybe not." Father had sat down to stuff his feet into his boots. "Time to wonder about that later. Now you wait here."

Before

CRITICAL READING STRATEGY
Connecting to Fictional Accounts
Strategic readers use what they know from their own experience and from what they have learned to connect with the fiction that they read. In this lesson, students use what they have learned about the 1906 earthquake to connect with the event as depicted in Laurence Yep's novel.

RESPONSE NOTES Read the first two paragraphs with students. At the end of each paragraph, stop and ask students to use their Response Notes to note connections between the fictional descriptions, the informational account, and the eyewitness accounts in the earlier lessons. As they refer to them, have them jot down the detail here and draw a line to the words in the story.

He started to get to his feet when the second tremor shook and he fell forward flat on his face. I heard the city bells ringing. They were rung by no human hand—the earthquake had just shaken them in their steeples. The second tremor was worse than the first. From all over came an immense wall of noise: of metal tearing, of bricks crashing, of wood breaking free from wood nails, and all. Everywhere, what man had built came undone. I was looking at a tenement house to our right and it just seemed to shudder and then collapse. One moment there were solid wooden walls and the next moment it had fallen with the cracking of wood and the tinkling of glass and the screams of people inside.

Mercifully, for a moment, it was lost to view in the cloud of dust that rose up. The debris surged against Miss Whitlaw's fence and toppled it over with a creak and a groan and a crash. I saw an arm sticking up from the mound of rubble and the hand was twisted at an impossible angle from the wrist. Coughing, Father pulled at my arm. "Stay here now," he ordered and started for Miss Whitlaw's.

❋ What is the strongest similarity or difference between this account and the ones you read in Lessons 46 and 47?

_____
_____
_____

❋ What are your feelings about Moonshadow's descriptions of the situation?

_____
_____
_____
_____

❋ Continue reading.

A strange, eerie silence hung over the city. The bells had stilled in their steeples, and houses had stopped collapsing momentarily. It was as if the city itself were holding its breath. Then we could hear the hissing of gas from the broken pipes, like dozens of angry snakes, and people, trapped inside the mounds, began calling. Their voices sounded faint and ghostly, as if dozens of ghosts floated over the rubble, crying in little, distant voices

ABOUT THE AUTHOR

Laurence Yep was born in San Francisco in 1948, where he grew up in a primarily African American neighborhood. Although Yep didn't live in Chinatown, he went to school there and knew it well. Yep was an avid reader of fantasy and science fiction as a young man and had his first science fiction story published when he was eighteen. Yep has said that he believes writing doesn't have to be based on the fantastic and extraordinary. Good writing can come out of the ordinary experience of everyday things. In this selection, Yep weaves the day-to-day experiences of a young boy with the extraordinary events of the 1906 San Francisco earthquake.

EXTRA SUPPORT

Differentiation If students need extra support connecting the fictional account with the information they've learned in the previous lessons, model with a think aloud: *In my Response Notes for this story, I wrote "hit San Francisco at 5:13 A.M." from Lesson 46. This story adds more details about the morning before the quake hit, like "soft, gentle twilight, dreamy colors and shapes."* Encourage students to make connections to the things that are similar and add things that are new in this account.

During

CONNECTING TO A STORY'S CHARACTER The story is told from Moonshadow's perspective. He is approximately 11 years old. Ask students to talk about what the descriptions reveal about the narrator of the story: *What do you learn about him? Did you compare his descriptions to what you read in the last two lessons?*

Ask them to read the next two excerpts, focusing on the narrator and how they, as readers, are connecting to Moonshadow's situation: *Do you feel afraid for him? Do you feel sympathy?*

As they finish reading the excerpts, ask students to explain their reactions to Moonshadow and to the other characters he describes: *Do you feel connected to him? Do you feel as if you are experiencing this with him? Why or why not?*

WRITER'S CRAFT

Word Choice Read aloud the last sentence that begins at the bottom of page 155: *Their voices sounded faint and ghostly, as if dozens of ghosts floated over the rubble, crying in little, distant voices for help.* Ask students to talk about what those words make them picture. How does it shape the mood of the story at this point? Invite students to find other examples of imagery in the selection (for example, on page 154: *Down the alley mouth, I could see the cobblestone street undulate and twist like a red-backed snake*; on page 155: *From all over, came an immense wall of noise*; on page 156: *One woman in a nightgown walked by, carrying her crying baby by its legs as if it were a dead chicken.*)

Talk about how Yep chooses words to create vivid pictures of the event in the reader's mind. Ask students to discuss whether or not they find it effective. Have them give reasons for their opinions.

EXTRA SUPPORT

Differentiation You may want to encourage visual learners to draw sketches of the image from the selection that made a lasting impression on them.

Response Notes

for help. Robin and I pressed close to one another for comfort. It was Miss Whitlaw who saved us. It was she who gave us something important to do and brought us out of shock.

She pressed her lips together for a moment, as if she were deciding something. "We must get those people out."

"It would take four of us weeks to clear tunnels for them," Father said.

"We'll draft help. After all, we were put on this earth to help one another," Miss Whitlaw said.

❋ List any additional connections you make to the characters' situation or feelings.

_____
_____
_____

❋ As you continue reading, jot down any connections you make to the characters.

We had gone to sleep on a street crowded with buildings, some three or four stories high and crowded with people; and now many of the houses were gone, and the ones that remained were dangerously close to falling too. There was a hole in the cobblestone street about a yard wide and twenty feet long. As we watched, a cobblestone fell over the edge, clattering ten feet to the bottom.

I heard one person compare it to being on the moon. It was that kind of desolate feeling—just looking at huge hills of rubble: of brick and broken wooden slats that had once been houses. On top of the piles we would see the random collection of things that had survived the quake: somebody's rag doll, an old bottle, a fiddle, the back of an upholstered chair . . . and a woman's slender wrist, sticking out of the rubble as if calling for help.

And then the survivors started to emerge, and I saw that there were as many hurt in mind as in body. Some people wandered out of the buildings almost naked, others still in their nightclothes. I saw one man with the lather on one side of his face, the other side already clean-shaven. In his hand was a lather-covered razor. One woman in a nightgown walked by, carrying her crying baby by its legs as if it were a dead chicken. Father caught her by the shoulder and gently took the baby from her.

"Fix her arms," Father told me. I set her arms so she could cradle the baby—as if the mother were a doll. Then Father put the baby back into her arms. She dumbly nodded her thanks and wandered on. ❖

✻ Another way of connecting is to imagine yourself as one of the characters in what you are reading. Imagine that you are the narrator Moonshadow. Take a minute to review what he is seeing and how he expresses his feelings about his situation. Then write the next scene in the novel as if you were Moonshadow.

_____
_____
_____
_____
_____
_____
_____
_____
_____
_____
_____
_____
_____
_____
_____
_____
_____
_____
_____

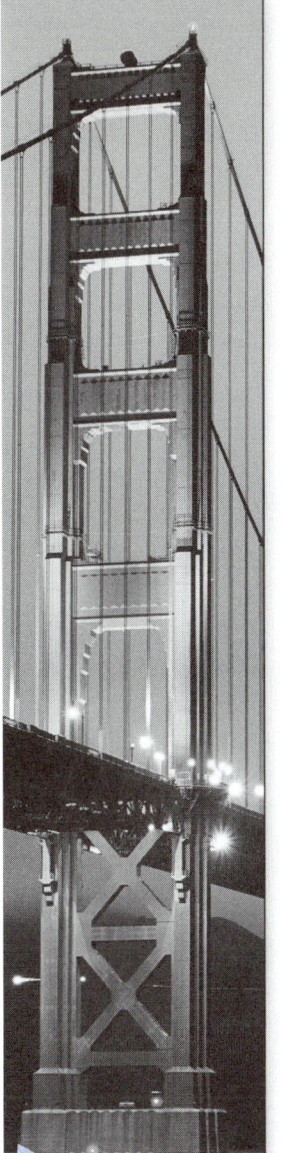

Connect to fictional accounts by comparing them to real events or by imagining yourself as one of the characters.

CONNECTING TO FICTIONAL ACCOUNTS 157

WRITING SUPPORT

Point of View As students prepare to write the story extension, remind them that they are writing their narrative from Moonshadow's point of view. They should use first-person point of view, using the pronouns *I* and *me*. Have them think about what they've learned about Moonshadow so far and encourage them to stay in character as they write from his point of view. Encourage them to use their imaginations to think of what Moonshadow would do next.

Quick Assess

✻ Were students able to make connections between the factual accounts in previous lessons with the fictional approach to the event?

✻ Did students describe the strongest similarity or difference thoroughly and explain the connection?

✻ Were students able to continue a creative narrative from the main character's point of view?

After

LISTENING/SPEAKING
CONNECTION Ask students to use the information they learned about the earthquake in the last three lessons and through any additional research to write a short script. First, have them think of their characters. They should create survivors who know each other, such as a family, or group of friends or co-workers, and create any other important background information for the characters. Then, using what they have learned about the 1906 earthquake, they can write a one-act play to perform in class.

MAKING CONNECTIONS 157

LESSON 49

Students will compare photographs of the same catastrophic event to connect visual details and write a descriptive poem that connects the images.

BACKGROUND KNOWLEDGE
Explain to students that photography began in the late 1830s and developed over the next 60 years from being practiced by a few to being a common way of sharing firsthand experiences with the rest of the world. At the beginning of the twentieth century, the Kodak Brownie, a user-friendly camera, was developed and mass-marketed for consumer use. By the time of the great earthquake, cameras were widely available and photographs have survived as a grim record of the disaster. However, color photography was rare at the time, and movie cameras were scarce, so most of the visual records are stills, black-and-white photos. The photographs in this lesson were taken in the early morning hours right after the earthquake and over the next several days. These photographs capture much of what is difficult to convey in words.

LESSON 49 CONNECTING THROUGH PHOTOGRAPHS

In the novel *Dragonwings,* Moonshadow captures many of the images of the morning of the quake through the use of **descriptive language.** For example, he describes how the pail "jumped and rattled like a spider dancing on a hot stove."

In this lesson, you will examine two photographs and see how connecting to visual images enhances your understanding of the earthquake.

✻ Study the photograph closely. What images stand out for you? Begin by listing four phrases that *describe* what you see:

1 _____
2 _____
3 _____
4 _____

✻ Using at least eight descriptive words from your list, write a four-line poem that captures what you see in this photograph.

Before

CRITICAL READING SKILL
Connecting Through Photographs
Students study the visual images presented in this lesson's photographs to help them make connections and understand what they have read about the event.

During

DESCRIBING THE VISUALS
Students learn strategies for "reading" visual texts through this activity. Ask students to use phrases to describe what they see in the photographs. Model using descriptive phrases that include images from the photographs: *the women standing at the top of the hill, the smoke off in the distance.* Then encourage students to use words from those phrases to write their poems.

Students can develop their list of details and then turn them into similes. Remind students that similes are comparisons that use *like* or *as.* Go over the example given on page 159 to make sure students understand how a simile is created.

✻ Study this photo carefully. Take a few minutes to look closely for specific details. List three details that show what has happened as a result of the earthquake. For example, one detail might be:

Piles of broken bricks

My three details are

1 _____
2 _____
3 _____

What do these details remind you of? What are these details *like?* When you use *like,* you are making a connection between a detail and something it suggests to you. You probably remember that this connection is called a **simile**. Here's an example: *Splinters of wood are like bits of driftwood left by the tide.*

✻ Write a statement in the form of a simile for each of your three details. When you finish, share your similes with a partner.

1 _____
2 _____
3 _____

Connect to visual images by describing and drawing comparisons to them.

CONNECTING THROUGH PHOTOGRAPHS 159

EXTRA SUPPORT

Differentiation Struggling readers often have a difficult time visualizing text because they are working hard to decode. To help students understand how to describe details in a photograph, show students a photo of something familiar and ask students to brainstorm words that describe what they see. Work with them to make these descriptions as concrete as possible. Use the words they contribute to write a poem together, determining which of the words will contribute the most visual power.

Quick Assess

✻ Were students able to use descriptive phrases to tell what they see in a photograph?

✻ Did students create a poem that captures what they see in the photo?

✻ Were students able to write effective similes, using details from the photo?

After

SOCIAL STUDIES CONNECTION

Invite students to find photographs of another important historical event (for example, the first moonwalk, the raising of the flag at Iwo Jima, or the *Hindenburg* bursting into flames). Have them describe what they see in the picture, using as many details as possible. Encourage them to tell how the picture helps them make connections and understand the event.

MAKING CONNECTIONS

LESSON 50

Students will read the Red Cross recommendations for surviving an earthquake and apply the information they have learned about the topic.

BACKGROUND KNOWLEDGE
Ask students if they and their families have special rules about what to do in case of a fire or another crisis. Invite students to discuss these safety rules, including fire drills at school and why we have them. Tell students that they are going to read some safety rules that will help keep people safe in the event of an earthquake.

VOCABULARY

structural mitigation techniques ways of making buildings safer

essential important, necessary

authorities people in charge, such as police officers and firefighters

eliminate get rid of

aftershocks small earth tremors that often follow an earthquake

Preview the vocabulary and talk with students about what each term means. Invite students to use each in a sentence, anticipating how it might be used in a list of earthquake safety preparations.

LESSON 50 — CONNECT TO INFORM FUTURE ACTIONS

You know that earthquakes can cause a great deal of damage. The shaking ground causes buildings and other structures to collapse. Fires result from broken gas and electric lines. In some cases, earthquakes cause fast-moving, giant ocean waves, called tsunamis, as the water heaves with the earth's movement. Extensive damage to property can result. Injuries to people and pets add to the destruction. All of the **connections** you've made in this unit focused on the reason earthquakes occur and the damage that results.

Let's focus now on connecting this knowledge of earthquakes and their results to how we can be better prepared for future earthquakes. The following excerpt is from one Red Cross website that details how to be prepared for an earthquake. In your **Response Notes,** mark with a star recommendations that you can put into effect fairly soon. Put a check beside recommendations that will take more time to implement.

"Safety Tips for Earthquakes" from the Rhode Island American Red Cross

PREPARE A HOME EARTHQUAKE PLAN

- Choose a safe place in every room—under a sturdy table or desk or against an inside wall where nothing can fall on you.
- Practice DROP, COVER, AND HOLD ON at least twice a year. Drop under a sturdy desk or table, hold on, and protect your eyes by pressing your face against your arm. If there's no table or desk nearby, sit on the floor against an interior wall away from windows, bookcases, or tall furniture that could fall on you. Teach children to DROP, COVER, AND HOLD ON!
- Choose an out-of-town family contact.
- Consult a professional to find out additional ways you can protect your home, such as bolting the house to its foundation and other **structural mitigation techniques.**
- Take a first aid class from your local Red Cross chapter. Keep your training current.
- Get training in how to use a fire extinguisher from your local fire department.
- Inform babysitters and caregivers of your plan.

160 LESSON 50

Before

CRITICAL READING SKILL
Connect to Inform Future Actions
Talk to students about how reading about disastrous events can help us prepare for them. Talk about what students have learned from reading the various accounts and studying the photographs in this unit. Talk about the fact that there are still things people need to do to make sure they're safe during an earthquake. Ask: *What would you need to do to stay safe? What types of things would you need to have on hand?*

RESPONSE NOTES As students read, have them note the things that they can prepare now and the things that would take more planning. You may want them to list things they can do on their own and things that would take the help of adults.

ELIMINATE HAZARDS, INCLUDING...
- Bolting bookcases, china cabinets, and other tall furniture to wall studs.
- Installing strong latches on cupboards.
- Strapping the water heater to wall studs.

PREPARE A DISASTER SUPPLIES KIT FOR HOME & CAR, INCLUDING...
- First aid kit and essential medications.
- Canned food and can opener.
- At least three gallons of water per person.
- Protective clothing, rainwear, and bedding or sleeping bags.
- Battery-powered radio, flashlight, and extra batteries.
- Special items for infant, elderly, or disabled family members.
- Written instructions for how to turn off gas, electricity, and water if authorities advise you to do so. (Remember, you'll need a professional to turn natural gas service back on.)
- Keeping essentials, such as a flashlight and sturdy shoes, by your bedside.

KNOW WHAT TO DO WHEN THE SHAKING BEGINS
- DROP, COVER, AND HOLD ON! Move only a few steps to a nearby safe place. Stay indoors until the shaking stops and you're sure it's safe to exit. Stay away from windows. In a high-rise building, expect the fire alarms and sprinklers to go off during a quake.
- If you are in bed, hold on and stay there, protecting your head with a pillow.
- If you are outdoors, find a clear spot away from buildings, trees, and power lines. Drop to the ground.
- If you are in a car, slow down and drive to a clear place (as described above). Stay in the car until the shaking stops.

IDENTIFY WHAT TO DO AFTER THE SHAKING STOPS
- Check yourself for injuries. Protect yourself from further danger by putting on long pants, a long-sleeved shirt, sturdy shoes, and work gloves.
- Check others for injuries. Give first aid for serious injuries.
- Look for and extinguish small fires. Eliminate fire hazards. Turn off the gas if you smell gas or think it's leaking. (Remember, only a professional should turn it back on.)
- Listen to the radio for instructions.
- Expect aftershocks. Each time you feel one, DROP, COVER, AND HOLD ON!
- Inspect your home for damage. Get everyone out if your home is unsafe.
- Use the telephone only to report life-threatening emergencies.

CONNECT TO INFORM FUTURE ACTIONS

EXTRA SUPPORT

Differentiation Read aloud each section of the selection and stop to discuss it with students. Make sure they understand what each bulleted item means. Encourage students to ask questions if they find unfamiliar terms. Invite them to speculate on why each item might be important. For example, ask questions such as the following: *Why is it important to keep a flashlight and sturdy shoes next to your bed?* (to be able to see if the lights go out, to be able to walk on debris outside if you have to leave your home)

During

PRIORITIZING INFORMATION

As students read the Red Cross recommendations, suggest that they think about the essential information. Which of the recommendations seem easy to do and which ones would be more difficult to implement?

After students have finished reading, have them prioritize the five most important tips. Then have them create their own guidebook.

MAKING CONNECTIONS

TEACHING TIP

Collaboration Have students work in pairs to do the preliminary brainstorming. They may also work in pairs or small groups to write the guide. Before students create their guidebook, talk with them about writing a guide. Note the use of bullets, simple directives, lists of supplies, and so on. Have them use the Red Cross guidelines as a model for their own.

Quick Assess

- Were students able to identify the essential elements of the Red Cross recommendations?
- Did students create a useful guide that would help their families in case of an earthquake?

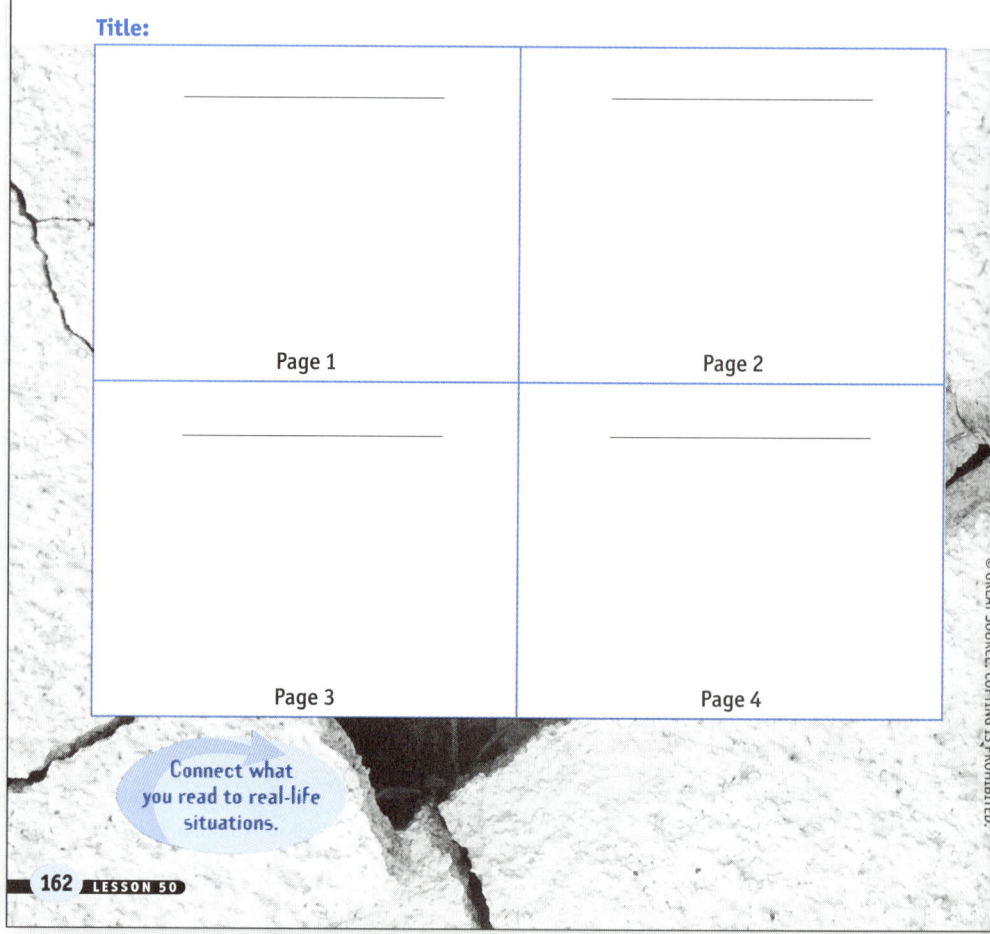

* List what you think are the six most important tips for you and your family to be prepared for earthquakes in the area where you live. When you finish, compare lists with a partner and make any changes or additions to your list that result from your conversation.

1 _____   4 _____
2 _____   5 _____
3 _____   6 _____

* Now design a guidebook to teach your family about how to be prepared for an earthquake. You have four pages in which to provide useful guidance for your family. Title the guidebook and put a heading on each page.

Title:

Page 1 | Page 2
Page 3 | Page 4

Connect what you read to real-life situations.

162 LESSON 50

After

READING/WRITING CONNECTION

Invite students to create a class guidebook or a poster for another type of crisis, such as a fire, a hurricane, or a flood. Encourage students to research the topic and find the essential steps a family can take to remain safe in time of crisis. Students can find information online or by contacting organizations with emergency procedures, such as the Red Cross or the local fire department. Students can publish or display their guidelines in school and in the community.

UNIT 11
EXPLORING MULTIPLE PERSPECTIVES

Lessons 51-55, pages 164-176

UNIT OVERVIEW
Reading five persuasive selections about environmental issues, students learn strategies for determining the elements of a convincing argument and applying them to their own writing.

KEY CONCEPT
Persuasive writers use a variety of strategies to make their arguments convincing to their audience.

CRITICAL READING SKILLS
by lesson

51 Identifying problem and solutions
52 Identifying convincing details
53 Examining alternate viewpoints
54 Using connections to persuade
55 Analyzing persuasion

WRITING ACTIVITIES
by lesson

51 Write a paragraph to evaluate an argument.
52 Write a persuasive note to convince family to use paper or plastic bags.
53 Write an opinion paragraph, using supporting details from an article.
54 Write the opening of a short story about the effects of a chemical hazard.
55 Write a persuasive letter.

Exploring Multiple Perspectives

Almost daily we hear news reports describing how air pollution and deforestation, the loss of forests due to excessive logging, are putting our environment at risk. Other stories tell about the depletion of natural resources such as water, oil, and healthy soil. Opinions vary about how we can best protect our natural resources. Some news reports provide facts about the issues. Other newspaper or magazine articles want to **persuade** you to accept certain viewpoints or engage in particular actions.

In this unit, you will read persuasive essays about environmental issues. As you read each article, you will learn more about the techniques of persuasion. You will also be asked to think about whether or not the authors are convincing. Which authors offer examples and evidence that persuade you to believe them, despite the **multiple perspectives** on environmental issues?

In addition to reading, you will apply techniques of persuasion to your own writing. You will try to convince others to consider your point of view about saving a particular natural resource.

Literature

- **"Are Plastic Bags Harming the Environment?"** reported by John Roach and written by Sara Ives (nonfiction article)

Environmental issues surround the use of plastic bags.

- **"Call of the Mall"** from *You Are the Earth* by David Suzuki and Kathy Vanderlinden (nonfiction excerpt)

Consumerism has an impact on the natural resources of our planet.

- **"To Drill or Not to Drill?"** by Steven R. Wills (nonfiction article)

This article examines the debate over drilling in the Arctic National Wildlife Refuge.

- **Harvest for Hope: A Guide to Mindful Eating** by Jane Goodall with Gary McAvoy and Gail Hudson (nonfiction excerpt)

Goodall discusses the use of pesticides in farming and the harmful effect on living creatures as well as on the food produced.

- **"Save Your Energy"** from *You Are the Earth* by David Suzuki and Kathy Vanderlinden (nonfiction excerpt)

This excerpt provides ideas for conserving energy.

ASSESSMENT To assess student learning in this unit, see pages 238 and 259.

LESSON 51

Students will read a persuasive essay to identify a problem and several solutions and describe their reaction to the writers' position.

BACKGROUND KNOWLEDGE

In the 1980s, plastic bags began to replace paper bags as the bag of choice in stores. Plastic bags cost less to produce, they take up less space, they block moisture, and they do not break open as easily as paper bags. Billions of plastic bags are used every year and most of them are discarded. Ask students how many times a day they use plastic bags and for what purposes. Have them also think about where they see discarded plastic bags and the impact of plastic bags on the environment.

VOCABULARY

environmentalists people who focus on ways to protect natural resources

drawbacks problems or disadvantages

staggering overwhelming or unbelievable

consumers those who utilize goods and services

biodegradable capable of breaking down, or decomposing, naturally

Write each vocabulary word on the board. Have students share what they know about each word. Confirm the definitions with a dictionary.

LESSON 51 — PROBLEM AND SOLUTIONS

You've probably heard this question asked many times at the grocery store: Paper or plastic? Maybe you've heard it so often that you don't even think about it any more. In the following essay, the authors ask you to consider how much we rely on paper products. But we rely on plastic as well. Plastic bags line our trash cans. They keep our bread and vegetables fresh. We use them to hold our lunches. Is paper a better alternative than plastic? Are there other alternatives available?

As you read "Are Plastic Bags Harming the Environment?" focus on what the authors are trying to persuade you to believe. One technique writers use is to describe the **problem** clearly and to offer **solutions.** Ask yourself: What is the *problem* the authors identify and what *solutions* do they suggest?

Underline words and phrases that emphasize the problem the authors identify. Circle any solutions they offer. In your **Response Notes**, write questions or comments you have about the writers' viewpoints.

"Are Plastic Bags Harming the Environment?"
by John Roach and written by Sara Ives

"Paper or plastic?" Nearly every time someone buys groceries, he or she is asked this question. The answer is not as easy as it may seem. According to environmentalists, plastic bags and paper bags both have drawbacks.

Plastic bags are everywhere. According to the Virginia-based American Plastics Council, 80 percent of groceries are packed in plastic bags.

"The numbers are absolutely staggering," said Vincent Cobb, a businessperson from Chicago who launched reusablebags.com. He notes that consumers use between 500 billion and 1 trillion plastic bags per year worldwide.

Plastic bags can be found in landfills, stuck on trees, and floating in the ocean.

What is the effect of all of these bags? Some experts say that they harm the environment. Plastic bags can take hundreds of years to break down. As they break down, they release poisonous materials into the water and soil.

Plastic bags in the ocean can choke and strangle wildlife. Endangered sea turtles eat the bags and often choke on them—probably because the bags look like jellyfish, the main food of many sea turtles.

In fact, floating plastic bags have been spotted as far north as the Arctic Ocean to as far south as the southern end of South America. One expert predicts that within ten years, plastic bags will wash up in Antarctica!

164 LESSON 51

Before

CRITICAL READING SKILL
Identifying Problem and Solutions
One way that a writer can structure nonfiction text is to present a problem and its solutions. In addition to presenting solutions, the writer usually offers an evaluation of each one. Explain that knowing the structure of an article can help the reader know what to expect and, therefore, understand the article better. In addition, the problem-solution structure is useful for taking notes.

RESPONSE NOTES Have students highlight or underline the last three sentences of the introductory text as a reminder of how to respond to the article. Advise students that the problem and solutions will be recorded in a chart later in the lesson.

164 UNIT 11

Despite these negative effects, plastic bags do have some advantages.

"Plastic grocery bags are some of the most reused items around the house," explained Laurie Kusek of the American Plastics Council.

Plastic bags hold school lunches, line trash cans, and serve as gym bags. These uses decrease plastic bag waste.

According to the Film and Bag Federation, a trade group within the Society of Plastics Industry, paper bags use more energy and create more waste than plastic bags.

Plastic bags require 40 percent less energy to produce than paper bags and cause 70 percent less air pollution, the group explained. Plus, plastic bags release as much as 94 percent less waste into the water.

Paper bags do, however, break down more quickly than plastic bags. They also don't strangle wildlife.

What, then, should people do?

While some experts have argued for placing a tax on plastic bags, others worry that the tax would cause people who make plastic bags to lose jobs. Some people also worry that making plastic bags more expensive (through taxes) would increase landfill waste because stores would start using paper bags again.

Another possible solution would be to use biodegradable plastic bags, a technology that has recently improved. "Biodegradable" means that the bags naturally break down, like, for example, a banana peel does when you leave it outside.

Perhaps the simplest solution for now, however, is to pack groceries in reusable bags, such as cloth tote bags.

※ Take a minute to list the types of paper products you use each day.

EXTRA SUPPORT

Differentiation Challenge students to find the sources cited in the selection. Ask them: *What are the sources for the information in the article? What point of view do you think each source may have? How would that affect the interpretation of the facts?* Encourage students to see that Vincent Cobb is responsible for a website that tries to convince people to reuse plastic bags, so he obviously thinks there is a big problem with discarded plastic bags. Laurie Kusek, who is also quoted, works for the American Plastics Council, so her point of view is likely to support the use of plastic bags. Help students understand that it's important to consider the sources used to make an argument.

During

PERSUASION
As students read the selection, ask them to identify the problems and solutions that are discussed in the selection. Have them think about these things: *Are the problems clearly presented? Which solutions seem as if they will work? Why?* After students have finished the selection, have them fill out the Problem-Solution Chart on page 166.

Students may then discuss the chart in pairs or small groups so that they can see that not everyone will identify the same solutions or find them convincing. Writing the paragraph after they complete the chart will help them consolidate their thinking. It will also encourage them to articulate their reactions to the selection and evaluate how convincing the case is.

TEACHING TIP

Using a Graphic Organizer: Problem-Solution Chart Seeing the problems next to the solutions will help students organize their thinking and evaluate the persuasiveness of the selection. While the selection focuses on one major problem, the proliferation of discarded plastic bags, it also talks about specific problems related to the broader topic. You may want to model filling in one of the problems and its solution: *On page 164, the text says that plastic bags can take hundreds of years to break down. I'll put that in the Problems column. On page 165, the text says that plastic bags can be made of biodegradable plastic, which breaks down more quickly. I'll put that in the Solutions column.*

Quick Assess

* Can students name the problems and identify the solutions offered (explicit or implicit)?

* Can students give examples from the selection to back up their opinion of whether or not the argument is convincing?

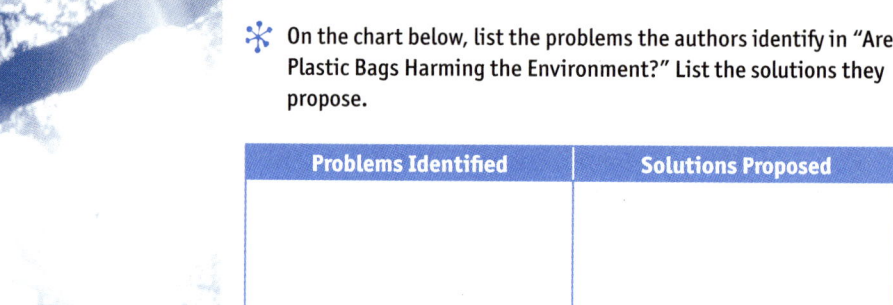

* On the chart below, list the problems the authors identify in "Are Plastic Bags Harming the Environment?" List the solutions they propose.

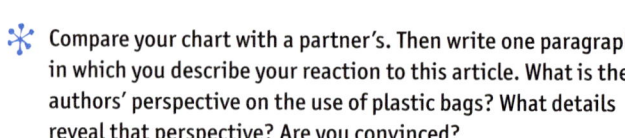

Problems Identified	Solutions Proposed

* Compare your chart with a partner's. Then write one paragraph in which you describe your reaction to this article. What is the authors' perspective on the use of plastic bags? What details reveal that perspective? Are you convinced?

> Determine the problems posed. Look for the solutions offered to help you understand the author's perspective.

After

APPLYING THE STRATEGY Have students use what they've learned from this article to come up with some strategies of their own for solving the problem of the growing number of discarded bags. They may want to start a campaign to make other students and teachers aware of the problem and offer some workable solutions. For example, students might want to create school posters that show facts related to plastic bag use. Encourage students to provide at least one solution on each poster, such as taking a reusable cloth bag to the grocery store, washing plastic bags and reusing them, or recycling them in other ways. For more solutions, students may even want to interview other students or local citizens who are involved with recycling.

CONVINCING DETAILS — LESSON 52

Make a mental picture of the pile of paper you use in a week. Remember that it takes wood and electricity to produce even a simple sheet of paper or a roll of paper towels. Now imagine how much wood and electricity it takes to produce the paper you use each *year.* How could you reduce your paper usage? What other resource-saving habits might you develop?

One strategy a writer uses in **persuasive writing** is to provide convincing details to readers. In the following article, the authors present facts about the consumption of natural resources. As you read, keep track of which **details** are convincing to you and which details you question. Use your **Response Notes** to raise questions and make comments about the details the authors provide.

"Call of the Mall" from *You Are the Earth*
by David Suzuki and Kathy Vanderlinden

. . . It can be fun to buy a great new outfit or the latest CD. But is that the only thing that's fun or has any value? For many people, it seems that it is. Buying more and more objects is a major way people today look for happiness and purpose in life. Look at these facts:

- Toy makers produce up to 6000 new toys each year. (That's on top of the old toys already for sale).
- Americans spend an average of 6 hours a week shopping. They spend just 40 minutes a week playing with their children.
- We can choose from more than 11,000 magazines and 25,000 supermarket items, including 200 kinds of cereal.
- North Americans will spend an average of two years of their lives just watching TV commercials.

But owning things by itself doesn't seem to make people happy. Buying something makes you feel happy for a little while. Then you have to buy something else to feel happy again. Meanwhile, all this shopping is eating up the Earth. Many natural resources, such as oil, trees, and aluminum, are used to make, advertise, and sell all those things we buy. Added to that is the waste these purchases create—the bags and boxes they come in, the advertising flyers, and the things themselves when we throw them away. This mountain of garbage gets burned in incinerators, dumped into lakes, or buried in the ground, where it contaminates the air, water, and soil.

LESSON 52

Students will read a persuasive essay, form an opinion on an issue, and justify their position with convincing details.

BACKGROUND KNOWLEDGE
Ask students to think about shopping. What items did they or their family purchase this week? Have them think about the way the purchases are packaged. For example, some stores wrap merchandise in tissue paper before putting the item into a bag. Some merchandise is sold in a box. Some products, especially toy items, are sealed in plastic and attached to paper backing. Have any students used recyclable shopping bags? What becomes of the packaging once they get the merchandise home? Talk about what effect all this packaging might have on the environment.

VOCABULARY
incinerators places for burning waste
contaminates makes something dirty or impure

Discuss the words and their meanings. For each word, invite students to write a sentence related to protecting the environment. After students have read the selection, allow them to revise their sentences.

Before

CRITICAL READING SKILL
Identifying Convincing Details
A writer's general statement of an argument may not be convincing to a reader. Instead, a good reader will look for convincing details by asking questions:

❖ Are the facts accurate and relevant?
❖ Do the facts support the argument?
❖ Are the facts appropriate for the audience?
❖ Does the writer stick to the facts or make sweeping generalizations that use such words as *all, always,* or *never*?

RESPONSE NOTES
Have students interact with the text by using their Response Notes to ask questions and comment on the details presented in the selection. Students should consider the list of questions in the previous column as they evaluate the details.

During

SUPPORTING AN ARGUMENT
After students have read the selection, have them fill out the chart, identifying the problems, the solutions, any convincing details the authors have presented.

Students will then use what they know to write a note to their family convincing them to see their point of view on the paper-or-plastic debate.

ABOUT THE AUTHORS
Born in 1936 in Vancouver, David T. Suzuki, PhD, is a well-known geneticist, author, environmentalist, and broadcaster. Dr. Suzuki's TV shows on science have been widely viewed in the U.S. and in Canada. He has also written more than 30 books. Kathy Vanderlinden has edited many fiction and nonfiction books for adolescents and children.

Quick Assess

- Did students identify convincing details in the selection?
- Did students list problems, solutions, and convincing details in the chart?
- Have students made a strong and convincing case to their families in their persuasive letters, using convincing details as well as stating problems and solutions?

- In the last 60 years, Americans alone have used up as large a share of the Earth's mineral resources as all people in the world used before that time.
- In the last 200 years, the United States has lost 85 percent of its old-growth forests, 50 percent of its wetlands, and 99 percent of its tall grass prairies.

Get the connection?

How convincing are the authors? Chart your understanding below.

Problems Identified	Solutions Proposed	Convincing Details

Now that you have read these authors' perspectives, consider how you would answer the question: paper or plastic? Write a note to your family to convince them to accept your viewpoint. Provide convincing details from your own experience or from those given by the authors to justify your perspective on the paper or plastic question.

Evaluate the details provided to help you understand the authors' opinions.

168 LESSON 52

After

PURPOSE AND AUDIENCE Before students draft a letter to their family, ask them to think about the audience *(their family)* and the purpose of the letter *(to convince their family to use paper or plastic bags)*. Point out that good writers keep their audience in mind as they write, making sure that they anticipate questions or problems the audience may have with their point of view. For example, does their family already know about the issue, or do they need to provide a little background? Remind students that part of the art of persuasion is to offer some solutions to the problems. Have them brainstorm possible solutions that are not too inconvenient or difficult to implement. Tell them to make sure to include convincing details to support their position.

READING/WRITING CONNECTION As a class, write a persuasive letter to local grocery and convenience stores convincing them that they should offer incentives to those who bring their own bags. Encourage students to cite convincing details from the selections to persuade their audience.

EXAMINING THE ALTERNATIVES — LESSON 53

Before you read the next article, ask yourself: What do I already know about the debate on drilling for oil in Alaska? Based on your prior knowledge of the topic, what questions do you have? Do you have an opinion about whether we should drill? Jot down your questions and opinions.

_____
_____
_____

Another strategy a writer might use in persuasive writing is to offer alternative positions for readers to think about. As you read the following article, highlight the alternatives the author points out about drilling for oil in Alaska. Make comments in the **Response Notes** about the perspectives offered.

"To Drill or Not to Drill" by Steven R. Wills

It is history class after lunch, and you are just falling to sleep. A large, fluffy hand reaches down and carries your history teacher away as she continues to describe the presidential election of 1868. Yes, you realize, this is a dream.

Suddenly you are behind the wheel of a massive SUV. You notice that you are running out of gas, and also notice a gas station just up ahead. You drive up to the pump, but find that a majestic Alaskan caribou is standing in your way. He's beautiful, but you need to fill up. It occurs to you that the only way you'll be able to get gas is to run him down.

The teacher shouts your name and you wake up, leaving a small puddle of drool on your desk.

Turns out your dream was also a metaphor—a visual symbol of the kinds of decisions lawmakers, oil companies, oil consumers, and environmental activists are facing today. "To drill or not to drill?!" *That* is the question.

At the heart of the problem is America's hunger for oil. The United States is, by far, the largest consumer of oil in the world—using more than 7,000,000,000 (yep, that's billion) barrels of oil each year. We use it to heat our homes and businesses, and to manufacture plastics, tires, ink, and synthetic fibers. And mostly, we use it to operate our cars, trucks, and other vehicles (almost five billion barrels each year).

EXAMINING THE ALTERNATIVES **169**

LESSON 53

Students will read and examine opposing viewpoints in an article.

BACKGROUND KNOWLEDGE

In 1960, a wildlife refuge of 8.9 million acres was established at the northern end of Alaska on the Beaufort Sea. This area preserves the wildlife of the region and provides recreational opportunities without endangering the land or its wildlife. In 1980, the area was named the Arctic National Wildlife Refuge and enlarged to 18 million acres. At least 45 different species of land and marine mammals, 180 species of birds, and 36 species of fish exist there. Some acres are designated for wildlife studies and oil and gas research. The area is rich in oil, and some people want to drill there. Invite students to write their questions and opinions about drilling at the top of page 169.

VOCABULARY

embargo a ban on something

tundra a treeless area between the icecap and the tree line of Arctic regions

migratory traveling from a colder climate to a warmer one

Use the Word Splash blackline master found on page 272.

Before

CRITICAL READING STRATEGY
Examining Alternate Viewpoints
Sometimes an argument is most effective when the presenter offers another viewpoint, or a counterargument. A counterargument argues against the main point. Ask students: *Why is it sometimes helpful to have an author offer various alternative solutions to a problem rather than taking just one position?* Point out that the presence of an alternative position strengthens the argument. It also gives further information with which the reader can make an informed choice.

RESPONSE NOTES Read the first four paragraphs with students. These set up the scenario for the arguments in this selection. Ask students to write in their Response Notes their first reaction to the "drill or not to drill" question. Then, as they read independently, suggest that they keep track of their reactions as the alternative positions are offered.

EXPLORING MULTIPLE PERSPECTIVES **169**

WRITER'S CRAFT

Organization Discuss with students the way that the author organizes his presentation of the alternate points of view on the issue of drilling for Alaskan oil. Talk about the metaphor, or analogy, on page 169. By connecting the debate to the image of the SUV that must run down the caribou to get to the gas station, Wills grabs the reader's attention. He follows this metaphor with some facts that set up the problem. Have students look at the way the different points of view are presented on page 170. Talk about how the author has created a dialogue of sorts with his "point-counterpoint" approach. Invite students to talk about whether they find this effective and why.

Response Notes

Although we import most of our oil from other countries, we realize that dependence gives the oil-producing countries a certain power over us. We learned that lesson from the oil crisis of the 1970s, caused by a Middle East oil embargo by the OPEC (Oil Producing and Exporting Countries) organization.

However, large oil reserves have been found under the frozen tundra of Alaska, on land, which, in 1960, was set aside to be protected as the Arctic National Wildlife Refuge (ANWR). When parts of ANWR were opened up to drilling in the 1980s, what followed was pollution, truck and drilling noise, chemical waste pits, and the 1989 disastrous oil spill from the *Exxon Valdez*.

Today, more oil reserves have been located on the ANWR, and sides are lining up to either support or oppose drilling for more oil. The opposing arguments sound like this:

No Drilling! Haven't we learned our lesson? The ANWR is rich in wildlife. It is home to bears (grizzly and Kodiak—both endangered), wolves, foxes, musk oxen, millions of migratory birds, and caribou. The caribou are of particular concern, since they move over the very areas targeted for drilling in order to reach their traditional breeding grounds.

The environment will be altered for other reasons, as well. You can't just pull oil from the ground—you need drilling platforms, trucking roads, pipelines, and a constant supply of heavy equipment. When will we finally take a stand and say, "Remember the *Exxon Valdez*? Not again! This last piece of wilderness must be preserved!"

Drill Away! We now have the ability to limit environmental damage. Trucking roads in the winter can be made of crushed ice, and supplies can be flown in by helicopter in the summer. Furthermore, high-tech drilling techniques mean that fewer drilling platforms need to be built. New pipelines can be elevated five feet off the ground so that wildlife can easily pass under. Also, the pipes will not be fitted with flat valves (which can fail and leak), but rather with loops that will limit the spill from any possible leak. Finally, all waste will be recycled.

No Drilling! Ice roads solve problems but create others, since they would require millions of gallons of precious fresh water—water that would likely come from the same sources that serve the plants of the tundra. Also, while high-tech devices help, they cannot eliminate accidents or potential disasters. Besides, who says drilling companies will follow all of these high-tech guidelines?

Drill Away! The new oil reserves are estimated to contain from 3.7 to 16 billion barrels of oil. That's anywhere from a six-month to two-year supply. Not only will that oil help curb our dependence on imports, but it will also generate big bucks for the local towns and people.

No Drilling! Why not increase the fuel efficiency of vehicles? A minor increase in auto and truck fuel efficiency would save more oil than would be found in the Alaskan reserves.

During

SUMMARIZING As students read, they are asked to examine alternative positions in the debate and decide which arguments are the most convincing. If they have difficulty doing this on their own, stop after each "Drill Away!" and "No Drilling!" section and ask them to summarize. Keep track of each alternative by listing the key points on the board or on an overhead. This activity is particularly valuable if you have struggling readers.

NO doubt this is a tough call, but a decision must be made about whether to drill on the ANWR. How would you face this problem?

✻ List the most persuasive details in the article for each of the positions in the debate. Share your list with a partner and discuss which alternative is most convincing to each of you and why.

Examining the Alternatives	
To Drill	Not to Drill

✻ Now that you have read about the debate, form an opinion about drilling in the Arctic National Wildlife Refuge. Write a paragraph explaining your opinion. Include details from the article that support your opinion.

_____
_____
_____
_____
_____
_____
_____
_____
_____

Examine the alternative perspectives the author uses to persuade you to consider an important problem and its potential solutions.

EXAMINING THE ALTERNATIVES 171

TEACHING TIP

Collaboration After students have completed their charts, have them share their chart with a partner. Have pairs discuss what they learned about each alternative. Have them take turns answering these questions: *Do you believe the author has presented one alternative more convincingly? Does one position have more persuasive details? After reading this article, what is your position on drilling for oil in Alaska?*

WRITING SUPPORT

Using Graphic Organizers Tell students that the chart they completed will help them think about what to include in their opinion paragraphs. Remind them that a good argument draws on convincing details to help persuade the reader.

Quick Assess

✻ Did students offer persuasive details for each alternative?

✻ Did students identify their opinion on the issues, explaining it with adequate support from the article?

After

LISTENING/SPEAKING CONNECTION Have students present an oral debate on the issue of drilling for oil in Alaska. Students can work in teams, with the team members preparing for the debate and then taking turns responding to counterpoints made by the other side.

RESEARCH CONNECTION Have students conduct a brief study on the use of petroleum products in their home or school. For example, have students chart the fuel costs associated with cars, school buses, and delivery trucks. Or have students find out the cost of heating or cooling a building. Make a class chart that tallies the total use over a period of time. Students can then prepare a report on the study they've conducted, along with some recommendations for ways in which they can learn to conserve and rely less on fossil fuels.

EXPLORING MULTIPLE PERSPECTIVES 171

LESSON 54

Students will read about a disastrous environmental event that occurred in the past that still has effects in the present.

BACKGROUND KNOWLEDGE
After World War II, many of the chemicals used as weapons during the war were used to fight crop-destroying insects. The intent was to increase the world's food supply, and that was one result. In 1962, Rachel Carson wrote of a different result in her book *Silent Spring*: the use of pesticides was negatively affecting the lives of plants and animals. Governments began to regulate their use, but the debate continues.

VOCABULARY
alliance partnership
bestowed gave
adversity hardship
impervious resistant
toxic poisonous
marauding raiding
leach seep into
PCBs chemical compounds that can build up in animal tissue
seminal influential

Preview the vocabulary words by finding each word in context in the selection and then discussing the meaning.

LESSON 54 — MAKING CONNECTIONS TO OUR LIVES

Farmers have become increasingly dependent on chemicals that help crops grow faster, protect them from insects or other pests, and increase yields. At the same time, some scientists and environmentalists have warned of the dangers of overusing chemical treatments. There are farmers who maintain organic farms, but the methods are more expensive and labor intensive. How conscientious are your family and friends about buying organic products? Does an organic label necessarily mean the product is chemical free? How is the issue of chemicals in food related to the earlier lessons about protecting our natural resources?

Writers know that readers respond when they can **make connections.** When a writer connects one situation to something the reader is familiar with, the author can make a persuasive case. Jane Goodall, the woman who is famous for her work with chimpanzees, has taken up another cause in science—our awareness of how food production affects our health and environment. Her perspective as a scientist affects what she writes and how she writes it.

As you read this excerpt from Goodall's book on the use of pesticides, highlight and write reactions in your **Response Notes** to the connections you make between what she describes, what you know about the use of chemicals, and how you think the issue relates to you.

from Harvest for Hope: A Guide to Mindful Eating
by Jane Goodall with Gary McAvoy and Gail Hudson

Growing Food with Poisons
Ever since World War II, when scientists first figured out that nerve gas used in warfare could be turned on crop-eating insects, the farm industry has become increasingly dependent on the chemical industry. And this has turned out to be an unholy—and a very destructive—alliance. Nature has bestowed all living things with the instinct to survive—adaptation to adversity is the key to evolutionary survival. When chemical pesticides are first introduced into an area, insect predators will quickly be poisoned and die. But gradually, after repeated applications, some insects will build up resistance. Just as overuse of antibiotics creates antibiotic-resistance in the bacteria that cause sicknesses in animals and human, heavy does of pesticides create pesticide-resistance in insects. After more than fifty years of farming with pesticides, there are whole populations of "pest" insects that have evolved to become

Before

CRITICAL READING STRATEGY
Using Connections to Persuade
Proficient readers recognize the ways that an author makes connections to readers' own lives to make a point. In this lesson, students will read a selection from Jane Goodall's book *Harvest for Hope,* in which she makes a highly technical subject very real for a general audience. As she discusses the facts, she makes strong connections to how these facts affect us in our everyday lives. As students read, they're asked to find examples of these connections and to evaluate their effectiveness.

RESPONSE NOTES
Ask students to look for places in the text where Goodall makes connections to things that are part of our daily lives. For example, in the second paragraph of the selection, she talks about how the chemicals escape into our environment, falling in *our rain and snowflakes,* drifting into *our backyards, our playgrounds.* Encourage students to write their reactions to what they are reading: how do these statements make them feel?

increasingly impervious to pesticides. The response of the farmer is to spray more often, and with increasingly more toxic pesticides. Nowadays, it's not uncommon for farmers to use three times as many chemicals as they needed forty years ago to kill off the same insects. It's the same situation with using chemicals to ward off marauding weeds, rodents, and diseases: Farmers are using more and more chemicals and finding them less and less effective. Each year, about three million tons of farm chemicals are applied to the surface of this planet.

And all these chemicals, of course, don't just stay on the farm: They escape into the environment. They evaporate into the jet stream and fall in our rain and snowflakes; they are lifted by the wind and drift into our backyards, our playgrounds, our preserved wild lands, and even our organic farms; they sink into the soil and leach into our groundwater, reservoirs, and wells; they find their way into our lakes, rivers, and oceans; and, of course, they can end up in the bodies of animals and people.

What's the collateral damage caused by these chemical assassins? For one thing, it's estimated that only 0.1 percent of applied pesticides reach the target pests, meaning all kinds of innocent bystanders suffer. Sometimes the immune and reproductive systems of honeybees are so compromised by pesticide exposure that they can't produce honey. Agricultural chemicals, combined with industrial and domestic chemicals, that enter the rivers and oceans weaken the immune systems of dolphins, whales, and thousands of other aquatic creatures. They cause birth defects in frogs and other amphibians—such as hind legs that are fused together or extra legs sprouting from their bellies or backs. When orcas are washed up on the shores of British Columbia their bodies are so contaminated with PCBs that they are regarded as hazardous toxic waste. And their calves die from drinking their mothers' toxic milk.

Farm chemicals kill of as many as 67 million American birds each year. I heard the other day that the songbirds that once greeted the spring in Iowa with their joyous chorus have virtually gone from the farming areas. In other words, farming chemicals are destroying our wild flora and fauna. The prophecy of Rachel Carson, in her seminal book, *Silent Spring*, has been fulfilled in many other places.

ABOUT THE AUTHOR
Jane Goodall, best-known for her work with chimpanzees in Africa, was born in London, England, in 1934. Her interest in animals, specifically chimpanzees, began early when her father bought her a toy chimpanzee named Jubilee, which she loved. Jubilee still sits on a chair in her home. See http://www.janegoodall.ca/index.html.

EXTRA SUPPORT
Differentiation For struggling readers, it may be important to read this selection aloud and stop to paraphrase what was read. Some paragraphs are complex, particularly the ones that describe the effects of chemicals on the environment. Help students comprehend the argument that Goodall is presenting. Ask students: *What is the author saying here? How does this tie to her point about the danger of pesticides?*

During

CONNECTING TO OUR LIVES
As students read, they should be thinking about how Goodall's topic affects the world today. Have students think about what they have learned so far in this unit. Ask them: *What is the environmental problem in this excerpt? Does Goodall present any solutions? Does she use convincing details to back up her argument?*

After students have read the selection once, have them review it and their Response Notes to complete an entry in the Double-Entry Log on page 174. Then brainstorm topic ideas for connecting what they've read to current issues.

EXTRA SUPPORT

Differentiation Model for struggling readers how to stop and summarize while reading. At the end of each paragraph, which you might want to read aloud, stop to offer a summary of the author's main point.

Paragraph 1. *Over time, chemical pesticides become less effective in controlling insects. The insects get used to the poison. Therefore, farmers have to use more and more chemicals.*

Paragraph 2. *The chemicals leave the farm and travel via wind and water. In other words, the chemicals reach many people and animals beyond the farm.*

Paragraph 3. *Only a very small amount of the pesticides actually reach the pests. The rest affects people and animals all over the world.*

Paragraph 4. *Farm chemicals affect our habitat by unintentionally killing off plants and animals.*

Finally, summarize the entire excerpt by prompting students with a question: *What is the author's opinion of farm chemicals?*

Quick Assess

* Did students make connections with the text in their Response Notes?
* Were students able to make connections to the problems of today?

❋ In the Double-Entry Log below, list the dangers Goodall discusses that made the strongest impression on you. In the right column, explain how you can connect these dangers to your life.

DOUBLE-ENTRY LOG

Goodall's example of dangers	Connections to my life

❋ Demonstrate how Goodall's discussion of chemical poisons is important to your life by using the space provided to write the beginning of a short story in which you are the main character. The story should focus on the effect of some chemical hazard on you, the main character.

Notice how the author makes connections to readers' lives to persuade them to be concerned about today's problems.

After

APPLYING THE STRATEGY
Encourage students to conduct additional research and express their opinion on an environmental issue. As they research their topic, have them ask themselves these questions: *What form of writing should I use to present the problem? How can I convince my audience that the problem needs to be solved? What actions or solutions could correct the problem?* Students might benefit from creating and using a graphic organizer to collect information.

PERSUADING OTHERS — LESSON 55

On average, each person in a developed country uses as much energy in six months as a citizen of a developing country such as Nepal uses in his or her lifetime.

As you read, underline the actions you are willing to take to reduce the amount of energy you consume. Underline, too, alternative ways to produce energy. In your **Response Notes,** list actions not included in the excerpt that you are willing to take to use less energy.

"Save Your Energy" from *You Are the Earth* by David Suzuki and Kathy Vanderlinden

What can we do? For a start, we can stop wasting energy. We can do this in simple ways, such as turning off lights when we aren't using them, lowering the thermostats in our homes at night, and using energy-efficient fluorescent lights whenever possible. We can also walk, skate, or bike more instead of riding in cars. It's a lot more fun to do these things, and it's good for our health and the Earth's health, too.

We can also make bigger changes as communities and nations. Instead of relying on fossil fuels, we can use energy sources that don't pollute and will never run out. For instance, in places near the ocean, the power of tides can drive turbines, which are wheel-like devices with blades that help them rotate. The turbines are connected to generators, which produce electricity. In windy regions, wind can also drive turbines to produce electricity. And best of all, the bountiful power of sunlight can be captured to heat and light homes, heat water, and generate electricity. Perhaps you have a calculator or a game that uses solar power. These sources of energy are being used in small ways today but show promise of having much wider uses in the future.

PERSUADING OTHERS 175

LESSON 55

Students will read a problem-solution essay to list ways to solve energy problems and write a persuasive letter about their environmental concerns.

BACKGROUND KNOWLEDGE
Discuss the meaning of *fossil fuels* (natural resources such as coal, natural gas, and oil). Explain that there is a limited supply of these resources, so people have spent decades looking for other sources of energy. Discuss some alternative energy sources, such as the sun, wind, and water. Invite students to talk about examples they have seen or heard about of machines or power fueled by alternative energy sources. Discuss the advantages and disadvantages for each energy source. Lead to a discussion of ways in which we might conserve energy.

VOCABULARY
thermostats devices that control temperature

energy-efficient uses as little energy as possible

generators machines that convert mechanical energy into electrical energy

bountiful plentiful

Find out what students know about energy-efficient appliances, as well as generators and thermostats.

Before

CRITICAL READING STRATEGY
Analyzing Persuasion Review with students the techniques of persuasion they have learned in this unit: presenting a problem and its solutions, using convincing details, giving a counter-argument, and making connections to personal experience. Tell students to notice which of these techniques Suzuki and Vanderlinden use in their persuasive writing about saving energy.

RESPONSE NOTES
Have students ask themselves as they read: *Is this something I am doing to save energy? Is it something my community is doing? If not, is it something we could do to make a difference?* In the Response Notes, have students comment whether the authors are effective in persuading them to save energy.

During

SORTING INFORMATION
Have students think about ways in which a society can conserve energy. Have them sort those ways into things individuals can do (such as walk, skate, or bike instead of riding in cars) and things people need to band together to accomplish (such as using water to power turbines). Encourage students to think of ways they might save energy that are not listed in the selection.

EXPLORING MULTIPLE PERSPECTIVES 175

TEACHING TIP

Reflecting Ask students to review their Response Notes for this unit in light of the persuasive techniques they have learned. Which technique(s) will they use in their letter?

EXTRA SUPPORT

Differentiation For students who need additional support, work with them to brainstorm their topic and the best way to present their recommendations. Have them create a list of the main points they are going to make and address any counterarguments. Work with them individually, or have them work with a partner, to draft their letters.

Quick Assess

* Did students list actions they're willing to take to conserve energy?
* Did students present an interesting project for the school to undertake?
* Did students name the problem and how this project provides potential solutions?
* Did students use convincing details and make relevant connections to their audience in order to provide a convincing case for conservation?

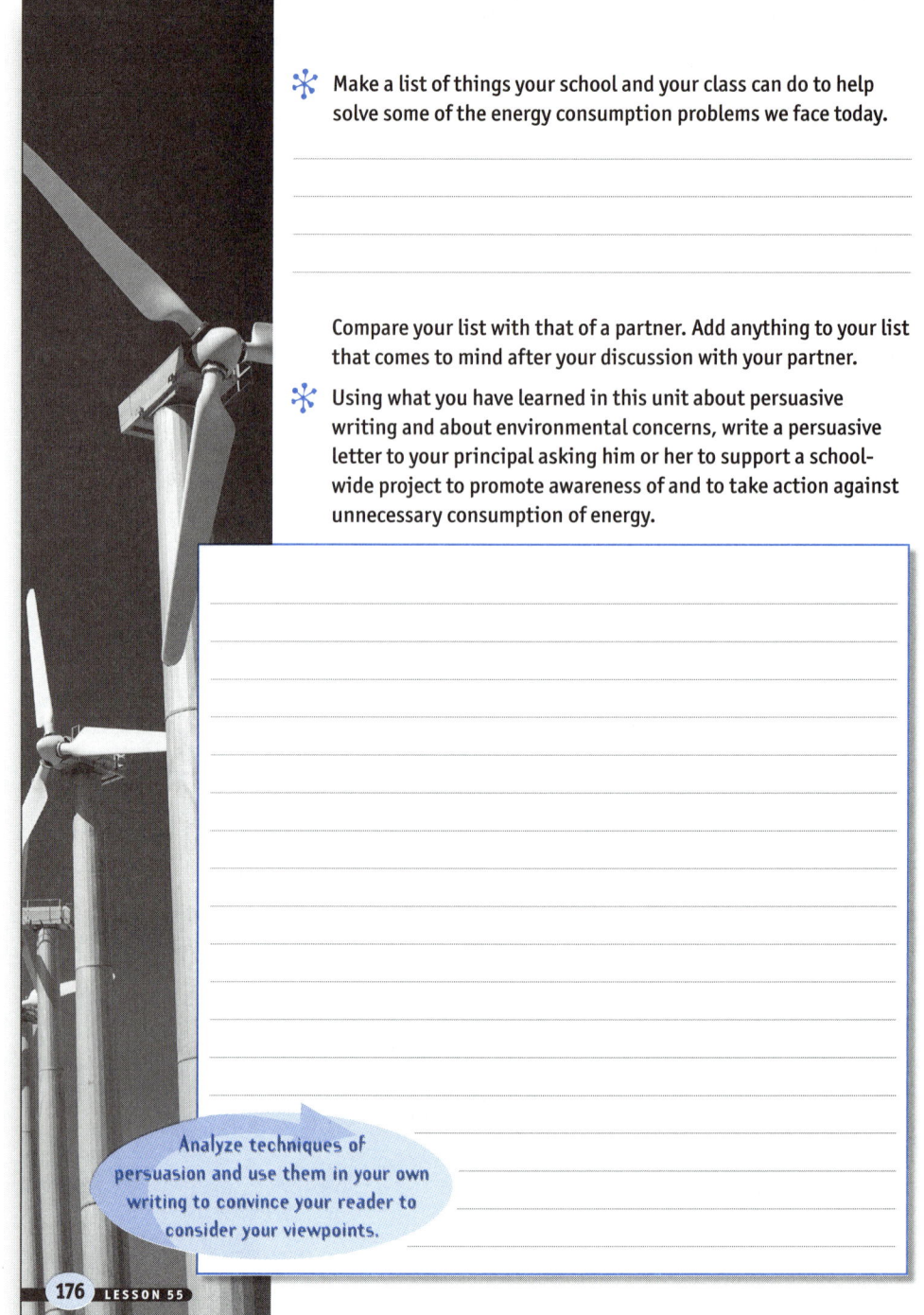

* Make a list of things your school and your class can do to help solve some of the energy consumption problems we face today.

Compare your list with that of a partner. Add anything to your list that comes to mind after your discussion with your partner.

* Using what you have learned in this unit about persuasive writing and about environmental concerns, write a persuasive letter to your principal asking him or her to support a school-wide project to promote awareness of and to take action against unnecessary consumption of energy.

> Analyze techniques of persuasion and use them in your own writing to convince your reader to consider your viewpoints.

176 LESSON 55

After

SCIENCE AND SOCIAL STUDIES CONNECTION Students may want to research other opinion pieces on the subject of the environment. Ask them to gather facts first and then write a persuasive essay on the topic. They can use the techniques they've studied in this unit. Have them illustrate their essays with photos and/or illustrations and allow students to share their essays with the class by presenting them orally or creating a display for the classroom or library.

UNIT 12
FOCUSING ON LANGUAGE AND CRAFT

Lessons 56–60 pages 178–192

UNIT OVERVIEW
The use of symbols is traced from the dawn of written language to modern literary writing.

KEY IDEA
Good readers recognize and understand the use of symbols in order to draw deeper meaning from text.

CRITICAL READING SKILLS
by lesson

56 Defining a concept
57 Focusing on symbols
58 Making connections
59 Focusing on figurative language
60 Focusing on literary symbols

WRITING ACTIVITIES
by lesson

56 Write an essay that reflects on reading and personal experience.
57 Create a symbolic representation of an abstract idea.
58 Write an essay that expands on a quotation from the text.
59 Write a poem that contains an image, simile, metaphor, and symbol.
60 Write a poem about a personal choice.

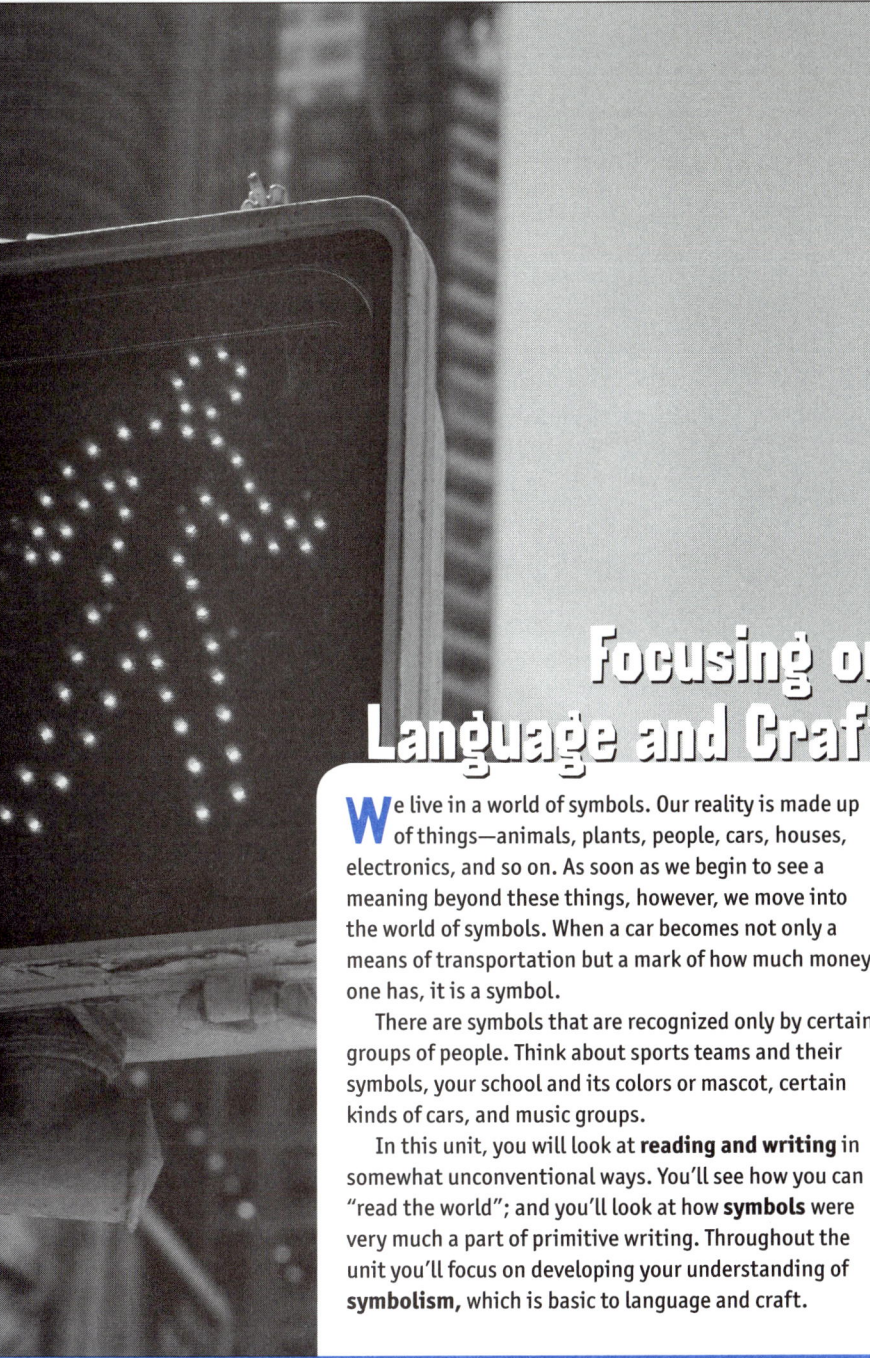

Focusing on Language and Craft

We live in a world of symbols. Our reality is made up of things—animals, plants, people, cars, houses, electronics, and so on. As soon as we begin to see a meaning beyond these things, however, we move into the world of symbols. When a car becomes not only a means of transportation but a mark of how much money one has, it is a symbol.

There are symbols that are recognized only by certain groups of people. Think about sports teams and their symbols, your school and its colors or mascot, certain kinds of cars, and music groups.

In this unit, you will look at **reading and writing** in somewhat unconventional ways. You'll see how you can "read the world"; and you'll look at how **symbols** were very much a part of primitive writing. Throughout the unit you'll focus on developing your understanding of **symbolism**, which is basic to language and craft.

Literature

- **"Martin Luther King Jr."** by Gwendolyn Brooks (poem)

Metaphors and imagery, symbolic uses of language, build this tribute to the slain civil rights leader.

- **A History of Reading** by Alberto Manguel (nonfiction excerpt)

A list of ways in which we "read the world" illustrates how symbols fill our lives.

- **"Symbols of Humankind"** by Don Lago (essay)

A speculation about the dawn of written communication asserts the importance of symbols through history and in the future.

- **"The Road Not Taken"** by Robert Frost (poem)

This famous poem about one man's choice provides a simple, powerful example of symbolism in literature.

ASSESSMENT To assess student learning in this unit, see pages 239 and 262.

LESSON 56

Students will think about what it means to read for understanding and identify symbols of meaning in the selections.

BACKGROUND KNOWLEDGE

In the first part of the lesson, students will explore their ideas of the word *reading*. Then, students will read a poem and an excerpt from a nonfiction book.

Throughout the reading and discussion of "Martin Luther King Jr.," provide background information about Dr. King as needed. Students should know these basic points in order to comprehend the poem:

* King was the leader of the civil rights movement of the 1950s and 1960s, inspiring people to unite in a stand against racial segregation.

* He led the March on Washington in 1963, where he gave his "I have a dream" speech in front of hundreds of thousands of supporters.

* King won the Nobel Peace Prize in 1964. He was killed in 1968.

Tell students that they will be doing an exercise in which they will think about what the concept of reading means to them.

Before

CRITICAL READING SKILL

Defining a Concept Use a word web to craft one or more definitions of *read*. Write the word *read* in the middle of a word web. Elicit students' help in collecting words and phrases that define reading, give examples of things to read, and state purposes for reading. Encourage students to think creatively about what they can "read"; for example, faces, maps, body language, and so forth.

As needed, support students as they work through the bullet points at the top of page 178. Students should continue their note-taking on a separate sheet of paper.

* When people learn to read, they gain the ability to learn anything. So, you could say that reading is a ticket to the world.

* When you read, you make sense of the letters and words. When I "read" a TV ad, I try to make sense of the images. So, reading images can be a way to make sense of a message.

* When scientists read signs in nature, they are better able to predict natural events, determine if the climate is changing, or chart an asteroid's course. So, reading signs in nature depends on knowing what to look for.

LESSON 56 — READING, IN OTHER WORDS

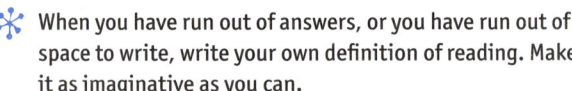

What do you mean by the word *reading*? With your classmates, come up with as many definitions or examples of reading as you can, and have someone post them on the board or on chart paper.

As you work, ask yourselves questions such as these:

- What does it mean for a child to learn to "read"?
- How is reading the words of a song different from reading a textbook?
- How is watching ads on television a kind of "reading"?
- What does it mean for a naturalist to "read" signs of animals in the woods?
- What does "reading" music mean?
- How is reading a novel like or different from reading a manual on setting up a new DVD player?

✻ Use this space for notes:

✻ When you have run out of answers, or you have run out of space to write, write your own definition of reading. Make it as imaginative as you can.

My definition of reading:

_____
_____
_____

Read Gwendolyn Brooks's poem about Martin Luther King, Jr., on page 179.

178 LESSON 56

Martin Luther King Jr. by Gwendolyn Brooks

A man went forth with gifts.
He was a prose poem.
He was a tragic grace.
He was a warm music.

He tried to heal the vivid volcanoes.
His ashes are
reading the world.

His Dream still wishes to anoint
    the barricades of faith and of control.

His word still burns the center of the sun,
    above the thousands and the
    hundred thousands.

The word was Justice. It was spoken.
So it shall be spoken.
So it shall be done.

※ Brooks writes, "His ashes are reading the world." What do you think she means by this phrase? There is no right or wrong answer; just say what you think. You'll come back to this poem later in the unit.

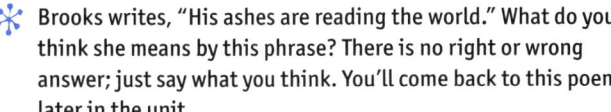

Alberto Manguel, in his book *A History of Reading,* writes that "reading letters on a page is only one of its many guises." He goes on to list many kinds of reading:

The astronomer reading a map of stars that no longer exist;
the Japanese architect reading the land on which a house is to be built so as
    to guard it from evil forces;
the zoologist reading the spoor of animals in the forest;
the card-player reading her partner's gestures before playing the winning
    card;
the dancer reading the choreographer's notations, and the public reading the
    dancer's movements on the stage;
the weaver reading the intricate design of a carpet being woven;

READING, IN OTHER WORDS

ABOUT THE AUTHORS

Gwendolyn Brooks (1917-2000) was born in Topeka, Kansas, and raised in Chicago, Illinois. After attending college, she worked at the *Chicago Defender,* an African-American newspaper, and published a weekly poetry column. Her early poetry collections garnered instant acclaim and she was awarded the Pulitzer Prize in 1950. Brooks taught creative writing at prestigious universities and was awarded many honors, but the heart of her work was never far from the racial dreams and realities of Chicago's South Side. As Poet Laureate of Illinois, she championed poetry education for inner-city schools. Go to http://www.poets.org for more information.

Alberto Manguel was born in Argentina in 1948 and raised in Israel, where his father was a diplomat. He is internationally known as an anthropologist, translator, novelist, and editor of literary anthologies. In 1992, his novel *News from a Foreign Country Came* won England's Society of Authors' prestigious McKitterick Prize.

TEACHING TIP

Relay Reading For the *History of Reading* excerpt, have students take turns reading lines aloud. Encourage all students to participate, repeating the lines until each student has had a chance to read.

During

TAKING NOTES Encourage students to write down insights on reading that are particularly meaningful to them. Students can use the notes to formulate their definitions.

RESPONSE NOTES Read aloud or ask a volunteer to read aloud "Martin Luther King Jr." before having students reread and respond to it. To help students develop a deeper understanding of the poem, ask them to speculate on the possible meanings of the images, such as *warm music*, *vivid volcanoes*, and *the center of the sun*.

FOCUSING ON LANGUAGE AND CRAFT

TEACHING TIP

Collaboration As students may not be familiar with each reference Manguel makes in his excerpt, have them form groups to research unfamiliar terms. You may want to split these references among groups:

* stars that are extinct
* evil forces and Japanese cultural beliefs (also known as *feng shui*)
* animal spoors
* choreographic notations
* dream interpretation

Have each group report their findings to the class. Then the class can discuss how the line relates to the larger concept of reading, in light of the new information.

the organ-player reading various simultaneous strands of music orchestrated on the page;
the parent reading the baby's face for signs of joy or fright or wonder;
the Chinese fortune-teller reading the ancient marks on the shell of a tortoise; ...
the psychiatrist helping patients read their own bewildering dreams;
the Hawaiian fisherman reading the ocean currents by plunging a hand into the water;
the farmer reading the weather in the sky—
all these share with book-readers the craft of deciphering and translating signs.

❋ Pick three of Manguel's examples of "reading" and draw the images they represent to you. In the top row of the chart below, write Manguel's words for the images you are sketching.

Example 1	Example 2	Example 3

WRITING SUPPORT

Visualizing Model a chart entry before students complete their charts on their own. For example, draw a smiling baby. Then, above the drawing, write *signs of joy*. Explain that students' drawings are subject to their own interpretation, so there are no "right" or "wrong" answers.

Manguel says "We all read ourselves and the world around us in order to glimpse what and where we are. We read to understand, or to begin to understand."

❋ Use this quotation as the beginning of a brief essay in which you explain what kinds of reading are important to you. Be as specific as you can as you elaborate on your ideas.

> Reading has a much broader meaning than simply deciphering text on a page.

WRITING SUPPORT

Elaboration Discuss the quote in the writing prompt, soliciting students' insights. Post these questions to prompt input:

❋ What kind of reading do people do, besides reading books, periodicals, or online sources?

❋ How does reading symbols and signs help you?

❋ What if we were not taught to read? How would life change?

Then use a think-aloud to model how to elaborate on an idea. For example, say: *Knowing how to read traffic signs is important to me. Beyond the obvious safety issues, they let me know when I should slow down for road construction and alert me to potential dangers in the road.*

Encourage students to jot down a few ideas before they start writing. If they have difficulty with elaborating on an idea, have them return to the posted questions.

Quick Assess

Do students' essays do the following:

❋ Assert at least one or two ideas about what reading means to them?

❋ Elaborate on their idea(s)?

❋ Show that they understand how reading plays an important role in their everyday lives?

After

READING/WRITING CONNECTION

Have students keep a reading journal for a period of time, recording daily occurrences when they read something besides text. Students should tell what they read, how they understood the information, and how the information affected them. Set aside time for students to share a journal entry with the class.

READING/ART CONNECTION

Have groups make collages with images and phrases that relate to reading. Students can start with the images they drew for the chart on *Daybook* page 180. Students can also use words and images from their own reading journals (see the previous activity). Have groups present their collages to the class, elaborating on how the images contribute to the concept of reading, beyond reading only text.

LESSON 57

Students will think about how writing has evolved and gain a deeper understanding of language symbols.

BACKGROUND KNOWLEDGE
Draw or display a few common symbols, such as the male and female figures that appear on public restroom doors. Ask students what they are. Then, ask students to speculate as to why, if most people in our society can read, we still use pictures to communicate. (Possible reasons: pictures are useful to people who do not read or do not read English, it's faster to understand a picture than read a word.) Then, explain that students will read part of an essay that explains how symbols were humans' first attempt at communication and why they are still useful today.

VOCABULARY
pictograph a picture that represents a familiar object

ideogram a picture that represents an idea

To prepare students to understand the difference between the concepts, have students look up the word parts for each vocabulary term. (Pictographs represent concrete objects, while ideograms represent abstract ideas.)

LESSON 57 WRITING AS WRITING

Most of us take writing for granted. We go to school, we learn to read and we learn to write. We don't question the existence of writing. It's strange to think that at one time, there was no such thing as writing.

Here is part of an essay that explains Don Lago's idea of how writing started. Read it, first without using the **Response Notes** column.

▶ Symbols of Humankind by Don Lago

Many thousands of years ago, a man quietly resting on a log reached down and picked up a stick and with it began scratching upon the sand at his feet. He moved the stick slowly back and forth and up and down, carefully guiding it through curves and straight lines. He gazed upon what he had made, and a gentle satisfaction lighted his face.

Other people noticed this man drawing on the sand. They gazed upon the figures he had made, and though they at once recognized the shapes of familiar things such as fish or birds or humans, they took a bit longer to realize what the man had meant to say by arranging these familiar shapes in this particular way. Understanding what he had done, they nodded or smiled in recognition.

This small band of humans didn't realize what they were beginning. The images these people left in the sand would soon be swept away by the wind, but their new idea would slowly grow until it had remade the human species. These people had discovered writing.

Writing, early people would learn, could contain much more information than human memory could and contain it more accurately. It could carry thoughts much farther than mere sounds could—farther in distance and in time. Profound thoughts born in a single mind could spread and endure.

The first written messages were simply pictures relating familiar objects in some meaningful way—pictographs. Yet there were no images for much that was important in human life. What, for instance, was the image for sorrow or bravery? So from pictographs humans developed ideograms to represent more abstract ideas. An eye flowing with tears could represent sorrow, and a man with the head of a lion might be bravery. ✦

✱ Now reread the first part of the essay. This time, beside each paragraph, use the **Response Notes** column to make a simple drawing (like a pictograph) that relates to the text.

182 LESSON 57

Before

CRITICAL READING SKILL
Focus on Symbol Explain that the next two lessons will focus on the history of writing. Before humans developed the text-based writing systems that are used today, humans wrote with pictures, or symbols. Model how to make a pictograph in response to the text. For example, read the first sentence and draw a twig. Direct students to read the essay, responding with pictures that relate to the text.

During

ABSTRACTIONS Before students begin the chart activity, briefly review the meaning of *abstract*. Explain that an abstract idea is something that is not tangible, such as an emotion or a way of acting or being. Give a few examples, such as *happiness, cleverness*, or *generosity*, to spark students' ideas for their lists.

Then model how these ideas can be represented as ideograms. For example, brainstorm concrete objects that students associate with *happiness*, such as a smiley face, a sun, or a flower.

✳ Compare your drawings with those of your partner or your group.
  ■ How similar are they?
  ■ How do they differ?
  ■ Can you tell from the drawings what the paragraph is about?

In the essay, Don Lago writes about the origin of *ideograms,* pictures that represent abstractions rather than concrete objects. He wrote, "Yet there were no images for much that was important in human life. What, for instance, was the image for sorrow or bravery? So from pictographs humans developed ideograms to represent more abstract ideas. An eye flowing with tears could represent sorrow, and a man with the head of a lion might be bravery."

✳ With your partner or group, make a list of some other abstract ideas that are as important in human life as sorrow and bravery.

✳ Write at least three items from your list here. For each one, design an *ideogram* that could represent that concept.

Abstract idea	Ideogram for the abstract idea

✳ Notice that this essay is titled "Symbols of Humankind." After reading the first part of the essay and working with the concept of ideograms, what do you think would be a good definition of the word *symbol*? Write your ideas here, then compare your definition with the definitions of your group.

Ideas can be expressed through pictures and words.

WRITING AS WRITING 183

ABOUT THE AUTHOR
Don Lago is an essayist who researches and writes about nature, science, and history. His travel memoir, *On the Viking Trail: Travels in Scandinavian America,* was inspired by Lago's attempt to connect with his ancestral memory after his father developed Alzheimer's disease. Lago lives near Flagstaff, Arizona.

WRITER'S CRAFT
Historical Fiction Explain that nobody really knows the story of how humans first wrote with symbols; the author has created a fictional scenario based on research findings. Point out that Lago has imagined characters, setting, and plot, in order to put the reader in the middle of a historical event (the advent of writing).

Quick Assess

✳ Do students' chart entries show an understanding of abstract ideas?

✳ Can students articulate how each of their ideograms represent an abstract idea?

✳ Do students' definitions show that they have considered the function and significance of symbols?

After

WRITING SUPPORT
Defining Suggest ways to define symbols, encouraging students to consider

✳ how they read and use symbols on an everyday basis;

✳ how symbols help people communicate;

✳ the significance of symbols within the historical development of human communication.

APPLYING THE STRATEGY
Have students reread a short nonfiction text they have already read, using pictographs and ideograms for response notes. Later, students can reflect on whether using symbols gave them a new or deeper meaning of the text. Encourage students who benefited from this exercise to continue the strategy with future readings.

READING/WRITING CONNECTION
Have students write a story or short play about learning to read or write. Students should include the following elements:

✳ a specific moment or event

✳ characters

✳ setting (modern day or long ago)

✳ a post-writing reflection on how literacy changes lives

FOCUSING ON LANGUAGE AND CRAFT 183

LESSON 58

Students will read more about the history of communication and reflect on their experiences with language.

BACKGROUND KNOWLEDGE
Ask students to share what they recall from the previous lesson, for example:

* humankind's first written communication was in the form of symbols;
* the first symbols were pictographs and ideograms;
* pictographs represent concrete objects, while ideograms represent abstract ideas.

VOCABULARY

syllabic having a set of symbols, each standing for a sound

alphabetic having a set of letters, each standing for a sound, that can be used to spell words

binary language the basic code of computer programming, which contains infinite combinations of the numbers 0 and 1

exobiologist a biologist who searches for life beyond Earth

interstellar between stars or planets

Remind students to use familiar words, such as *alphabet* and *biology,* and word parts, such as *bi* ("two") and *exo* ("out of"), to determine the definitions.

LESSON 58 — WRITING GOES EXTRATERRESTRIAL

The story of "Symbols of Humankind" continues in Don Lago's essay. Read this final part of the essay, using your **Response Notes** column in the usual way. Make notes, ask questions, notice any ideas new to you, and make connections to what you already know or have experienced.

Symbols of Humankind by Don Lago (continued)

The next leap occurred when the figures became independent of things or ideas and came to stand for spoken sounds. Written figures were free to lose all resemblance to actual objects. Some societies developed syllabic systems of writing in which several hundred signs corresponded to several hundred spoken sounds. Others discovered the much simpler alphabetic system, in which a handful of signs represented the basic sounds the human voice can make.

At first, ideas flowed only slightly faster when written than they had through speech. But as technologies evolved, humans embodied their thoughts in new ways: through the printing press, in Morse code, in electromagnetic waves bouncing through the atmosphere and in the binary language of computers.

Today, when the Earth is covered with a swarming interchange of ideas, we are even trying to send our thoughts beyond our planet to other minds in the Universe. Our first efforts at sending our thoughts beyond Earth have taken a very ancient form: pictographs. The first message, on plaques aboard Pioneer spacecraft launched in 1972 and 1973, featured a simple line drawing of two humans, one male and one female, the male holding up his hand in greeting. Behind them was an outline of the Pioneer spacecraft, from which the size of the humans could be judged. The plaque also included the "address" of the two human figures: a picture of the solar system, with a spacecraft emerging from the third planet. Most exobiologists believe that when other civilizations attempt to communicate with us they too will use pictures.

All the accomplishments since humans first scribbled in the sand have led us back to where we began. Written language only works when two individuals know what the symbols mean. We can only return to the simplest form of symbol available and work from there. In interstellar communication, we are at the same stage our ancestors were when they used sticks to trace a few simple images in the sand.

We still hold their sticks in our hands and draw pictures with them. But the stick is no longer made of wood; over the ages that piece of wood has been transformed into a massive radio telescope. And we no longer scratch on sand; now we write our thoughts onto the emptiness of space itself.

Before

CRITICAL READING SKILL
Making Connections Explain that this is a continuation of the previous lesson. As the text is dense with linguistic and historical details, you may want to use this process for each paragraph:

* Read it aloud.
* Solicit questions from students.
* Check comprehension by having students summarize main point(s).

RESPONSE NOTES
Have students reread the paragraph and respond with questions or comments. Suggest that they stop at the end of each paragraph to make some notes.

During

WRITING SUPPORT
Expanding on a Quote Paraphrase the meaning before students complete the prompt. For example,

Prompt 1 Ask what Lago means by "where we began." (*Like the earliest writings, interstellar communication relies on pictographs.*) Then ask students whether or not they agree.

✲ Choose one of the following quotations taken from the second part of Don Lago's essay and expand on it. Use the quotation as a starting point to explore your own ideas about what Lago says. Use specific incidents or examples from your own experience.
  1. "All the accomplishments since humans first scribbled in the sand have led us back to where we began."
  2. "Written language only works when two individuals know what the symbols mean."
  3. "And we no longer scratch on sand; now we write our thoughts onto the emptiness of space itself."

Writing has evolved from simple pictographs to symbols conveying our deepest thoughts.

TEACHING TIP
Collaboration Have students choose which quote they will write about, then form groups accordingly. Creating a word web, students can brainstorm ideas about the quote.

✲ One student writes the quote in the middle of a large piece of paper.

✲ Each student connects one word or phrase to the quote in the space surrounding it.

✲ Students draw their own connections and make new associations from others' words and ideas.

EXTRA SUPPORT
Differentiation If students seem to have difficulty finding connections to the text, ask broad questions that elicit the importance of the topic.

✲ *Imagine that it took days or weeks to write and send a message instead of minutes. How would your life be different?*

✲ *Why would interstellar communication be important?*

✲ *If you were communicating with another planet, what message would you send?*

Quick Assess
✲ Do students use specific examples to support their writing about a quotation from the Lago excerpt?

After

ART CONNECTION Return to the third paragraph of the excerpt and review how the plaque on the *Pioneer* depicts humans' identity and origin. Ask: *If you were to have a symbol that depicts who you are or where you are from, what would it be?* Students should develop and draw a personal symbol, accompanied by a written explanation. Encourage them to consider

✲ pictographs of things they like to do;

✲ ideograms of concepts that are important to them.

LISTENING/SPEAKING CONNECTION Invite students to conduct further research on the origin of symbols and communication. Groups can research their topics online:

✲ the origin of letter shapes in an alphabet

✲ the Roman numeral system

✲ the computer binary system

✲ International Distress Signals

✲ a state or nation's flag

Have students create a poster containing example(s) of the related symbols. Students can then present their research findings to the class.

FOCUSING ON LANGUAGE AND CRAFT 185

LESSON 59

Students will write a poem that uses imagery, figures of speech, and symbolic language.

BACKGROUND KNOWLEDGE
Ask students what they learned from the previous two lessons (writing has progressed from pictographs to our current alphabetic system; symbols are still used to communicate messages). Explain that students will now apply their knowledge of symbols in a common way: writing a poem.

LESSON 59 — FROM IMAGE TO SYMBOL

In this unit you have looked at reading and writing in somewhat unconventional ways. You have looked at *reading* as a way of making meaning from many aspects of our universe, rather than just making meaning from texts on a page. You have read that *writing* is made up of the symbols we use to represent both things and ideas.

In this lesson you're going to write a series of simple statements that will become a poem illustrating the definitions of *image, simile, metaphor,* and *symbol*.

STEP ONE: THE IMAGE
Definition: An image describes how something looks, sounds, feels, smells, or tastes. It presents a specific sensory description.

* Choose something, such as an animal, plant, or object that you can describe. Write a simple sentence about your subject.
   Example: The *heron* stands tall, unblinking in the early morning sun.
   Write a sentence that describes the subject, or the image, you have chosen:

   _____
   _____
   _____

STEP TWO: THE SIMILE
Definition: A simile is a stated comparison. It compares one thing with another using the words "like" or "as."

* Use the subject you described and write a simile using "like" or "as."
   Example: The heron *is like* a mysterious stranger, barely visible through the mist.
   Write a sentence that compares your subject to something else (simile):

   _____
   _____
   _____

186 LESSON 59

Before

CRITICAL READING SKILL
Focus on Figurative Language
Explain that figurative language xpresses, compares, or represents something or someone with something else. Figurative language can include images, similes, metaphors, and literary symbols.

During

Model the steps by choosing a subject and completing a poem with students' suggestions.

Step One: The Image Ask a volunteer to read the definition of *image*. Then point out the two images in the example (*standing tall, early morning sun*). For more examples of images, you may want to revisit "Oranges" by Gary Soto on *Daybook* page 19.

Step Two: The Simile Ask a volunteer to read the definition of *simile*. Then point out the simile in the example, along with the phrase that explains the connection between a heron and the sun (*barely visible through the mist*).

Step Three: The Metaphor Review the definition and point out how the example line includes a phrase that connects the subject to its metaphor (*it is a shadow*).

STEP THREE: THE METAPHOR

Definition: A metaphor is an implied comparison. It speaks of one thing in terms of another.

Look again at the poem about Martin Luther King, Jr., in Lesson 56 and find these lines that are all metaphors:

> He was a prose poem.
> He was a tragic grace.
> He was a warm music.

Notice how Gwendolyn Brooks uses them to build her impressions of King.

❋ Write another comparison for your subject, but don't use "like" or "as."

Example: On the ground, it is a shadow of itself, emerging and fading in the swirling fog.

Write a sentence with another comparison without using "like" or "as" (metaphor):

_____
_____
_____

STEP FOUR: THE SYMBOL

Definition: A symbol means both what it is and something else. It stands for something beyond the concrete image.

❋ Write one more simple sentence about your subject. This time be aware of all that you have already written.

Example: The heron shifts, rises on unfolding wings—*the stranger floats away.*

Write a last sentence describing something your subject does; try to take the image to a new level so that it becomes a symbol.

_____
_____
_____

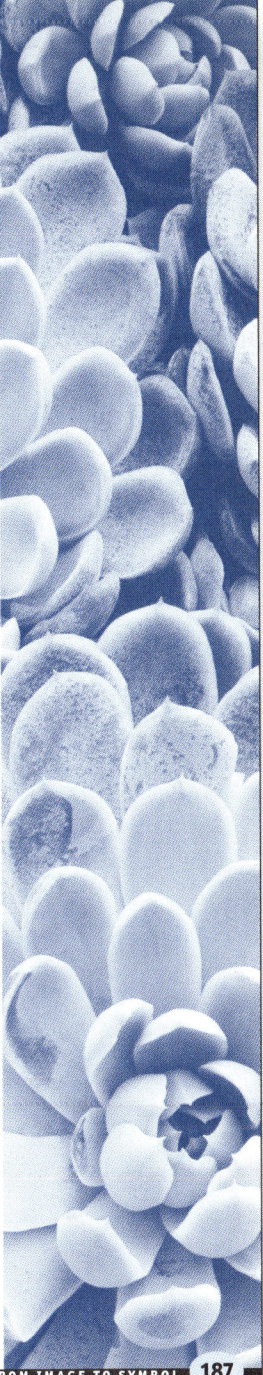

FROM IMAGE TO SYMBOL 187

TEACHING TIP

Collaboration Have students form groups of four to complete the poem together. After modeling the steps, have each group decide on a subject. Then, groups can decide on the image, simile, metaphor, or symbol that will describe their subject. Each student can choose a step and craft the corresponding line. At step five, have students assemble the group's poem, critique, and revise their poem accordingly.

To form their metaphors, encourage students to generate a list of things they associate with their subject. The item with the strongest connection to the subject can be the metaphor.

Step Four: The Symbol Go through the definition and discuss how the qualities of a stranger (elusive, mysterious) can also be attributed to a heron. As students brainstorm symbols for their subjects, offer a list of those commonly used in poetry:

❋ for *love*, a rose or a heart

❋ for *peace*, a dove

❋ for *war*, a hawk

❋ for *life*, water

❋ for *birth*, a sunrise

❋ for *death* or *old age*, a sunset.

Step Five: Putting it All Together Explain how the example's title reflects the image of the bird as it rises out of the mist and into the early morning brightness.

FOCUSING ON LANGUAGE AND CRAFT

WRITER'S CRAFT

Line Breaks Point out how the line breaks of "The Radiant Bird" create an interesting shape that may suggest the shape of a bird. Encourage students to experiment with the line breaks in their own poems, using them to create a relevant shape or isolate key words or phrases.

STEP FIVE: PUTTING IT ALL TOGETHER

✳ Give your poem a title that conveys the idea of the evolving symbol. Below is an example of the finished poem illustrating image, simile, metaphor, and symbol.

The Radiant Bird

Image: The heron stands tall, unblinking in the early morning sun

Simile: The heron is like a mysterious stranger, barely visible through the mist.

Metaphor: On the ground, it is a shadow of itself, emerging and fading in the swirling fog.

Symbol: The heron shifts, rises on unfolding wings— the stranger floats away.

Write your finished poem here. Don't forget the title!

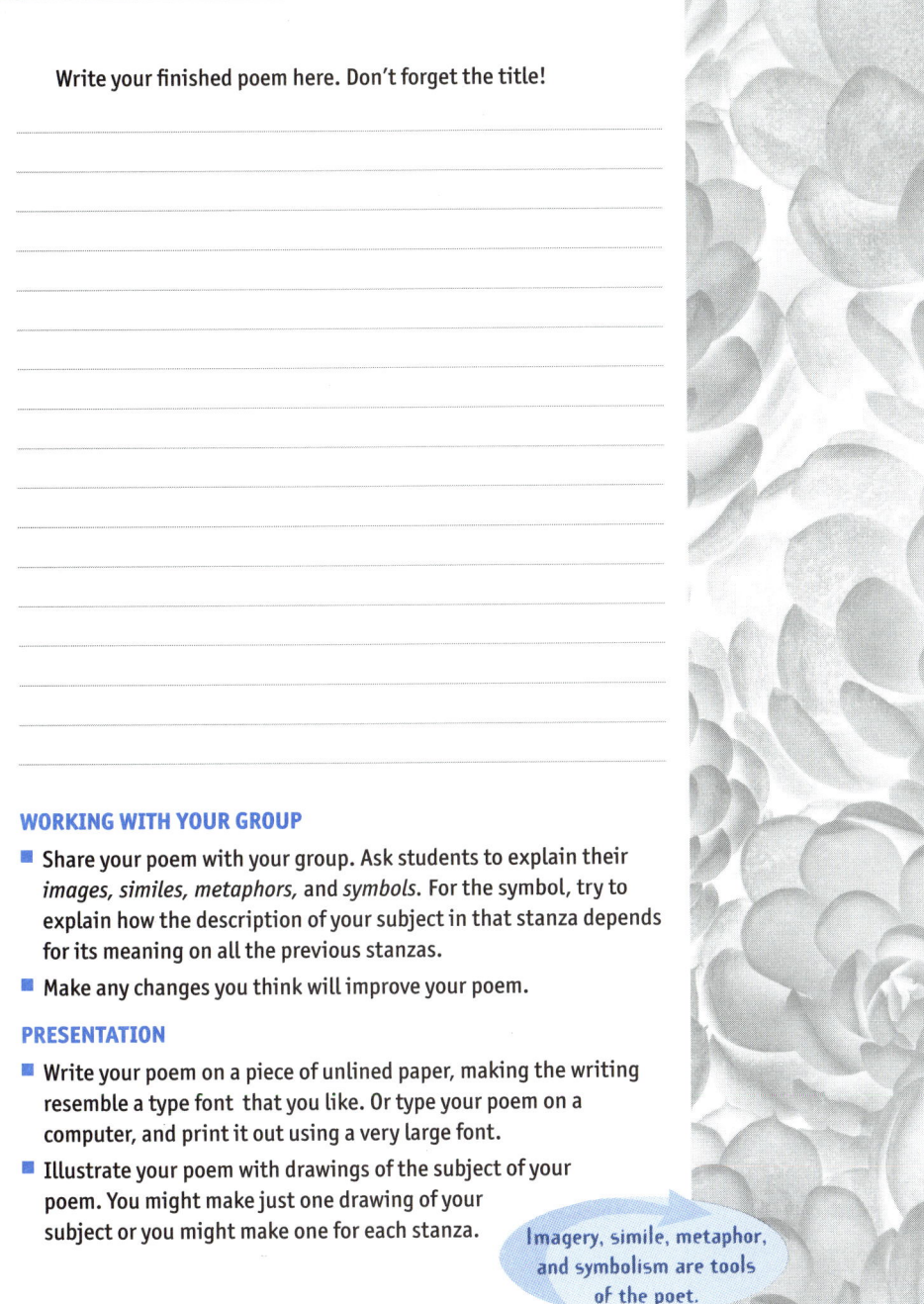

TEACHING TIP
Collaboration If students crafted parts of a collaborative poem, have the group review the finished piece together. Ask: *Do all your images lead up to the symbol?* Students can revise the poem together. Have them list possible titles and choose the best one.

Quick Assess
* Do students understand the difference between an image, simile, metaphor, and symbol?
* Does students' figurative language give thoughtful description of their subjects?

WORKING WITH YOUR GROUP
- Share your poem with your group. Ask students to explain their *images, similes, metaphors,* and *symbols.* For the symbol, try to explain how the description of your subject in that stanza depends for its meaning on all the previous stanzas.
- Make any changes you think will improve your poem.

PRESENTATION
- Write your poem on a piece of unlined paper, making the writing resemble a type font that you like. Or type your poem on a computer, and print it out using a very large font.
- Illustrate your poem with drawings of the subject of your poem. You might make just one drawing of your subject or you might make one for each stanza.

Imagery, simile, metaphor, and symbolism are tools of the poet.

FROM IMAGE TO SYMBOL 189

After

APPLYING THE STRATEGY Shuffle and distribute the finished poems, so each student has a poem that is not his or her own. On a separate sheet of paper, have each student write sentences explaining the poem's image, simile, metaphor, and symbol. Students can also write a sentence about the way the title relates to the images in the poem.

Return the poems to their owners, along with the completed analyses. Then discuss the activity, asking these questions:

* Did your analyzer understand your poem correctly?
* How does it feel to have your poem analyzed by someone else?

LISTENING/SPEAKING CONNECTION Stage a class "poetry blitz" with each student practicing and performing his or her own poem for the class. Challenge students to recite their poems, and encourage them to add movement that "shows" the words. After every student has performed, blitz the walls with their poems.

FOCUSING ON LANGUAGE AND CRAFT **189**

LESSON 60

Students will read a well-known poem that uses figurative language to make connections with its meaning.

BACKGROUND KNOWLEDGE

Ask students if they've ever known or read about someone who made a difficult choice. You may want to reread Langston Hughes's "Thank You, M'am" in Lesson 13. Ask: *What were the two options? What made it hard to choose between the two? What was the final choice, and why?*

Explain that students will be reading a well-known poem about a man who makes a choice.

LESSON 60 WRITING A POEM

"The Road Not Taken," one of Robert Frost's best-known and best-loved poems, speaks to all of us. Who hasn't had difficulty making a decision at some point? Read and listen to this poem, first without making any notations.

The Road Not Taken by Robert Frost

Two roads diverged in a yellow wood,
And sorry I could not travel both
And be one traveler, long I stood
And looked down one as far as I could
To where it bent in the undergrowth;

Then took the other, as just as fair,
And having perhaps the better claim,
Because it was grassy and wanted wear;
Though as for that the passing there
Had worn them really about the same,

And both that morning equally lay
In leaves no step had trodden black.
Oh, I kept the first for another day!
Yet knowing how way leads on to way,
I doubted if I should ever come back.

I shall be telling this with a sigh
Somewhere ages and ages hence:
Two roads diverged in a wood, and I—
I took the one less traveled by,
And that has made all the difference.

Response Notes

✻ Reread the poem, this time paying closer attention to how the narrator describes the two roads. First, circle words and lines that tell about the first road. Then underline words and phrases that tell about the second road. Finally, use the **Response Notes** column to record your questions, connections, and thoughts about the meaning of the poem.

Before

CRITICAL READING SKILL

Focus on Literary Symbols Read the poem aloud or play a voice recording of the poet himself reading the poem. Let the rhythm and the rhyme of the lines create their own effect. Then briefly discuss what the poem is about, making sure that students understand these points:

✻ The narrator is faced with two roads.

✻ He takes the second, less-traveled road.

✻ He is sure he'll never return to the first road.

Then explain that the poem is about more than just choosing between two roads. Say: *There is a symbol in this poem. It stands for something deeper than what is said in the poem.* Explain that the symbol will be discussed later in the lesson.

RESPONSE NOTES Students should make the usual text interactions, focusing on the description of each road. Model a potential entry by writing "bends—can't see where it goes" under the column for the first road.

* You have been working with the idea of *symbol* in poetry. What word in this poem is a symbol? Remember that to be a symbol, a word must stand both for itself and something beyond its literal meaning.

   The symbol is _____.

   It means _____.

   In a few sentences, tell what this poem means to you.

   _____
   _____

Talk with your partner or group about the meaning of this poem. Share some stories about choices you have made when you had to decide which of two "roads" to take. The discussion will be preparation for writing your own symbolic poem.

PREWRITING Think about a choice you made in your life when you really had two options. The choice had consequences. State both options:

Option 1: _____

Option 2: _____

* Tell which option you took and what difference it has made in your life.

   _____
   _____
   _____

* Explain how you now feel about your choice. How has it changed your life? (Remember, Frost said his choice "made all the difference," but he doesn't tell us what that difference was.)

   _____
   _____
   _____

ABOUT THE POET
Robert Frost (1874-1963) was one of the United States' most widely read and highly celebrated poets of the 20th century. Born in San Francisco, Frost moved to Massachusetts at age 11, following the death of his father. It was there that he started writing poetry as a high school student. He briefly attended college but made his living mainly through teaching and working on his farm in New Hampshire.

Frost made New England his home for most of his life, and his poetic images reflect the starkness and beauty of the region's wooded landscape. Though he won four Pulitzer Prizes (among other top honors), Frost has been consistently characterized as a thoughtful man who wrote about simple, yet meaningful, experiences.

EXTRA SUPPORT
Differentiation Allow students to attempt the first prompt on page 191 independently. For students who may have difficulty finding the symbol and meaning, refer them to the chart you created for the Response Notes, and ask questions such as:

* Between what two things is the narrator choosing?
* How do the roads represent making a choice between two options?

WRITING A POEM 191

During

SYMBOLS Ask: *Can a split in a road be similar to making a choice in life? How?* Then discuss the narrator's choice, having students share the description they've noted for each road. Ask students how each image says something about choosing between two options.

WRITING SUPPORT
Prewriting Help students brainstorm topics for their poems by listing common situations in which young adults make choices:

* taking up or quitting a sport or extracurricular activity
* keeping or breaking ties with a friend
* what to do in an emergency

FOCUSING ON LANGUAGE AND CRAFT

WRITING SUPPORT

Symbols in Poetry Use a think-aloud to model finding a symbol that fits your choice. For example, say: *My choice was a* tough *choice to make. Something else that's tough is a rock. So, a rock could be my symbol.*

Encourage students to also describe their choice and then brainstorm objects or symbols that fit the description.

Quick Assess

* Do students understand that the two roads are the main symbol of the Frost poem?

* Do students list two distinct options they were faced with when they made their choice?

* Can students articulate the consequences of the choice they made?

WRITING THE SYMBOLIC POEM Think of a symbol that can stand for the choice you had to make. Frost chose "two roads." Think of something that has meaning in its own right, such as *morning,* but also has a larger, symbolic meaning, such as, perhaps, *a beginning.*

* Use the symbol you have chosen to tell about your choice. In your poem, tell
  - what the choices were
  - which choice you made
  - what difference your decision has made in your life
  - how you feel about that choice now

You may wish to use the form of Frost's poem as a model. When you finish, share your poem with your classmates.

Writing a symbolic poem helps you understand the meaning of literary symbols.

After

APPLYING THE STRATEGY Have groups choose an additional poem by Frost. Collections are available at Bartleby Great Books Online: www.bartleby.com/people/Frost-Ro. Each group can analyze the poem's imagery and present it to the class. Students may want to copy the poem on a poster and add an illustration.

Studying an Author

Reading several works by a single author helps you concentrate on the craft of writing, giving you ideas for different types of stories you can write.

Will Hobbs draws from his life experience, from research he has done, and from people he has known. He loves to hike, go whitewater rafting, and write books. As of 2005, he had written fifteen novels and two picture books. Many of his novels have won numerous awards. But he does not write for awards; he writes for his readers. He says, "My first hope for my novels is that they tell a good story, that the reader will keep turning the pages and will hate to see the story end. Beyond that, I hope to be inspiring a love for the natural world. I'd like my readers to appreciate and to care more about what's happening to wild creatures, wild places, and the diversity of life."

UNIT 13 STUDYING AN AUTHOR

Lessons 61–65, pages 194–208

UNIT OVERVIEW
In this unit, students examine the writing style of Will Hobbs, his stories about real life experiences, and his skill at bringing ideas to life in print.

KEY IDEA
Studying an author's work can lead to a better understanding of the author's style, genres, and the craft of writing in general.

CRITICAL READING SKILLS
by lesson

61 Exploring stories derived from other stories
62 Appreciating real-life stories
63 Understanding genre
64 Analyzing characters in stories
65 Revising stories

WRITING ACTIVITIES
by lesson

61 Create a continuation of a story.
62 Draft an Experience Snapshot.
63 Recast the Experience Snapshot in another genre.
64 Describe a character.
65 Revise the Experience Snapshot.

Literature

- ***The Maze*** by Will Hobbs (novel excerpt)

Rick Walter, a troubled teen in a detention center, reads the Greek myth of the great inventor Daedalus, his son Icarus, and their experiment with flight. After Rick leaves the detention center, he finds himself in a predicament similar to Icarus's, as he attempts to rescue a friend.

- ***Jason's Gold*** by Will Hobbs (historical fiction excerpt)

While traveling to the Yukon Terrritory in 1897 in search of his brothers, teen Jason Hawthorn stumbles across a cabin inhabited by two recently deceased prospectors.

- ***Kokopelli's Flute*** by Will Hobbs (fantasy excerpt)

Tep, a young boy, finds a small stone flute in an ancient cave. When he begins to play the flute, magical things begin to happen.

- ***Downriver*** by Will Hobbs (novel excerpt)

Eight teens take a rafting trip through the Grand Canyon. The ways the teens cope with the dangerous situations they encounter reveal their varied characters.

- ***Bearstone*** by Will Hobbs (novel excerpt)

Cloyd, a Native American teen, is fascinated by an old Colorado rancher's way of life.

ASSESSMENT See page 240 for a writing prompt based on this unit.

LESSON 61

Students will read about a troubled teen and analyze the story within the story to make connections to the character.

BACKGROUND KNOWLEDGE
Retell the Greek myth of Icarus and Daedalus: Imprisoned in a maze, inventor Daedalus and his son, Icarus, devise wings made of wax and bird feathers to effect their escape. As the pair begins their flight, Daedalus warns his son to avoid the excessive heat of the sun. Perhaps due to the exuberance of youth, Icarus flies too high where the sun melts the wax that holds his wings together. The unfortunate boy plunges into the sea and perishes.

VOCABULARY
fashioning making, forming, shaping
intoxicated very excited
levitate to rise and float in the air
riddled filled with holes; perforated
thermal a column of warm, rising air. Thermals form over hot, flat surfaces, such as the floor of a canyon, lifting soaring birds and hang gliders.

Point out that "fashion" and "intoxicated" in this context have different meanings than those students might know from other contexts. Have students jot down these definitions in their Response Notes for reference.

LESSON 61 — STORIES FROM OTHER STORIES

Where do writers get their ideas? Often they adapt a story, creating new characters in a new setting, but using the old story as a base. Science fiction and fantasy writers, for example, sometimes create their stories from myths and legends. They change the original stories to fit their purposes and to give the old stories new meanings. Will Hobbs says that he wanted to write because "I loved reading. If you like reading stories, you too might start thinking, I want to try that. I want to write a story." Some of Hobbs's novels are clearly connected to stories he has read.

In *The Maze,* Rick Walker is a troubled 14-year-old. Until he was 10, his grandmother raised him. When she died, he was placed in a series of foster homes. As the novel opens, he is sent to Blue Canyon Youth Detention Center for a minor offense. There, he spends a lot of time in the library, where Mr. B. befriends him and recommends books. As you read the excerpt, jot down in the **Response Notes** any questions or reactions you have.

from *The Maze* by Will Hobbs

Rick realized he'd gone on longer than usual with his reading warm-up. He turned to "Escape from the Maze" and read from the point where the greatest inventor of all time, Daedalus, was **fashioning** wings for himself and his son, Icarus, so they could fly out of the elaborate puzzle they were imprisoned in.

The wings worked all too well. Once they'd left their island prison behind, Icarus became **intoxicated** with the sensation of flight and started outflying the birds.

Suddenly Rick recalled that he'd heard this story before. His grandmother had read him a version of it when he was little.

He knew all about the intoxication of flight from way back, from a dream that had come almost nightly. In the dream he always had a miraculous, inexplicable power inside himself: he could actually fly. In the dream all he had to do was spread his arms and he'd begin to **levitate** higher and higher until he was hovering above the earth. Then he was not only hovering but actually flying above the fields and the treetops and the towns, weightless and peaceful and free.

Dream-flying had been his own great escape—he'd figured that out—a childish fantasy that had been gradually dying over the years and was nearly dead. He couldn't remember having had the flying dream a single time at Blue Canyon.

Rick remembered how Icarus' escape was going to end but he kept reading anyway. Ignoring his father's calls from below, Icarus flew higher and higher

---

Before

STORY STRUCTURE To help students make sense of the story's complicated structure, point out that the narrator provides four insights into the character: the Greek myth, Rick's thoughts about the myth, his flying dream, and Mr. B's comments. Have students create graphic organizers to sort out the elements.

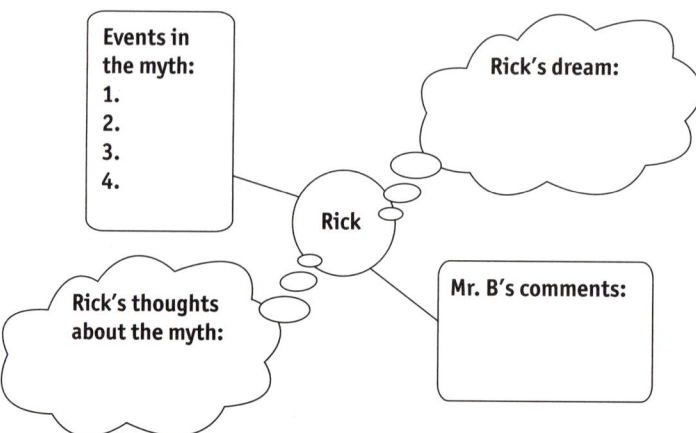

until the sun melted the wax holding the invention together, and the boy fell into the sea.

Now Rick realized why he found the story of Icarus so appealing. His own life was a puzzle riddled with dead ends. His own life was a maze.

"From the expression on your face," Mr. B. said from his desk, "you're enjoying that book."

Almost always they talked about what Rick was reading. "Yeah," he said, "I kind of like it."

"So, what do you think of Greek mythology?"

"I can relate to it."

"How so?"

"Things just happen to people for no good reason. Because some god or other gets ticked at them."

"That's the way the ancient Greeks looked at the world, Rick, but we're not ancient Greeks. Americans believe you make your own luck, you know."

Rick didn't really believe it.... "I suppose."

"Hang in there, Rick. Your break will come. And when it does, you have to be willing to go for it. To see your break for what it is and dare to ride it with all that you've got."

※ Write two things you know about Rick from this excerpt. What is he like?

___

Rick runs away from the correctional facility when he learns that other inmates plan to beat him up for reporting that a guard was taking bribes. He ends up in The Maze, a labyrinth of canyons and rock formations in Canyonlands National Park in Utah. There he meets Lon Peregrino, an avid hang glider, who is releasing six condors into the wild in an attempt to restore the population of this endangered species. Rick is entranced by the beauty of the condors' flight, especially one he names Maverick who dares to fly higher and farther than the others. Yet, Lon is worried about Maverick's flying too close to the sun. Rick asks him about it.

"Isn't that what happened to Icarus, in the story from Greek mythology?"

"You know about Icarus! I love that story. But I have this theory, Rick.... I never bought the bit about the sun melting the wax that held the wings together. Everybody knows that as you go higher up in the atmosphere, it gets colder, not warmer."

ABOUT THE AUTHOR

Born into an Air Force family in 1947 as the third of five children, Will Hobbs grew up "all over the map" of the United States and gained a love of wild things and places at an early age. As a child, he enjoyed hiking, fishing, baseball, and books and roamed the out-of-doors at every possible opportunity. All the works featured in this unit were named Best Books for Young Adults by the American Library Association. To learn more about the author, visit http://www.willhobbsauthor.com/.

WRITING SUPPORT

Gathering Information To help students respond to the prompt, point out Rick's pessimistic view of the world at the end of the first part of the excerpt. Ask: *Why do you think Rick connects so strongly with the idea that he has no control over his life? What events in Rick's background might have contributed to this attitude?* Encourage students to consider these ideas in writing about Rick.

During

STORY SETTING The Maze, a section of Canyonlands National Park, is often described as "a thirty-square-mile puzzle in sandstone." This tangle of canyons offers a beautiful but daunting experience for only the hardiest and most well-equipped adventurers. Have students locate Canyonlands National Park using a globe, map, or atlas. Explain that the area around The Maze is a desert that is home to a variety of interesting plant and animal species, including California condors and living dirt called Biological Soil Crust. For more information about Canyonlands National Park, visit the website at http://www.canyonlands.national-park.com/.

WRITING SUPPORT

Prewriting To prepare for writing story continuations, have students work with partners in a Think-Pair-Share exercise:

1. **Think** Have students jot down new information about Rick. Ask: *What does Lon's interpretation of the myth suggest to Rick? How might Rick use this idea to get out of the maze?*

2. **Pair** Have partners share ideas from the Think step and brainstorm events for the story continuation.

3. **Share** Invite pairs to share their ideas with the class and write them on the board or overhead.

Encourage students to use their own paper so they are not limited by the space in the *Daybook*.

Quick Assess

✷ Did students' Response Notes include questions or reactions?

✷ Did students list two things they learned about Rick?

✷ Did students' Response Notes include connections between the myth and Rick's thoughts?

✷ Did students compose plausible continuation stories?

Response Notes

"It's just a story, Lon."

"What if it *wasn't?* The Greeks were about the smartest people who ever lived, and Daedalus was the most brilliant inventor who ever lived. His time might have been thousands of years ago, but let's give him the credit he's due. Suppose for a minute that the Icarus story is a poetic account of something that *actually happened.*"

"That would be amazing."

"Imagine for a moment that Daedalus actually built two devices, very much like modern hang gliders, one for himself and one for his son."

"I like this theory of yours."

"Here's what happened. Very simply, Icarus got caught in a thermal he wasn't experienced enough to handle. It took him up and up, who knows how many thousands of feet up—"

"And then he tucked and tumbled into the sea."

"That's it."

"Icarus flew out of a maze, you know." ✧

✷ On the surface, this selection is about Icarus and Maverick, but on a deeper level it may be a story about Rick. Talk with a partner about the connections you see among the mythological characters of Daedalus and Icarus and the present-day fictional characters, Rick and Lon. Write your connections in the **Response Notes**.

✷ Rick cannot stay in Canyonlands forever. He will need to find his way out of that maze. Write a possible continuation of the story, based on what you have read and the connections you have made.

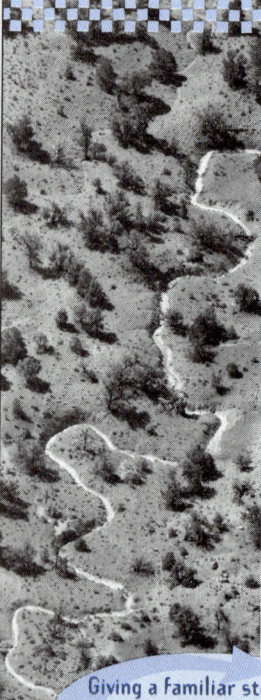

Giving a familiar story new twists allows the author to add layers of meaning.

196 LESSON 61

After

LITERATURE CONNECTION Invite students to read other Greek myths and think of ways they might influence modern teens like Rick. Encourage students to create dioramas or other visual representations of the myths and share them with the class, along with their thoughts about how modern teens might connect with the myths.

REAL-LIFE STORIES — LESSON 62

Will Hobbs says, "About half of my ideas for stories come from my own life experiences, and the other half come from reading, as I learn more about whatever has sparked my interest." Life experience and research are obvious in all of Hobbs's novels.

Although Hobbs hiked all around The Maze in Canyonlands National Park, he did not hang glide. The life experiences he used for the hang gliding scenes included reading, imagining, and observing three hang glider pilots.

This excerpt begins after a rough launch, as Rick leaves the cliffs where he picked up the wind. As you read about Rick's flight to rescue Lon, made more dangerous because a storm is developing, think about how Hobbs puts you in the scene and increases suspense. Circle any words or phrases that make you feel as if you are there. Underline words or phrases that make the scene suspenseful. Write comments in the **Response Notes** about anything else that catches your attention.

from The Maze by Will Hobbs

After five rising revolutions he was satisfied that he was high enough above the cliffs to glide away from them and head for Jasper Canyon.

You're still alive, he told himself as he broke to the east and began to soar toward the Standing Rocks. A powerful wave of exhilaration washed over him. He suddenly realized he was whooping and shouting like a wild man, grinning from ear to ear. "Yes!" he was screaming. "Yes!"

On his left and below, a very large bird was flying in his direction. As it neared he saw the broad wings, the distinctive wing tips, the featherless gray head. Lon's missing condor, he realized. It was M1, returning home in advance of the storm.

A glance at the variometer told him he had risen from 6,200 feet at launch to 7,560. Concentrate, he told himself. Stay focused. Take a deep breath. This is just the beginning.

Over the Standing Rocks the glider took a powerful buffeting. He clung tight as the wing shuddered with the turbulence. The variometer kept chirping as the glider was rocked by more and more turbulence. Still, he pushed back slightly from the bar and kept rising. He needed altitude. It was taking all his strength to hang on to the control bar and fly the glider. He knew now for certain that he was inside a thermal, a very powerful thermal.

Rick saw the earth's spinning, dizzying retreat below him, and he fought the panic that accompanied his sudden loss of equilibrium.

REAL-LIFE STORIES 197

LESSON 62

Students will read more of the teen's story to understand how writers use techniques to create an experience in words.

BACKGROUND KNOWLEDGE
Explain that hang gliding is one of the simplest forms of human flight. All a pilot needs is a specially constructed wing made of rip-stop nylon or Mylar over an aluminum frame, a mountain, and the ability to jog a few feet, carrying the 50-60 pound glider. The pilot of a hang glider, which is also called a kite, hangs from the frame of the kite in a harness. By moving the body forward and backward and from side to side, the pilot alters the center of gravity of the kite which allows the pilot to control its speed, direction, and altitude. Hang gliding is as risky as scuba diving or motorcycling, but those who master its intricacies can fly for many years. For more information, visit http://www.all-about-hang-gliding.com/faq.htm

VOCABULARY
variometer an instrument used to monitor altitude during flight
buffeting beating
turbulence boisterous or unsettled air
equilibrium a state of balance

After discussing the definitions, use each term in a sentence that relates to flight.

Before

CRITICAL READING SKILL
Real-Life Stories Explain that real-life stories tell about events that have really happened or about events that could actually occur. Although Hobbs has never flown a hang glider himself, his story reads as though from firsthand experience. One way the author accomplishes this is through careful research about the sport. Another way is through effective word choices that help readers relate to experiences they may never have had. To model identifying elements of this craft, say, for example: *The sentence "A powerful wave of exhilaration washed over him" reminds me of the feeling I experienced in the ocean.*

Invite students to share other examples of effective word choices and feelings those words inspire. Then remind students to make connections with the text in their Response Notes.

STUDYING AN AUTHOR 197

EXTRA SUPPORT

Differentiation Have visual learners create a diagram that shows the various elevations mentioned in the story. Encourage students to download pictures of cloud and land formations mentioned in the story to use as illustrations for the diagram. Invite students to create models of hang gliders in various altitudes described in the excerpt and mount them on the diagram at appropriate locations.

Response Notes

Keep fighting, he told himself. Keep flying it. Don't let it get away from you. He didn't know if he was strong enough to keep the wing tips down. One or the other kept threatening to go too high on him. He kept yanking hard on the side he wanted to bring down.

Ride it! Fight it!

Up, up, up he went, on an increasingly powerful column of rising air. He checked the variometer. He was at eleven thousand feet and climbing at a rate of a thousand feet per minute.

Eleven thousand feet!

It was getting cold. His face was cold, his teeth were cold.

High enough! There was a river below, but he couldn't tell which one. It was all a sickening blur.

He had to break out, find Jasper Canyon.

Rick pulled his weight over the bar, but the variometer kept chirping. A glance told him he was rising now at a rate of eighteen hundred feet per minute.

The turbulence was getting worse, much worse.

Ride it! Fight it!

. . .

Twelve thousand, thirteen thousand, fourteen thousand feet. It was becoming nearly impossible to hang on to the bar and keep the wings down. He didn't know how much longer he could hang on. He had to start thinking about the parachute.

Icarus, he thought ruefully. I'm pulling an Icarus. "Wasn't ready to fly a thermal," Lon had said.

Sixteen thousand feet. It was cold, cold, and getting harder to breathe.

From the variometer he glanced up and saw the base of a massive cumulus cloud not so far above. He could picture exactly what was going to happen, and soon. He was going to be inside that cloud and unable to tell up from down. Tucking and tumbling.

This is the way I'm going to die.

Wildly he forced his body as far forward of the control bar as he possibly could. He spread his hands wide and held on with all his strength.

Finally, finally, the glider nosed down. He heard the buzzing that told him he was losing altitude.

He kept his body forward of the bar, kept fighting the glider down. It felt like he was dropping fast, fast.

Suddenly the nose dived much more steeply than he wanted it to, and his stomach went into free fall. He pushed his body back, but not too far back. More than anything he didn't want to stall the glider.

Abruptly he found himself in relatively stable air, and realized what had happened. He'd just gone over the falls, and was free of the thermal. ✦

198 LESSON 62

During

READERS' THEATRE To help students develop a deeper understanding of this adventure tale, invite pairs of students to prepare presentations of its various scenes as Readers' Theater. Ask each pair to decide how to read an excerpt of approximately 20 lines to show suspense. There are several ways to do this; encourage students to be creative. They might have one person take the role of the narrator and one read what Rick is thinking, or they might divide the reading into segments that make sense to them. Allow students to change the words slightly if they need to. For example, they might want the character reading Rick's thoughts to say "I have to break out. Find Jasper Canyon!" instead of "He had to break out, find Jasper Canyon."

Allow time for rehearsal. Pairs could present to the class or in small groups. After all pairs have presented, have a class discussion about the techniques they used to show the action and suspense.

SHARE RESPONSE NOTES Invite students to discuss their Response Notes with partners or in groups. Encourage them to compare the writer's language and their personal connections.

❋ Did you feel as if you were flying with Rick? Or could you imagine watching him soar above you? If so, that is because Hobbs used certain techniques to convey an experience in words. He used specific names of places. He focused on sensory details, and he used strong verbs to tell what was happening. With a partner, complete the first two columns of the following technique chart. Leave the third column blank for now.

TECHNIQUES USED TO CREATE AN EXPERIENCE IN WORDS

Technique	Hobbs's Examples	My Examples
Use specific names, places, and things	Jasper Canyon	
Focus on sensory details (how the experience sounded, looked, felt, and so on)	whooping and shouting	
Use strong verbs	fight, force	

❋ Now it's your turn. Plan and draft an Experience Snapshot. Think about an experience that you know well enough to recreate for a reader. Don't just describe it; use some of the techniques that Will Hobbs used to create an experience. Your experience can be one you actually had or one you have read about or imagined. Once you have an experience in mind, fill in the third column of the chart to help you plan what you will write. In the space below, write a draft of your Experience Snapshot.

_____
_____
_____
_____
_____
_____
_____

Writers recreate experiences for the reader by providing specific names and places, focusing on sensory details, and using strong verbs.

REAL-LIFE STORIES 199

WRITING SUPPORT

Word Choice As students work on their Experience Snapshot drafts, remind them to check off each example they recorded in the chart and add more ideas as they write. Remind students of the powerful word choices Hobbs uses in *The Maze*. Form peer conference groups and have students give each other suggestions for adding realism to their drafts. Suggest using a thesaurus to find different or more expressive terms.

Quick Assess

❋ Did students identify suspenseful words and phrases?

❋ Did students' Response Notes include comments about the real-life aspects of the story?

❋ Did students complete their techniques chart?

After

SCIENCE CONNECTION Invite students to learn more about the science of hang gliding. Suggest that they conduct research through books, hang glider publications, or the Internet. Then they can create diagrams and other visuals to explain technical aspects of the sport in a presentation.

STUDYING AN AUTHOR 199

LESSON 63

Students will read a historical fiction story and a fantasy to compare the writing techniques employed in each kind of story.

BACKGROUND KNOWLEDGE

Help students find the Yukon Territory on a globe or a map. Point out that the area is located in one of the coldest parts of the world. Briefly recount the history of the Klondike Gold Rush that began in July of 1897 when miners returned from the Yukon with bags of gold. This event inspired "gold fever" in thousands of young people. Getting to the gold fields was a very dangerous undertaking. Although approximately 100,000 gold-seekers set out for the Yukon, only 30,000 completed the trip. For more information, visit websites such as http://www.explorenorth.com/library/ya/bl22y.htm.

VOCABULARY

tarp a piece of heavy canvas

spooked scared away; startled

scavengers animals that eat decaying food

obliterated wiped out; obscured

Discuss each word by asking these questions: *Over what could you put a tarp? Why? What animals spook easily? What kind of animals are scavengers? Why would you obliterate something?*

LESSON 63 — STORIES IN DIFFERENT GENRES

Will Hobbs likes to try new things, including finding different ways to tell stories. He has written fantasy, adventure, historical fiction, and mystery novels. How does he know which genre to use? The story suggests the **genre**. For example, he told an interviewer that when he wrote *Jason's Gold* he wanted "the sort of realism that could only be achieved by basing incidents in the novel on actual incidents from the Klondike gold rush." Hobbs included historical characters in the novel, such as the writer Jack London and the con man Soapy Smith.

Jason's Gold features 15-year-old Jason Hawthorn, who travels from New York to Seattle in 1897, planning to meet his brothers and beat other prospectors to the Klondike gold fields. When he arrives, his brothers have already left. Jason heads to the Yukon on his own, determined to find his brothers and his fortune.

Life is harsh for the prospectors who are unprepared for the rugged terrain and deep cold of the Yukon. Jason is smart and resourceful, and he gets some good breaks with help from Jack London and others he meets on the trail. But not everyone is so fortunate, as Jason discovers when he and his husky King hunt for the moose that will keep them alive. What they find is based on a true story. Note in the **Response Notes** any of Hobbs's writing techniques that you recognize from the last lesson. Remember, also, to note your questions and reactions.

from *Jason's Gold* by Will Hobbs

It was a gray day, threatening snow. It had warmed up to twenty below or even ten, he guessed. He was in despair of ever overtaking the two moose. As he turned another in the endless bends along the frozen river, he stopped dead in his tracks. He realized he'd lost the will to continue.

Something up ahead, it seemed, didn't quite fit the landscape—a crude log cabin at the edge of a clearing and slightly above the river.

Another mirage.

But the mirage wasn't going away. Maybe there *was* a cabin there.

He trudged closer. Yes, it really was a cabin, an extremely small one. His heart leaped, but then he realized there was no smoke coming from it. Never mind, they could be away hunting.

Look inside this cabin, then turn back around.

Up close, he was stunned to see a beaten trail leading from the cabin to the river, and the unmistakable tracks of snowshoes. There really *was* someone here!

Before

CRITICAL READING SKILL

Understanding Genre Recall several stories the class has read and specify the genre for each story. Ask: *Was this genre the best choice for the story? Why?* For one story, name a different genre and ask students how the story would be different if told through another genre. For example: *How might* The Maze *differ if Will had chosen to write it as a science fiction novel or a historical account?*

HISTORICAL FICTION

Explain that the genre of historical fiction is used for stories that did not really happen but could have happened. These stories combine factual settings, events, and people with fictional ones. For example, Will Hobbs explains at the end of his novel that the two frozen men are based on an account of two corpses discovered in another part of the Yukon. He kept the incident but changed the location and added details drawn from real people added to details he made up.

Have students recall what historical facts they know about the Klondike Gold Rush. Then have them use a T-chart to speculate on what elements of *Jason's Gold* are factual and what are fictional. Interested students could do further research to confirm their guesses.

"Hello?" he cried. "Is anybody in there?"

There were no windows to peek through. A piece of heavy tarp served for the door.

As his mitten pushed the canvas to one side, light fell on two bearded men in fur coats and fur hats. Startled, Jason jumped back, lost his grip on the tarp. "Ho in there!" he cried out—no reply. Once again he pushed the tarp aside. The bearded men were sitting on rounds of wood, right there, right there in front of him.

A cooking pot was suspended over a fire, but the fire had gone out.

The men weren't moving, he realized, and in the next instant he saw why. They were frozen solid.

He cried out in terror, then clamped his mouth shut. If the moose were close by, he'd spooked them.

He dropped the canvas over the opening and retreated. He stood there frozen by fright, with the husky puzzling at him. All he could think about was that this was how *he* was going to end up, and Charlie too.

He had to get one of those moose.

Wait, there might be some way to identify these two. Their kin would want to know.

He crawled back inside with the two men sitting by the dead fire. There was a piece of shoe leather sticking out of the ice in the bottom of their cooking pot. This was what starvation looked like.

Here, on the log wall, was what he was looking for—a message scrawled in pencil and punched over a nail:

> *Ours is the folly. Left Fort Simpson on the Mackenzie River. Seeking Dawson but lost. Too far, too late. Skin boat crushed by ice. Seen no game in weeks. Lack strength to continue.*
> *God bless,*
> *Samuel Whittaker and Villy Champlain*
> *November, 30, 1897*

They'd written this message less than two weeks before. They had died, maybe, only days ago. Where was Fort Simpson? Where was the Mackenzie River?

Jason folded the paper and put it in the pocket of his coat, then secured the tarp over the door to keep the scavengers out. He started upstream, more desperate than ever to catch up with those moose. But then it started snowing, and heavily. Before long, all trace of their tracks was obliterated. ❖

Jason's Gold is **historical fiction** set in a specific time and place in history, the 1897 Klondike Gold Rush. It uses actual details to add realism to the fictional story. Jason Hawthorn did not exist, but many like him did.

STORIES IN DIFFERENT GENRES 201

During

KOKOPELLI To build background for the fantasy, explain the significance of the Kokopelli figure in Native American cultures. Hopi legend identifies Kokopelli as an insect-like creature whose flute heals and draws heat from the center of the Earth to help things grow. His name comes from *koko* for the wood of the flute, and *pilau* for the hump on his back that represents the bag of seeds he always carries. His invisible presence is felt whenever life comes forth from seeds.

RESPONSE NOTES Define the elements of fantasy: magical interventions or powers, impossible or larger-than-life events, and vivid, dreamlike images. Suggest that students include in their Response Notes the writer's techniques in *Kokopelli's Flute* that qualify it as a fantasy. They might also note writing techniques that make the story seem real.

TEACHING TIP

Collaboration To further develop background for the excerpt, use a Jigsaw cooperative learning activity. Form "expert groups."

1. Have each expert group choose a historical figure related to the Klondike Gold Rush: Jack London, Soapy Smith, etc.
2. Each group researches the person and their relationship to the Gold Rush.
3. Rearrange groups so that each new group contains at least one student from each "expert group."
4. Experts share their research with their new groups.

STUDYING AN AUTHOR 201

✳︎ How has Hobbs recreated the experience for you? Explain in a short paragraph the techniques he used to weave history into an adventure story.

_____
_____
_____
_____
_____

Will Hobbs has also written **fantasy**, a genre characterized by talking animals and magical events. Hobbs wanted to write a novel that incorporated a magical flute and the legendary character Kokopelli, who was important to the ancient people of the Americas for his life-giving seeds. Hobbs, therefore, had to use elements of fantasy in *Kokopelli's Flute*.

Tepary Jones (Tep) finds a small stone flute in an ancient cave near his home in New Mexico. Although drawn to the flute, he waits until he is in his room that night to try it out. His only companion is his pet ringtail, Ringo, an animal like a raccoon who is an excellent hunter of mice. Read this once, just to get a sense of the story.

Response Notes

from Kokopelli's Flute by Will Hobbs

I turned my attention from Ringo to the ancient flute in my hands. It was only about four and a half inches long, so smooth, so ancient.... I was about to put the flute to my mouth when Ringo swooped down and knocked it free. The ringtail grabbed for it, but I'd already snatched it up. He sprang to my desktop a few feet away and started waving his tail like a battle flag.

I remember putting the flute to my lips and blowing on it a minute or two. The notes I was producing sounded as pure as falling water. I remember starting to feel dizzy... the room started spinning and reeling, and I was bucking like I was being ripped open and turned inside out. Next thing I knew, I had the sensation of having long black whiskers radiating out from my face. These whiskers almost hurt, they were so sensitive. My nose was twitching. I was aware of an alien scent, musky, overpowering, and close.

By now I was in a panic at whatever was happening, and Ringo was looking at me differently, strangely, starting to make those high-pitched ringtail hunting noises that sound like crackling static.

WRITING SUPPORT

Organization To help students organize their thinking in response to the prompt, have them look over their Response Notes and identify ideas that seem to go together. For example, they should have notes about writing techniques discussed in Lesson 62: using sensory details, choosing powerful words. Encourage students to create an outline:

I. Specific places and things
   A.
   B.
   C.
II. Sensory details
   A.
   B.
   C.

Then they can mark each item with IA, IB, or IC, etc. to show where their notes belong in the outline.

I didn't feel anything like myself, and when I looked at my hands, I could see why. I was looking at the five-clawed fingers of . . . a rat. I felt the bottom of my spine moving, and out of the corner of my eye I could see a long, bushy tail.

I jumped from the bed to the floor, but Ringo jumped just as quick. There was only a foot between us, and there was murder in his eye. "It's me!" I yelled at him. "It's Tep!"

* Reread the excerpt. Mark the text where you find characteristics of the fantasy genre.

* Read the Experience Snapshot you drafted in Lesson 62. Outline the changes you would make in your writing if you were to rewrite it as fantasy or historical fiction or another genre you know well. Write or sketch a few notes for yourself in the space below.

* Rewrite your Experience Snapshot in a different genre, using your notes above.

> Writers choose a genre to help them tell a story in a certain way. They select details for the story that fit that genre.

STORIES IN DIFFERENT GENRES 203

WRITING SUPPORT

Characteristics of Genres Use a chart to help students define the many fictional genres. In the first column, list genres students recognize with examples. Label the other columns with elements of the genres.

Genres and examples	Real events or people	Made-up events or people	Set in the future	etc.
Historical fiction: *Jason's Gold*				
Fantasy: *Kokopelli's Flute*				
Realistic fiction: *The Maze*				
Science fiction:				
etc.				

Invite students to help you complete the chart. Then discuss common and unique elements of the genres.

Quick Assess

* Did students write organized paragraphs about the techniques used in *Jason's Gold*?

* Did students reflect their knowledge of genre in their writing.

After

APPLYING THE STRATEGY

Stories in Different Genres Propose a generic story topic such as an athlete who overcomes obstacles to reach a personal goal or a hero/heroine who helps hundreds of people. Have students brainstorm elements of the story that might appear in each genre they named. Then have students write the story in the genre they feel is best for the story. Invite partners to recast each other's stories in different genres.

STUDYING AN AUTHOR 203

LESSON 64

Students will consider how writers develop their fictional characters, identify traits, and assign descriptive details to their own characters.

BACKGROUND KNOWLEDGE

Ask students to recall a time when they "got in over their heads" and found themselves in situations that were more challenging than they had anticipated. Ask: *What feelings did you notice during the challenge? What did you do to handle the situation? How did other people respond to the challenge?* Explain that this story deals with such a situation. In fact, the teens in this episode literally get in over their heads!

VOCABULARY

hole in this context, a place where the water swirls rapidly in a circle, creating suction that is dangerous for rafters

speared in this context, to position precisely

eddy a small whirlpool; water with a circular motion

thrashing a beating

landfall to reach shore

berserk crazy; out of control

After providing the definitions, divide students into groups. Assign one word to each group. Without revealing the word, have each group act out the word and have the class guess the word.

Before

CRITICAL READING SKILL

Character Traits Explain that characters' traits include their gender and physical traits, actions and thoughts, and the relationships they form with other characters. Assign seven groups, one for each character mentioned in the excerpt. After students read and record Response Notes for all the characters, have each group work together to create a character sketch for their assigned character. Encourage groups to prepare visual aids, such as drawings, role-plays, or diagrams to use as they present their characters to the class.

LESSON 64 CHARACTERS IN STORIES

Compelling characters are essential to a good story. They do not need to be likeable, but they should be interesting. You wonder what will happen to them or how their actions will change the story. Developing **characters** can be hard work.

Will Hobbs told an interviewer, "For those kids in *Downriver*, I wrote pages and pages on each one before I ever started writing that story." *Downriver* tells the story of several teenagers with various problems. They have come together from all over the United States to an outdoor education school in Colorado, Discovery Unlimited. After experiencing whitewater rafting with Al, the leader, they decide that they can raft the Grand Canyon on their own, without a permit or expert leadership. They steal the rafts and van and leave Al behind—until he catches up with them far downriver. On the Colorado River, they learn whom to trust and whom to fear, and they learn about their own inner resources.

Sixteen-year-old Jessie narrates their story. The excerpt that follows is from the early part of their trip down the Grand Canyon, while they still feel confident about their ability and while they still have enough food for the trip. But then they hit a wild stretch of the river. Jessie and Troy are in one boat and the others are in the other boat. As you read, get a sense of who the characters are. Write your impressions and questions in the **Response Notes.**

from Downriver by Will Hobbs

We could hear another rapid coming, but we couldn't see it because it was on a sharp turn. "Should we scout it?" I asked Troy. He wagged his head. He was taken with the string of successes behind us, and having too much fun rowing to want to pull the boat to shore, tie it up, and go for a look. We rounded the bend in the center of the river and caught sight of a major hole only thirty or so feet in front of us.

There was no time to cock the boat and row to either side. All Troy could do was hit the hole straight on. I speared my weight to the very front as we dropped into the hole, and then I felt the oddest sensation. We had stopped moving. We were surfing in place. Suddenly the hole spun us sideways, and one side of the boat lifted up in the air as the low side was filling with water. My eyes met Troy's for a minute. He was at a loss. I lunged for the high side, to try to put some weight on it. Just as suddenly, the hole spit us out. "Bail!" Troy yelled. We were suddenly knee-deep in water.

Around the bend came the paddle raft, only they were on the inside of the turn as they approached the hole. They would have missed it, but they were paddling like crazy to line up for it on purpose. When they dropped into it, the hole spun them sideways too. They had no more control than a stick of driftwood. The black underside of their boat showed for a moment, and then the boat turned over. They'd flipped!

I saw swimmers. A couple of people were bobbing along in the river; Adam was hanging onto the chicken line on the overturned boat. Troy bent his back to the oars and towed toward an eddy, so we wouldn't be swept downstream. "Bail!" he yelled. "Boat's too heavy to row! Bail!"

I bailed like mad with that big bucket, and Troy caught the eddy. As the swimmers approached us, he rowed out into the current and I hauled Rita aboard. Troy intercepted Adam, who was clinging to the paddle raft. "We hit the hole straight on," Adam protested. "I don't know what happened."

Freddy and Pug, I could see, had reached the shore on their own, but where was Star?

"Over there!" I yelled, and pointed at Star in the river.

We dragged Star in. She was so weak, she couldn't help herself at all. She wasn't built with any insulation against that icy water, and as it turned out, she'd been held in the hole and given a thrashing.

We made a quick landfall, as Freddy and Pug ran downstream to join us. There was no beach there. It wasn't really a camp, but we had work to do, with the paddle raft to overturn, and little time—the sun was down from the canyon. We were all shivering, especially Star, whose eyes weren't even focusing. We had to get to the dry bags under the paddle raft, and put on some dry clothes. It took all of us, minus Star, to turn the boat over. Any kind of beach would've been handy, but there was a deep drop-off right at the bank. We had to use a lot of ropes, and pull on them with all our strength. For a while it looked like we wouldn't succeed. Three times the boat came about halfway up and then stalled. Adam said to Troy, "I sure hope that gear boat of yours never flips. It weighs about three times as much as this one."

We gave it one more try, and this time Pug went berserk, giving a ferocious battle cry and pulling on his rope like a Goliath. His mighty legs dug for traction, and in the end he fell into a pile of sharp rocks as the boat fell rightside up against the bank.

Pug came up full of scrapes and scratches, but he thought nothing of them, being the man of the moment and the recipient of truckloads of praise. He was beaming. That butch marine crewcut of his, about a month grown out, made him seem like a little fuzzball kid in a giant body, a little kid who only wanted the rest of the gang to like him. Rita went over to him and raised his right arm like a boxer's in triumph, then felt his biceps. "Hot stuff," she declared.

CHARACTERS IN STORIES 205

EXTRA SUPPORT

Differentiation For students who need extra support in following the action in the story, suggest that they work in groups to create sequence charts or storyboards to show how the events link together.

WRITING SUPPORT

Organize Ideas To help students organize their Response Notes, suggest that they write each character's name when he or she first appears in the story. Then have them leave some space before writing the next name. Remind students that Jessie is the narrator. As they encounter more information about the characters, have students add notes under each name.

During

CHUNKING THE READING Explain that one technique of managing a very detailed text is to break it into sections, or "chunks." Advise students to read the selection in small chunks, pausing between them to draw, make notes, or otherwise clarify the actions and events. At the end of ech section, students should pause to ask themselves questions such as these:

* What is this section about?
* Do I understand what I just read, or should I reread it?

STUDYING AN AUTHOR 205

WRITING SUPPORT

Prewriting Have partners share the Experience Snapshots they started in Lesson 62. Encourage them to imagine characters in their snapshots have partners brainstorm details that might communicate the character or characters' traits. Encourage them to include the kinds of traits the author mentions to the interviewer.

Quick Assess

* Do students' Response Notes include their impressions of each character?
* Do students' Response Notes include comments and questions?
* Are students' character descriptions complete?

* Discuss with a partner your impressions of the characters. Add other comments to your **Response Notes.**

When Hobbs told the interviewer that he had written pages and pages about the characters in *Downriver,* the interviewer asked if he wrote dialogue as well. Hobbs replied, "Both—the way they would talk, what they would wear, the kind of music they would listen to, the kind of friends they would have, what sorts of trouble they would have gotten into—just kind of jamming on ideas about everything on that kid."

* Choose one character who plays a role, or could play a role, in your Experience Snapshot from Lesson 62. For that character, jot down the kinds of descriptive details Hobbs wrote for his characters.

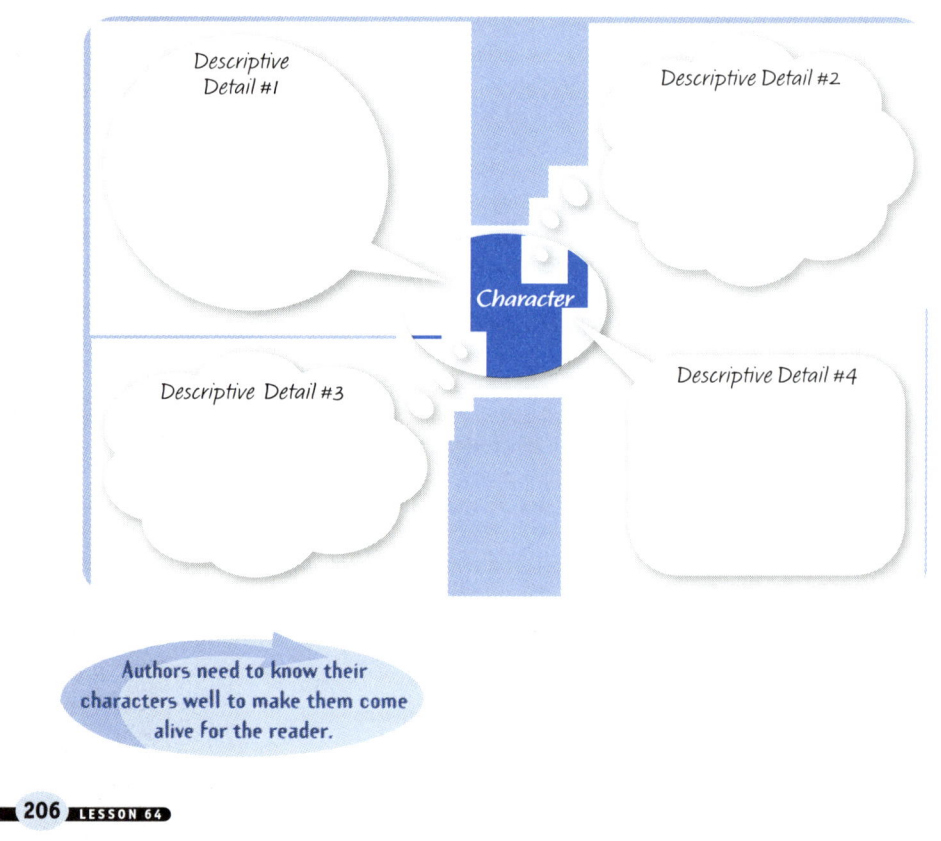

Authors need to know their characters well to make them come alive for the reader.

206 LESSON 64

After

APPLYING THE STRATEGY

Characters in Stories Ask students to think about someone they know very well, such as a friend, parent, or sibling. Have them consider the kinds of traits discussed above and those mentioned by Hobbs in the interview. Then have each student create a written or oral character sketch of the person they chose. Encourage students to draw or download action pictures that represent the person to illustrate their sketches.

LESSON 65: REVISING STORIES

Will Hobbs wrote three complete drafts of *Downriver* before he felt that he had the narrator and the plot that he wanted. While he does not revise all of his books as extensively, he often stresses the importance of revision. In this lesson, you will use his advice to revise your Experience Snapshot.

Bearstone tells the story of Cloyd, a 14-year-old Native American boy sent to live in the mountains of Colorado with an old rancher. An early draft of the novel contains the following paragraph:

> He made a cut in the dozen or so peach trees, about a third of the way through. He didn't want them to die. He just wanted the leaves to wither and yellow, and the peaches to shrivel.

✳ What do you know about Cloyd's feelings from this paragraph? What do you know about his motivation? Write your answers.

_____
_____

The published novel contains this paragraph:

> He cut through the skin of the nearest tree and winced as he withdrew the saw. Beads of moisture were forming along the edges of the fresh wound. From one to the next he ran with the saw roaring at full throttle, and he cut each of the twenty-two peach trees most of the way through. Each time, as the saw's teeth bit into the thick bark, he hollered with hurt as if he felt the saw himself. He didn't want to cut them down, he wanted them to die slowly. Before they died, their leaves would yellow and the peaches shrivel, and they would look just like his grandmother's peaches.

✳ Now, what do you know about Cloyd's feelings and motivation? How does this paragraph make you feel? In the space below, write your answers to these questions.

_____
_____
_____

REVISING STORIES 207

LESSON 65

Students will learn about the writer's process and how revision improves a story.

BACKGROUND KNOWLEDGE
Explain the difference between revising and editing. Say: *When Will revises his writing, he doesn't worry about spelling or grammar at that point. He thinks only about how well he communicates his ideas and images. He looks at things like the order in which he says things, the descriptive details he includes, when he wants to introduce a new thought, and the words he chooses to convey his story.*

Explain that the purpose of editing is to clean up the revision by checking spelling and mechanics, sentence structure, and word choice. A good writer learns to edit his or her writing after revising.

VOCABULARY
winced drew back, as if in pain
wound a cut or tear on outer surface
full throttle at top speed

After discussing the meanings, invite students to think of synonyms and applications for each term.

Before

CRITICAL READING SKILL
Revising Stories Ask students to think of something they have learned that took a lot of practice to perfect, such as holding a paint brush or the bow of an instrument, or passing a basketball to another player. Ask: *How did you feel about all that practice when you were doing it? What were the results of the practice? Was it worth the effort? Why or why not?* Explain that revising one's writing is similar to practicing a skill; practice leads to proficiency. Tell students that the more they revise their writing, the easier revising will be for them the next time.

STUDYING AN AUTHOR

Quick Assess

✻ Did students respond to the questions completely?

✻ Do students' Experience Snapshot revisions show evidence of revision?

The second paragraph is a revision. Will Hobbs explains, "Revision does not mean throwing out everything you have written and starting over. The part that I'd done well in the first version, I saved: 'their leaves would yellow and the peaches shrivel.' You learn to recognize what was good, and shouldn't be abandoned."

Review what you have drafted in this unit:

- a snapshot recreating an experience, real or imagined
- the same snapshot written in a different genre
- details about a character who plays a role in your Experience Snapshot

Decide what to keep and what to abandon. Revise one of your Experience Snapshots. You may want to use some of the techniques Will Hobbs used in the excerpts you read in this unit:

- putting a new twist on an old story
- providing specific names and places
- focusing on sensory details
- using strong verbs
- creating character sketches
- revising

✻ Write your revised snapshot here.

Writers can make their writing more effective by starting with a vision in the early drafts and continually refining the story through revisions.

During

ANALYZING A MODEL Have students connect Hobbs's first draft to his final revision. Help students identify revisions that Hobbs made. Point out, for example, that he

✻ added details (*winced as he withdrew the saw, beads of moisture, roaring at full throttle*)

✻ replaced words (*cut through the skin* in place of *made a cut*; *most of the way through* in place of *about a third of the way through*)

Ask: *Are the author's revisions effective? Why? Which version gives you the better picture of the events?* Then invite students to discuss their observations with partners.

After

REFLECTING Invite students to reflect on other writing they have done. Encourage them to apply several of the revising strategies in this lesson to an earlier piece of writing. Afterward have students discuss their revisions with you, a writing partner, or a small group.

UNIT 14
ASSESSING YOUR STRENGTHS

Lessons 66-70, pages 210-222

UNIT OVERVIEW
As students read and respond to a short story by Cynthia Rylant and write a short story of their own, they will demonstrate what they have learned and reflect on their growth as readers and writers.

KEY IDEA
Good readers and writers draw upon multiple strategies as they read the writing of others and write on their own.

CRITICAL READING AND WRITING SKILLS
by lesson

66 Interacting and connecting with a story
67 Studying an author's craft
68 Focusing on language and craft
69 Writing a short story
70 Revising and reflecting

WRITING ACTIVITIES
by lesson

66 Write about a connection between characters.
67 Make a prediction about the story.
68 Write responses to the story.
69 Plan and draft a story.
70 Write a reflection.

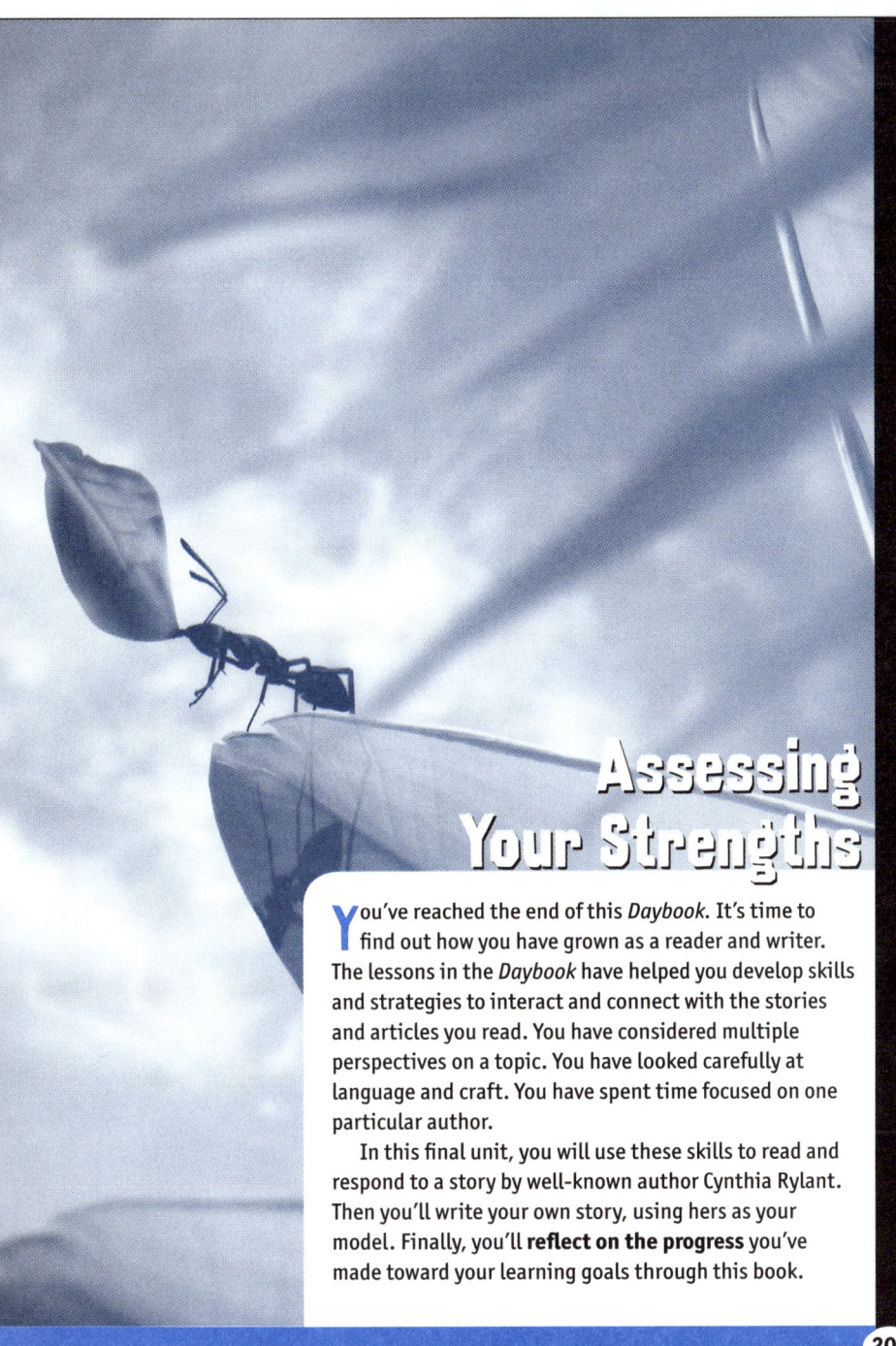

Assessing Your Strengths

You've reached the end of this *Daybook*. It's time to find out how you have grown as a reader and writer. The lessons in the *Daybook* have helped you develop skills and strategies to interact and connect with the stories and articles you read. You have considered multiple perspectives on a topic. You have looked carefully at language and craft. You have spent time focused on one particular author.

In this final unit, you will use these skills to read and respond to a story by well-known author Cynthia Rylant. Then you'll write your own story, using hers as your model. Finally, you'll **reflect on the progress** you've made toward your learning goals through this book.

Literature

- *"Shells"* by Cynthia Rylant (short story)

In this story, a teenage boy whose parents have died struggles with the uneasy relationship he has with his aunt with whom he now lives.

LESSON 66

Students will read the first part of a story to make connections to other stories and their own experiences.

BACKGROUND KNOWLEDGE
Review with students what they've learned in previous lessons about interacting and making connections with the text. Make sure that students understand that interacting with the text means making predictions, asking questions, recording ideas, and noting feelings. Making connections involves drawing on experience to connect with characters in or other elements of a story.

VOCABULARY

dully in a depressed or sad way

gawked stared in disbelief

condominium apartment-like home

talc powder

prejudiced being biased against someone or something

Presbyterian member of a Protestant church

grieve mourn

assured promised

Discuss how students can use context clues, word parts, or a dictionary to determine the definitions.

LESSON 66 — INTERACTING AND CONNECTING WITH A STORY

A As you read the first part of "Shells," pay attention to the conflict that exists between the characters. Try to imagine yourself in Michael's place. How would you feel? As you read, **interact** with the story by jotting down your first impressions and questions in the **Response Notes**.

"Shells" by Cynthia Rylant

"You hate living here."

Michael looked at the woman speaking to him.

"No, Aunt Esther. I don't." He said it dully, sliding his milk glass back and forth on the table. "I don't hate it here."

Esther removed the last pan from the dishwasher and hung it above the oven.

"You hate it here," she said, "and you hate me."

"I don't!" Michael yelled. "It's not you!"

The woman turned to face him in the kitchen.

"Don't yell at me!" she yelled. "I'll not have it in my home. I can't make you happy, Michael. You just refuse to be happy here. And you punish me every day for it."

"Punish you?" Michael gawked at her. "I don't punish you! I don't care about you! I don't care what you eat or how you dress or where you go or what you think. Can't you just leave me alone?"

He slammed down the glass, scraped his chair back from the table and ran out the door.

"Michael!" yelled Esther.

They had been living together, the two of them, for six months. Michael's parents had died and only Esther could take him in—or, only she had offered to. Michael's other relatives could not imagine dealing with a fourteen-year-old boy. They wanted peaceful lives.

Esther lived in a condominium in a wealthy section of Detroit. Most of the area's residents were older (like her) and afraid of the world they lived in (like her). They stayed indoors much of the time. They trusted few people. Esther liked living alone. She had never married or had children. She had never lived anywhere but Detroit. She liked her condominium.

But she was fiercely loyal to her family, and when her only sister had died, Esther insisted she be allowed to care for Michael. And Michael, afraid of going anywhere else, had accepted.

Oh, he was lonely. Even six months after their deaths, he still expected to see his parents—sitting on the couch as he walked into Esther's living room,

---

Before

CRITICAL READING SKILL
Interacting and Connecting with a Story One of the literary elements writers use in creating stories is conflict. In this lesson, students will identify the problem between the characters and speculate on how it will be resolved. Ask students to think about times they have disagreed with someone at home. That experience will help them prepare to read the story.

RESPONSE NOTES
Remind students that they can interact and make connections with the story in different ways. They can

* record their impressions;
* ask questions;
* make inferences;
* identify with the characters;
* make connections to other stories;
* make predictions.

See *Daybook* page 227 for tips on marking text.

waiting for the bathroom as he came out of the shower, coming in the door late at night. He still smelled his father's Old Spice somewhere, his mother's talc.

Sometimes he was so sure one of them was somewhere around him that he thought maybe he was going crazy. His heart hurt him. He wondered if he would ever get better. And though he denied it, he did hate Esther. She was so different from his mother and father. Prejudiced—she admired only those who were white and Presbyterian. Selfish—she wouldn't allow him to use her phone. Complaining—she always had a headache or a backache or a stomachache.

He didn't want to, but he hated her. And he didn't know what to do except lie about it.

Michael hadn't made any friends at his new school, and his teachers barely noticed him. He came home alone every day and usually found Esther on the phone. She kept in close touch with several other women in nearby condominiums. Esther told her friends she didn't understand Michael. She said she knew he must grieve for his parents, but why punish her? She said she thought she might send him away if he couldn't be nicer. She said she didn't deserve this. But when Michael came in the door, she always quickly changed the subject.

One day after school Michael came home with a hermit crab.* He had gone into a pet store, looking for some small, living thing, and hermit crabs were selling for just a few dollars. He'd bought one, and a bowl.

Esther, for a change, was not on the phone when he arrived home. She was having tea and a crescent roll and seemed cheerful. Michael wanted badly to show someone what he had bought. So he showed her.

Esther surprised him. She picked up the shell and poked the long, shiny nail of her little finger at the crab's claws. "Where is he?" she asked.

Michael showed her the crab's eyes peering through the small opening of the shell.

"Well, for heaven's sake, come out of there!" she said to the crab, and she turned the shell upside down and shook it. "Aunt Esther!" Michael grabbed for the shell.

"All right, all right." She turned it right side up. "Well," she said, "what does he do?"

Michael grinned and shrugged his shoulders.

"I don't know," he answered. "Just grows, I guess." His aunt looked at him.

"An attraction to a crab is something I cannot identify with. However, it's fine with me if you keep him, as long as I can be assured he won't grow out of that bowl." She gave him a hard stare.

"He won't," Michael answered. "I promise." ❖

---

* **The hermit crab** is a type of crab that doesn't have a very hard shell. Not a true crab, it uses other animals' old shells for protection. As the hermit crab grows in size, it must find a larger shell.

INTERACTING AND CONNECTING WITH A STORY **211**

During

SHARING INSIGHTS After students have read the lesson's selection, have them use their Response Notes to respond to the first prompt on page 212. Once students have completed their response, have them form discussion groups to talk about their connections.

Then have each group share the connections they made to characters in other stories with the class.

ABOUT THE AUTHOR
Cynthia Rylant has written about her childhood in her autobiography, *But I'll Be Back Again*. Rylant, born in 1954, grew up in West Virginia, and she and her mother lived with her grandparents until Cynthia was eight. After high school, Rylant went on to get her bachelor's degree from what is now the University of Charleston. She received her master's degree in English from Marshall University and a Master of Library Science degree from Kent State University in Ohio. More than her degrees, Rylant credits her childhood in West Virginia, the influence of her grandparents, and her love of animals as the sources of inspiration for much of her writing. For more about Rylant, see *Daybook* page 213.

EXTRA SUPPORT
Differentiation Ask students to share what they know about hermit crabs. Invite students to find pictures of hermit crabs on the Internet or in books from the library. Talk about what the word *hermit* means (someone who lives by himself or herself, cut off from everyone). Have students speculate on why this animal is called a hermit crab and what meaning that might have in the story.

ASSESSING YOUR STRENGTHS **211**

WRITER'S CRAFT

Making Connections Tell students that writers often use details from real life in fictional stories. Ask students to find several examples of realistic details. For example, point out that Michael acquires a hermit crab from a pet shop. Discuss how real-life details help readers interact and connect with the story.

TEACHING TIP

Using a Graphic Organizer
Two-Column Chart Making a chart helps readers organize story elements. Have students use the chart to connect the newest addition to the household (the hermit crab) to Michael and Aunt Esther, using details from the story.

Quick Assess

* Did students find realistic details from the story to make personal connections in their Response Notes?
* Did students make logical connections to characters in other stories?
* Were students able to connect characters?

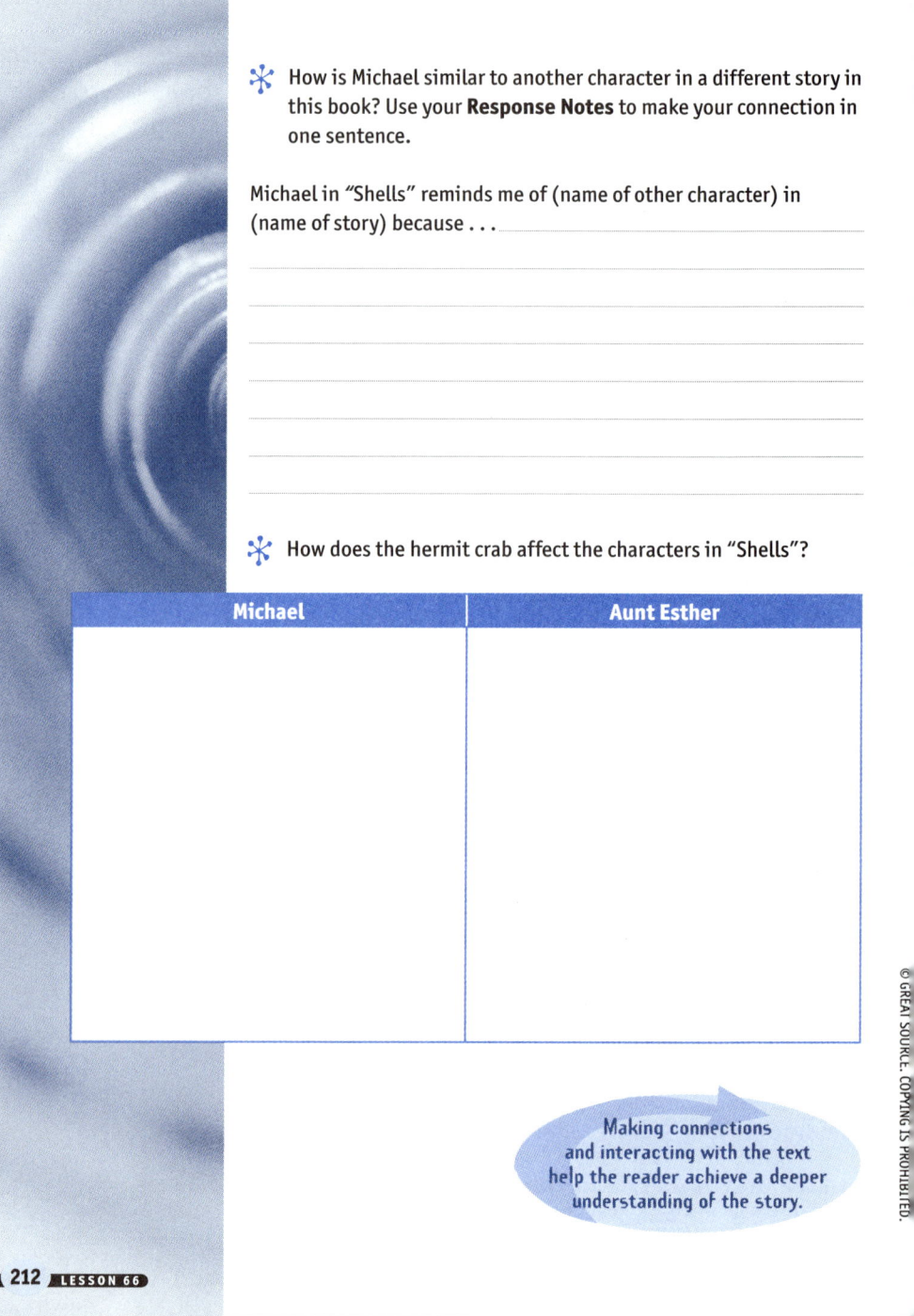

* How is Michael similar to another character in a different story in this book? Use your **Response Notes** to make your connection in one sentence.

Michael in "Shells" reminds me of (name of other character) in (name of story) because . . .

* How does the hermit crab affect the characters in "Shells"?

Michael	Aunt Esther

Making connections and interacting with the text help the reader achieve a deeper understanding of the story.

212 LESSON 66

APPLYING THE STRATEGY Ask students to think about a conflict in another story they have read. Have students make a two-column chart to compare the conflict to the one in Rylant's story. Then have them share the charts in their discussion groups.

212 UNIT 14

STUDYING AN AUTHOR'S CRAFT — LESSON 67

Before reading the rest of the story, think about the hermit crab that Michael brought home. Did you have any idea when he brought it home that it might take on the role of another character in the story? Read about the author to learn why she may have written a role for a hermit crab. In the **Response Notes,** write any connections you notice between the author's life and her writing.

ABOUT THE AUTHOR

It's not surprising that Cynthia Rylant used a hermit crab in her story. She loves animals, and you will find many in her books. Rylant has said that taking walks with her dogs helps her writing. It's always important to see how she uses animals. Some, like Sluggo, become metaphors; others just add interest to the story. Cynthia Rylant has been a teacher, a librarian, and a writer. When she isn't writing, she enjoys watching movies, as well as whales, dolphins, and sea otters. So her attraction to a sea creature is understandable.

You may have read books by Cynthia Rylant, like *Missing May* or *When I Was Young in the Mountains.* She writes for younger children as well as for teenagers and adults. She didn't read much when she was a child. "There just weren't that many books around," she remembers. "No public library, no money to buy books—no bookstores, anyway." Instead, she spent her time playing, something she now says is the best thing for young writers to do. There were some stories available for her in the form of Archie and Jughead comic books and paperback romance novels. So she earned her "training" as a writer with comics from the local drugstore, buying them "three for a quarter—plus Danny Alderman who lived behind me used to trade me a big pile of his for a big pile of mine."

STUDYING AN AUTHOR'S CRAFT 213

LESSON 67

Students will read about an author to understand how a writer develops characters with realistic thoughts and feelings.

BACKGROUND KNOWLEDGE

Cynthia Rylant is a prolific author who has published picture books, poetry, short stories, novels, and nonfiction. Check students' familiarity with Rylant by asking what they know of her and her books. Some students might remmeber reading her illustrated books for younger readers such as *When I Was Young in the Mountains, The Relatives Came,* and the Henry and Mudge books. Ask what students know about her books for young adults such as *Missing May* (a Newbery Award winner), *Something Permanent* (a collection of poems and photographs), and *I Had Seen Castles.* Readers interested in nonfiction might be interested in her autobiography or *Appalachia: The Voices of Sleeping Birds,* which received a *Boston Globe-Hornbook* Nonfiction Award.

Before

STUDYING AN AUTHOR'S CRAFT

Rylant employs her love for animals to create a part for a hermit crab. As students read about the author's life, encourage discussion of why the author chose such an unusual animal for this story. This will help students understand the comparisons that the author wants readers to make about the characters.

During

CHARACTER DEVELOPMENT

Have students use their Response Notes to make connections between the story and the author's life.

Have students form groups and discuss their connections before making their predictions. Have them refer to the connections they made to inform their discussions.

ASSESSING YOUR STRENGTHS 213

EXTRA SUPPORT

Differentiation Some students may have difficulty connecting the hermit crab to Michael. Remind students that the comparison is based on the crab's characteristics. Prepare students to see how the hermit crab stands for the character Michael. Both of them wear a protective shell to protect themselves from the outside. Use a think-aloud to help them make the connection: *Michael has just lost his parents. It says that his heart hurt him. He withdraws from people into a protective shell, just like the hermit crab, to protect himself from hurting even more.*

Quick Assess

* Did students express their ideas clearly?
* Did they list more than one way that the crab would or would not help Michael?
* Did students make connections between Michael and the hermit crab?

* Do you think the hermit crab will help Michael with his problem? In what ways? List your ideas.

Animal characters, real or imaginary, can add a deeper dimension to a story.

214 LESSON 67

STUDYING THE AUTHOR Invite students to find out more about Cynthia Rylant. Have them connect what they find out about her with one or more of the books that she's written. Students can then share their information during a time set aside for author study.

214 UNIT 14

FOCUSING ON LANGUAGE AND CRAFT — LESSON 68

An author can let you know what a character is feeling in several different ways. Most times, an author will use more than one of these techniques in a single piece of writing. The author can express a character's feelings by having the character speak directly in dialogue, describing how the character feels, or telling what the character is doing or how he or she is acting. As you read the rest of the story, focus on the how the author conveys Michael's thoughts and feelings.

In the **Response Notes**, jot down clues that show how Michael's feelings are changing.

"Shells" by Cynthia Rylant (continued)

The hermit crab moved into the condominium. Michael named him Sluggo and kept the bowl beside his bed. Michael had to watch the bowl for very long periods of time to catch Sluggo with his head poking out of his shell, moving around. Bedtime seemed to be Sluggo's liveliest part of the day, and Michael found it easy to lie and watch the busy crab as sleep slowly came on.

One day Michael arrived home to find Esther sitting on the edge of his bed, looking at the bowl. Esther usually did not intrude in Michael's room, and seeing her there disturbed him. But he stood at the doorway and said nothing.

Esther seemed perfectly comfortable, although she looked over at him with a frown on her face.

"I think he needs a companion," she said.

"What?" Michael's eyebrows went up as his jaw dropped down.

Esther sniffed.

"I think Sluggo needs a girl friend." She stood up. "Where is that pet store?"

Michael took her. In the store was a huge tank full of hermit crabs.

"Oh my!" Esther grabbed the rim of the tank and craned her neck over the side. "Look at them!"

Michael was looking more at his Aunt Esther than at the crabs. He couldn't believe it.

"Oh, look at those shells. You say they grow out of them?" We must stock up with several sizes. See the pink in that one? Michael, look! He's got his little head out!"

Esther was so dramatic—leaning into the tank, her bangle bracelets clanking, earrings swinging, red pumps clicking on the linoleum—that she attracted the attention of everyone in the store. Michael pretended not to know her well.

He and Esther returned to the condominium with a thirty gallon tank and twenty hermit crabs.

LESSON 68

Students will study an author's language and craft to understand how a writer resolves conflict between characters.

BACKGROUND KNOWLEDGE

Activate prior knowledge by asking students to share their own experience with taking care of pets. Encourage them to talk about special food, equipment, and any chores they have to do related to their pets. Ask them if they think it's a good idea for Michael to have acquired the pet hermit crab. Have them give reasons for their opinions. Then have them make predictions about how the crab may help the characters resolve their problems.

VOCABULARY

intrude break in on

linoleum a type of floor covering that's like tile

founding father the originator of an institution or movement

phenomenon exceptional or unusual occurrence

distinguish tell something apart

Have students use the Word Splash on page 272 to familiarize themselves with the vocabulary.

Before

CRITICAL READING SKILL
Focusing on Language and Craft

Explain the techniques writers use to convey characters' emotions. For example, they use dialogue and descriptions of characters' thoughts and actions. Ask students to find clues in this passage that lead them to believe that Michael is changing his mind about Aunt Esther. Challenge them to think about the role the crab plays in effecting this change.

RESPONSE NOTES
Encourage students to think of ways in which Michael's "shell" resembles a hermit crab and to note or highlight places in the text that support that connection. Have them consider the title of the story and why the author used the plural form of the word *shell*.

EXTRA SUPPORT

Differentiation In some cultures, people do not keep animals as pets the way we do. The concept may require extra explanation for students unfamiliar with this concept.

Response Notes

Michael figured he'd have a heart attack before he got the heavy tank into their living room. He figured he'd die and Aunt Esther would inherit twenty-one crabs and funeral expenses.

But he made it. Esther carried the box of crabs.

"Won't Sluggo be surprised?" she asked happily. "Oh, I do hope we'll be able to tell him apart from the rest. He's their founding father!"

Michael, in a stupor over his Aunt Esther and the phenomenon of twenty-one hermit crabs, wiped out the tank, arranged it with gravel and sticks (as well as the plastic scuba diver Aunt Esther insisted on buying) and assisted her in loading it up, one by one, with the new residents. The crabs were as overwhelmed as Michael. Not one showed its face. Before moving Sluggo from his bowl, Aunt Esther marked his shell with some red fingernail polish so she could distinguish him from the rest. Then she flopped down on the couch beside Michael.

"Oh, what would your mother think, Michael, if she could see this mess we've gotten ourselves into!"

She looked at Michael with a broad smile, but it quickly disappeared. The boy's eyes were full of pain.

"Oh, my," she whispered. "I'm sorry."

Michael turned his head away.

Aunt Esther, who had not embraced anyone in years, gently put her arm about his shoulders.

"I am so sorry, Michael. Oh, you must hate me."

Michael sensed a familiar smell then. His mother's talc. He looked at his aunt.

"No, Aunt Esther." He shook his head solemnly. "I don't hate you."

Esther's mouth trembled and her bangles clanked as she patted his arm. She took a deep, strong breath. "Well, let's look in on our friend Sluggo," she said. They leaned their heads over the tank and found him. The crab, finished with the old home that no longer fit, was coming out of his shell.

❋ Review your Response Notes. How did Cynthia Rylant convey Michael's feelings to the reader?

_____
_____
_____
_____

During

MAKING CONNECTIONS After students have finished the activity at the bottom of page 216, make a class list of their ideas on the board or overhead. Discuss the class list, with examples from the story. Then have students complete the activities on page 217. Have them share their ideas in groups or as a whole class. Finally, review the information about Cynthia Rylant found on page 213 and discuss how knowing her background adds to their understanding of the techniques she uses to develop the characters and their problem.

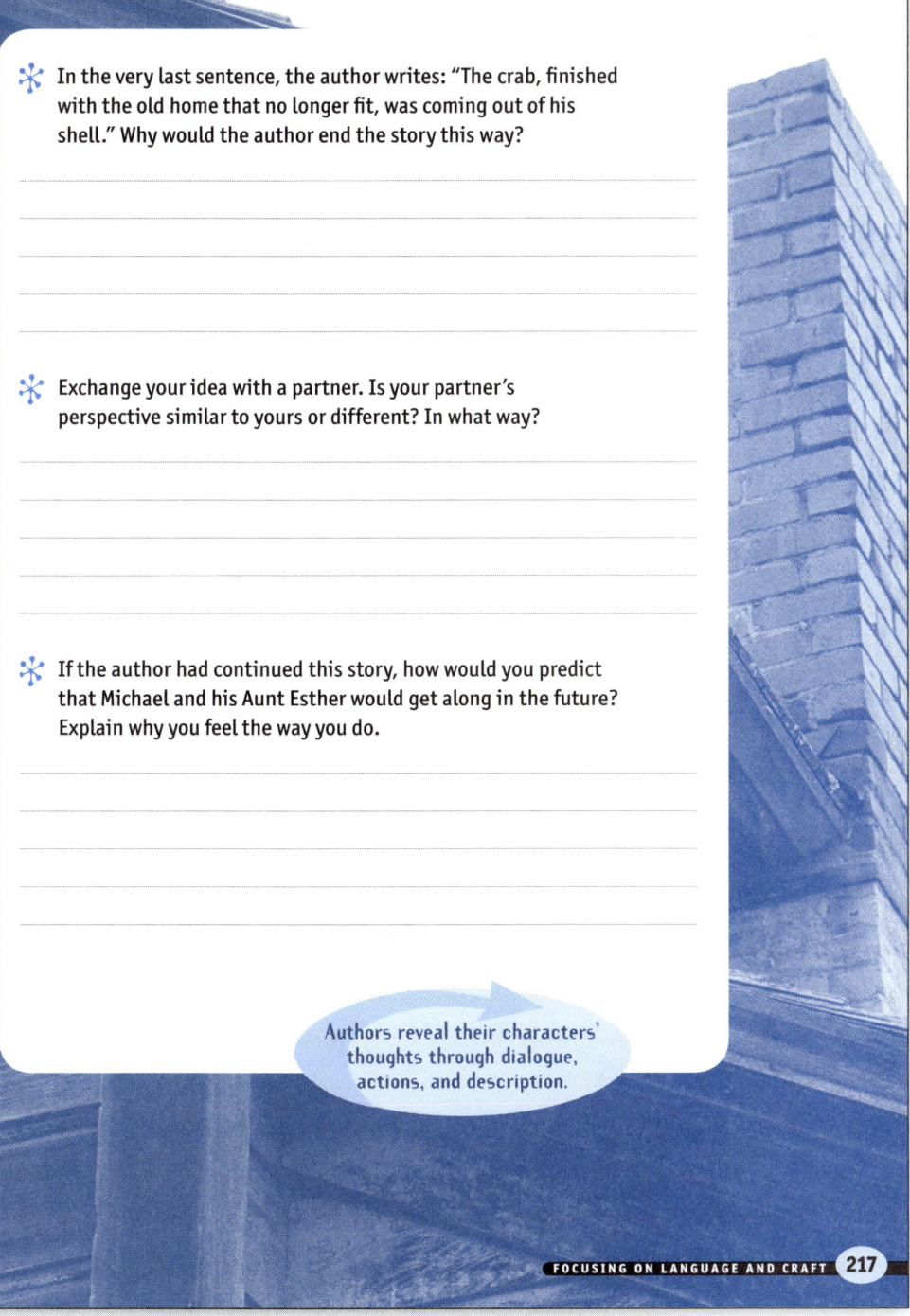

* In the very last sentence, the author writes: "The crab, finished with the old home that no longer fit, was coming out of his shell." Why would the author end the story this way?

_____
_____
_____
_____

* Exchange your idea with a partner. Is your partner's perspective similar to yours or different? In what way?

_____
_____
_____
_____

* If the author had continued this story, how would you predict that Michael and his Aunt Esther would get along in the future? Explain why you feel the way you do.

_____
_____
_____
_____
_____

Authors reveal their characters' thoughts through dialogue, actions, and description.

FOCUSING ON LANGUAGE AND CRAFT

TEACHING TIP

Collaboration Have students work in pairs to articulate their predictions before they write them. Encourage partners to support their predictions with details from the story. You may want students to fill out Character Map (a web that has places to collect information about aspects of a character) for Michael and Aunt Esther. Ask students to think about these questions: *What is Michael like? Why? What feelings does he express toward Aunt Esther in the beginning? in the ending? What is Aunt Esther like? Why? How does Aunt Esther act toward Michael in the beginning? in the ending?* Remind students to compare the characters' development. Then have students write their continuation of the story independently.

Quick Assess

* Did students use the Response Notes to interact and make connections with the text?
* Were students able to express how the author uses a hermit crab to describe Michael?
* Were students' continuations based on the information in the story and inferences they've made?

After

APPLYING THE STRATEGY
Ask students to look at the story again, this time focusing on the character of Aunt Esther. Have them think about how the hermit crab could be used to describe her as well as Michael. Ask students to list ways in which Aunt Esther's behavior suggests that she too lives in a "shell." Have students defend their viewpoint with details from the story.

READING/WRITING CONNECTION
Have students brainstorm descriptive words and phrases about an animal, using a cluster. Then encourage them to use those descriptive words and phrases in a short paragraph to draw comparisons to a person.

ASSESSING YOUR STRENGTHS

LESSON 69

Students will use the strategies they have practiced in the *Daybook* to write an original story that is modeled on "Shells" by Cynthia Rylant.

BACKGROUND KNOWLEDGE

Review the story elements students have studied in the *Daybook*: setting, point of view, characterization, plot, conflict, and theme. Point out each element in "Shells":

Setting: Present day; Aunt Esther's condominium in Detroit

Point of View: Third-person

Characters: Michael, Aunt Esther, and Sluggo, a hermit crab

Plot: Michael, age 14, moved in with his Aunt Esther after his parents died. Michael is lonely and buys a hermit crab. To his surprise, Aunt Esther takes an interest in Sluggo and buys more hermit crabs.

Conflict: At first, Michael and Aunt Esther don't get along. They don't begin to understand each other until they find a mutual interest.

Theme: People who hide their true feelings because they are afraid of being hurt need to trust someone who reaches out to them.

LESSON 69 GETTING READY TO WRITE

Effective writing starts with a plan. To get started on your own story that includes two characters facing a problem and an animal (or imaginary creature) that could help solve the problem, use this chart to plan your story.

Setting (time and place)

Characters (2)

The problem

Animal or imaginary creature description

How the problem will be solved

Before

CRITICAL WRITING SKILL

Prewriting Have a volunteer read aloud the introduction at the top of page 218. Then brainstorm story ideas that connect with problems young people might experience. Ask students to brainstorm possible solutions for each problem on the list.

After the brainstorming sessions, invite students to share their story ideas with you before they fill in their plan.

WRITING THE BEGINNING

❋ Before you write the beginning to your story, exchange the chart you made on page 218 with a writing partner. Respond to each other's ideas and write down at least one good suggestion your partner can use.

❋ Using "Shells" as a model, think of where you will begin your story. Notice how author Rylant began her story in the middle of a situation (Michael had moved in with his aunt).

WRITING SUPPORT

Beginning the Story Have students use the planning chart on page 218 to help guide their writing. You may wish to distribute other graphic organizers, such as a Plot Diagram (see page 271). Have students read again the beginning sentences of the story on page 210. Remind them that using dialogue is a good technique for beginning a story. In "Shells" the dialogue presents the problem and creates the tension and suspense that keep the story moving along.

During

WRITING THE STORY As students plan their stories, have them think about the role an animal (real or imaginary) will play in resolving the problem for the main character(s). If students did the activity under Reading/Writing Connection on page 217, have them review their animal cluster and corresponding paragraph. Suggest they use the same animal to compare to the character(s) in their story.

MORE WRITING SUPPORT

Criteria for a Story Before students continue their story, provide the following criteria for a good story.

A well-written story will

※ establish the setting;

※ develop the characters;

※ unfold the plot events;

※ establish the point of view;

※ present a theme.

A well-written story will also show the traits of effective writing:

※ creative ideas, developed with details

※ good organization—beginning, middle, and end

※ appropriate voice

※ thoughtful word choice

※ fluent sentences

※ correct mechanics, usage, and grammar

Quick Assess

※ Were students able to complete their plans?

※ Did students use their prewriting and planning tools to organize their writing?

※ Did students complete a first draft?

CONTINUING YOUR STORY
Now continue your story, adding an interesting element (a pet like Sluggo or an imaginary creature), who will take the role of a character in the story. Then use specific details to show how the animal helps solve the problem. (For example, in "Shells," a hermit crab must find a new home.) Be sure you have considered the suggestion you received from your writing partner on page 219.

Making a plan for writing is a useful strategy.

220 LESSON 69

After

WRITER'S CRAFT Have students use books or stories they have read to find good examples of how an author has developed setting, plot, characters, conflict, and so forth. They can write short descriptions of the author's technique, with examples, and post them on a bulletin board or class website. Classmates can use the postings as inspiration for their own writing.

REVISING AND REFLECTING — LESSON 70

A very important step in writing is to look at a draft to see how it can be improved. This is called **revision** because you **see** *(vision)* your writing **again** *(re-)*. If possible, set your story aside for a day or two before revising it. You may want to share your story with a writing partner to find more ways to improve it. Use this list before preparing your final copy.

- Does the beginning get my attention so I want to read more? If not, how could I improve it?
- Do I stay on topic? If not, where do I get off topic?
- Do I use vivid verbs to show action? Where are some places that I could use stronger verbs?
- Do I use specific, concrete details and sensory language to make my piece come alive? Where could I use more details?
- Is the ending satisfying? Does it sound "finished"? If not, what could I do to create a better ending?
- Does my dialogue (if I used any) sound realistic? If not, how can I change it?
- Are my sentences complete? Do I use a variety of sentence types and lengths? If not, where do I need to make changes?
- Have I checked my writing for spelling and punctuation errors?

✳ Think about a good title for your story. Why did the author title hers "Shells"? Ask your writing partner if your title captures the meaning of your story.

✳ After you have made changes to your story, make a final, neat copy in your best handwriting or on a computer. Your class may want to publish the stories in a class book, titled *Our Best Short Stories*.

LESSON 70

Students will revise their stories and reflect on their progress as readers and writers.

BACKGROUND KNOWLEDGE
Review with students the many stories that they have read. Encourage students to talk about the qualities of their favorite stories. Write the things students share on a chart labeled *Qualities of a Good Story*.

Then review the criteria you discussed in class in the previous lesson and have students draw on those criteria as they go over their drafts independently before meeting with you or a partner.

Before

CRITICAL WRITING SKILL
Revising Review the difference between revising and editing. Compare the difference to remodeling a house and cleaning the house. Revising means that the writer checks to see that the ideas are in place, the organization of ideas is appropriate, and the voice matches the purpose and audience. Tell students this is their chance to look back over their draft and make changes to improve it. Then have students work in pairs to review each other's story, using the checklist.

During

PREPARING THE FINAL COPY
Remind students that even professional writers find it very difficult to make revisions. Have students set aside their work for a time before making the final edits. This strategy can yield fresh insights into making final changes to improve the piece.

When students have finished making their changes, have them proofread their copy carefully for conventions. ▶▶▶

Quick Assess

✵ Did students use the criteria, the checklist, feedback from their peers, and their own ideas to improve their stories?

✵ Did students write a title that complemented their stories?

✵ Did students submit a final copy of their stories?

✵ Were students able to identify a strategy they have perfected in the *Daybook*?

✵ Did students write a paragraph reflecting on their growth as a reader and writer?

A FINAL REFLECTION
In a final reflection, identify one strategy you have perfected during your work with the *Daybook*. Think about whether you have met the most important goal: that you now really *like to* read and write. Write a paragraph reflecting on your growth as a reader and writer.

Reflection is a vital part of learning to read and write effectively.

After

They can exchange their story with a peer editing partner to help correct something they have overlooked.

Once students have given their story an interesting title and prepared their final copy, they should submit their writing for your evaluation.

LOOKING FORWARD Ask students to think about what they have learned about themselves as readers and writers. How can they apply what they've learned? Invite students to set goals for future reading and writing. Use their personal goals as discussion points for your student conferences.

Becoming An Active Reader

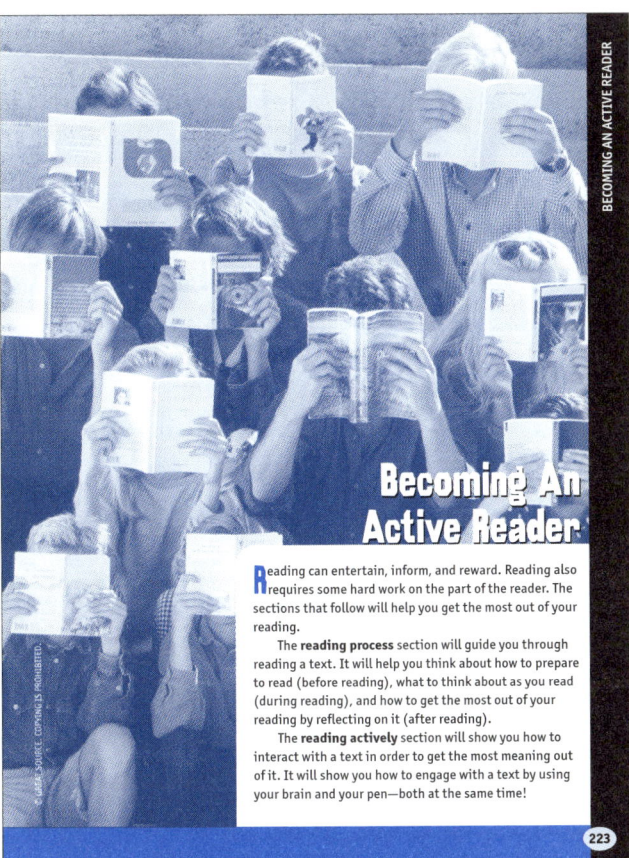

Reading can entertain, inform, and reward. Reading also requires some hard work on the part of the reader. The sections that follow will help you get the most out of your reading.

The **reading process** section will guide you through reading a text. It will help you think about how to prepare to read (before reading), what to think about as you read (during reading), and how to get the most out of your reading by reflecting on it (after reading).

The **reading actively** section will show you how to interact with a text in order to get the most meaning out of it. It will show you how to engage with a text by using your brain and your pen—both at the same time!

THE READING PROCESS

The Reading Process has three parts: **Before Reading, During Reading,** and **After Reading.**

1. BEFORE READING

❋ **Preview the Material**
Look over the selection before you read. Does the selection look like a short story or other work of fiction? If so, look at the title, introduction, and illustrations. Does the selection look like nonfiction? If so, look for headings, boldfaced words, photos, and captions. Also, ask yourself how the information is organized. Is the author comparing or contrasting information about the topic? Is the information presented in a sequence using signal words like *first, second, third,* and *finally*? Understanding how an author has organized information will help you to recognize key points as you read.

❋ **Make Predictions**
When you make predictions, you actively connect with the words on the page. Think about what you already know about the subject or the images. Then, think of yourself as a text detective, putting together what you know with new details in the text. Predict what you think will happen: why an event caused something to happen or what might come next in a series of events.

❋ **Set a Purpose**
Begin by reviewing what you already know about the topic or situation in the text. Then, think about what you want to find out.

QUESTIONS TO ASK YOURSELF BEFORE READING
- Before I read this material, what do I think it is going to be about?
- After looking over the selection, what do I already know about this subject?
- What should I be thinking about as I read?

2. DURING READING

❋ **Engage with the Text**
As your eyes look at the words, your brain should be working to make connections between the words and what you already know. Have you had an experience similar to that of one of the characters in a story you are reading? Do you know someone like the character? Have you read another book about the topic? You will also want to connect what you read to the predictions you made before reading. *Confirm, revise, predict again* is a cycle that continues until you finish reading the material. All of these questions will go on inside your head. Sometimes, though, it helps to think out loud or write.

❋ **Monitor Your Understanding**
As you read, stop from time to time and ask yourself, "Do I understand what I just read?" If the text doesn't make sense, there are several steps that you can take.

- Go back and reread the text carefully.
- Read on to see if more information helps you understand.
- Pull together the author's ideas in a summary.
- Retell, or say in your own words, the events that have happened.
- Picture in your mind what the author described.
- Look for context clues or word-structure clues to help you figure out hard words.

This takes some practice. Remember, to be a successful reader, you must be an active reader. Make an effort to check your understanding every so often when you read a new selection.

QUESTIONS TO ASK YOURSELF WHILE YOU ARE READING
- What important details am I finding?
- Which of these ideas seem to be the most important?
- Does this information fit with anything I already know?
- What do I see in my mind as I read this material?
- Do I understand the information in the charts or tables? Does it help me understand what I am reading?

3. AFTER READING

❋ **Summarize**
Reread to locate the most important ideas in the story or essay.

❋ **Respond and Reflect**
Talk with a partner about what you have read. What did you learn from the text? Were your predictions confirmed? What questions do you still have? Talking about reading helps you better understand what you have read.

❋ **Ask Questions**
Try asking yourself questions that begin like this:

Can I compare or contrast . . . evaluate . . . connect . . . examine . . . analyze . . . relate . . .

❋ **Engage with the Text**
Good readers engage with a text all the time, even when they have finished reading. When you tie events in your life or something else you have read to what you are currently reading, you become more involved with your reading. In the process, you are learning more about your values, relationships in your family, and issues in the world around you.

QUESTIONS TO ASK YOURSELF AFTER READING
- What was this article about?
- What was the author trying to tell me?
- Have I learned something that made me change the way I think about this topic?
- Are there parts of this material that I really want to remember?

READING ACTIVELY

Make the effort to stay involved with your reading by reading actively. Your mind should be busy reading the text, making connections, making predictions, and asking questions. Your hand should be busy, too. Keep track of what you are thinking by "reading with your pen." **Write** your reactions to the text or connections that you can make. **Circle** words you don't understand. **Draw** a sketch of a scene. **Underline** or **highlight** an important idea. You may have your own way of reading actively. You may develop a style that works better for you, but here are six common ways of reading actively.

MARK OR HIGHLIGHT The most common way of noting important parts of a text is to write on a sticky note and put it on the page. Or, if you can, mark important parts of a text by highlighting them with a marker, pen, or pencil. You can also use highlighting tape. The highlighted parts should provide a good review of the text.

ASK QUESTIONS Asking questions is a way of engaging the author in conversation. Readers who ask a lot of questions think about the text more and understand it better. "Why is the writer talking about this?" "Is this really true?" "What does that mean?"

REACT AND CONNECT When you read, listen to the author and to yourself. Think about what you are reading and relate it to your own life. Compare and contrast what the text says to what you know.

PREDICT Readers who are involved with the text constantly wonder how things will turn out. They think about what might happen. They check their thoughts against the text and make adjustments. Sometimes the author surprises them! Making predictions helps you stay interested in what you are reading.

VISUALIZE Making pictures in your mind can help you "see" what you are thinking and help you remember. A chart, a sketch, a diagram—any of these can help you "see." Sometimes your picture doesn't match what you think the author is telling you. This is a signal to reread to check your understanding of the text.

CLARIFY As you read, you need to be sure that you understand what is going on in the text. Take time to pull together what you have learned. Try writing notes to clarify your understanding. Another way of checking to see that you understand is to tell someone about what you have read.

GLOSSARY

acrobatic able to move like an acrobat; exceptionally agile
adjacent to next to, connected to
adversity hardship
aftershocks small tremors that often follow an earthquake
aglus hole in a piece of ice where a seal comes up for air when swimming under the ice
alliance partnership
alphabetic having a set of letters, each standing for a sound, that can be used to spell words
anonymous without an identity
apathy a feeling of not caring
Apollo a theater in Harlem
assured promised
at bay cornered
authorities people in charge, such as police officers and firefighters
autobiography an author's story of his or her own life
Ay, Dios Spanish exclamation of surprise or amazement
barbed wire fence wire with many sharp points
barge a large, flat-bottomed boat used to carry heavy loads
barracks a large, plain, temporary building
bear the lash be beaten
belie misrepresent
bellowed yelled
benevolent kind, giving
berserk crazy; out of control
bestowed gave
binary language the basic code of computer programming, which contains only combinations of the numbers 0 and 1
biodegradable capable of breaking down, or decomposing, naturally
bold fearless; brave
bonjour French word for "hello" or "good day"
bountiful plentiful
breadwinner family member who earns most of the money a family needs to survive
brimming full, almost overflowing
brouhaha huge fuss
buffeting pushing as if repeatedly striking
bustled buzzed with activity; was crowded and busy
candidly honestly
carnie mildly insulting slang term for "carnival worker"
cataracts waterfalls
ceramic made from clay
chador [chah DOR] garment worn by women and girls to cover their hair and shoulders
char a type of fish in the trout family
characteristics (of a genre) the features that define a genre
characterization the way an author reveals information about the people, animals, and imaginary creatures in a story
cocoon a protective cover or case, such as that which shelters an animal during its pupa stage

commingled mixed
condominium apartment-like house
connection relationship based on similar experiences
consumers those who utilize goods and services
contaminates makes something dirty or impure
context the circumstances or events that make up the environment within which events takes place
conviction a strong belief
convulsion violent upheaval
cooing talking in an overly happy way; similar to "baby talk"
coveted longed for, desired
critical reading and writing strategies skills that involve understanding and evaluating material outside a text one is reading or writing
critics people who write reviews of other people's work
cross-stitch a kind of embroidery
crucial important; essential
crystal high quality glass
cupie-doll an early 1900s doll with a rotund body and a wisp of hair
debilitating weakening
debris remains of something that's been destroyed
defiant defying or showing resistance to authority
details information used to support the main idea of an argument
descriptive language words that capture images
dialogue conversation(s) between characters in a story
discrimination attitudes and actions based on prejudice rather than on an individual's merit
dispel to scatter; drive away
dissever to separate, to cut apart
distinguish tell apart
drawbacks problems or disadvantages
draw conclusions to come up with a summary of a situation based on information given
dully in a depressed or sad way
eddy a small whirlpool; water with a circular motion
eerie spooky, scary
eliminate get rid of
embargo a ban on something
embittered harboring feelings of anger and resentment
emerged came out
emotional language language that evokes feelings
energy-efficient using as little energy as possible
environmentalists people who focus on ways to protect natural resources
epistle poem a letter written as a poem
equilibrium a state of balance
erupted released suddenly
ese Spanish slang for "you." The use here is similar to that in the greeting "Hey, you!"

essential important, necessary
exobiologist a biologist who searches for life beyond Earth
extraterrestrial beyond Earth
facts information that can be proved
fantasy a type of fiction featuring imaginary worlds and magical or supernatural events
farm team a minor-league team
fashioning making, forming, shaping
financial security having enough money to live a comfortable life
first-person point of view the telling of a story in which the narrator is one of the characters and calls himself or herself "I"
flank side
floe a large piece of floating ice
foreboding a feeling that something dreadful is about to happen
foreigner a person from another country
fortify strengthen
fortitude strength
fossil fuels energy resources formed in the earth from remains of long-dead plants and animals
founding father the first to start something
fractures breaks
freak show a display of unusual creatures, such as a two-headed dog, commonly found at a fair
French knots on samplers an allusion to a common symbol of home—the words "Home, Sweet Home" cross-stitched in a wall hanging; French knot is a particular type of stitch made with yarn or floss
full throttle to run at top speed
funneled came from various directions toward one point
furrow a long, narrow, shallow trench in the ground
gawked stared in disbelief
generators machines that convert mechanical energy into electrical energy
genre a type of writing
geyser a hot spring that shoots water or steam into the air
girders big beams that support a building or bridge
global view having a broad perspective
gorge deep narrow passage
graphic novel a story presented as a cartoon
grieve mourn
grim serious, gloomy
groping feeling around with fingers or hands
grudge an attitude of anger or bitterness toward someone
half-coy acting shy
historical fiction fiction set in the past, in a time of important historical events
hole in this context, a place where the water swirls very rapidly in a circle, creating suction that is very dangerous for rafters
honeycombs the waxy structures in which bees store honey
horizon line where ground meets sky; in this case, the edges of the area that could be seen
humanity human qualities

identity a person's answers to the questions "Who am I?" "Where do I belong?" and "How do I fit in?"
ideogram a picture that represents an idea
impelled moved or urged to do something
impenetrable unable to be passed through
impervious resistant
in a fix in trouble
incinerators a place for burning waste
inevitable impossible to avoid
intensity very strong feeling
interacting with a text to "carry on a conversation" with a text; a strategy for effective reading that involves circling, underlining, and writing notes
interstellar between stars or solar systems
interview a one-on-one meeting in which someone is asked questions about himself or herself
intoxicated excited in an obsessed way
intrude break in on
jangles harsh, metallic sounds
Jesse Semple a character in many of Hughes's stories
Kabul [KAH bul] capital city of Afghanistan
kayak a native American canoe with a wooden frame covered by animal skins and propelled with a paddle
kinsmen relatives, members of one's family
landfall arrival at shore after a journey by water
Langston Hughes a poet (1902–1967) who was an influential presence in the Harlem Renaissance, a movement based in New York City that celebrated African American life and culture
Le bateau est sur l'eau. French for "The boat is on the water."
leach seep into
Lenox and 7th Harlem streets
levitate to rise and float in the air
linoleum a type of floor covering that's like tile
locomotion the ability to move around from place to place
lope run with a steady rhythm
maiden an unmarried woman
make inferences a reading strategy that involves making reasonable guesses by putting together something you have read in a story with something you know from real life; "reading between the lines"
making connections a reading strategy that involves comparing what you are reading to something you already know
Malali [mah LAH lee] legendary young girl who gave Afghani troops the courage to defeat an enemy in 1880
marauding raiding
masonry bricks and stones
meditation deep reflection
menacing threatening
migratory traveling from a colder climate to a warmer one
multiple perspectives different points of view in a story that allow a reader to look at a moment or event from more than one angle

muscular dystrophy a fatal disease that gradually weakens all muscles in the body
narrator a storyteller
naysayers people who say something is impossible
obliged to you thank you
obliterated wiped out; obscured
ominously in a threatening way
on the sly secretly
oncologist a doctor who specializes in cancer diagnosis and treatment
oppressiveness heaviness, burden
out of kilter out of order
Oya-oya! Japanese exclamation meaning "my goodness!"
pass a permission form
PCBs chemical compounds that can build up in animal tissue
permeated filled
persistent keeping at it
personal narrative a short prose piece in which a writer expresses personal thoughts and makes connections
perspective the point of view or angle from which you see a subject
persuade to try to convince others to feel the same way you do
persuasive writing writing that attempts to persuade a reader of the validity of an argument by using persuasive details
pertinacity ability to stick with it
phenomenon unusual occurrence
pictograph a picture that represents a familiar object
pivoting turning around
point of view the vantage point from which a story is told
plot how the characters and events in a story are connected
prediction an educated guess about upcoming events that is based on background knowledge and clues from the present
prejudiced feeling strongly about something, regardless of any facts to the contrary
Presbyterian member of a particular Protestant church
pretense pretending something isn't what it is
purpose an author's intent in writing a piece
queasy having nausea
queue a ponytail once worn by Chinese men
quiver tremble or shake
ramshackle rundown, not sturdy
raza-style part-Spanish for a hand-shake style expressive of a Latino culture
reading for meaning reading with focus and effort to discover and understand an author's message
rebellious tending to go against the rules
recounted reviewed; retold
reflecting taking time to think about what you have read
relish a feeling of enthusiasm or delight
Renaissance man a person who is accomplished in many areas, both arts and sciences.

repertoire a performer's collection of abilities
respite a short time of rest
revision looking at a draft again in order to find ways to improve it
riddled filled with holes; perforated
rouge makeup that reddens cheeks
runt a scrawny creature. The runt of a litter of puppies is the smallest.
saludo de vato Spanish for a special head nod expressive of a Latino culture
scavengers animals that eat dead and decaying plants and animals
scholars people who make a living doing research in colleges and universities
Scotland Yard/MI 5 security forces of the British government
second-person point of view the telling of a story in which the reader is one of the characters and is the "you" referred to in the story
seminal influential; important development
sensory language language that appeals to the reader's senses
sepulcher a grave or tomb
seraphs angels, heavenly beings
setting the time and place of a story
shalwar kameez [SHAHL wahr kah MEEZ] a long, loose shirt and trousers worn by either a man or a woman
sheepish embarrassed
shrine a place for worship
simile a technique of figurative language in which the characteristics of one thing are described in terms of something else using the word like or as
solemnly seriously
somber darkening
speared in this context, to position precisely
spooked scared away; startled
sprint burst of speed
staggering overwhelming, unbelievable
steadfast firm, constant, unwavering
steeples pointed towers on churches
stereotypic not original or having no individuality; trite
stitching a decoration made from thread
story elements the essential parts that make up a story
strategic reading using a repertoire of skills and strategies to make decisions about how to approach texts
strivings intense efforts
structural mitigation techniques ways of making buildings safer
summarize to find the main idea of a text and restate it in your own words
Sweet Flypaper of Life a book of Harlem photographs by Hughes and photographer Ray DeCarava
symbolism the use of symbols to communicate ideas
symbols images or objects that represent other things
syllabic having a set of symbols, each standing for a sound
talc powder

Taliban (TAL ih bahn) ruling party in Afghanistan from 1996–2001. A member of the party is a Talib (TAL eeb).
tangible something that can be touched
tarp a piece of heavy canvas
taunts insulting remarks intended to anger
tempest storm
tenement a rundown building where poor people live
theme the main topic or message that is explored through the characters and plot of a story
thermal a column of warm, rising air. Thermals form over hot, flat surfaces, such as the floor of a canyon, offering soaring birds and hang gliders a literal lift.
thermostats devices that control temperature
thicket a place where plants grow very close together
third-person point of view the telling of a story in which the narrator is not part of the story: a limited third-person narrator reveals the thoughts and feelings of only one character; an omniscient third-person narrator reveals the thoughts and feelings of several characters
thrashing a beating
tiered stacked up
toddle to walk unsteadily like a toddler
toshak (TOH shawk) a mattress used as a bed, chair, or couch; similar to a futon
toxic poisonous
trauma emotional shock
tremendous great
Trés bien. Parlez-vous français? French for "Very good. Do you speak French?"
tundra a treeless area between the icecap and the tree line of Arctic regions
turbulence boisterous or unsettled air
Underground formal name for London's subway system
undulate roll like a wave
unwonted unusual
variometer an instrument used to monitor altitude during flight
ventured forth set out on a new adventure
ventured tried, said
visual information messages presented with visual images
visualizing a reading strategy in which a reader makes pictures in his or her mind of a text
visual text a collection of visual images that present a coherent message
whiff an inhaling of air; in this context "take a whiff" means to smell something
winced to have shrunk or drawn back, as if in pain
wound a cut or tear in the outer layer of a plant
wretched badly made

ACKNOWLEDGMENTS

10 Excerpt from "The Computer Date" from *A Summer Life* by Gary Soto. Copyright © 1990 by University Press of New England.

11, 13, 16 "Seventh Grade" from *Baseball in April and Other Stories*, copyright © 1990 by Gary Soto, reprinted by permission of Harcourt, Inc.

19 "Oranges" from *New And Selected Poems* © 1995 by Gary Soto. Used with permission of Chronicle Books, LLC, San Francisco. Visit ChronicleBooks.com.

22 Excerpt from *Living Up the Street* by Gary Soto (Dell, 1991), © 1985 by Gary Soto. Used by permission of the author.

26, 29 From *The Breadwinner* by Deborah Ellis. Copyright © 2001. Used by permission of Groundwood Books.

35 "Vietnam War Memorial" from "Journey Through Hartsong" by Mattie J.T. Stepanek. Used by permission of Hyperion Books.

40, 42, 44 Excerpts from *Year of Impossible Goodbyes* by Sook Nyul Choi. Copyright © 1991 by Sook Nyul Choi. Reprinted by permission of Houghton Mifflin Company. All rights reserved.

45, 48 "Thank You, Ma'am" from *Short Stories* by Langston Hughes. Copyright © 1996 by Ramona Bass and Arnold Rampersad. Used by permission of Hill and Wang, a division of Farrar, Straus and Giroux, LLC.

54 With permission of Robert W. Peterson and *Boys' Life*, April 1997, published by the Boy Scouts of America.

58 Used by permission of Primedia History Group.

62 Copyright © 1996 by Sharon Robinson. Reprinted by permission of HarperCollins Publishers.

65 Lucille Clifton, "jackie robinson" from *Good Woman: Poems and a Memoir 1969-1980*. Copyright © 1987 by Lucille Clifton. Reprinted with the permission of BOA Editions, Ltd., www.BOAEditions.org.

70, 73, 75 "Poem Book", "Name all the People", "Line Break Poem", "Epistle Poem", from *Locomotion* by Jacqueline Woodson, copyright © 2003 by Jacqueline Woodson. Used by permission of G.P. Putnam's Sons, A Division of Penguin Young Readers Group, A Member of Penguin Group (USA) Inc., 345 Hudson Street, New York, NY 10014. All rights reserved.

77 "Mother to Son" from *Collected Poems* by Langston Hughes. Used by permission of Random House Inc.

80 "Long Live Langston" by Wesley Boone from *Bronx Masquerade* by Nikki Grimes. Used by permission of Penguin Putnam.

82 From *Bronx Masquerade* by Nikki Grimes. Used by permission of Penguin Putnam.

86 "The Princess of Light" from *The Dancing Kettle and Other Japanese Folktales* retold by Yoshiko Uchida, illustrated by Richard C. Jones.

90 From *The Invisible Thread* by Yoshiko Uchida. Reprinted with the permission of Simon & Schuster Books for Young Readers, an imprint of Simon & Schuster Children's Publishing Division. Copyright © 1991 Yoshiko Uchida.

93 From *Journey Home* by Yoshiko Uchida. Reprinted with the permission of Margaret K. McElderry Books, an imprint of Simon & Schuster Children's Publishing Division. Text copyright © 1978 Yoshiko Uchida.

96 From *Desert Exile: The Uprooting of a Japanese-American Family* by Yoshiko Uchida. First published by University of Washington Press, 1982. Reprinted with permission.

99 From a conversation with Yoshiko Uchida. Reprinted with permission.

102 "Birthday Box," copyright © 1995 by Jane Yolen. First appeared in *Birthday Surprises: Ten Great Stories to Unwrap*, published by Morrow Junior Books. Reprinted by permission of Curtis Brown, Ltd.

107 "The Key to Everything" from *The Complete Love Poems of May Swenson*. Copyright © 1991, 2003 by The Literary Estate of May Swenson. Reprinted by the permission of Houghton Mifflin Company. All rights reserved.

109 www.JaneYolen.com, copyright © 2000 by Jane Yolen. Reprinted by permission of Curtis Brown, Ltd.

113 Excerpt from *Island of the Blue Dolphins* by Scott O'Dell. Copyright © 1960, renewed 1988 by Scott O'Dell. Reprinted by permission of Houghton Mifflin Company. All rights reserved.

118 Excerpts from *Ice Drift*, copyright © 2005 by Theodore Taylor, reprinted by permission of Harcourt, Inc.

121 Reprinted with the permission of Atheneum Books for Young Readers, an imprint of Simon & Schuster Children's Publishing Division, from *True Believer* by Virginia Euwer Wolff. Copyright © 2001 Virginia Euwer Wolff.

124 From *The Terrorist* by Caroline B. Cooney. Published by Scholastic Press/Scholastic Inc. Copyright © 1997 by Caroline B. Cooney. Reprinted by permission.

129 "Homeless," copyright © 1987 by Anna Quindlen, from *Living Out Loud* by Anna Quindlen. Used by permission of Random House, Inc.

134, 137 Courtesy of Cartoon Books.

140 NBM Publishing.

148, 151 Text copyright © 1995 by Eagle Productions. Used by permission of HarperCollins Publishers.

151 From "Three Fearful Days", edited by Malcolm Barker. Used be permission of Sunset Publishing Corp.

154 Copyright © 1975 by Lawrence Yep. Used by permission of HarperCollins Publishers.

160 © Copyright The American National Red Cross. All rights reserved.

164 Roach, John & Ives, Sara/National Geographic

167, 175 Excerpt from *You Are the Earth*. Copyright © 1990 by David Suzuki and Kathy Vanderlinden. Published by Breystone Books, a division of Douglas & McIntyre Ltd. Reprinted by permission of the publisher.

169 Excerpt from *Odyssey*'s April 2004 issue: Future Power, © 2004, Carus Publishing Company, published by Cobblestone Publishing, 30 Grove Street, Suite C, Peterborough, NH 03458. All Rights Reserved. Used by permission of the author.

172 From *Harvest for Hope* by Jane Goodall with Gary McAvoy and Gail Hudson. Copyright © 2005 by Jane Goodall and Gary McAvoy. By permission of Warner Books, Inc.

179 "The Last Page" from *A History of Reading* by Alberto Manguel, copyright © 1996 by Alberto Manguel. Used by permission fo Penguin, a division of Penguin Group (USA) Inc.

179 Reprinted by Consent of Brooks Permissions.

182, 184 Reprinted by permission of Don Lago.

190 "The Road Not Taken" from *The Poetry of Robert Frost* edited by Edward Connery Lathem. Copyright © 1969 by Henry Holt and Company. Reprinted by permission of Henry Holt and Company, LLC.

194, 197, 200 Text Copyright © 1998 by Will Hobbs. Used by permission of HarperCollins Publishers.

202 Reprinted with the permission of Atheneum Books for Young Readers, an imprint of Simon & Schuster Children's Publishing Division from *Kokopelli's Flute* by Will Hobbs. Copyright © 1995 Will Hobbs.

204 Reprinted with the permission of Athenuem Books for Young Readers, an imprint of Simon & Schuster Children's Publishing Division from *Downriver* by Will Hobbs. Copyright © 1991 Will Hobbs.

207 Reprinted with the permission of Atheneum Books for Young Readers, an imprint of Simon & Schuster Children's Publishing Division from *Bearstone* by Will Hobbs. Copyright © 1989 Will Hobbs.

210, 215 "Shells" from *Every Living Thing* by Cynthia Rylant. Reprinted with the permission of Simon & Schuster Books for Young Readers, an imprint of Simon & Schuster Children's Publishing Division. Copyright © 1985 Cynthia Rylant

ILLUSTRATIONS

137: © Great Source; **142 *m*:** © Laszlo Kubinyi. Reprinted by permission of Houghton Mifflin Company. All rights reserved.

All additional art created by AARTPACK, Inc.

PHOTOGRAPHY

Photo Research AARTPACK, Inc.

cover, 1: © Royalty-Free/Corbis.

Unit 1 9: © Duncan Smith/Getty Images; **10*t*:** © Donna Day/Getty Images; **10*b*:** © Itstock/InMagine; **11:** © Donna Day/Getty; **12:** © Royalty-Free/Corbis; **13:** © Royalty-Free/Corbis; **14:** © Tom Merton/Getty; **15:** © Tom Merton/Getty; **16:** © Getty Images; **17:** © Photodisc/InMagine; **18:** © Getty Images; **19:** © Photodisc/InMagine; **20:** © Photodisc/InMagine; **21:** © Royalty-Free/Corbis; **22:** © Royalty-Free/Corbis; **23:** © Royalty-Free/Corbis

Unit 2 25: © Julio Lopez Saguar/Getty; **26:** © Paula Bronstein/Getty; **27:** © Thorne Anderson/Corbis; **28*l*:** © Paula Bronstein/Getty; **28*r*:** © Paula Bronstein/Getty; **29:** © Le Segretain Pascal/Corbis Sygma; **30:** © Le Segretain Pascal/Corbis Sygma; 31: © Paula Bronstein/Getty; **32:** © Hulton Archive/Getty; **33:** © Bettmann/Corbis; **34:** © Royalty-Free/Corbis; **35*t*:** © Royalty-Free/Corbis; **35*b*:** © Joyce Naltchayan/Getty;

36: © Royalty-Free/Corbis; **37:** © 1993 PhotoDisc, Inc.; **38:** © 1993 PhotoDisc, Inc.

Unit 3 39: © Debra McClinton/Getty; **40:** © Getty Images; **41:** © Getty Images; **42:** © Royalty-Free/Corbis; **43:** © Megumi Takamura/Getty; **44:** © Photodisc/InMagine; **45:** © Stockbyte/InMagine; **46:** © Getty Images; **47:** © Getty Images; **48:** © Jules Frazier/Getty; **49:** © Comstock, Inc. 1998; **50:** © Jules Frazier/Getty; **51:** © Tom Morrison/Getty; **52:** © Royalty-Free/Corbis

Unit 4 53: © Bettmann/Corbis; **54:** © Royalty-Free/Corbis; **55:** © Bettmann/Corbis; **56:** © Comstock/InMagine; **58:** © Royalty-Free/Corbis; **59:** © Bettmann/ Corbis; **60:** © Royalty-Free/Corbis; **61:** © Royalty-Free/Corbis; **62:** © Michael Matisse/Getty; **63:** © Phil Schermeister/Corbis; **64:** © Michael Matisse/Getty; **65*t*:** © Kaz Chiba/1997 PhotoDisc, Inc.; **65*b*:** © Bettmann/Corbis; **66:** © Royalty-Free/Corbis; **67:** © Bettmann/Corbis; **68:** © Flip Schulke/Corbis

Unit 5 69: © Royalty-Free/Corbis; **70:** © Royalty-Free/Corbis; **71:** © Royalty-Free/Corbis; **72:** © Alexander Walter/Getty; **73:** © Alexander Walter/Getty; **74:** © Ultraviolent/Getty; **75*t*:** © Royalty-Free/Corbis; **75*b*:** © Royalty-Free/Corbis; **76:** © Royalty-Free/Corbis; **77:** © Getty Images; **78:** © Getty Images; **79:** © Getty Images; **80:** © Getty Images; **81*t*:** © Sami Sarkis/Getty; **81*b*:** © Sami Sarkis/Getty; **82*t*:** © Royalty-Free/Corbis; **82*b*:** © Royalty-Free/Corbis; **83:** © Royalty-Free/Corbis; **84:** © Royalty-Free/Corbis

Unit 6 85: © Corbis; **86:** © Andrew Garn/Getty; **87:** © Jeremy Maude/Getty; **88:** © Jeremy Maude/Getty; **89:** © Getty Images; **90:** © Corbis (U.S. War Relocation Authority); **91:** © Santokh Kochar/Getty; **92:** © Bettmann/Corbis; **93:** © Corbis; **94*l*:** © Seattle Post-Intelligencer Collection; Museum of History and Industry/Corbis; **94*r*:** © Seattle Post-Intelligencer Collection; Museum of History and Industry/Corbis; **95:** © Getty Images; **96*t*:** © Brandxpictures/InMagine; **96*b*:** © Special Collections Dept., J. Willard Marriott Library, University of Utah; **98:** © Brand X pictures/InMagine; **99:** © Jeremy Maude/Getty

Unit 7 100: © Jeremy Maude/Getty; **101:** © Hulton Archive/Getty; **102:** © Getty Images; **103:** © Getty Images; **104:** © Stockdisc/InMagine; **105:** © Getty Images; **106:** © Jan Stromme/Getty; **107:** © Royalty-Free/Corbis; **108:** © Jan Stromme/Getty; **109:** © Royalty-Free/Corbis; **110:** © Royalty-Free/Corbis; **111:** © 1993 PhotoDisc, Inc.; **112:** © Tom Brakefield/Getty; **113:** © Royalty-Free/Corbis; **114:** © Tom Brakefield/Getty; **115:** © Royalty-Free/Corbis; **116:** © Image Source/Getty

Unit 8 117: © Brian Bailey/Getty; **118:** © Image100/InMagine; **119:** © Image100/InMagine; **120:** © Getty Images; **121:** © Janis Christie/Getty; **122:** © Janis Christie/Getty; **123*t*:** © MedioImages/Getty; **123*r*:** © MedioImages/Getty; **124:** © Terry Vine/Getty; **125:** © Digital Vision/Getty; **126:** © Ryan McVay/Getty; **127:** © Alexander Benz/zefa/Corbis; **128:** © Digital Vision/Getty; **129:** © Terry Vine/Getty; **130*l*:** © Terry Vine/Getty; **130*r*:** © Terry Vine/Getty; **131:** © Kevin Forest/Getty; **132:** © Kevin Forest/Getty

Unit 9 133: © Photonica/Getty; **134*t*:** © Image Source/Getty; **134*b*:** © Image Source/Getty; **136:** © Image Source/Getty; **137*t*:** © Photodisc Green/Getty; **138*b*:** © 2005 Comstock Images; **139:** © Image Source/Getty; **140*l*:** © Spencer Grant/PhotoEdit; **143:** © Comstock Images; **143*t*:** © MedioImages/Getty; **143*m*:** © MedioImages/Getty; **143*b*:** © 1993 PhotoDisc, Inc.; **144:** © Digital Vision/Getty; **145:** © Digital Vision/Getty; **146:** © Digital Vision/Getty

Unit 10 147: © Bettmann/Corbis; **148:** © Inter-Network Media/Getty; **149:** © 1999 PhotoDisc, Inc.; **150:** © InterNetwork Media/Getty; **151:** © Getty Images; **152:** © Bettmann/Corbis; **154:** © Royalty-Free/Corbis; **155:** © Royalty-Free/Corbis; **156:** © Royalty-Free/Corbis; **157:** © 1999 PhotoDisc, Inc.; **158*l*:** © 1999 PhotoDisc, Inc.; **158*m*:** © Bettmann/Corbis; **159*t*:** © Getty Images; **159*r*:** © 1999 PhotoDisc, Inc.; **160*t*:** © Spencer Grant/PhotoEdit; **160*b*:** © 1999 PhotoDisc, Inc.; **161:** © Getty Images; **162:** © Brand X Pictures

Unit 11 163: © Photodisc/InMagine; **164:** © Royalty-Free/Corbis; **165:** © Royalty-Free/Corbis; **166:** © Tracy Montana/PhotoLink/Getty; **167:** © Tracy Montana/PhotoLink/Getty; **168:** © Pete Starman/Getty; **169:** © Tom Brakefield/Getty; **170:** © 1993 photodisc, Inc.; **171:** © Brand X Pictures/InMagine; **172:** © 1993 photodisc, Inc.;

173: © Philip Wallick/Corbis; **174:** © Royalty-Free/Corbis; **175*t*:** © Russell Illig/Getty; **175*b*:** © Royalty-Free/Corbis; **176:** © Getty Images

Unit 12 177: © Royalty-Free/Corbis; **178:** © Getty Images; **179:** © Flip Schulke/Corbis; **180:** © Getty Images; **181:** © Royalty-Free/Corbis; **182*t*:** © Nick Koudis/Getty; **182*b*:** © Nick Koudis/Getty; **183:** © R H Productions/Getty; **184:** © Photodisc/InMagine; **185:** © Chad Baker/Ryan McVay/Getty; **186:** © Brandxpictures/InMagine; **187:** © Tony Sweet/Getty; **188:** © Ingram/InMagine; **189:** © Tony Sweet/Getty; **190*t*:** © Royalty-Free/Corbis; **190*b*:** © Royalty-Free/Corbis; **191:** © Royalty-Free/Corbis; **192:** © William Manning/Corbis

Unit 13 193: © Brandxpictures/InMagine; **194:** © Jack Hollingsworth/Getty; **195:** © Pixtal/InMagine; **196:** © Royalty-Free/Corbis; **197:** © Royalty-Free/Corbis; **199:** © Royalty-Free/Corbis; **200:** © Ablestock/InMagine; **201:** © Ablestock/InMagine; **204:** © Photodisc/InMagine; **205:** © Getty Images; **206:** © Ken Redding/Corbis; **207:** © Royalty-Free/Corbis; **208:** © Royalty-Free/Corbis

Unit 14 209: © Royalty-Free/Corbis; **210:** © Kaz chiba/Getty Images; **211:** © Creatas Images/2006 Jupiterimages Corporation; **212:** © 2004 Comstock ImagesLLC; **213*b*:** © Creatas Images/2006 Jupiterimages Corporation; **213*r*:** © Royalty-Free/Corbis; **214:** © Kaz chiba/Getty Images; **215:** © Ken Usami/Getty; **216:** © 2004 Comstock ImagesLLC; **217:** © 2001 Brand X Pictures; **218:** © Kaz chiba/Getty Images; **219:** © Kaz chiba/Getty Images; **220:** © Ken Usami/Getty; **221:** © TRBfoto/Getty; **222:** © 2001 Brand X Pictures

Becoming an Active Reader 223: © Photodisc Green/Getty; **224–226:** © Kaz chiba/Getty Images; **227:** © Lonely Planet Images/Getty

TEACHER'S EDITION

cover, i: © Royalty-Free/Corbis; **iii-vii, x-2:** © 1993 PhotoDisc, Inc.; **227:** © Tony Sweet/Getty; **228:** © Royalty-Free/Corbis; **229-240, 246-269, 271-272:** © 1993 PhotoDisc, Inc.; **241-245:** © Getty Images; **270:** © Royalty-Free/Corbis. **247, 255, 265:** illustrations by Tim Robinson.

RESOURCES

WRITING PROMPTS   228

Unit 1	Response to Literature	229
Unit 2	Character Sketch	230
Unit 3	Personal Narrative	231
Unit 4	Character Sketch	232
Unit 5	Persuasive Letter	233
Unit 6	Response to Literature	234
Unit 7	*See the writing assessment prompt on page 112.*	
Unit 8	Story Continuation	235
Unit 9	Persuasive Letter	236
Unit 10	Expository Essay	237
Unit 11	Expository Essay	238
Unit 12	Descriptive Essay	239
Unit 13	Response to Literature	240
Unit 14	*See the writing assessment prompt on page 218.*	

ASSESSMENTS   241

Answer Keys   243

Scoring Chart   246

Pretest   247

Reading Strategy Assessments

Assessment	Administer after . . .	
1 Interacting with the Text	Unit 2 or Unit 9	253
2 Making Connections	Unit 3 or Unit 10	256
3 Exploring Multiple Perspectives	Unit 4 or Unit 11	259
4 Focusing on Language and Craft	Unit 5 or Unit 12	262

Posttest   264

REPRODUCIBLE GRAPHIC ORGANIZERS   270

WRITING PROMPTS

The following Writing Prompts are designed for use at the end of each unit of the *Daybook*. You can assign the prompt in a single class period, or you may prefer to have students write over a period of two or three days with time for peer conferences, revising, editing, and reflecting.

Since each prompt is based on the literature and strategies from the corresponding unit, assign the prompt when students have finished the unit. Allow students to refer to their *Daybooks* so they can use the selections as they write.

Please note: The Writing Prompts for Unit 7 and Unit 14 are contained within those units.

* **Evaluation criteria accompany each prompt.**
  Go over the criteria with students before they begin each assessment so they can use the criteria to inform their writing. Tell students to use resources such as dictionaries or computer programs to check spelling and grammar.

UNIT 1: Building Your Repertoire
WRITING PROMPT

LITERATURE CONNECTION
- "A Summer Life"
- "Seventh Grade"
- "Oranges"
- *Living Up the Street*

Response to Literature

Think about the selections by Gary Soto. Could you relate to the young people in the stories and poem? Did they seem realistic to you? Would you recommend Gary Soto's writing to someone else your age? Why or why not?

Responding Write a review of Gary Soto's writing and based on what you've read in Unit 1, make a recommendation to other students your age. Be specific about which pieces you would recommend and why. Be sure to give specific reasons for your opinion. Support your opinion with examples and quotations from at least one of the selections. Your closing should draw your main points together.

Evaluation Criteria

The writer responds directly to the prompt and

- develops and supports the main points, using examples from at least one selection
- organizes the review logically (beginning, middle, ending)
- uses an objective writer's voice to convince the reader
- makes effective word choices
- varies sentence structure and writes fluent sentences
- edits and proofreads for accurate copy

UNIT 2: Interacting with the Text
WRITING PROMPT

LITERATURE CONNECTION
- *The Breadwinner*
- "The Vietnam War Memorial"
- "Ain't I a Woman?"

Character Sketch

In Unit 2, you read about some special people and thought about what made each of them remarkable. Think about a person you know or someone you have read about who is remarkable. Make some notes about the person's characteristics, what his or her relationship is to you, and why you consider this person remarkable.

Responding Write about the remarkable person you know. In the beginning paragraph, introduce the person and explain what his or her relationship is to you. In the middle part explain and provide examples for why you consider this person remarkable. Be specific about what makes this person special. Include details of things the person has done and what the person is like. In your closing, restate the main reason why the person is someone you want your reader to know.

Evaluation Criteria

The writer responds directly to the prompt and

* develops and supports the ideas with details and examples
* organizes the sketch logically (beginning, middle, ending)
* uses a personal writer's voice that appeals to the reader
* makes effective word choices
* varies sentence structure and writes fluent sentences
* edits and proofreads for accurate copy

UNIT 3: Making Connections
WRITING PROMPT

LITERATURE CONNECTION
- "Thank You, Ma'm"

Personal Narrative
Think about Roger, the young man in "Thank You, Ma'm." He finds himself in trouble, but someone steps in and takes the time to talk to him and give him some direction in his life. Think about a time when someone helped you in a way that really made you think about your choices.

Responding Write a personal narrative, telling about a time when someone stepped in to help you and made a difference in your life. In your narrative, remember to make the sequence of events clear. First explain what the problem was and then what the person did to help you. Remember to include details to help your reader picture what happened. In your closing, draw a final conclusion on why you believe the person helped change your life.

Evaluation Criteria
The writer responds directly to the prompt and

* develops and supports the ideas
* use transition words such as *therefore, because,* and *in conclusion* to connect ideas
* uses a personal writer's voice that connects with the reader
* makes effective word choices
* varies sentence structure and writes fluent sentences
* edits and proofreads for accurate copy

UNIT 4: Exploring Multiple Perspectives
WRITING PROMPT

LITERATURE CONNECTION
- "Hero on the Ball Field"
- *"Henry Aaron Remembers"*
- "jackie robinson"
- "Lady, That's Jackie Robinson!"

Character Sketch

In Unit 4, you explored different perspectives on Jackie Robinson. In the last lesson of the unit, you selected three words that could describe Jackie Robinson, based on what you had read about him. Turn back to page 68 of your *Daybook* and look at the words you wrote. Think about how they reflect your sense of Jackie Robinson.

Responding Write a character sketch of Jackie Robinson. Tell what kind of person you think he was, include details you learned about him, and how people might think of him if he were playing ball today. Be sure to include your own views as you look back at each writer's perspective of this man and his accomplishments. Your closing should leave your reader with a clear understanding of your perspective.

Evaluation Criteria

The writer responds directly to the prompt and

- develops and supports the ideas with details and examples from the selections
- organizes the sketch logically (beginning, middle, ending)
- uses an objective writer's voice that conveys the writer's point of view
- makes effective word choices
- varies sentence structure and writes fluent sentences
- edits and proofreads for accurate copy

UNIT 5: Focusing on Language and Craft

WRITING PROMPT

LITERATURE CONNECTION
- *Locomotion*
- "Mother to Son"
- *Bronx Masquerade*

Persuasive Letter

Think about what you learned about poetry in Unit 5. Imagine that you read an editorial against the study of poetry. The writer argues that students should spend more time on science and math and less time on "nonsense" like poetry. The writer asks, "Will poetry help you think better or more creatively?"

Responding Write a letter to the editor. Make a case for why it is important to study poetry. Use examples from the selections in Unit 5 to give specific details to support your point of view. Sum up your viewpoint in the closing and ask for a specific action. Remember to use the five parts of a letter:

- the heading (the date)
- the greeting (*Dear Editor:*)
- the body (express your point of view)
- the closing (*Sincerely,* or *Yours truly,*)
- your signature

Evaluation Criteria

The writer responds directly to the prompt and

- develops and supports the position with examples from the selections
- organizes the letter logically (states a position, supports the position, wraps up)
- uses an objective, polite voice to convince the reader
- makes effective word choices
- varies sentence structure and writes fluent sentences
- edits and proofreads for accurate copy
- uses a conventional letter format

UNIT 6: Studying an Author
WRITING PROMPT

LITERATURE CONNECTION
- "The Princess of Light"
- *The Invisible Thread*
- *Journey Home*
- *Desert Exile*

Response to Literature
Yoshiko Uchida has said that she wants to give young Asian Americans a sense of their own history, but she also writes for a broader audience with the intention of celebrating "our common humanity." Think of the selections by Yoshiko Uchida that you read in Unit 6 and reflect on how well you think she has succeeded in meeting her goals.

Responding Write a review of one of the works you read by Yoshiko Uchida in Unit 6. Evaluate the piece based on whether the author meets her goals, and give reasons for why or why not you would recommend it to others. Use examples from the selection, including quotations, to support your viewpoint. Your closing should draw your main points together.

Evaluation Criteria
The writer responds directly to the prompt and

- develops and supports the main points, using examples from the selection
- organizes the review logically (beginning, middle, ending)
- uses an objective writer's voice to convince the reader
- avoids wordiness and repetition of words
- varies sentence lengths and beginnings
- edits and proofreads for accurate copy

UNIT 8: Expanding Your Repertoire
WRITING PROMPT

LITERATURE CONNECTION
- *Ice Drift*
- *The Terrorist*

Story Continuation
IIn Unit 8, you read excerpts from two novels, *Ice Drift* by Theodore Taylor and *The Terrorist* by Caroline Cooney. Both endings leave the reader wondering about what could happen next. Choose your favorite excerpt, and imagine the next event.

Responding Choose one of the excerpts that appear in Unit 8 and think of a logical event that could happen next. Then continue the story by adding a new scene. As you plan your writing, consider the following:

* maintain the setting and characters
* use the same narrator's voice
* connect the event to the story

Evaluation Criteria
The writer responds directly to the prompt and

* develops and connects the ideas to the story
* uses sequence words such as next, meanwhile, during, or after to show the order of events
* uses the narrator's voice
* uses synonyms and pronouns to avoid repeating words
* varies sentence lengths and beginnings
* edits and proofreads for accurate copy

UNIT 9: Interacting with the Text
WRITING PROMPT

LITERATURE CONNECTION
- *Bone*
- *The Borden Tragedy*
- "Annabel Lee"

Persuasive Letter
You have learned new strategies to read visual texts. You studied the style and design techniques of graphic novels and learned how the authors use dialogue, narration, and sound. You also learned that the essential reading and writing strategies you have been studying apply as well to graphic novels.

Responding Write to the School Book Purchasing Committee in favor of adding graphic novels in the school library. In a persuasive letter, use your best arguments to persuade the committee that graphic novels help students become better readers and writers. Use examples from the graphic novels that you've explored in Unit 9. Remember to use the five parts of a letter:

- the heading (the date)
- the greeting (*Dear Committee:*)
- the body (your argument supported by examples)
- the closing (*Sincerely,* or *Yours truly,*)
- your signature

Evaluation Criteria
The writer responds directly to the prompt and

- develops and supports the argument with examples from the selections
- organizes the letter logically (beginning, middle, ending)
- uses an objective, polite voice to convince the reader
- choose words that are appropriate for the audience and purpose
- varies sentence structure and writes fluent sentences
- edits and proofreads for accurate copy

UNIT 10: Making Connections
WRITING PROMPT

LITERATURE CONNECTION
- *America's Great Disasters*
- *Three Fearful Days*
- *Dragonwings*
- "Safety Tips for Earthquakes"

Expository Essay

In Unit 10, you read about the 1906 San Francisco earthquake. If you were going to tell someone else about what happened, what would be the main points you would want to make? What details would you include?

Responding Write an expository essay about the earthquake. Write a strong beginning that focuses on the big picture of what happened. In the middle part, include details to help the reader picture the disaster and aftermath, using the photographs, information, and eye witness accounts in Unit 10. Conclude with a powerful image or prediction for your reader. Be sure to give your essay a title.

Evaluation Criteria

The writer responds directly to the prompt and

- develops and supports the ideas with details from the selections
- catches the reader's attention with a strong beginning
- uses a knowledgeable voice to convey information
- makes effective word choices
- varies sentence structure and writes fluent sentences
- edits and proofreads for accurate copy
- titles the essay

UNIT 11: Exploring Multiple Perspectives
WRITING PROMPT

LITERATURE CONNECTION
- "Are Plastic Bags Harming the Environment"
- "The Call of the Mall"
- "To Drill or Not to Drill"
- *Harvest for Hope: A Guide to Mindful Eating*
- "Save Your Energy"

Expository Essay
In Unit 12, you read about the danger of many of our consumer habits. These habits are using up our natural resources, and we're creating more trash than we know what to do with. We are all part of the problem, and we all must be part of the solution.

Responding Think of a consumer-related problem that threatens our environment. You can draw on the problems and proposed solutions discussed in the selections in Unit 12, but you may also think of your own. Write an essay in which you state the problem clearly. Support your position about the problem. Then offer one or more solutions that can help reduce or eliminate the problem. Your conclusion should make a call for an action based on your solution.

Evaluation Criteria
The writer responds directly to the prompt and

- states the problem clearly and supports the solution(s)
- organizes the essay logically (beginning, middle, ending)
- uses a confident voice that persuades the reader to take action
- makes effective word choices
- varies sentence structure and writes fluent sentences
- edits and proofreads for accurate copy

UNIT 12: Focusing on Language and Craft

WRITING PROMPT

LITERATURE CONNECTION
- *A History of Reading*

Descriptive Essay

Alberto Manguel's book *A History of Reading* talks about different ways in which people "read" the world. Reading isn't always about what's on the printed page. Think of the ways we use our "reading skills" to study the people we see, the places we visit, and even the things we hear.

Responding Write a description of a place you've visited. Think about what it looks like, sounds like, feels like, and smells like. Use sensory language and vivid imagery in your description to help create a clear picture of the place for your reader. Your conclusion should leave your reader with a lasting impression.

Evaluation Criteria

The writer responds directly to the prompt and

- develops and supports the ideas with sensory details
- organizes the essay logically (beginning, middle, ending)
- uses a knowledgeable voice to describe a real place
- chooses vivid verbs and specific nouns
- writes sentences that flow and are easy to read aloud
- edits and proofreads for accurate copy

UNIT 13: Studying an Author
WRITING PROMPT

LITERATURE CONNECTION
- *The Maze*
- *Jason's Gold*
- *Kokopelli's Flute*
- *Downriver*
- *Bearstone*

Response to Literature
Think about which one of the excerpts from the books by Will Hobbs is your favorite. What was it about the excerpt that caught your attention and held your interest? What connections did you make? How did your favorite selection compare with the others?

Responding Write a response to your favorite excerpt that explains to a classmate why you want to read the whole book. Be sure to mention the genre (fantasy, historical fiction, or realistic fiction) and whether that contributes to why you like it. Support your choice with specific details, dialogue, and descriptions from the excerpt. Your conclusion should convince the reader to read the book.

Evaluation Criteria
The writer responds directly to the prompt and

* develops and supports the choice with details from the excerpts
* concludes the essay with a convincing statement
* uses a confident voice to convince the reader
* makes effective word choices
* varies sentence lengths and beginnings
* edits and proofreads for accurate copy

OVERVIEW OF ASSESSMENTS

The *Daybook* assessments are designed to help you evaluate students' progress toward understanding what they read. The assessments include a Pretest, four Reading Strategy Assessments, and a Posttest, as described below. Each assessment includes one or two passages that were created for the assessment and are based on the types of selections found in the *Daybook*.

PRETEST

The Pretest has one long and two short, paired literature selections. This test is designed to be administered at the beginning of the school year. Because each of the sixteen questions covers a particular reading strategy, the test can help you determine students' beginning levels and indicate what you might need to emphasize in your teaching. The test also provides a baseline for measuring students' progress through the *Daybook*.

READING STRATEGY ASSESSMENTS

These assessments can help you monitor students' progress and inform your teaching plans for using the *Daybook*. Each assessment requires students to apply a particular reading strategy to a selection of literature. Units not listed below are assessed only through the more appropriate method of the writing prompts (see page 225). The following list shows the strategy focus of each assessment and suggests when to administer the assessment.

Assessment	To be administered after . . .
1. Interacting with the Text	Unit 2 or Unit 9
2. Making Connections	Unit 3 or Unit 10
3. Exploring Multiple Perspectives	Unit 4 or Unit 11
4. Focusing on Language and Craft	Unit 5 or Unit 12

Note: If you administer the assessment after completing the first unit and students do not score well, you may want to administer the assessment again after the second unit of instruction for the same strategy.

ASSESSMENTS 241

POSTTEST

The Posttest contains the same types of selections and the same number of questions as the Pretest and measures the same strategies. It should be administered at the completion of the *Daybook* to help determine how much progress students have made.

DIRECTIONS FOR ADMINISTERING ASSESSMENTS

To administer, distribute copies of the test pages to each student. Have students write their name at the top of each page. Then have students read the selections and answer the questions. For multiple-choice questions, students should choose the best answer to each question and circle the letter of the answer. For written-response questions, students should write their answers in complete sentences on the writing lines provided on the test page.

DIRECTIONS FOR SCORING ASSESSMENTS

All multiple-choice items are worth 1 point each; written-response questions are worth 2 points each. (A partially correct written response may be awarded 1 point.) Use a copy of the Scoring Chart on page 244 to record students' scores.

Pretest & Posttest—Add the total number of points earned and write the result under "Points" on the Scoring Chart for each test. To find the "Percent," multiply the total points × 5. (For example, 15 points × 5 = 75%).

Reading Strategy Assessments—Add the total number of points earned and write the result under "Points" on the Scoring Chart for each assessment. To find the "Percent," multiply the total points × 10. (For example, 7 points × 10 = 70%).

Students should score at least 70% correct on each test. For students who score 70% or lower, you may want to analyze the test responses more closely and focus instruction on particular strategies.

PRETEST ANSWER KEY

Multiple Choice (1 point each)

Item	Answer	Reading Strategy
1	C	Making Connections: Setting
2	A	Making Connections: Point of View
3	D	Interacting with the Text: Making Inferences
4	A	Focusing on Language and Craft: Simile and Metaphor
5	B	Interacting with the Text: Visualizing
6	D	Making Connections: Theme

Written Responses (2 points each)

7	Answers vary.	Acceptable responses will describe Brendan's character by naming two character traits that may be plausibly inferred from the text and will support each trait with evidence from the story. (Making Connections: Character)
8	Answers vary.	Acceptable responses will make a prediction about Nathaniel and Hank's friendship and will support the prediction with at least one detail from the story. (Interacting with the Text: Making Predictions)

Multiple Choice (1 point each)

Item	Answer	Reading Strategy
9	B	Exploring Multiple Perspectives: Inside Perspective
10	B	Focusing on Language and Craft: Simile and Metaphor
11	A	Exploring Multiple Perspectives: Outside Perspective
12	D	Focusing on Language and Craft: Simile and Metaphor
13	C	Exploring Multiple Perspectives: Outside Perspective
14	A	Interacting with the Text: Summarizing

Written Responses (2 points each)

15	Answers vary.	Acceptable responses will give two reasons why, according to the author of the passage, teaching ballet was a good career. (Exploring Multiple Perspectives: Personal Account)
16	Answers vary.	Answers will vary. An acceptable response will mention two details to support the idea that a ballet career is unlike for most girls. (Exploring Multiple Perspectives: Outside Perspective)

ANSWER KEY 243

READING STRATEGY ASSESSMENTS ANSWER KEY

ASSESSMENT 1   Interacting with the Text

Answers: 1–A   2–C   3–B   4–C   5–D   6–B   (1 point each)

Written responses   (2 points each)

7   **Answers vary.**   Acceptable responses will indicate that Michael is in a hospital and the person speaking to him is a doctor or nurse.

8   **Answers vary.**   Acceptable responses will make a prediction about what Mark will do (for example, he will ask someone to call 911 and then try to help anyone in the cars who is injured) and will explain why the prediction is reasonable.

ASSESSMENT 2   Making Connections

Answers: 1–D   2–B   3–A   4–A   5–C   6–B   (1 point each)

Written responses   (2 points each)

7   **Answers vary.**   Acceptable responses will describe two or more relevant facts from the story. Examples: Uncle Ike had not been around for 10 days. No one at the university had seen him for weeks. His backpacking gear was at his house. His basement lab was messy, as if he'd left suddenly.

8   **Answers vary.**   Acceptable responses will identify a character trait of Uncle Ike's (such as his sense of responsibility) that is revealed at the end of the story and will give evidence to support the character trait.

ASSESSMENT 3   Exploring Multiple Perspectives

Answers: 1–B   2–D   3–A   4–D   5–C   6–B   (1 point each)

Written responses   (2 points each)

7   **Answers vary.**   Acceptable responses will describe the author's attitude toward President Roosevelt, as expressed in the passage. Example: The author seems to feel that Roosevelt was positive and reassuring, and he acted on his promises to rebuild the nation.

8   **Answers vary.**   Acceptable responses will explain the lesson about sacrifice and doing without that Suzanne learned from her grandfather and will tell how it relates to her life and her concern about her new sneakers.

ASSESSMENT 4   Focusing on Language and Craft

Answers: 1–B   2–D   3–C   4–D   5–B   6–A   (1 point each)

Written responses   (2 points each)

7   **Answers vary.**   Acceptable responses will explain the meaning of the title "The Barrier," which refers to a difference in race or color.

8   **Answers vary.**   Acceptable responses will compare the speakers of the two poems and suggest that they both see something they want but cannot have, both are discouraged, and both know that prejudice keeps them from pursuing their goals.

POSTTEST ANSWER KEY

Multiple Choice (1 point each)

Item	Answer	Reading Strategy
1	D	Making Connections: Setting
2	A	Making Connections: Point of View
3	C	Focusing on Language and Craft: Simile and Metaphor
4	B	Interacting with the Text: Making Inferences
5	C	Interacting with the Text: Visualizing
6	A	Making Connections: Theme

Written Responses (2 points each)

7 **Answers vary.** Acceptable responses will restate or paraphrase Pam's description of Dominic and explain why this description is accurate. (Making Connections: Character)

8 **Answers vary.** Acceptable responses will make a plausible prediction in two sentences of what might happen next in the story. (Interacting with Text: Making Predictions)

Multiple Choice (1 point each)

Item	Answer	Reading Strategy
9	A	Exploring Multiple Perspectives: Outside Perspective
10	C	Focusing on Language and Craft: Simile and Metaphor
11	B	Interacting with the Text: Summarizing
12	C	Exploring Multiple Perspectives: Inside Perspective
13	A	Focusing on Language and Craft: Simile and Metaphor
14	D	Exploring Multiple Perspectives: Problem and Solution

Written Responses (2 points each)

15 **Answers vary.** Acceptable responses will answer yes and will include two details that support the claim that middle and high school students eat too many unhealthy snacks. (Exploring Multiple Perspectives: Outside Perspective)

16 **Answers vary.** An acceptable response will accurately paraphrase the author's solution and explain why the author favors the solution. (Exploring Multiple Perspectives: Problem and Solution)

READING ASSESSMENTS SCORING CHART

Daybook 7

CLASS _____

TEACHER _____

Student Name	Pretest			Assess 1		Assess 2		Assess 3		Assess 4		Posttest	
	Date	Points	%		%		%		%		%		%

DIRECTIONS: Read this passage about what happens when three students try to work together. Then answer questions 1–8.

When Three's a Crowd

In the beginning, the skit project sounded great. Mr. Johnson explained that we would choose an issue we had studied in our American history class and develop a ten-minute skit around it. "You can work in groups of two or more. But let's get this straight right from the start: there will be no freeloading on this assignment!" warned Mr. Johnson. "I expect each member of the group to do an equal portion of the work."

As Mr. Johnson spoke, I turned around and looked at Hank. He smiled and nodded his head, sealing the agreement that he and I would work together. A minute later, when Mr. Johnson gave us a chance to form our groups, Hank and I pushed our desks together and started planning.

"So, Nathaniel, what issue should we do?" Hank asked. I already knew he'd leave the decision to me, because I'm a total history buff and he's not. But I was also confident that Hank would really sink his teeth into whatever topic I picked, and we'd come up with a fantastic skit.

I didn't hesitate. "How about the way the Civil War tore some families apart? You know, one son joins the Union army, and the other joins the Confederate army."

"Yeah, that would definitely make an awesome skit, Nathaniel," said Hank. "And it would be perfect for the two of us. You would be one brother, and I'd be the other."

As Hank spoke, I noticed that Brendan was headed our way, with a self-satisfied expression on his face. "Whoa, Hank and Nathaniel, the makings of one dynamite group. And the only missing ingredient is . . . ME!"

With my back to Brendan, I rolled my eyes at Hank, but he didn't take the hint. I half expected he wouldn't. Hank and Brendan had gotten friendly since they both made varsity basketball. Hank had been my best friend since preschool, but he didn't include me when he hung out with Brendan—and that was fine with me. I considered Brendan a jock, and he obviously put me in the nerdy geek department. I had to give Hank credit, though; he did an impressive job of juggling friendships with two really different guys.

But with the three of us working together, the juggling got trickier, because Brendan and I clashed immediately. When he heard what topic I'd selected, Brendan announced that he and Hank should play the brothers, and I would be the boys' father. As soon as Hank went along with the suggestion, I was outvoted—and felt completely betrayed. My resentment was fueled by the fact that their basketball schedule made it difficult to plan the after-school meetings we needed to write and rehearse the script.

When the meetings got underway, things went from bad to horrible. While I hadn't really expected Brendan to contribute much to writing the script, Hank's dismal effort was a huge disappointment. He never took the skit seriously. Instead he kept allowing Brendan to distract him with jokes, gossip, and horseplay.

I finally reached my limit on the day before the performance. Hank, Brendan, and I had agreed to memorize our lines on our own and then meet at Hank's house for a rehearsal. And while I had my lines down cold, it became obvious to me as soon as we did our first run-through that Hank and Brendan had never practiced. With all the coolness I could muster, I zipped my script into my backpack and headed for the door. "Since I can't memorize your lines for you, I'm going to take off," I announced. Walking home, I felt like a animal just freed from a cage.

My abrupt departure must have lit a roaring fire under Hank and Brendan because our skit performance the next day was amazing. Each of us delivered our lines flawlessly, as if we had spent days rehearsing. As the audience applauded loudly, I glanced at over at Hank, who was smiling at me with a mixture of satisfaction and embarrassment. I thought about smiling back, but instead I looked away.

Later, in the cafeteria, I found Hank and sat down with him. I had made up my mind to congratulate him when Brendan spotted us and walked over. Looking straight at me, Brendan said, "Hey, Geek, our skit rocked! Everyone says Hank and I really know how to act." Turning to face Hank, he added, "I think maybe we deserve some kind of award!"

It was one of those moments when you're desperate for the perfect comeback to put the guy in his place, but your mind's a total blank. Fortunately, Hank came through. "Yeah, like, if there's one for freeloading," he told Brendan, "we'd win hands down." ❖

✤ QUESTIONS 1–6: Circle the letter of the best answer to each question.

1. **What is the setting at the beginning of the story?**
   A the cafeteria
   B Brendan's house
   C Mr. Johnson's classroom
   D Hank's house

2. **This story is told from which narrative point of view?**
   A first-person narrator
   B second-person narrator
   C limited third-person narrator
   D omniscient third-person narrator

3. Look at the illustration and read the text in the word balloon. Which of these best describes the character's way of speaking?
   A hushed and soothing
   B annoyed and whiny
   C polite and hesitant
   D loud and enthusiastic

4. In the story, Nathaniel says, "Walking home, I felt like an animal just released from a cage." The simile is a way of saying that he felt —
   A relieved to get away from Brendan and Hank.
   B ashamed of the way he'd behaved at the rehearsal.
   C confused about what he should do next.
   D worried that Brendan and Hank might look for him.

5. When Brendan approached Hank and Nathaniel in the cafeteria after the skit, the expression on his face was most likely —
   A a look of concern.
   B a huge grin.
   C an embarrassed smirk.
   D a look of irritation.

6. What is the main message of this story?
   A Practice does not always make perfect.
   B It's not possible for work to be fun.
   C Different people have different talents.
   D It's wrong to let someone do your work for you.

❋ QUESTIONS 7 and 8: Write your answers on the lines.

7. Describe Brendan's character. Name two of his main character traits and give evidence from the story for each trait you list.

8. Do you think Nathaniel and Hank will remain friends? Make a prediction and cite evidence from the story that supports your prediction.

DIRECTIONS: Read these two passages about ballet dancers. Then answer questions 9–16.

PASSAGE 1

Just a Dream

The Fates were surely playing a practical joke the day they put my parts together. On the one hand, they gave me a short, sturdy body and not an ounce of grace. On the other hand, they gave me a heart yearning to dance. I wanted to be a ballerina. But like a fish that wants to fly, I was a born mismatch.

Along with my lack of physical gifts, I had a father who kept tight hold of every penny he earned. Though we were always well fed and adequately clothed, we were never allowed any "extras." For my three brothers, who loved baseball, this meant sharing a single bat and glove. For me, this meant no possibility of ballet lessons.

My mother had always seemed to back my father's thriftiness, so I never imagined she understood my longing to dance. Then just a month after my high school graduation, my father died unexpectedly. After his funeral, my mother stunned me by giving me three hundred dollars—a lot of money at the time. She urged me to make my dance dream come true.

Within weeks, I'd moved to New York City, rented a tiny flat, and found a job as a waitress. Every day I worked the breakfast and lunch shifts, finishing up just in time to take a ballet class at Carnegie Hall. It was a beginners' class filled with older women looking for a new hobby or a way to get in shape. My ballet teacher, Madame Rochas, who'd enjoyed a brief career as a ballerina before her marriage, regarded me as a curiosity. After my fourth lesson, she asked me to stay after class. "Tell me, Nina," she began when the others had left. "What is it you expect to get from your lessons?"

Without knowing how ridiculous I sounded, I assured Madame Rochas I was determined to become a ballerina. Her response crushed me. "Nina, you must be realistic. A ballerina needs long limbs and flexible muscles, and she must start training as a young child. Your shape and your age are against you." When her words registered, Madame Rochas gently touched my hand and said, "But if you love the ballet, there are other careers for you. You can make the dances. You can teach the dancers. If doing these things would satisfy you, stay in New York. Take classes, watch classes, and go to the ballet whenever you can."

As devastating as it was to hear, the advice Madame Rochas gave me that day became my road map. I spent the next three years in New York. By the time I left and returned to my hometown, I was ready to open my own ballet school and share my love of dance with other dreamers. The thirty years I've spent as a teacher have given me tremendous satisfaction, and I am proud of the excellent reputation I've earned. But even now, I cannot resist the temptation to dream about the ballerina I could have become if the Fates weren't such practical jokers. ❖

PASSAGE 2

A Demanding Career

Many girls dream of becoming a famous ballerina. This is easy to understand, since ballerinas appear to live glamorous lives. They wear gorgeous costumes and perform dazzling steps to beautiful music. Yet, for a variety of reasons, most girls who dream of a ballet career never reach the stage.

Perhaps the biggest reason is that becoming an accomplished dancer requires many years of training. By the age of ten, any future ballerina must be willing to take at least three dance classes each week, even in summer. Not surprisingly, most young girls lack the discipline to follow such a strict routine. Others simply have too many other interests they want to pursue. Either way, girls who find the demands of ballet training too time-consuming are usually happy to give up the dream.

Many of these girls abandon hope reluctantly after they realize that no amount of training will lead to a ballet career. Why not? Although ballet is beautiful to watch, it is a grueling athletic activity. It requires a combination of natural abilities: strength, speed, and flexibility. Not every aspiring dancer has such abilities. Musicality, or the ability to move gracefully to music, is another trait every would-be dancer must have. Also, in the ballet world, there is a strong bias toward dancers who have long legs and arms, a slender neck, and highly-arched feet. No matter how talented, dancers without these natural qualities are likely to be passed over in competition.

There are still other roadblocks in the way. The hardest truth dancers must face is the shortage of jobs. There just aren't enough ballet companies around to employ the talented dancers who want to join them. Also, dancers lucky enough to join these companies know their careers will be short. Because ballet is so physically demanding, most dancers retire by at least age 40. At that point, they must be ready to find another career to fill out their working years.

A ballet career is far beyond the reach of most young dancers, and the best ballet teachers let their students know this right from the start. As a hobby or a form of exercise, however, just about anyone can benefit from and enjoy ballet.

QUESTIONS 9–14: Circle the letter of the best answer to each question.

9. In Passage 1, the author focuses primarily on which of these?
   A presenting facts about the ballet world
   B telling the story of her life
   C giving her opinions of ballet dancers
   D describing someone she knows

10. In Passage 1, the author states that she was *like a fish that wants to fly* in order to —
    A make the reader laugh.
    B show how hopeless her dream was.
    C describe her appearance.
    D compare swimming and flying.

11. According to Madame Rochas, what prevented the author of Passage 1 from becoming a dancer?
    A She was too old to begin ballet training.
    B She did not have enough self-discipline.
    C She did not move in a musical way.
    D She did not take enough ballet lessons.

12. Which idea from Passage 1 is a *metaphor*?
    A I had a father who kept tight hold of every penny he earned.
    B Every day I worked the breakfast and lunch shifts.
    C My ballet teacher regarded me as a curiosity.
    D The advice Madame Rochas gave me became my road map.

13. Passage 2 is best described as what kind of writing?
    A a retired dancer's commentary on her career
    B a young ballet student's personal account of her experiences
    C an outsider's view of what it takes to become a ballerina
    D the biography of a ballerina

14. Which is the best summary of Passage 2?
    A A girl who wants to become a ballerina must be willing to spend years training for this career. She must have certain abilities and physical gifts. However, the shortage of jobs makes a ballet career unlikely for most girls.
    B Ballet seems like a glamorous career, so many girls dream of becoming a ballerina. Most girls happily give up the dream after a while. And by the age of 40, even successful dancers must look for other work.
    C The most successful ballerinas have long, flexible limbs; highly-arched feet; and the ability to move gracefully. Most ballet students take classes to get exercise and never hope to become ballerinas.
    D Girls who dream of becoming a ballerina spend years taking dance classes. When they become ballerinas, they wear gorgeous costumes and perform dazzling steps. They make a grueling physical activity look beautiful.

QUESTIONS 15 and 16: Write your answers on the lines.

15. Do you think teaching ballet was a good career alternative for the author of Passage 1? Give two reasons for your answer.

16. Imagine you know a young girl who dreams of becoming a ballerina. Which details from Passage 2 would you use to convince the girl that her dream will probably not come true? List two convincing details from Passage 2.

READING STRATEGY ASSESSMENT 1

INTERACTING WITH THE TEXT

DIRECTIONS: Read this passage about something that happened during a school trip. Then answer questions 1–8.

Accidental Friends

For 150 eighth-grade students and their teachers from Takoma Park Middle School in Maryland, the pool party was meant to be just a bit of icing on the cake. The main events of their week-long field trip to Florida were visits to the Kennedy Space Center and an amusement park. But on the third day of the trip, the party at the hotel pool took a dramatic turn that two students will never forget.

Michael Sobalvarro, age 14 and a nonswimmer, planned to stay in the shallow end of the pool. But without realizing it, he drifted over to the place where the pool floor dropped off in a steep incline. Suddenly, Michael found himself in water over his head, and he felt himself sinking below the surface. Trying to keep his cool, Michael stayed still until he floated back to the surface. But when he yelled for help, his lungs filled with water and he sank again. Sure he was about to drown, Michael thought about his parents. He thought of all they'd done for him and of their great hopes for his future. Then, at the bottom of the pool, Michael blacked out.

Meanwhile, Michael's 13-year-old classmate, Mark Berry, was swimming in the deep end. A strong swimmer who had recently earned a Boy Scout merit badge in lifesaving, Mark spotted something dark at the bottom of the pool. Realizing it was Michael, Mark shouted for someone to call 911. Then he swam down to Michael, grabbed his shoulders, and pulled him to the edge of the pool. There, another student lifted Michael's unconscious body from the water, and a teacher began administering CPR. Michael came around quickly, spitting out the water he had swallowed.

After a day spent resting, Michael was ready to join his classmates. When he saw Mark for the first time since the accident, Michael hugged him and thanked him for saving his life. Mark downplayed the importance of his quick and cool-headed actions, saying that anyone else in his place would have done the same thing.

Perhaps that's true, but the accident formed a bond between the boys. They weren't really close friends before the event, but they now shake hands or stop to talk when they see each other at school. The accident affected the boys in other ways, too. Michael immediately enrolled in swimming lessons, and Mark made plans to put the experience to good use by taking a summer job as a lifeguard.

✷ **QUESTIONS 1–6:** Circle the letter of the best answer to each question.

1. Which of these questions is answered in the text?
   A Which two Takoma Park students will never forget the pool party?
   B Did the hotel swimming pool have a lifeguard?
   C How deep was the deep end of the swimming pool?
   D What did the Takoma Park students do at the Kennedy Space Center?

2. Which of these is the best summary statement of the second paragraph?
   A Michael Sobalvarro thought he was drowning, and he thought about his parents.
   B Michael Sobalvarro tried to stay calm, but then he yelled for help, taking water into his lungs.
   C Michael Sobalvarro, who couldn't swim, drifted into water over his head.
   D Michael Solbalvarro swallowed water and blacked out.

3. Visualize the moment when Mark comes to Michael's rescue. Based on the information in the passage, which of these best describes Michael's appearance?
   A His face looks terrified as he grips Mark's shoulder.
   B His eyes are closed and his body is limp.
   C He is crying and reaching out toward Mark.
   D He looks dazed as Mark pulls him to the edge of the pool.

4. Which detail about the boys is most important to include in a longer summary of the passage?
   A Mark is older than Michael.
   B Mark made plans to work as a lifeguard.
   C The accident formed a bond between Mark and Michael.
   D Michael signed up for swimming lessons.

5. Based on the information in the passage, you can predict that Michael will —
   A take another trip to Florida.
   B join the Boy Scouts.
   C save someone's life someday.
   D become a better swimmer.

✳ Use these illustrations to answer questions 6 and 7.

6. Look at the second picture. Based on the information in the passage, which reply fits best in Mark's word balloon.

   A BOY, ARE YOU LUCKY I TOOK LIFESAVING!
   B IT'S NO BIG DEAL. I'M GLAD YOU'RE OKAY.
   C NEXT TIME, BE SURE TO STAY IN THE SHALLOW END.
   D IT FEELS KIND OF COOL TO BE A HERO.

✳ **QUESTIONS 7 and 8:** Write your answers on the lines.

7. Tell what is happening in the first picture. Where is Michael, and who is speaking to him?

8. Suppose Mark Berry is riding down the street on a bicycle when he witnesses an accident involving two cars. What will Mark most likely do? Predict what he will do and tell why you think so.

READING STRATEGY ASSESSMENT 1

READING STRATEGY ASSESSMENT 2

MAKING CONNECTIONS

DIRECTIONS: Read this passage about a very unusual event. Then answer questions 1–8.

Invisible Trouble

At first Uncle Ike's disappearance didn't concern us. It was summertime, after all, and he'd probably gone backpacking in the canyons. Uncle Ike often did this when he was starting a new project and needed some uninterrupted quiet time to think. A science professor and a bachelor, Uncle Ike seldom thought to tell anyone where he was going or when he might return.

Still, after weeks with no word from Uncle Ike, Mom got worried. She stopped by his office at the university, but no one there had seen him. Then she went to Uncle Ike's house and found his backpacking gear in his closet. Mom also noticed that his basement laboratory was a mess, as if he had suddenly left in the middle of an experiment.

Back at our house, Mom leafed though our photo album. "I don't know what else to do," she explained as she removed a recent photo of her brother from the album and slipped it into her purse. "I'm going to the police station to report that Uncle Ike is a missing person."

After Mom left, the phone rang. I answered it and heard, "Hey, Lucy, Uncle Ike here."

"Uncle Ike!" I yelled. "Where are you? Mom was just at your house looking for you!"

"I must have just missed her. I was taking a walk around the block, trying to make a decision," Uncle Ike explained. "And now, I need a little assistance from you or your mom."

"Mom's not here, She went to fill out a missing person report on you!" I exclaimed.

"I was afraid of that," muttered Uncle Ike. "Look, I need you to come to my house and meet me downstairs in my lab. I'll explain my predicament when you get here."

Five minutes later, I jumped off my bike, hurried into Uncle Ike's house, and scrambled downstairs. Straining to see in the dimness of the basement, I yanked on a cord that was dangling from an overhead light. The light illuminated Uncle Ike's messy lab table, but I couldn't see him anywhere. Then, eerily, a plastic spray bottle levitated off the table and drifted toward me. I tried to scream, but my utter terror prevented me from making a sound.

"Don't be alarmed, Lucy, I can explain." Uncle Ike's reassuring voice was coming from the direction of the spray bottle, which had stopped drifting and now hung suspended in the air. "I got a little ahead of myself with one of my experiments. I've been trying for years to develop an invisibility spray. As you can see—or rather, as you can't see—I finally succeeded."

I stepped toward the floating spray bottle and passed my hand through the empty space around it. Then the bottle moved closer to me and into my open hand.

"Take the bottle, Lucy," Uncle Ike's voice instructed me gently. "It's visibility spray, the antidote to my invisibility. I've worked around the clock for the last ten weeks to develop it. Now, please, before your poor mother gets here with the police detectives, spray me from head to toe."

Fascinated, I did as he said, pumping the spray bottle vigorously and filling the air with a fine mist. Gradually, the outlines and then the details of Uncle Ike's form materialized. He was rotating around slowly to make sure I didn't miss a single spot. By the time Uncle Ike was completely visible again, not a drop of the spray was left; I had emptied the bottle.

After giving me a hug of gratitude, Uncle Ike immediately grabbed a different spray bottle and opened his lab notebook to two note-covered pages. He aimed the bottle and started spraying. Before my eyes, the notes vanished. Then Uncle Ike opened the bottle and poured the rest of its contents down the sink. Heaving a sigh of relief, he exclaimed, "No more sprays, no more notes, no more invisibility experiments. I've learned my lesson!"

"But Uncle Ike, invisibility is awesome. It's like a super power!" I protested. "Why destroy what you've discovered? Your spray could make you a billionaire!"

"That's what I thought too, at first," Uncle Ike explained. "But then I thought about how dishonest people might use invisibility. Cheating, stealing, spying—with invisibility, the possibilities are endless! I'd never forgive myself if I unleashed such a terrible power on the world. I'll gladly pass on becoming a billionaire."

At first, I didn't think Uncle Ike was making sense. But he's a smart guy, so I decided to keep an open mind. Later, when I read a newspaper story about some bad guy's evil deed, I imagined how much worse things might have been if that guy had used invisibility. Uncle Ike had definitely made the right choice.

QUESTIONS 1-6: Circle the letter of the best answer to each question.

1. Where do most of the events involving Lucy take place?
   - **A** in Uncle Ike's office
   - **B** at Lucy and Mom's house
   - **C** at the police station
   - **D** in Uncle Ike's house

2. What can you tell about Mom in this story?
   - **A** She tends to worry needlessly.
   - **B** She cares a lot about her brother Ike.
   - **C** She gives Lucy too much responsibility.
   - **D** She is often moody and unhappy.

3. This story is told from which narrative point of view?
   - **A** first person
   - **B** second person
   - **C** limited third person
   - **D** omniscient third person

4. What did Uncle Ike do with his lab notes?
   - A He destroyed them with invisibility spray.
   - B He let Lucy read them.
   - C He washed them down the drain.
   - D He turned them over to the police.

5. How did Lucy feel at first when Uncle Ike announced his decision to her?
   - A amused and accepting
   - B afraid and suspicious
   - C disappointed and confused
   - D relieved and happy

6. Which sentence best expresses the theme of this story?
   - A Doing the right thing is always an easy choice.
   - B Knowledge must be used wisely.
   - C Wealth and intelligence usually go together.
   - D Smart people often use bad judgment.

QUESTIONS 7 and 8: Write your answers on the lines.

7. Describe two facts in the story that led Mom to report Uncle Ike's disappearance to the police.

8. Describe a character trait of Uncle Ike's that is revealed at the end of the story. Give evidence from the story to support the trait you describe.

READING STRATEGY ASSESSMENT 3

EXPLORING MULTIPLE PERSPECTIVES

DIRECTIONS: Read these two passages about the Great Depression, a difficult time in United States history. Then answer questions 1–8.

PASSAGE 1

Years of Loss and Fear

The Great Depression of the 1930s may be long gone, but it is an era of American history that will never be forgotten. Just three months before the decade began, a combination of factors threw the economy off balance. All across the country, like tumbling dominoes, thousands of businesses and farms went bankrupt and banks failed. People who had kept their money in banks lost their savings. Millions lost their jobs until, by 1932, one of every four households had no wage earner. Those hit hardest by the disaster also lost their homes. Forced onto the streets, many homeless families fell apart. As a result, countless children were left to fend for themselves, begging for pennies, food, or shelter.

In 1932, President Herbert Hoover faced reelection. He also faced the fear and resentment of millions of impoverished Americans. Hoover could point to little he had done to relieve their suffering. However, his opponent, Franklin Roosevelt, promised to rebuild the country's ruined economy. Predictably, Roosevelt defeated Hoover. In a stirring inaugural speech, Roosevelt tried to reassure Americans that better days lay ahead. "The only thing we have to fear," he declared, "is fear itself."

Roosevelt's New Deal projects created jobs for the unemployed. At the same time, these projects helped improve living conditions all over the United States. Workers built dams, bridges, and hospitals. They replanted forests and dug wells. They created parks, hiking trails, and wildlife refuges.

Recovering from the Great Depression took a decade. By 1942, the United States was pulling out of its long and difficult slump. Americans were grateful to put the years of loss and fear behind them, but they would never forget the Great Depression. ✤

PASSAGE 2

An Unforgettable Lesson

I'll never forget the day Dad brought me to Grandpa's house on the way home from the shoe store. I was making a fuss about my new sneakers because Dad had refused to buy the ones I wanted, insisting instead on a cheaper pair. Hearing what the problem was, Grandfather suggested a walk. "We'll break in those shoes and calm down a bit," he explained gently.

As we walked, Grandpa recalled his childhood, growing up in the 1920s in a comfortable home, the oldest of five children. His father owned a car dealership, and his mother ran her busy household with a great sense of fun. "But then," Grandpa said, "came the Great Depression."

His parents felt the effects immediately, losing their entire savings when the local bank failed. The same thing happened to many of their neighbors and friends, and these losses doomed his father's business. "After all, broke people don't buy new cars," Grandpa pointed out with a bitter laugh." And when the family's savings vanished, so did the sense of fun in his house. His father strung together an endless series of odd jobs—shoveling snow in the winter, cleaning sidewalks in the summer—to bring in a few dollars every week. His mother took in laundry and sewing. But with five growing children, there was never enough. Grandfather watched helplessly as the constant worry and struggle broke his parents' spirits.

One night in 1933, when Grandfather was 14, he left his parents a goodbye letter and sneaked out of the house. "I wasn't running away, Suzanne," he insisted as we walked. "I wanted to stay more than anything, but I was another mouth to feed. It was time to take care of myself."

Not knowing where to go, Grandpa headed to the railroad station. When a freight train started to roll out, he hopped aboard an open boxcar. "I was so frightened and lonely," Grandpa explained. Eventually, though, he fell asleep on the train. He woke early the next morning as the train pulled into a station near Fort Wayne, Indiana. It was the start of a dreary new life. Grandpa spent the next three years on the move, doing odd jobs when he could find them. He slept mostly outside in the open, usually alone, or sometimes in makeshift camps with other homeless folks.

Finally, Grandpa got a break when he stopped at a relief society for a free meal. The director befriended him and arranged for him to join the Civilian Conservation Corps, one of Roosevelt's New Deal programs. Soon he was working on a highway construction crew. "I earned $30 a month," Grandpa said proudly. "I kept just $5 and sent the rest to my family."

Grandpa and I had reached the corner, a good place to turn around and head back to his house. Reaching down to muss my hair, he winked and said, "That was a difficult way to learn about sacrifice and going without, but it was an unforgettable lesson."

No more so than the lesson Grandpa taught me that day. ❖

❋ QUESTIONS 1–6: Circle the letter of the best answer to each question.

1. **Passage 1 is best described as what kind of writing?**
   - A a poetic portrait
   - B an outsider's account
   - C a biography
   - D a personal account

2. **Which statement from Passage 1 reflects a conclusion drawn by the author?**
   - A Thousands of businesses and farms went bankrupt.
   - B Roosevelt promised to rebuilt the economy.
   - C Recovering from the Great Depression took a decade.
   - D Americans would never forget the Great Depression.

3. Passage 2 is best described as —
   A a memoir.
   B an outsider's perspective.
   C a poetic portrait.
   D a commentary.

4. What attitude does the author of Passage 2 express toward her grandfather?
   A generosity
   B resentment
   C impatience
   D respect

5. Which action by Grandpa was most helpful for solving his family's problems during the Great Depression?
   A leaving home
   B getting a free meal at a relief society
   C joining the Civilian Conservation Corps
   D doing odd jobs when he could find them

6. In Passage 2, the author includes many details of her grandfather's experiences during the Great Depression to —
   A make his life look happier than it probably was.
   B show how bravely he coped with hard times.
   C compare his problems to those of other people.
   D show how much better his life was as an adult.

QUESTIONS 7 and 8: Write your answers on the lines.

7. Describe the attitude that the author of Passage 1 expresses toward President Roosevelt. Use details from the passage to support your views.

_____
_____
_____
_____

8. In Passage 2, what lesson do you think Suzanne learned from her grandfather? Tell how it related to her life.

_____
_____
_____
_____
_____

READING STRATEGY ASSESSMENT 3 261

FOCUSING ON LANGUAGE AND CRAFT

DIRECTIONS: Read these two poems. Then answer questions 1–8.

Ships That Pass in the Night

OUT in the sky the great dark clouds are massing;
    I look far out into the pregnant night,
Where I can hear a solemn booming gun
    And catch the gleaming of a random light,
That tells me that the ship I seek is passing, passing.   5

My tearful eyes my soul's deep hurt are glassing;
    For I would hail and check that ship of ships.
I stretch my hands imploring, cry aloud,
    My voice falls dead a foot from mine own lips,
And but its ghost doth reach that vessel, passing, passing.   10

O Earth, O Sky, O Ocean, both surpassing,
    O heart of mine, O soul that dreads the dark!
Is there no hope for me? Is there no way
    That I may sight and check that speeding bark
Which out of sight and sound is passing, passing?   15

    — Paul Laurence Dunbar (1872–1906)

The Barrier

I MUST not gaze at them although
    Your eyes are dawning day;
I must not watch you as you go
    Your sun-illumined way;

I hear but I must never heed   5
    The fascinating note,
Which, fluting like a river-reed,
    Comes from your trembling throat;

I must not see upon your face
    Love's softly glowing spark;   10
For there's the barrier of race,
    You're fair and I am dark.

    — Claude McKay (1890–1948)

QUESTIONS 1–6: Circle the letter of the best answer to each question.

1. In the poem "Ships That Pass in the Night," the ship is a metaphor for something that —
   - A gives you strength.
   - B represents an opportunity.
   - C protects you from harm.
   - D prevents you from making progress.

2. What do the images of "clouds massing" and "pregnant night" represent in "Ships That Pass in the Night"?
   - A sleep and peacefulness
   - B companionship and love
   - C greed and selfishness
   - D darkness and the unknown

3. Which words best describe the mood of "Ships That Pass in the Night"?
   - A happy and peaceful
   - B sad and worried
   - C disheartened and hopeless
   - D confident and bold

4. In "The Barrier," the "fascinating note" (line 6) refers to —
   - A a written letter.
   - B a bird's song.
   - C a musical instrument.
   - D a woman's voice.

5. In "The Barrier," what is the main feeling expressed by the speaker?
   - A joy
   - B wistfulness
   - C optimism
   - D resentment

6. What does the speaker in "The Barrier" reveal about himself?
   - A He is black, but he is attracted to a woman who is white.
   - B He has experienced failure, but he is expecting to become successful.
   - C He is poor, but he is attracted to a woman who is wealthy.
   - D He has disappointed himself, but he is still trying to follow his dreams.

QUESTIONS 7 and 8: Write your answers on the lines.

7. Why do you think Claude McKay titled his poem "The Barrier"? Explain your answer.

8. What do the speakers of these two poems have in common, in terms of their attitudes and feelings? Use details from the poems to support your views.

DIRECTIONS: Read this passage about what happens when three friends get together for a trip to the mall. Then answer questions 1–8.

Afternoon at the Mall

When I answered the telephone on the third day of spring vacation, Jasmine's voice took me by surprise. "Pam, I am so-o-o bored!" she exclaimed. "How about going to the mall with me this afternoon? We'll have a blast and, don't worry, my mom says she can drive us."

So, after weeks of acting as if I had disappeared from the face of the earth, Jasmine suddenly remembered me. It never occurred to me that Jasmine might have some other motive for inviting me to the mall.

A couple of hours later, the familiar car pulled up in front of my house and Jasmine's mom beeped the horn. I ran outside, opened the car door, and jumped in. Turning to greet Jasmine, I was startled to discover myself face-to-face with Dominic Russo! But before I could say anything, Jasmine, sitting on the other side of Dominic, reached across and tapped me on the knee. "Turns out Dominic is as bored as we are!" Jasmine explained a bit too enthusiastically. "I told Dominic you would have invited him yourself, if you knew."

"Hm-hmm," was my only response. Grasping Jasmine's ulterior motive, I felt like a hungry little kid who has just dropped a double-scoop ice cream cone on the ground. The facts were obvious: Dominic was Jasmine's latest crush. Jasmine wanted to hang out with Dominic. Jasmine's mother allowed Jasmine to have friends who were boys, but not boyfriends; so Jasmine was using me to spend time with Dominic.

"So anyway, I thought we could check out the pet shop first—they always have the most a*dor*able kittens—and maybe we could play a few arcade games...." Jasmine was working hard to keep up a steady stream of chatter as we drove along, trying to keep her mother from figuring out that I was too mad to respond. With a twinge of satisfaction, I noted that Dominic didn't offer Jasmine even a syllable of assistance. Although Dominic was definitely easy on the eyes, he wasn't much of a conversationalist.

A few minutes later, we walked into the mall through the Randolph's Department Store entrance. I was more than a bit disarmed when Jasmine flashed me a blindingly bright smile, grabbed my elbow, and steered me to the jewelry counter, with Dominic trailing along behind us. "There are some earrings here I saw last week that are *so you!*" Jasmine assured me. "I *really* think you should buy them!"

The earrings, a pair of silver hoops, really were attractive. I lifted them from the display rack and, looking in the mirror, held them up to my ears. "They're *perfect*, and such a *bargain!*" said Jasmine, and I had to agree. So, after paying fifteen dollars for the hoops, I went back to the mirror and put them on.

No sooner had I tossed my head to set the earrings dangling than Jasmine was ready to move on, but this time she grabbed Dominic's elbow. "Come on," she murmured sweetly as she led us out of Randolph's. Steering Dominic to the right toward the movie theater, Jasmine added, "I noticed that *The Knight's Impossible Quest* is playing here. Let's go see it! The next show starts in about 10 minutes."

I felt my jaw drop to the floor. Having just spent fifteen dollars on the earrings, I had less than two dollars left in my wallet. "Jasmine," I began, feeling my throat tightening with irritation. "If I had known we were going to a movie, I would have never bought the earrings! Now I'm practically broke!"

Maintaining her grip on Dominic's elbow, Jasmine didn't even pretend to sympathize with my predicament. "Oh, *Pamela*, relax, this is a *mall* for goodness sake. I'm sure you can find lots of things to do until the movie's over. Anyway, my mom's picking us up in front of the Randolph's entrance in two and a half hours, so be sure to meet Dominic and me right here after the movie." With that, they turned around and headed for the box office to buy their movie tickets.

And what did I do? I dug a couple of quarters out of my wallet and headed for the pay phone. A few minutes later, as I walked out of Randolph's to wait for my mother to come and pick me up, I tried to imagine what Jasmine's explanation would be when *her* mother asked what had happened to me. ❖

✳ QUESTIONS 1–6: Circle the letter of the best answer to each question.

1. What is the setting at the beginning of the story?
    - **A** the mall
    - **B** Jasmine's car
    - **C** an ice cream shop
    - **D** Pam's house

2. This story is told from which narrative point of view?
    - **A** first-person narrator
    - **B** second-person narrator
    - **C** limited third-person narrator
    - **D** omniscient third-person narrator

3. In the story, Pam says, "I felt like a hungry little kid who has dropped a double-scoop ice cream cone on the ground." Pam's statement is a way of saying that she —
   - A was hungrier than she realized.
   - B knew she was behaving childishly.
   - C felt a big, unexpected disappointment.
   - D wished she weren't so clumsy.

4. Look at the illustration and read the text in the speech balloon. Which of these best describes the character's way of speaking?
   - A calm and soothing
   - B enthusiastic and assured
   - C amused and giggling
   - D bossy and mean

5. When Jasmine announces that she wants to go to a movie, the expression on Pam's face is most likely —
   - A embarrassed and nervous.
   - B happy and excited.
   - C shocked and angry.
   - D bored and tired.

6. Which sentence best expresses the theme of this story?
   - A Thoughtless, selfish people do not make good friends.
   - B Friendship is more important than possessions.
   - C It is always better to save your money than spend it.
   - D You should be willing to give a good friend a second chance.

✻ QUESTIONS 7 and 8: Write your answers on the lines.

7. How does Pam describe Dominic in this story? Does her description seem accurate? Tell why or why not.

8. What do you think will happen when the movie ends? Write two sentences that predict what will happen next, based on what you have already read.

DIRECTIONS: Read these two passages about snack foods in school. Then answer questions 9–16.

PASSAGE 1

Should Schools Sell Unhealthy Snacks?

Chocolate chip cookies, candy, and potato chips—what do these snack items have in common? First, they have little or no nutritional value. Second, when consumed in excess, they can contribute to obesity. And third, they're easily purchased in vending machines and student stores in schools across the country.

However, many schools have recently begun to examine the issue of snack sales. They're doing so at the urging of frustrated parents who would like to keep their kids from eating unhealthy food at school. Health experts are also weighing in against junk-food sales at schools.

So how serious is the problem, anyway? According to a study by the Center for Science in the Public Interest, 85 percent of drinks sold in school vending machines have almost no nutritional value. The study found that 70 percent of beverages sold were sugary drinks and 14 percent were diet. Only 17 percent were water or milk. Recent agreements with soft drink companies may help to remove sodas and other sugary beverages from schools over the next several years, but what about the snack foods? Of foods sold in vending machines, 42 percent were candy, 25 percent were chips, and 13 percent were bakery-type sweets, such as cookies and doughnuts. By comparison, healthier food choices were scarce. For example, just two percent of food items sold were low-fat baked goods, and only one percent were nuts or trail mix.

Additional evidence suggests that many students find the readily available junk food just too tempting to pass up. In a poll of students aged 13 to 17, slightly more than two-thirds, or 67 percent, say they buy junk food and beverages at school. They also buy junk food at the movie theater, the mall, the bowling alley, the hockey rink, and just about everywhere else they go. About 23 percent describe themselves as eating "a great deal" of junk food each week.

Taken all together, these data are an alarm signaling a threat to young people's well being. As health experts point out, nearly one-third of American children are overweight, or at risk of becoming so. Junk foods and drinks, the experts say, play a major role in weight problems.

So why don't schools just stop selling junk food? Some are planning to do so, but others are finding the junk food habit a bit harder to break. Why? Because schools get to keep a share of the profits earned from food and beverage sales. These funds are often used to support valued school activities, such as clubs, sports teams, and art programs.

Are junk food sales at school a problem that needs to be solved? If so, what's the best way to solve it? Middle and high schools everywhere are trying to answer these questions. ❖

PASSAGE 2

Help Us Make Healthy Choices

There's no doubt about it: middle school is a lot tougher than elementary school. There's more homework. There's no recess. And the teachers expect us to take more responsibility for ourselves.

Along with the added responsibility, however, come some privileges. For me, one of the best privileges is treating myself to a snack right in the middle of the day. When I was in elementary school, I never imagined I would be able to buy a candy bar from a student store or get a bag of chips from the cafeteria vending machine. But I can in middle school.

Now the school committee is talking about making some serious changes. At their last meeting, a group of parents and professionals spoke. They claimed it was irresponsible for the school to raise money for clubs and sports teams by selling junk food to students. They said the school was vacuuming up dollar bills at the expense of the students' well being. A doctor claimed that every year she sees more and more overweight teens who get that way by eating too much junk food. Then a dentist pointed out that kids who start drinking more sugary drinks in middle school also start getting more tooth decay and more cavities. For these adults, the solution was simple: no more junk food in school.

Eliminating all the unhealthy snacks is a bad idea. Why? Since middle-school students will eventually grow up and face a world filled with junk food, we need to develop the ability to make healthy choices about how we snack. It is unrealistic to think that keeping unhealthy snacks away from middle schoolers will turn us into adults who never eat unhealthy snacks. After all, most adults with healthy eating habits do, at least occasionally, choose a not-so-healthy treat.

A better alternative would be to make healthy snacks available at school, too. Besides chips, candy, and sodas, the vending machines or store could sell nuts, fruits, granola bars, low-fat baked goods, milk, and water. Posters that spell out the nutritional value of different snacks could be displayed nearby. These changes, along with the nutrition unit taught each year in health class, are enough to help students learn to make healthy choices about snacks. After all, making healthy choices is one of the responsibilities we take on as we become adults.

QUESTIONS 9–14: Circle the letter of the best answer to each question.

9. In Passage 1, the author includes a number of facts that —
   - **A** strongly suggest that selling unhealthy snacks in schools is a bad idea.
   - **B** equally balance arguments for and against selling unhealthy snacks in schools.
   - **C** demonstrate that most schools don't sell too many unhealthy snacks.
   - **D** shows how difficult it is to measure the nutritional value of snacks sold in schools.

10. Which statement from Passage 1 is a metaphor?

    A Many schools have begun to examine the issue of snack food sales.
    B Many students find the junk food too tempting to pass up.
    C These data are an alarm signaling a threat to young people's well being.
    D Schools keep a share of profits earned from food and beverage sales.

11. Which is the best summary of Passage 1?

    A Middle and high schools sell snack foods in school to earn money for activities. Some of the snacks are healthy, but some lack nutritional value.
    B Studies show that many middle- and high-school students are buying unhealthy snacks at school. As parents and health experts voice their concerns, many schools are starting to examine the issue.
    C Most middle and high schools sell snacks in vending machines and in student stores. The snack food choices range from candy to low-fat baked goods.
    D Middle and high schools sell a lot of unhealthy snacks, such as candy and cookies. Studies show that most students would rather have fruit.

12. In Passage 2, the author's approach is to —

    A present facts and allow the reader to draw a conclusion.
    B offer several different solutions to a problem.
    C use facts and reasoning to support an opinion.
    D make a strongly emotional argument.

13. In Passage 2, the metaphor "the school vacuuming up dollar bills" suggests which of these?

    A greed   C cleanliness
    B success   D happiness

14. In Passage 2, the parents and professionals suggest that the school should —

    A teach students how to choose healthy snacks.
    B have students bring snacks from home
    C offer more healthy snacks than junk food.
    D stop selling all junk food.

QUESTIONS 15 and 16: Write your answers on the lines.

15. Does Passage 1 suggest that middle- and high-school students eat too many unhealthy snacks? List two details that support your answer.

16. Explain the author's solution to the junk food problem, as presented in Passage 2, and tell why the author thinks it is a good solution.

REPRODUCIBLE GRAPHIC ORGANIZERS

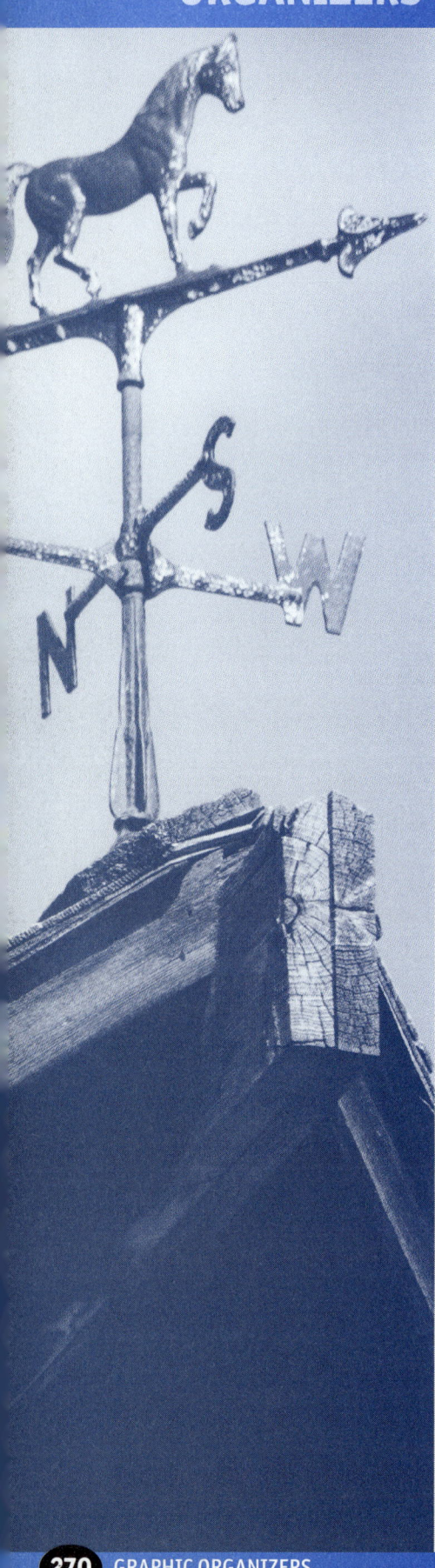

Graphic organizers are great for helping students organize their thinking, whether they are analyzing something they've read; planning their own writing; or exploring relationships among words, phrases, and ideas.

PLOT DIAGRAM, Page 270

Keeping track of the events of the plot helps readers comprehend and remember the action of the story. While many stories have the five-part structure presented in unit 3, some stories may have fewer or more parts. This diagram can also be used for planning the writing of a story.

WORD SPLASH, Page 272

Use this graphic to preview the vocabulary in something students are about to read. First give students the list of key vocabulary that they may not know but will need to understand in order to get the key concepts in the story. Then provide them with definitions or have them find their own definitions to write next to the words. Ask them to suggest the subject of the article and tell why they think so, accounting for all of the words and phrases. Once you have discussed the possibilities, read the selection independently or as a group. Discuss students' guesses and how close they are to the actual text. Make sure students understand that the point of the activity is to get them thinking about the words; it is not about guessing correctly. Surprises should be welcome. They will inspire interesting discussions about word meanings and language.

PLOT DIAGRAM

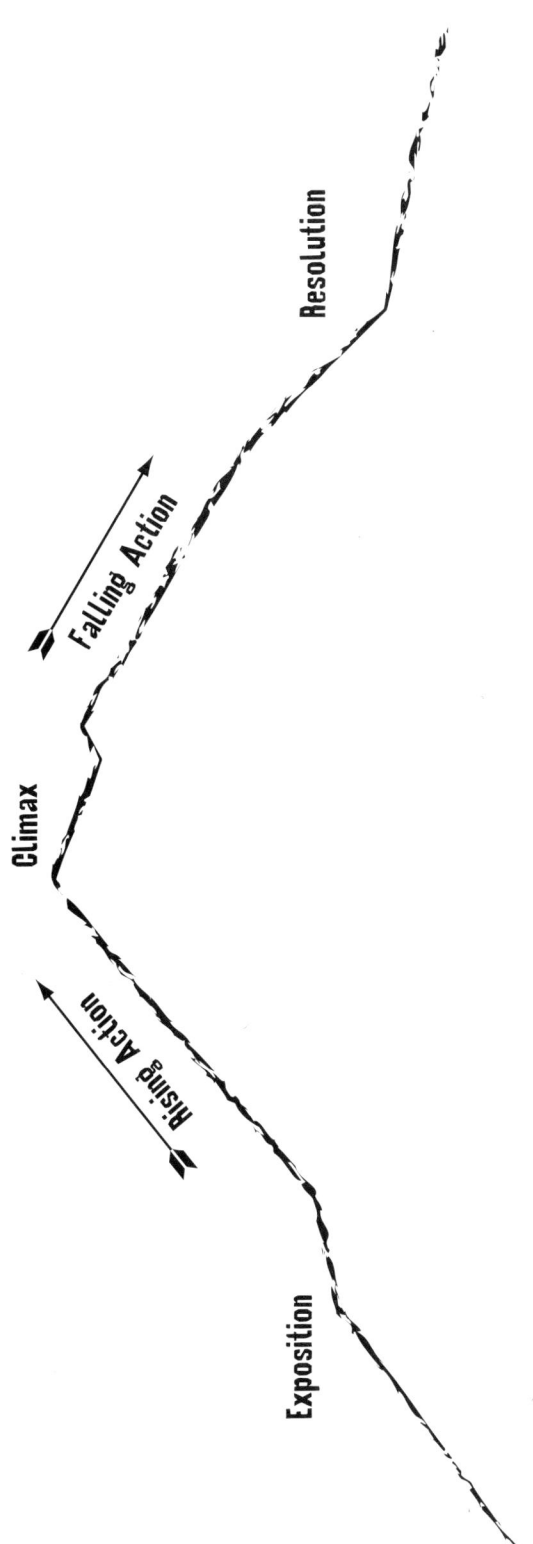

GRAPHIC ORGANIZERS

WORD SPLASH

SELECTION VOCABULARY

Write the selection vocabulary on the lines below. Write a definition for each word. Read the words and their definitions and then guess what the selection will be about. Remember, all the words will be used in the selection. Compare your guess with your classmates and talk about the reasons for each person's guess. Then read the selection to see if anyone's guess was close to the topic.

Word　　　　　　　　　　**Definition**

What the selection will be about

INDEX

"Ain't I a Woman?" 32
from *America's Great Disasters,* 148, 151
"Annabel Lee," 145
"Are Plastic Bags Harming the Environment?" 164
autobiography, 62, 90
Barker, Malcolm, 151
from *Bearstone,* 207
biography, 54
Birmingham, Nan, 67
"Birthday Box," 102
from *Bone,* 134, 137
from *Borden Tragedy, The,* 140
from *Breadwinner, The,* 26, 29
from *Bronx Masquerade,* 80, 82
Brooks, Gwendolyn, 179
"Call of the Mall," 167
from *Call of the Wild, The,* 112
characterization, 45, 91, 205, 213
Choi, Sook Nyul, 42
Clifton, Lucille, 65
collaboration, 11, 21, 23, 31, 38, 43, 50, 56, 60, 64, 71, 73, 76, 78, 92, 105, 108, 114, 122, 135, 142, 144, 150, 153, 162, 171, 180, 185, 187, 189, 201, 216
compare and contrast, 47, 61, 113, 114, 145, 152
connection, 82, 109
context, 40
Cooney, Caroline, 124
counterargument, 169
critical reading and writing strategies, 9, 101
descriptive language, 158
from *Desert Exile,* 96
details, 167
dialogue, 143

differentiation, 12, 15, 17, 20, 23, 27, 33, 35, 36, 44, 56, 63, 68, 72, 79, 83, 87, 88, 91, 94, 111, 119, 123, 128, 132, 135, 138, 146, 152, 155, 159, 161, 164, 165, 173, 176, 185, 198, 201, 211, 214, 216
from *Downriver,* 204
from *Dragonwings,* 154
draw conclusions, 54
Ellis, Deborah, 26, 29
emotional language, 129
epistle poem, 75
Ethier, Brian, 58
facts, 54–55
fantasy, 202
fiction, 10, 26, 29, 40, 42, 80, 82, 86, 93, 112, 118, 124, 134, 137, 154, 194, 197, 200, 204
first-person point of view, 42, 59
Frost, Robert, 190
Geary, Rick, 140
genre, 137, 200, 201, 203
Goodall, Jane, with Gary McAvoy and Gail Hudson, 172
graphic novel, 137, 140
Grimes, Nikki, 80, 82
from *Harvest for Hope: A Guide to Mindful Eating,* 172
from "Henry Aaron Remembers," 58
"Hero on the Ball Field," 54
historical fiction, 201
from *History of Reading, A,* 179
Hobbs, Will, 194, 197, 200, 202, 204
from "Homeless," 129
Hughes, Langston, 45, 48, 77
from *Ice Drift,* 118
identity, 86
interact with a text, 10, 70, 102, 106, 118–119, 133, 210

interview, 58, 99
from *Invisible Thread, The,* 90
from *Island of the Blue Dolphins,* 113
Ives, Sara, 164
"jackie robinson," 65
from *Jason's Gold,* 200
from *Journey Home,* 93
"Key to Everything, The," 107
from *Kokopelli's Flute,* 202
"Lady, That's Jackie Robinson!" 67
Lago, Don, 182, 184
from "Living Up the Street," 22
from *Locomotion,* 70, 75
London, Jack, 112
"Long Live Langston," from *Bronx Masquerade,* 80
make inferences, 67, 87, 134, 177
making connections, 13, 39, 42, 46, 52, 69, 82, 102, 106, 109, 121, 147, 148, 149, 154, 160, 172, 184, 210, 212, 216
Manguel, Alberto, 179
"Martin Luther King Jr.," 179
from *Maze, The,* 194, 197
memoir, 22
"Mother to Son," 77
multiple perspectives, 16, 53, 124, 127, 152, 163
narrator, 143
nonfiction, 62, 67, 90, 96, 109, 129, 140, 148, 151, 160, 164, 167, 169, 172, 175, 178, 182, 184
O'Dell, Scott, 113
"Oranges," 19
personal narrative, 69
perspective, 16, 53, 63, 83, 106, 127
persuade, 163
persuasive writing, 167

INDEX

Peterson, Robert, 54
plot, 48
Poe, Edgar Allan, 145
poetry, 19, 35, 65, 69, 70, 75, 77, 107, 121, 145, 179, 190
point of view, 42, 120, 124, 157
"Porscha's Journal," from *Bronx Masquerade,* 82
prediction, 13, 14, 26, 27
from "Princess of Light, The," 86
problem and solution, 164, 166
purpose, 99, 168
Quindlen, Anna, 129
reading actively, 11, 54, 93, 102
reading for meaning, 117
reading process, 10, 224
reflecting, 37, 209
repertoire, 9
revision, 76, 221
Rhode Island Red Cross, 160
"Road Not Taken, The," 190
Robinson, Sharon, 62
Rylant, Cynthia, 210, 215
"Safety Tips for Earthquakes," 160
Sandler, Martin, 148, 151
"Save Your Energy," 175
second-person point of view, 42
sensory language, 93

setting, 40, 41, 138, 195, 218
setting a purpose, 16, 82, 118
"Seventh Grade," 11, 13, 16
"Shells," 210, 215
short story, 11, 13, 16, 45, 48, 102, 210, 215
simile, 159
Smith, Jeff, 134, 137
Soto, Gary, 10, 11, 13, 16, 19, 22
sound (as conveyed in a graphic novel), 143
speech, 32
from *Stealing Home,* 62
Stepanek, Mattie, 35
story elements, 39, 194, 195, 218
strategic reading, 25
summarize, 32, 170, 174
from *Summer Life, A,* 10
Suzuki, David, and Kathy Vanderlinden, 167, 175
Swenson, May, 107
symbolism, 177
symbols, 177, 187, 190, 191, 192
from "Symbols of Humankind," 182, 184
Taylor, Theodore, 118
from *Terrorist, The,* 124
"Thank You, Ma'm," 45, 48
theme, 51–52, 96

third-person point of view, 42
from *Three Fearful Days,* 151
"To Drill or Not to Drill," 169
traits of effective writing, 55, 76, 91, 94, 97, 104, 116, 139, 156, 170, 199, 201, 205
from *True Believer,* 121
Truth, Sojourner, 32
Uchida, Yoshiko, 86, 90, 93, 96, 99
"Vietnam War Memorial," 35
visual information, 133
visualizing, 34, 40, 180
visual text, 133
vocabulary, 10, 13, 16, 19, 22, 26, 29, 32, 34, 40, 42, 54, 58, 62, 67, 70, 75, 77, 80, 82, 86, 90, 93, 96, 99, 102, 109, 112, 118, 121, 124, 129, 134, 140, 145, 148, 151, 154, 160, 164, 167, 169, 172, 175, 180, 194, 197, 200, 204, 207, 210
Wills, Steven R., 169
Wolff, Virginia Euwer, 121
Woodson, Jacqueline, 70, 73, 75
writer's craft, 12, 17, 36, 46, 49, 55, 57, 74, 88, 91, 104, 120, 122, 127, 156, 170, 183, 188, 199, 220
Year of Impossible Goodbyes, 40, 42
Yep, Laurence, 154
Yolen, Jane, 102, 109
from *You Are the Earth,* 167, 175